*"We didn't know we were making memories.
We were just having fun."*

—A.A. Milne

# WHAT A RIDE!

## My Amazing Life with The Original Right Stuff, Chuck Yeager

by Chuck Yeager's Favorite Co-Pilot,
## VICTORIA YEAGER

WHAT A RIDE!
My Amazing Life with The Original Right Stuff, Chuck Yeager

© 2024 The Right Stuff Publishing. All Rights Reserved.
This book or parts thereof may not be reproduced in any form, stored in any retrieval system, or transmitted in any form by any means—electronic, mechanical, photocopy, recording, or otherwise—without prior written permission of the publisher, except as provided by United States of America

The Right Stuff Publishing

Book Cover Concept: Ricardo Rallo, @i9star.mkt
Book Design and Formatting: TeaBerryCreative.com

ISBN: (paperback) 979-8-9864982-4-9
ISBN: (hardcover) 979-8-9864982-5-6
ISBN: (eBook) 979-8-9864982-6-3

*This book is dedicated to my late great husband,
General Chuck Yeager, who always wanted to write a
book about us, but we were too busy enjoying life to sit
down and chronicle it, so now here it is, in part.*

*As you would say, Charlie, with your smile that still
lights up the world, obviously so very heartfelt,
as is mine from me to you: A simple thank you, Charlie.
You have given me, and continue to give me, so much.*

# TABLE OF CONTENTS

| | | |
|---|---|---|
| PART I | BEGINNINGS | 1 |
| PART II | HIGH SIERRA | 15 |
| PART III | FISHING | 29 |
| PART IV | MARRIAGE & HAVING KIDS | 44 |
| PART V | HIS KIDS | 64 |
| PART VI | PEOPLE | 70 |
| PART VII | HUNTIN' | 159 |
| PART VIII | FLYING | 178 |
| PART IX | MILITARY | 231 |
| PART X | EVENTS | 297 |
| PART XI | GERMANY, FRANCE & SPAIN | 338 |
| PART XII | OTHER VOICES | 363 |
| PART XIII | PHOTOS | 368 |

PROLOGUE

## VICTORIA'S BACKGROUND

I was a city kid—grew up in a mixed (religion and color) neighborhood in Philadelphia with three older brothers who hated me, and often some male strays who would stay with us for a month to a year from the U.S. and various countries around the world. I never saw a real cow till I was eight, had no clue how asparagus grew till after I met Chuck Yeager. I went to public school through first grade, till it got dangerous. Thereafter, my dad drove me every morning on a wild ride to make the train on time. Starting at age 8, I rode the train by myself to an exclusive girls school on the Main Line, a very wealthy, snobby suburb where my family belonged to all the exclusive clubs.

To keep me busy, tire me out, and expose me to a variety of skills, Mom had me take various extracurricular lessons: horseback riding, sailing, piano, dance, skiing, and more. But mostly, the neighborhood kids and I played outside and after we outgrew our backyards, often in the street, touch football, baseball, having fun.. From a very young age, I did volunteer work and traveled around the world, from sailing in Nova Scotia to studying monkeys in Nepal, to attending various U.N. and other international meetings with my mother, including in Kenya, South Africa, Denmark, Australia, and Yugoslavia.

Both my parents graduated from the University of Pennsylvania; my father with a law degree, my mother with a master's degree in psychiatric social work at age 19. Mom consulted around the world on alcoholism and drug abuse prevention and convinced First Lady Betty Ford to go public with her alcoholism and drug addictions.

My travel was eclectic: from living with tribes in Africa for short stints to climbing Mt Kilimanjaro, to boogie boarding the Zambezi, to getting a human trafficker (who had tried to break my shoulder and had put a loaded gun to my head) put in prison in Southeast Asia, to visiting the Louvre; to afternoon tea at the Ritz or the Savoy in London, to dining with princes, dukes, earls, billionaires, artists, actors and writers. With an MBA from Columbia University, my career has been varied: investment banking, financial/marketing and valuation consulting, acting, writing, producing and directing. I acted in *Witness*, *Blades: Just When You Thought It Was Safe to Putt* and other movies, starting at age 3 on *Uncle Pete's*, a kiddie T.V. show in 1961 hosted by character actor Peter Boyle's father.

As a fourth-year student (senior) at the University of Virginia, I began flying lessons. After seven to eight hours of dual, I kicked the CFI (certified flight instructor) out and said, "I got this." No, what really happened was the CFI got out and said you're on your own. Surprisingly, I was quite confident I'd be fine.

I asked her before doing any cross country, "How do you get into a spin? How do you get out of it?"

She responded succinctly, "You get into a spin, you die."

Me: "Ah. Then how do you get into a spin so I can prevent it?"

She refused to respond. I never went back.

Imagine then that 20 years later, I meet the man whose job it was to get in and out of spins: Chuck Yeager.

## PART I

## BEGINNINGS

## MOST OFTEN ASKED QUESTION: HOW DID GENERAL YEAGER AND YOU MEET?

I went hiking one spring day in March 2000, in the foothills of the High Sierra, to commune with the miracle of nature and enjoy the beautiful spring wildflowers and magnificent, crisp, clear sunny day. I was negotiating a deal as a producer with a network regarding a female Indiana Jones-type character in a tale involving Bible-based spirituality. I wasn't comfortable with the network's behavior, so I was trying to decide if I should just walk away from a significant amount of money.

As I was walking up the hill on a trail where I rarely saw anyone else, a handsome, fit, older man was walking down. The sun was behind him, creating an ethereal radiance. Or maybe it was just his lovely, contagious smile and exquisite blue-green eyes. I saw blue; he said green.

"Great day!" I greeted him.

"I just got back from Australia." (He literally had driven home from the airport, dropped his bag, and come for a walk.)

"I just got back from Africa," I countered. "What were you doing in Australia?"

"Teaching software guys," this handsome man said.

"Oh! I was volunteering, helping tribes. I need to refill my coffers. Could you get me a job? I can teach software," I said.

"No, no, I'm not a software guy; I'm a fighter pilot. I'm Chuck Yeager."

My mind was racing. Is "Chuck Yeager" a common name in the military? Is he *the* Chuck Yeager? Wait, who was Chuck Yeager?

As my mind kept pinballing, I asked, "Okay, will you take me up in a fighter jet?"

Stunned, he replied, "No, no—that costs tens of thousands of taxpayer dollars!"

I answered, "I pay taxes."

He looked at me quizzically, debating, chose: "I gotta go," and continued down the trail.

I quickly said, "Okay. You won't get me a job. You won't take me up in a fighter jet. You want to go hiking tomorrow?"

He looked at me, looked at his watch, and said, "It's 3 o'clock. That's my truck down there. We'll meet there at 3 p.m. tomorrow. It's got an X-1 on it. Do you know what that is?"

I hesitated, pondering. "I used to be so good in school…No…"

He gave me a clue: "Broke the sound barrier."

Without thinking, I exclaimed, "Oh! That's right! That's you! I saw the movie."

He was still dubious, squinted his eyes and challenged: "What movie?"

I got this: "*The Right Stuff*?"

Satisfied, "That's right," he said and again continued down the trail.

I started up, thrilled.

He stopped, called out, "Now, wait a minute!"

I stopped. Uh oh.

He continued, "I'm older than you are; you can't go too fast." (I was 41 then; he was 77.)

I responded, "We're fifty feet from the start of the trail. You think I stopped to talk to you?" I shook my head. "I'm tired!"

He smiled, probably wondering what he was getting himself into.

I think I skipped the next three and a half miles around that hill, thrilled I'd be hiking with this oh-so-attractive, interesting man the next day.

That night, I did a little research on the internet, such as it was in those days, to make sure I was right and to learn anything more about *the* Chuck Yeager.

The following day, I had been waiting for twenty-one minutes when he showed up at the start of the trail. For those long twenty-one minutes, I was contemplating the options and possibilities. What if he never shows up? He didn't have my number to call and cancel; something may have come up. If I call his office, if I can find a number, if he has a number, his secretary would say, "Sure, sure," and not believe me. (Little did I know then this was a very apt thought.)

Or maybe he didn't like my feisty?? playful?? sense of humor.

Or…

How long do I wait before I'm so annoyed he's late that meeting up would be counterproductive? I was brought up that you better be in the hospital or dead if you're late.

If I go the way I was going when I met him, then I'll get exercise, and if he shows up late, maybe he'll just go the direction he was going the day before and we'll meet up again.

As I was analyzing my options, at 3:04 p.m., he drove up and parked across the road. I got out of my car and ran across the road into his outstretched arms. He gathered me up in a big, warm, loving, safe hug and never let me go for the next almost 21 years. But I get ahead of myself.

He was wearing aftershave, which gave me an idea of what he thought this was. I thought that was sweet. It never occurred to me—I just thought I want to know this guy.

As we started up the trail, me first, the first thing he said was, "I'm never getting married again."

I responded, "Works for me. I'm never getting married." (I had not seen one marriage anywhere that I wanted to emulate.)

As I look back on that, I think the next sound I heard was God rolling on a cloud, laughing. We make plans and God laughs.

We continued talking about everything and nothing I remember—I just remember the feeling and it was euphoric.

When we had made the full loop, taking in the great smell of the oldest single-span wooden-covered bridge in the country (1862), Chuck asked me if I wanted to go flying. I said, "Sure."

We dropped my car off at his house on the way and headed to the airport. I watched while he inspected the plane. At one point, I was at the other end of the plane. He waggled the wings. I thought he was flirting with me, trying to get my attention, and laughed a little.

He wasn't. I realized muuu-uch later, perhaps years, he was checking to make sure the wings wouldn't fall off in flight.

We pulled the plane out, got in, which is no easy feat, but I had taken ballet as a kid and was the youngest, so could fit anywhere if I wanted to go (almost including the glove compartment), and taxied off to the runway.

He did the run-up (checking the plane's functions before takeoff). It was a dual-controlled airplane, so there was a stick in the backseat with me. At one point, he moved the stick back and forth and around. It was a small space, so the stick touched each of my thighs. I thought he was flirting with me again.

Yet again, he wasn't. He was making sure there were no impediments to moving the controls to fly the plane, especially in any emergency. Sigh.

We took off and he showed me the sights, including where we had just hiked. I was quiet, taking it all in, proverbially pinching myself at the realization that I was flying not only with a beautiful, handsome, charming, witty man, but this man was also Chuck Yeager!!!!!! I was making sure I was fully present. I kept telling myself as though I might forget. Interestingly, it was the first time I flew in a small airplane and didn't get sick. Clearly, I trusted this pilot.

We landed, put the plane to bed, and as we drove to his house, he asked if I wanted to stay for dinner. Sure. Or yes, thank you.

We stopped at his daughter's house, which then was on the same property, and had dinner with her and her two kids.

For dessert, we had my all-time favorite: ice cream. But not just any ol' ice cream. We had Chuck Yeager's homemade vanilla gelato. To die for.

I finished my ice cream before Chuck did and he nonchalantly offered me a bite of his with his spoon. I said, "No, thank you." He said, "Why not?" I teased, "Because you licked it."

I noticed his grandson perk up—not used to anyone saying no to his grandfather, let alone teasing him, although I didn't smile—to see how Grandpa would react. Grandpa just nonchalantly kept eating his ice cream.

Every now and then, the kids and their mother would imitate a turkey gobble sound and the turkeys outside would respond. After a few of these, Chuck looked at me, wondering what I was thinking of his "crazy" family. Pretty funny.

After dinner, we went back to his house, where I had parked my car, and sat on the swing on his deck, watching the deer, dove, and quail, chatting a little, a very peaceful ending to a lovely day.

As I left, Chuck gave me a copy of the sequel to his autobiography, *Press*

*On! Further Adventures in the Good Life,* to read. I thought this would be a great friendship. He had other things in mind.

## SKINNY DIPPING

Following my dinner with Chuck and his family, he had no way of getting a hold of me or I him, so a few days later, when he said he would be back, I boldly went by his property. He drove in after me, told me to get in his car and we went hiking. Phew!

We hiked and had lunch or dinner a few more times.

One day we decided to go swimming in the river.

After we hiked back, the park ranger, whom we knew, said, "Someone reported two people skinny-dipping. Did you see them?"

Chuck replied, "Oh, someone saw us?"

The ranger was shocked and managed to stutter, "Ch-Ch-Chuck! You weren't…" The concept—or picture in his head—of Chuck Yeager, age 77, skinny-dipping with someone 35 years younger was too much for him.

Chuck just smiled. The ranger looked desperately at me as if to say, say it ain't so. He did not want that picture in his head. I just smiled. That was fun.

## OUR FIRST NIGHT TOGETHER

It got too late to drive home, so Chuck offered for me to spend the night in the guest room. Before he met me, he had been looking for a companion—someone he could pay and who would be there to take care of him if he needed help. Chuck knew his four kids wouldn't take care of him—they had not helped to take care of his wife, their mother, Glennis, when she got sick and passed. On one of our daily hikes, he pointed out one of the gals he had thought about approaching to hire as a companion because she looked like a hippy desperately in need of a shower, a place to live, a job, and some money. Chuck and I sure met in the nick of time.

I said, "If I'm spending the night, I'm spending it with you."

Chuck's eyes got wide. He was speechless; he couldn't believe his good fortune.

After a lovely night, he, being a morning person, brought me, definitely not a morning person, tea in bed. (Chuck YEAGER-ism #110: "Now it takes me all night to do what I used to do all night.")

It was his way of making sure I got up and out when he did. I sure understood that.

We repeated this for about a week, although him bringing me tea in bed lasted for the next twelve to fifteen years. Then, for the subsequent five to eight years, I brought him coffee in bed.

At the end of this week, Chuck asked me to housesit while he flew (literally) to Argentina with a bunch of guys in a private jet to hunt dove. After a few days of huntin' dove, he called me from the plane on the flight back and said, "I hope my favorite house sitter doesn't move out when I get back." Music to my ears. I was staying in a guest house at a friend's, trying to decide what and where my next adventure would be in the world. (Chuck YEAGER-ism #132: It's huntin', not huntinG".)

And that was that. I used to joke; I was looking for a house to rent and he came with the house.

I had a choice, after that, of doing the deal with the network and hitting my head against their wall or hanging out with Chuck Yeager. I chose wisely.

My life was already interesting, yet solitary, full of adventures, but now my greatest adventure was beginning: life with The Original "Right Stuff", General Charles E. "Chuck" Yeager.

One of his great friends, the first I met, had spent the night before they flew to Argentina, so we all had dinner together. Tony was a handsome, witty, analytical, charming man, born on the same day as, but 11 years younger than, Chuck.

He told Chuck I was a keeper because I looked him in the eye when I shook his hand. And I wasn't intimidated, nor was I overwhelming; I had class and elegance. Needless to say, after I heard what Tony had said, I liked that guy.

Living with Chuck while reading his book, Chuck would ask me where I was in *Press On!* and then he'd tell the whole story. It was surreal and perfect. I thought this might be fun to do with several authors; stay at their house (not in the same type of relationship though) and have them expound on where I was in their autobiography.

I next read *Yeager: An Autobiography*. Same results. It also gave me a head start and a clue as to Chuck's character and view on life. Check.

It occurred to me recently that I didn't have to "get to know" Chuck to find out if he had integrity, was generous, kind, interesting, loyal, affectionate and the like (which he was), or mean, dishonest, dissembling, and/or disrespectful (which he was not). His fame, book, and life preceded him.

## DINING WITH CHUCK

Shortly after his Argentina trip, Chuck, a great cook, grilled some sort of meat for lunch. While cooking, he served me a piece with a fork while keenly observing me.

After we sat down, I waited for him to start eating so I could figure out how to proceed. At a very young age, I had learned to wait for the hostess to start so I could follow suit with the correct silverware.

I asked, "No knife?"

He replied, "No. It's tender enough for a fork."

Dubiously, I cut it with the fork—he was right, as usual, it was tender—and took a bite. Different. Delicious. But different.

I smiled at him.

He asked, "Do you like it?"

I answered, "Yes. Thank you—it's delicious."

He continued, "Do you know what it is?"

I replied, "Well, it's almost filet mignon or beef, but not really."

He nodded approvingly. "That's right."

I waited, then asked: "What is it?"

"Elk. Backstrap. Choice stuff. Yearling cow elk—I shot it—still had milk on its mouth."

I looked at him, blinked, mind racing, no answers forthcoming, and after several seconds, queried, "What's a yearling cow elk?"

He got a kick out of me, the city kid, but was impressed I was willing to try it and didn't pick up my skirts and run in horror at his attempt to shock.

We continued eating.

Chuck didn't say a word.

I decided I was not going to say anything.

When I was going out with guys, I would keep a conversation going during a meal. Then, after a few meals, for whatever reason, I would just be tired or in a quiet mood and rely on the guy. Dull. Couldn't start a conversation. Hadn't had many adventures or opinions in life or, more than that, hadn't viewed life itself as an adventure.

I decided this time, with Chuck, I wasn't going to wait to see if I was the only conversationalist in the family.

Chuck did not say a word the whole time we ate. Neither did I. And I thought, "Well, if he thinks I'm dull, so be it." And I enjoyed my elk backstrap immensely.

Once Chuck finished, he sat back and told me stories. Fascinating, humorous. Amazing. Seriously amazing.

And, as I got to know Chuck, rather than think I was dull, he was grateful I didn't chat away or ask silly mundane questions (like what's your favorite airplane) distracting him from eating his delicious, well-earned backstrap. That day, I passed two tests: tries new food easily, doesn't chatter about not much.

John, a friend whom we helped get an air base egress road repaved, told me: "When you two came out to support the bicycle race on Chuck Yeager Road, Chuck (and I) saw people in the crowd, who had recognized him, approaching to talk with him. He put down his sandwich, sat back and was very gracious. I could see him just used to never being able to finish a meal in public. I thought this remarkable man, this hero, never gets any peace, never gets to eat his lunch."

Chuck definitely was the scintillating one…*after* he ate.

## NAMES — WHAT TO CALL EACH OTHER

After about four months together, I didn't feel comfortable saying endearments yet. In fact, Chuck tried one early-ish and it shocked both of us so much he didn't do that again for a long time. But I also didn't want to call him "Chuck" like everyone else.

I quickly found a good nickname: "Charlie". No one else called him that (except the French I was to learn later and a few in the U.S. military early on until they glommed onto "Chuck"). And I noticed Chuck hadn't liked it when some acquaintance had called him "Charlie" a couple months before, but…

So, one day, I tried it out. Seeming almost to leap for joy, he let out a small whoop, obviously elated. "Charlie" it was. Ever after, whenever someone else heard me call Chuck "Charlie" and tried to get too familiar by using my nickname for him, Chuck or I made it clear only I could call him "Charlie". Chuck was quite down with that. (The surviving members of the French Maquis, who were part of the group that had saved F/O [Flight Officer] Chuck Yeager's life in 1944 and had called him "Charlie"—sounding like "Sharlee"—in 1944, were also a rare breed, part of our inner circle, and allowed to call Chuck our special nickname.)

By contrast, Chuck could never quite find a suitable nickname for me. He often called me "uh…Victoria," which I understood. My mother would go through all the names of my three older brothers before she got to mine when she was calling me. I'd tease her, "Mom. I'm the only girl! It should be easy!"

Sometimes Chuck called me "Little Yeager". I'd call him "Big Yeager".

He always wanted to name a plane after me. But we didn't own a plane and neither of us, sure as heck, wanted him to go back into combat to name a plane, although he did joke about it. Every time he said something like that, I heard loud and clear, yet simply and deeply, "I love you." I knew his actions would support his words if I indicated it was important to me.

## HOLIDAYS

Before Chuck, I seemed to have always ended up on my own on many holidays or with a guy who was not generous of spirit—let alone of pocketbook—so the first year, it was important to me to celebrate every holiday. And I was mature enough not to think if he loved me, he'd know what to get me. I wrote down suggestions. For my birthday: great moist yellow two-layer cake with one layer of thick chocolate buttercream or ganache icing and one layer of vanilla thick buttercream or ganache icing and a friendship ring. I can't remember what I got him for Father's Day, but I did email two "sons" to wish him a Happy Father's Day. We carved pumpkins for Halloween. For Thanksgiving, turkey and dressing (NOT oyster dressing either) and excellent pumpkin pie. For Christmas, more turkey and dressing. For Christmas, I can't remember what was on my list. But I got him lots of presents, useful things he liked. He often didn't open some till April. We also made ornaments. New Year's Eve; we kissed at midnight wherever we were. In fact, we'd be asleep; Chuck, with his accurate inner clock, would wake up seconds before midnight, we'd kiss and go back to sleep. For his birthday, I put together a celebration, cake, friends, not sure what presents. For Valentine's Day, sometimes a piece of jewelry given him to give to me, a beautiful card and a gesture. For Easter, we painted eggs and got malted milk balls for me, a chocolate bunny for him and, later, fantastic Easter-themed petit fours.

Chuck, bless him, not only did as I asked, but was happy to do so. I realized, though, that Chuck gave me a present or two every time he came home from a trip I wasn't on or "just because" when we were home if he saw something he thought I'd like. I did the same. To have to do it on a specific day became silly with unnecessary pressure.

After that first year, I never worried about celebrating amateur Hallmark days again. We did celebrate Chuck's birthday because it was great fun. And we did have birthday cake on or vaguely near my birthday.

# COMMITMENT

One day, while Chuck was in the shower, a woman called. I answered the phone and clearly, she was put off. She asked for Chuck. Her tone was a bit rude as she asked me who I was. I told her my name and asked her for her name. She announced it with authority.

Well, you can't out-snob me. I grew up in one of the snootiest areas of the country, had spent time in Europe with titled folks, and went to girls' school with the "mean girls"—lots of training. So I took the phone to just outside the bathroom and called, "Honey! Telephone!" No answer—he couldn't hear me, of course, but she sure could hear the shower. I walked back to the kitchen and said, "I'm sorry; he's busy. Can he call you back?"

"Tell him I called."

"Your number?"

"He knows it." And she slammed the phone. So much for that potential competition.

I really don't know what possessed me—that is not my style at all, but she was so mean and they had been merely friends. Most importantly, either a guy wants to be with me or he doesn't.

He called her back. I could hear her yelling at him through the phone. This woman's husband had hunted with Chuck and died 20 years before. This woman, like many, didn't hunt, fish, or fly; wanted to use Chuck to show him off at cocktail parties and obviously, they weren't the right fit. By contrast, before meeting Chuck, I had been to enough cocktail parties, met enough famous people, and just liked learning new skills, new viewpoints, and having fantastic new adventures with a truly great man.

A few days later, Chuck wrote a note to this woman. He left the envelope open. I sure contemplated reading it but didn't. When Chuck came home, he asked if I had read it. I told him no. He asked, "Why?" I explained, "That's your deal, your privacy." Yet, I do wish I had asked at that point if I could read it—it would have been insightful. He was a great writer. He did tell me the gist of it; as he phrased it, "I broke my plate."

That night, Chuck and I were in each other's arms, lying down, when he said, "Now, you can't be with anyone else."

I replied, "Okay. And neither can you." He hadn't had anyone say that to him so directly and clearly. I could see a slight smile; he was very pleased with my response.

One time, while we were lying in bed, Chuck ordered, "Bring those knockers over here!" Momentarily, I thought, "Wha—? What's a knocker?" Then I burst into peals of laughter. He always delighted in my laughter but looked at me with that quizzical look again. "I don't have anything on my body that's big enough to knock," I sputtered. "My knees don't even knock!" As I was saying all that, I brought over what I did have, best I could, while continuing my fit of giggles.

## IT'S OVER

About a month after our first High Sierra trip, Chuck, out of the blue, told me, "You have to move out."

Me: "Oh? Why?"

Chuck: "Because we're not married."

I considered this. The only time we had discussed it was that first day hiking together: we were either never getting married again or never getting married. A vow with this man. Unbelievably, I said, "I guess…I think I could marry you." Another new adventure.

Taken aback, not expecting that reply, he responded, "No, no…you just have to move out."

Me, completely confused: "Right this second, or can I take a little time to find a place?"

Chuck, also not expecting this response, said, "Yeah."

I boldly asked him, "Do you love me?"

He answered, "No."

Me, now completely in shock: "Oh." Then, "I have to go for a walk," and almost ran out the door. I hiked around the property while I cried.

When I returned, he said, "You're like a little kid. You always run out the door. Can't we discuss this?"

I replied, "What is there to discuss? I love you. You don't love me. That makes me sad, but I'll find a place."

That night, we were intimate. I'm not sure why I...but it was lovely, and I guess deep down, part of me didn't believe him and I most definitely trusted him.

The next day, he went to the office and I got the paper to look for a place to live and made some calls for some consulting work. He came home for lunch and asked me what I was doing.

"You want me to move out, so I'm looking for a place to live and some work."

He looked stern, torn, and finally uttered, "You don't have to rush."

I had a doctor's appointment, so I left...even more confused.

For some reason, as I waited in the reception area for the doctor, I, the only one there, told the receptionist the story. She was older, kind, and seemed wise.

She said to me very pointedly, "Don't you move out until he physically throws you out!"

Me: "I'm not comfortable with that—I'd seem like a stalker or something."

She repeated, "Mark my words." It was a small town; maybe she knew something.

After the appointment, I thanked her and went home.

Chuck walked in and I said, again, no idea what prompted me except an idea that perhaps outside forces were at work on him: "I think you do love me."

He half smiled and asked, "What is love?"

I kissed him on the cheek and said, "Just this." And then, "It doesn't mean we have to get married, or you have to buy me anything, or me you. It's very, very simple."

Chuck smiled, full of joy, then laughed his overwhelmingly beautiful laugh that filled my whole being with great warmth.

And that was that.

The kindly receptionist's instincts and then mine were right. Others were telling Chuck to get me out because of jealousy and because their incomes had decreased. He now had someone to play with, so was doing far fewer paying talks, appearances, etc., for money. I was an oddity— I didn't want his money; I wanted him.

## PART II

# HIGH SIERRA

## FIRST TIME

The first time I trekked into the High Sierra to fish for golden trout was with Chuck; it was such a wonder. We had been together just under three months at that point.

We had hiked often at higher elevations the month leading up to Chuck's annual High Sierra trip to get him in shape. I sure wished I could go, but it was a boys' trip.

Tuesday. Shopping from the list for the trip. He was leaving Friday.

Wednesday: Two people canceled. Chuck looked at me and said: "Would you like to go?"

"YEEESSSS!" My head screamed, but I wasn't sure if he was kidding. Slightly more calmly, I answered, "Sure."

Then: Gasp! I did not have good hiking boots. No time to break them in. Or to break me in. I scrambled. Shoes never fit me. I tried every boot within a fifty-mile radius. Oddly, the cheapest ones fit the best. They weren't the greatest—not very deep tread, but…they'd just have to do.

Other than in Africa, I had been camping maybe once. So when Chuck asked if I wanted to go on his annual fishing/trekking trip into the Sierra, I was thrilled. After years of traveling all over the world, this invitation opened up an entirely new world and experience for me. Chuck even had a small booklet he had composed/written over the years listing supplies to bring on this trip he had taken almost annually for 55 years.

Chuck's daughter asked me dubiously what I planned to do about…well… menses, although she used another term. It's the reason she didn't go camping anymore. I replied, "I don't know, but plenty of women have done it before over the centuries, so I'll figure it out. I'm not going to let it limit me." Baffled, she wasn't keen on that answer.

On Thursday, we flew over the target High Sierra lakes to make sure the snow and ice had melted enough for fishing. Check. I think Chuck was also testing my tolerance for thin air to make sure I didn't get mountain sickness. I didn't. Check.

When we returned, we loaded our packs and sleeping bags according to Chuck's well-worn and tested booklet and one overnight bag for Friday night—which we would spend in a motel in Lone Pine, Nevada.

On Friday, we picked up Chuck's younger brother, Hal, at the Reno airport and set out for Lone Pine, driving through some interesting, historic towns in Nevada.

I was the first gal Chuck had brought into the Sierra on the annual boys' trip. He had taken Glennis and the kids on family trips often over the years, but on this trip, which, in the last few years, had the group returning from the trek on July 4; Chuck had taken no females.

We had a hearty dinner Friday night in Lone Pine with the motel owners, their son, M, who was going to accompany us, and some friends.

The next morning, after our last big breakfast, we drove up to the portal and started hiking. We were a large group—some were just hiking to the pass, having lunch with us, and returning the same day. When we started out, my pack was forty pounds. Chuck's, Hal's, and M's were each around fifty pounds or more.

As we walked, Chuck gave me a few pointers. One guest a few years back had raced up the first day while Chuck walked slowly. Chuck passed the rabbit, who was puking his guts out from the altitude change. Several, including his brother, had gotten mountain sickness over the years—taking care of getting them off the Sierra had almost ruined the trip.

Every few switchbacks, Chuck would ask me if I wanted a "blow" (which meant a breather). That was my cue. I'd say, "Yes," and stop to rest.

He would sit on a rock. I found sitting down okay—it was getting back up with the forty-pound pack on my back that was challenging, so I learned to just stand for my rest.

We'd rest for a minute or two, then move on. Some of the others went on ahead.

Chuck liked to tell the story this way: "Victoria would say to me: 'You look bad, or you look like hell—let me take some of the weight in your pack,' and took five pounds out of my sack and put it in hers. She did this a few times so she ended up with fifty-five pounds and I ended up with thirty-five pounds."

(Although it makes for an amusing story about the new kid, me, I assure you; this is not true. Chuck was too kind and caring to do this to me.)

Chuck would also tell people that fifteen pounds of mine was "crampax," as he calls those supplies.

(I assure you…this might be true.)

This go-and-blow happened several times as we gained three thousand feet from nine thousand to twelve thousand feet in about four miles to Cottonwood Pass. My own pace is a little faster, but my feet most likely had blisters—boy, did they hurt. I decided that they may hurt, but there was nothing dangerous like infection. I was partly afraid to take my boots off to put on moleskin—afraid I'd never get them on again. I had played enough field hockey in new shoes to know I better have a good supply of moleskin on this trip.

One of the hikers was a doctor—I asked him. His response (unbelievably) was: It just means you are walking too fast. Slow down. If I had walked any more slowly, I would have been going backwards/downhill. I don't know why I thought he would know what he was talking about; he was a cardiologist, not a foot doctor. And not that good a cardiologist at that.

It was an arduous climb. When I stumbled over a rock, Chuck would say (Chuck YEAGER-ism #133): "Want us to paint that a neon color for you!" I turned to him in mock indignation, laughing.

When we got to the pass, what a relief. Spectacular view. Lots of snow. Chuck found a dry boulder. We sat down in the sun and ate our sandwiches—the last ones we would have for at least two weeks. Deeeelicious. Chuck took a quick nap with my lap as a pillow, as he did for the rest of our lives when we were out in nature.

We bade our farewells and four of us continued on. At a certain point when we were climbing again, I was in the rear of the group—I about fainted (that pesky menses). I sat down and regained my equilibrium. I was short on iron and oxygen, for sure.

We ran into a guy whom the group usually saw towards the end of the trip—he brings in lots of goodies. It was his last day, so he gave us a few chocolates. We would have been more receptive ten days in, but now it was just more weight. I still gratefully accepted some of it—one never knows. (I had been stuck in the outskirts of Bagan, Myanmar, visiting the myriads of temples without sufficient food or water to the point of almost not making it. One never forgets that.)

The rest seemed downhill. And it was. Eight miles. We descended one thousand feet.

When we got to camp, there was no rest for the weary. We started putting up our tents, gathering firewood, and getting out food. When I thought we were mostly done, I got on a rock and removed my boots. Ah, relief. But: Oh my goodness. I had blisters…on blisters…on blisters.

That's when Chuck told me to go help M get some water for camp: Ramen noodles, hot chocolate…Ahhhhhhh. Oops. Was he kidding? I dreaded putting my boots back on to go down the relatively short hill, but I did not want Chuck to regret bringing a "female" into the Sierra.

He looked over, saw me in bare feet, well, really couldn't see my bare feet through all the blisters, and was stunned. Chuck could not believe how awful or awfully painful my feet looked.

But more, he couldn't believe I hadn't complained.

I could see he catalogued that on the plus side. As I look back on our lives, I realize we tested each other a lot in a sense before we got married. My father always said never marry someone you haven't seen go through a trauma; that will tell you his/her true character and what to expect when things aren't always rosy.

M said he had some slippers I could wear. I was soooo grateful, wondering why I hadn't thought to bring some (that fit!). Too big, M's slippers worked in camp but I found it too difficult to walk down to the water safely in them. Spraining an ankle would not help the trip. And barefoot—too many prickly pines, leaves, etc., on the ground. I started out—trying to get there, but M said he was fine handling it on his own.

I quietly, meekly, asked Chuck if it was all right if I stayed close to camp and continued gathering wood instead. Yes.

Relief, again.

Supper, since we weren't near any streams with golden trout, was ramen noodles as well as beef jerky, almonds, raisins, and hot chocolate with marshmallows. I forewent the jerky, too tough for me, and the hot chocolate—chocolate's caffeine would keep me up all night no matter how tired I was. The altitude might be enough to overcome to try to sleep.

Hal offered that we use the soup and hot chocolate from his bag. I thought bemusedly: that's a lot of trust that we'd share ours later.

Silly me. Sounded nice until Chuck clued the new kid (me) in: "He's just trying to lighten his load. Say, 'No.'" Ah. I adored Chuck protecting me from others. Especially from Hal.

Chuck and I went to bed right after supper. We changed into our pajamas and huddled together to keep warm. It was a lovely night. Except for the altitude, I eventually slept pretty darn well.

The next morning, we had oatmeal (grits for Hal), coffee, and tea and packed up after filling our canteens. I delayed putting on those boots as long as possible.

Yeowww-ch. That was what I was thinking, but it didn't get voiced.

Some of the rock and tree formations were so intricate, they greatly inspired the imagination. At one point, we were talking to Hal seated on a rock. Chuck stepped back and caught himself—or I caught him. It was a long drop.

The High Sierra is such glorious country. We came around a hill and crossed a meadow of blue, white, and red flowers. Very marshy in areas, so we had to be careful not to get wet.

Chuck gave us a couple of "Attaboys" to get over the next hill. "Attaboys" are Werther's butterscotch candy—you get one to encourage you to get over the hill or one after you have achieved it. Hal brought a similar candy, too—a chocolate version.

M and Hal got way ahead of us. We didn't mind too much—they could set up camp. And if we didn't arrive, they'd know how to backtrack to find us.

I preferred being alone with Chuck.

This day, it rained. So Chuck set up the tarp under which we waited it out. We also built a fire to keep warm. When I say we, I mean he did and I helped. Frigid rain. I was so grateful to be with a *very* knowledgeable guy with whom I felt, and was, safe.

When the rain lightened up, we took down the tarp and continued on. Chuck was a great leader. Knowing I was exhausted, cold, a little wet, feet hurting, but not complaining, he distracted me and started talking about the new regulations—no (camp) fires above 10,000 feet. Almost all of the wood is below that, so why have that regulation? The fish are above 12,000', so that makes for longer hikes to get lunch and dinner each day. Then Chuck told me stories of when he brought Glennis and the kids up. One year, there was so much snow around Rocky Basin Lakes that the boys built a tunnel inside the snow to slide down from the top of the cliff to the lake.

We hiked up to our next stop. I immediately removed my shoes and stood on a rock, airing out the blisters. We built a big fire. Viktor Belenko, the Russian defector, when he had been on one of these trips with Chuck, called it the B.S. (the full word) fire because usually, the guys would talk B.S. around it into the night.

A gorgeous night—starry. Many satellites going by. Some shooting stars, some planes.

The next morning, I put my ouch, boots, ouch, back on, climbed down to the stream to wash up a little and brought some water up for tea, coffee and oatmeal. We ate, packed, filled our canteens and continued on towards Funston Lake (our next camping spot for a week). As we crested the hill and were descending the other side, we stopped for some almonds, raisins, and jerky. Lunch.

We continued for about ten minutes when Chuck proclaimed: "It's going to hail in five minutes."

His brother said, "No, I think it'll hold off. We should be at Funston in three hours." So M and he continued hiking.

Chuck ignored them and started setting up the tarp. I helped Chuck. As much as I wanted to forge ahead, I had no doubt whatsoever Chuck was right.

To the second, five minutes later, le deluge! Chuck and I were under our tarp, nice and comfy.

Hal and M came running back. We shouted: "No room! No room!" but of course, we let them under—it was a tight fit. There is a photo somewhere.

I kidded Hal: "You doubted your brother's take on the weather?"

He just shook his head at himself. "You'd think I'd know better after all these years (67 at that time to be exact)."

After about thirty minutes, the rain and hail subsided, so we gathered the tarp and set out again. We reached Funston in the afternoon and the usual campsite area about forty-five minutes after that. We unpacked. We'd be here for at least a week.

Then we headed up to the lake to get dinner by fishing for the famed golden trout. A little easier climb without the pack.

## CHUCK TEACHES VICTORIA HOW TO FISH

That third evening of the fourteen days especially sticks out in my mind. Chuck was teaching me how to fish. I had only been fishing once—on a kid trip, age 15, in France. No one on that trip knew how to fish. I think I caught an old boot with no treasure inside. Very disappointing.

While Chuck was using a fly rod, he decided I should start on a spinning rod. We fished side by side while he gave me pointers now and again. I could throw medium distance pretty well; consequently got the spinner out into the lake pretty far. Chuck had warned me: "Don't let it sink and get caught on a rock. We don't have that many lures for the spinner." And laughed.

Terrified we'd starve if I lost the spinner, I reeled it in quickly.

Chuck: "Not so fast; the fish aren't on the top." The next toss, then, still terrified, I tried to slow down.

Chuck: "Not so fast!" I tried again.

I watched Chuck catch a couple of goldens (trout). Watching him concentrate on putting his rod together, carefully choosing his fly, tying the fly on in his unique way, casting, stripping (which with a fly rod essentially means retrieving)…well, that is poetry in motion.

Then, Chuck watches the fish take notice of his fly in the clear, frigid waters of this lake and plays with the fly, attracting the fish to consummate and bite the fly…

Fish on! The fish jumps a little, trying to shake the hook. Zigs. Zags. Chuck plays him, clearly enjoying it all, exuding great joy. Woo hoo! Once the fish is worn out, Chuck has me hold the fly rod—not going to trust me to take the fish off and not lose it. I agree.

Chuck bleeds the fish, then strings the first catch on a stick and secures the stick by burrowing one end in the sand under the water in the shallow edge. This keeps the fish cold and wet. Well. We have Chuck's dinner. He looks at me and orders: "Catch a fish!"

He turns to his rod and checks the fly and the line for glitches before he tosses it out again. His line floats to the surface of the lake. He lets the tip sink and when he thinks it has sunk far enough, he starts bringing it in in spurts to make his fly appear as food, a bug, to the fish.

I continue tossing and retrieving…still too fast. After watching me through several exercises in good tossing and not-so-good retrieving, Chuck warned, "You'll have to learn how to fish if we're going to go to Alaska in two months!"

Alaska. For as long as I could remember, I had always wanted to go to Alaska. I couldn't figure out how to do it well. Europe was easy—historic places, museums, great food, friends. Alaska was resplendent scenery. I received all sorts of invitations but just not from the right person. Until Chuck. Prior to our trip in the Sierra, within a month of knowing him, out of the blue, he asked, "Want to go fishing in Alaska?"

I liked doing just about anything with Chuck, but add going to a place I had always wanted to go, with someone who knew it well and with his friend, Tony, traveling by helicopter? I couldn't say "Yes" fast enough! Now the coveted Alaska trip was threatened, I became very motivated. I had to learn how to fish. And fast. Occasionally, I took Chuck a little too seriously.

The umpteenth time the reel came skipping across the top, Chuck said, "You have to let it sink so it gets to the fish, gets their attention."

I tried again. Here came the spinner skipping merrily.

After the umpteenth-plus-one time, Chuck, with great patience, said, "When it hits the water, count to three before you start reeling."

The next cast, I dutifully counted to three and let the spinner sink. Chuck, music to my ears, said, "Atta girl. Now reel."

No fish.

Chuck: "That was good. Try again." I tried using the counting-to-three method. I was thinking, 'This is too much like work. What happened to napping with the rod next to you until you feel a tug?' Actually, my attitude, at 42, was: this is too sedentary. I want to go exploring the hills. But this was also dinner, so had purpose.

After several more attempts, finally, halfway in, I felt a tug. I was elated!

"I GOT A FISH!" Now, what do I do? I tugged back.

Chuck looked over, assessed the situation and said: "That's not a fish; that's a rock."

Me: "It's a fish!"

A few more tugs, my rod tip bending a little each time…"See!"

Chuck replied: "That's a rock!"

I insisted: "It's a fish!"

Chuck, with his famous quizzical look of great bemusement re me, asked: "Can't you tell the difference between a fish and a rock?"

As I was seriously contemplating how to describe the scientific differences, Chuck broke into this heavy thinking and said: "A fish wiggles!"

Simple. And brilliant in its simplicity, as usual.

Me? I took a break.

As Chuck told the story: "Victoria threw down the rod and said, 'Get your own goddamn fish!' and stomped off."

While that last sentence isn't entirely true, it was funny.

I had ten days to learn to fish for the Alaska trip—it wasn't a bad start.

## ALONE AT LAST *(in the High Sierra)*

On the fifth day, Chuck had decided he wasn't going to move on to the next camp, Crabtree Lake; he was staying put. So I was staying put. Hal wanted to climb Mt. Whitney one last time, so M and he pushed off. While I would have liked to climb it as well, 111 switchbacks didn't sound like fun, but more importantly, not without Chuck.

I was a bit worried—what if something happened to Chuck? What would I do? I certainly didn't know my way out. If I left him, yikes for him and for me. If I stayed without help…

Prior to leaving, M split up the food. Only apparently, he didn't know how to count. Or maybe he did. I didn't want to rock the boat too much, but they took the skillet and far too much. I pointed it out, so got some supplies back.

I wish they had left sooner. It was the best week ever—just the two of us, Chuck and me.

We learned later that at Crabtree, Hal and M ran into forty Boy Scouts, or Boy Sprouts as Chuck would say, camping there. Chuck often had this sixth sense. For me, one does not trek three days one way to be in a crowd. So I was even more glad Chuck and I stayed put alone together.

One time, I dropped an Attaboy candy on the ground, picked it up and wiped it off on my pants before popping it in my mouth. I looked up and saw Chuck silently watching me, looking at my pants, then at me and laughing with great mirth. We had been camping for over a week—He was right; it was questionable as to which was less dirty or sanitary—my pants or the ground.

One time, while Chuck took a nap, I hiked around, being very careful not to get lost. I grew up in a city and am quick to find my way in most cities. Country? Especially on a cloudy day…not so much. M, who grew up and lived by those hills, had said he got lost, which had my attention and concern—if he can get lost…I couldn't figure out how, though—all the draws led up to Funston Lake. He also said he had seen bear scat. Hmmm.

But I did hike over to the next draw and turned right to go away from the lake. I kept looking back so I had the correct sight picture to return. I found large boulders that looked like someone had placed them there—like Stonehenge. I looked over the cliffs, careful that nothing happened to me—how would Chuck ever find me, get help, etc.? I then hiked up to the lake, went around it, and back down the draw where our tent was. Safe.

Chuck had brought a sun shower, using me as the excuse—and I gladly accepted being the excuse. But it was he who loved it for shaving. And frankly, I did like washing my hair in warm water. That second week, we didn't have to put it in a secluded spot—it was just us. And that was quite pleasurable and, frankly, sensual, showering in the middle of the Sierra in the warm sun. One time, we were in the tent in the middle of the day and a guy came looking for us—calling out Chuck's name. We stayed quiet—we were definitely not ready or even dressed…for company. Thank goodness he didn't come to the tent. That would have been…interesting.

After a bit of time, after the guy left, we were hungry—we wanted to go get fish for dinner. We got dressed, found him at the lake and said hello. We didn't explain when he said he came looking for us. Chuck smiled. I smiled. It was a recurring theme with us.

The guy got the message and never came down to our camping area again. Smart man.

## POACHED GOLDEN TROUT

One of the days, another friend, T, hiked all the way in just for the day. While we had taken three days to get to where we were camping, after ten days of hiking to get food twice a day, I thought I could probably do it in a day as well, if I had to, without the forty pounds.

T had heard about how Chuck cooked golden trout and was keen to have some. She arrived just after we had gotten back to our camp with lunch. Her eager face fell when she saw we were boiling it. Chuck had let the others take the only skillet because he wanted to try the fish the way the Germans had prepared it when he was stationed there 1954-57 and 1966-68: boiling. Chuck had another name that escapes me now, but I renamed it the snobbish, better-sounding or tastier-sounding "poaching."

She dutifully tasted it and liked it so much Chuck and I barely got any and had to go back to fish for dinner. To be fair, it was delicious. After lunch, T hiked back to the portal from which she came.

* * *

While we were there, some government agency had flown some folks up in a helicopter and set up camp next to Funston to fix the repeater station above Funston. Each day, the helicopter would fly up to Funston, pick up the personnel, then fly the personnel to the repeater station. They all left for a couple of days, so Chuck went exploring on his own. The huge tent was full of supplies; nothing exciting except, at best, peanut butter. No jelly.

I hiked up to the repeater station from Funston—took me about forty-five minutes. All that expenditure for the helicopter when the personnel could have easily hiked up.

After another glorious five days, we packed up and retraced our steps back, sad to be leaving our idyllic spot, looking forward to a nice meal, great pressurized showers, and our own bed at home.

That night, the motel owners served us a huge meal at their house. However, the steak was inedible—couldn't chew it. I so wanted to be able to.

The next day, on our drive back, we stopped at IHOP in Reno for lunch before we put Hal on the plane. As Chuck walked in, an airline pilot recognized him, said hello and asked how many hours Chuck had in flight. It was so unimportant to Chuck; he guessed 10,000 hours.

The airline pilot said, "That all?" Chuck retorted, "I did all my own take-offs and landings." (Each airline pilot doesn't do everything every time since there are two pilots generally in commercial airlines and some airplanes have automatic landing capabilities.) That stopped the smart aleck's nonsense.

## PURE WATER

I'd be remiss if I didn't mention the highlight of our second trip into the High Sierra. The year before, Chuck had been exploring and found water gushing out of the side of a rock like a forceful spigot that you could not turn off. It was remarkable. A majestic fountain. Although about a twenty-minute hike farther from Funston Lake, we camped near the fountain the second year. The water tasted great and, while it was frigid for a shower, it was so forceful, I did get my hair wet and then, after shampooing, rinsed in nanoseconds, making the freezing cold water bearable.

Unfortunately, we had three boys on our trip in their 40's. Two of them wanted to hike down to another river, move along and hike up another draw. Chuck told them the last person who did that ended up with a broken neck. Two of them still went. I hiked down with them till it got too difficult. The tallest was sure I could make it. I could just jump across these chasms with death below. I chose to return the way I came. Turns out, they did not go all the way to the creek but took a shortcut another way. Before I left, they wanted the stores of food and water I had brought for me. I contemplated this, usually willing to help, but this time I said no. I had to hike back up by myself, dangerous in itself, and might need them. Why didn't they bring any for themselves? One was experienced, the other a doctor. A little concerned that I was alone, I rather rejoiced that I was alone and without those two. I went slowly up the draw, stopping at each of the creek's tiny waterfalls, analyzing the waterflow.

After about the right time had passed, Chuck, sure I would be smart enough not to go the whole way and break my neck, asked the third guy, who had remained, if he saw me. The boy said, "I see a head moving. then stopping to examine the creek every few feet." Satisfied, very relieved, and amused, apparently Chuck laughed and said, "Yep. That would be Victoria."

# PART III
## FISHING

## ALASKA

In early August 2000, we flew to Anchorage. Our friend Tony picked us up and brought us a few minutes away to his house on a slight hill on a lake. Rita, his wife, was a great cook. Dinner was delicious, with a splendid view of Campbell Lake, watching float planes taking off and landing.

Tony put on one of Chuck's favorite songs, Jim Ed Brown's *"Doggone My Soul, How I Love Them Old Songs"*, and Chuck and I danced to it. Tony was stunned—he'd never seen his friend dance (great dancer) or so happy.

Chuck and I went downstairs, unpacked and got our gear ready. The next morning, we had a fairly early breakfast and headed down the hill in Tony's backyard, where his helicopter was waiting.

We put on our hip waders and packed our gear, the drinks, and sandwiches. Two of Tony's grandkids, ZZ and Oney, ages about nine and eleven, joined us. The first time, Chuck put me in the front seat. Ever after, he took the front seat for safety in case something happened to Tony. He never said anything but. ...

We took off, gained speed, ascended above the lake, and headed out. Along the way, we saw beluga whales, bald eagles, moose, and bears, many of these animals with their offspring. We flew over bald eagles' nests, rivers, glaciers, shrubs, and mountains.

It was breathtaking.

As we hovered over one river, we looked to see if there were fish. There weren't any visible, so we continued on. We passed several rivers until we found one with fish.

We landed, waited the required two minutes for the helicopter to shut down, and got out.

Chuck and Tony helped me put my rod together with my fly-fishing reel and the right fly, an egg-sucking leech.

I was learning to fly fish and caught a lot of trees, grass and debris. Tony, very patiently, would go across the river or behind me and retrieve my fly. I started getting the hang of it and catching fish on the fly rod.

Real fishing, as Chuck would say. Now that was fun.

Chuck, of course, caught some right off the bat. He loved fishing. I marveled as I once again observed Chuck so focused, concentrating, at one with the fish, catching lots of them. I knew with him, we wouldn't starve. Ever. In fact, the next year in the Sierra, with six of us (too many), Chuck was the only one who caught fish and generously shared.

I was casting okay—it was a narrow river. Chuck was coaching me.

Tony got busy helping his grandkids learn to fish. Little Oney caught one and we had to hold onto him, or the fish would have dragged him down the river and out to sea. So very cute. He brought in that big silver salmon with lots of coaching from Grandpa Tony and General Chuck.

I did a little better with the eggs from Oney's fish as bait. Those silvers like to try to shake that hook loose any which way they can and zing down the river, letting out the line, then swimming fast back up, so you have to reel very fast to keep the line taught.

Chuck and I used six-weight rods, so a lot more lively and fun.

We took a break to eat Rita's delicious halibut sandwiches. I tried hard not to eat her cookies, but to no avail; they knew my name. The sun was shining, the flowers were out...Within a few hours, we all caught our limit, loaded up and took off.

We saw moose, bears, cubs, and eagles on the way back. One bear could hear us but couldn't see us, so she stood up on her hind legs, swatting at the air to make us go away, protecting her three little cubs. Brave Momma.

We landed at a river to clean the fish and lighten our load. Tony had his own efficient way to clean them, so we helped by staying out of his way. We also explored and found a small rock that looked like a long monkey face.

When Tony was finished and had fed the river the carcasses, we headed home. Tony cooked some of the fresh salmon on the grill.

Best. Salmon. Ever.

First time I ever really liked salmon (other than gravlax). Cooked properly, not too done. Fresh.

The next two days were similarly great. Then we helicoptered to Tony and Rita's summer cabin on Two Lakes. We landed on a glacier, drank some fresh water, and enjoyed the view. I held my breath as Chuck jumped a crevasse. I went around. To get to Two Lakes, one had to traverse a pass where there were pieces of twenty-seven airplanes whose pilots had thought they could make it through the pass in inclement weather. They couldn't.

We fished for a very bony fish, pike. Hard to eat.

While I enjoyed the overnight, I was glad to return to Anchorage and more helicopter fishing for silvers (salmon).

We saw many interesting sights from the helicopter over the years. One time, we saw a guy fishing. As we flew downriver, there was his picnic table all set up for lunch. Farther downriver, around the corner, we saw a bear heading towards the lunch table. We wondered how that scenario ended. The table was only set for one.

Another time, we saw a lone wolf, but it was a bit nuts; it tried to jump up on the skid.

Life is amazing. For the first 42 years of my life, I wanted to go, but never got, to Alaska. Then, for the next fifteen, we averaged two to five times a year, almost always one of those each year was with Tony, helicopter fishing, until both men passed.

So glad I waited for the right person with whom to go!

I'll always remember my first fish and my first kiss in Alaska!

## HONEYMOON IN ALASKA

In August 2003, just after Chuck and I got married (wedding details in Part IV), an acquaintance flew us up to Anchorage from the lower forty-eight. We kid about it now that Jim took us on our honeymoon. The next day, we flew in Tony's helicopter east, then south past blueberry fields where there was no sign of humans. Exquisite.

We were fishing on a little river. I went downriver away from the crowd of four, then stepped into the river. At one point, I turned to return upriver, but the boot parts of my hip waders were stuck in the mud, so I ended up sitting up to my chest in the water. I was so shocked (very cold, fed by glaciers); I didn't get up as quickly as I should have, which might have lessened the drenching.

I finally got my boots and me out and walked back to the helicopter. Everyone else was still fishing.

Tony's coat came below my knees, so he gave it to me to wear. It wasn't cold out—a gorgeous, sunny day. I put on the coat, did the girls' school-undress-under-the-coat maneuver where nothing private was revealed, and hung my clothes up to dry.

Jim called out, "Victoria, I hooked a fish; come reel it in!"

I yelled back, without thinking: "I can't! I'm not wearing any underwear!" (That's when Chuck would say my mouth wasn't connected to my brain. He was right!)

Jim replied, "Well, I've never heard that excuse before!"

Chuck, Tony, and Jim laughed about that for years.

Yes, I did, too.

## BRISTOL BAY FISHING

After 2001, we were often guests the end of June, first week of July at a fishing lodge on Bristol Bay, Alaska, now owned by one of the former pilots, Jerry. Several times, we were lucky to have a private jet take us there and back.

One year, there were two co-CEOs of a large corporation, one former CEO of one of the largest corporations, a former governor and his wife (who had muscled in on the trip), some sons of the above, Chuck Yeager, and me.

When you go fishing with folks, you sure get to know them well.

Some of the memories of that trip are:

There was great competition as to who caught the biggest fish. Archie, former Chairman of a Fortune 100 company, asked me how big my fish was. I told him. Then, to be polite, I asked Archie how big his fish was. Miraculously, his was half a pound more. That's when Chuck clued me in with Chuck YEAGER-ism #134: "The first guy to answer never stands a chance!" In other words, NEVER answer first. We laughed. And I learned.

Another time, I caught a line. I pulled it in and realized there might be a fish on the other end of the broken line. I started pulling it in hand over hand. One of the young, newer guides was trying to figure out how to tie it onto my rod instead of hand over hand. He kept telling me to stop while he was not accomplishing getting it tied to my rod.

Fortunately, the owner of the lodge, an expert, experienced fisherman, was there and backed me up when I said, "That's how they did it for thousands of years ere now and they didn't starve." What I needed, I told him, was a can or something to wrap the line around in case the fish took off. I didn't want to lose the fish and I couldn't hold on barehanded—that would just severely damage my hands before the fish got away.

Archie's son, Steve, noticed and said, "I think that's the fish I lost—my line broke."

The line had broken close to the rod, so there was a lot to pull in. The good news was that it was a sinking line, thus very heavy, causing the fish to have already tired. I slowly pulled the fish in with the young guide trying to hover. I told him to get out of the way. The fish tugged a little. The green guide tried to jump in. I shooed him away.

The fish was ginormous; Steve immediately jokingly claimed his stake, "I should get half credit!"

Me: "Oh sure! You only wanted that AFTER you saw how big he was. And you lost him!"

Steve: "That's my line you're bringing him in on." We bantered good-naturedly a little more, both happy to capture the fish and Steve's line.

At dinner, when everyone was giving me kudos, I gave Steve half-credit, to his great delight.

*  *  *

Before one of the dinners, about five days into the trip, the guys were having guy talk about clothes, how women dress, clearly "wanting it." I jumped in, "Seriously?" They realized then that I was there. Oops.

I said, "So, do you think wearing tight clothes is intentionally inviting?"

One of the adult kids: "Yes."

I assured all: "Well, I can guarantee you, I'm not! My jeans were loose when we arrived!"

Everyone laughed. The food was excellent. I'm sure we all gained weight that week, so they could all relate.

*　*　*

We did a lot of fly-outs to different scenic rivers, lakes and ocean spots and saw plenty of bear fishing in the places we fished. I often got to take off and land the float planes (with Jerry as instructor pilot), so it was pretty exciting.

One time, we were fishing on the side of a river, close to the mouth, with a few strangers fishing on the other side. They started yelling at us. We turned and saw a bear fishing slowly towards us. The guide told us to follow him slowly in the opposite direction. The other four or five in our group did so.

Chuck was happily fishing and didn't want to leave—the bear wasn't that close. I stayed with Chuck, but the bear kept approaching and got quite close, about twenty yards—usually, they'll see a human and veer off. This one didn't. So, we pulled in our lines and headed slowly away—zigzagging so it didn't look as though we were running off.

Another time, we rescued an eagle. After we fished for grayling and rainbows down a river, we were making our way by boat to the rendezvous spot when we spied a young eagle caught in an Indian fishing net.

Chuck tenderly removed the net and gave the eagle to the governor, who held the frightened eagle in a jacket to keep it warm and prevent its talons from scratching the governor. When we came upon the takeout spot, we managed to get the governor with the eagle, as well as the rest of us, into the truck.

At the lodge, we let the eagle go. He looked at us, shook his head, and hopped off. We weren't sure he was long for this world, being a little bit crippled.

The next year, when we were there, an adult eagle showed up walking toward us. The lodge owner said no eagle had shown up before. The governor was sure it was his buddy. And why not?

One year, the host flew us to Nome, Alaska. After lunch, overlooking the water, everyone else went shopping. Chuck and I did a cursory look through the stores, saw the prices, and immediately went searching for General Jimmy

Doolittle's boyhood home (a less expensive endeavor). General Doolittle was known for World War II's Tokyo Raid, being the first to develop instrument flying, changing the World War II air combat strategy in Europe, thus turning the war around, among other accomplishments.

Two people told us two different sites. The discrepancy came because the house in which General Doolittle grew up had been located in one spot, and after he moved away, the house was relocated to another spot. A very tiny, dark, two-story house.

We heard about General Doolittle's boxing in town as a boy. He had to; he was a little guy, and it was a rough town. Probably still is. His size, though, was perfect for flying. After retirement, Jimmy and Chuck hunted together. They did long drives to the hunts, so had plenty of private time together and a mutual admiration. General Doolittle had saved F/O Yeager's career during World War II.

## THE DREADED BROCCOLI!

Another evening at the Alaska lodge, Archie said in no uncertain terms, "Don't give me broccoli!" It was already on his plate, so he left it. The young daughter of the owner was clearing the dinner plates and Archie remarked how he, like Daddy (Chuck's and my nickname for Pres. George H.W.) Bush, hated broccoli and, at their age, they can refuse to eat broccoli.

I pulled the gal aside and whispered, "Don't give him dessert. He didn't eat his broccoli."

Archie's son knew something was up, so watched carefully.

This was some of the guys' umpteenth trip to this lodge, so they knew what great menus were being served. The gal served everyone the eagerly anticipated, delicious dessert.

Correction: she served the delicious dessert to everyone…except Archie. Then she started to leave.

Archie exclaimed, "Hey! What about me?" A few others chimed in to help.

Without skipping a beat, this seventeen-year-old wisp of a girl immediately turned around and scolded Archie, ex-Chairman of Conoco Philips, one of the largest corporations in the world: "You didn't eat your broccoli!" Everyone burst out laughing.

She was perfect. Chuck loved it!

Archie and his son loved it—people rarely took on his father. Like most Chairmen, they are often surrounded by kowtowing people. Archie, after his initial surprise, also burst out laughing. The gal relented and gave him his dessert. Without him having to eat his broccoli.

Archie decided I was okay.

But I'm pretty sure he still doesn't eat broccoli.

## MORE HELICOPTER FISHING IN ALASKA

We had a great week fishing. Monday, we went fishing, transported by helicopter, in some rivers nearby. It was a wet day, but as Chuck said: "The fish are already wet, so they don't care."

We took a break from fishing to eat lunch. Fortunately, the rain stopped to let us.

For dinner, we had a great fresh halibut dish and fresh corn on the cob.

The next day, we headed out—some clouds. By late morning, the sun was peeking out. All Anchorage natives were thrilled—they had had thirty days straight of rain—a record for summer.

We didn't catch much, but the halibut sandwiches, superb weather, snow-capped mountains, red flowers, eagles, and moose made for a perfect day. While flying, I spotted two wolves. Tony, our friend and helicopter pilot, didn't believe me. He couldn't have *two* passengers with excellent eyesight!

We circled—he thought they might be coyotes. Definitely young-ish as they were playfully running around. They were wolves. Tony was impressed. We also saw an eagle's nest with young ones and a Momma bear with her young-un. We had seen her on the same road (from the air) three times in a row.

Fishing and the outdoors don't get any better than that. We were catching fish, the sun was bright, the mountains visible, and some of the fish were jumping (and the cotton is high…oops, just had to break into an Ira Gershwin song)—putting on an excellent show.

I caught the first fish—rare when I'm with Chuck. I also caught the biggest fish…until 3 p.m. And the coolest was I watched the fish follow my fly, so I changed the pace of my stripping, and then the fish…snatched it and hooked himself. I set the hook a couple of times, though, just to make sure. It took a while to tire this big boy out. My arm got a bit tired, but I was loving it. He was a jumper. Each time he jumped, I held my breath while trying to keep the line taught, but not too taught…and he never got off till we bled him and took him off.

I danced the victory dance, teasing that I had to enjoy the moment because someone might catch a bigger one for the day and my "biggest" record would be short-lived.

We tried to take photos, which felt like Keystone Cops. By the time J got the camera out and figured out how to shoot it while holding our cell phone… Tony dropped the slippery fish. He picked it up and J took the photo, but the fish was muddy. So Tony washed the fish, which took some doing; the mud was pretty darn sticky. And we all posed again—Chuck pointing to himself even though this one was MY fish. And we got the photo.

A few hours later, at three or so, Chuck caught a fish probably bigger than mine. Yup, my record was short-lived. It, too, was a beauty!

## TSIU RIVER, ALASKA: *September 2010*

What an adventure! We flew a Gooney Bird, DC-3, (with Chuck as pilot) and landed on a spit between the Tsiu River and the Pacific Ocean to get to the lodge. The next day, Chuck and I took the ATV seven miles to the mouth of the Tsiu River. Each year, because of the harsh winter weather, the river course changes—a couple years before, it was four miles to the mouth. We ran into the others from the lodge coming back—they had started at the ungodly hour of 5:30 a.m.

Chuck wisely said: the fish don't know what time it is—and they'll be there whenever we arrive. The report from mid-river was good fishing early and then the fish quit biting.

And then—wham! They were biting like crazy—very fresh, very large fish!

(Two rods were bought and brought in from Cordova—Number 9, instead of the number 7s the other guests broke). Chuck and I were fishing on Number 6s, so a little more sporty.

There's nothing like throwing out a lure or a fly, reeling or stripping…a fish grabs it, and you feel that tug. Got one! And then it flips. Do I still have it? Tug-yes! Another energetic flip and jump! Trying to hold on but not too tight—that's how the rod or line gets broken or the hook rips out of the fish's mouth. Woo hoo! Then you actually get it ashore and weigh it. If a male and over thirteen lbs., we keep it. As soon as the hook has been removed and the decision made, we either bleed it and take it up to the box or set it loose. Many are a bit tired after our game, so we have to encourage them to swim; they are free of the lure or fly. We aim them so their gills start working and they are headed out to the fish hole, not the net. One fish floated for a bit towards the net. Oh dear! But then it realized it didn't have to play dead… and took off. Phew!

On to the next. Toss, reel, reel…TUG! Woo hoo! And the play begins again.

Chuck and I had a blast; silver salmon like to jump and run and flip. Beautiful silver fish. If they have barnacles, they are considered even fresher. As they swim up the river, they slowly turn red, spawn in the lake, and then die.

So the fresher from the ocean, the better tasting the fish.

Chuck did some funny moves—like the fish was so big he had to haul it over his shoulder and walk towards the beach. I pretended the same when we each had a large fish on. It was fun. Adrian, our fishing guide, got some great shots.

Have to be careful, though—sometimes it looks like footing is flat and it can suddenly be a big gully up to your…well, eyeballs if you're not careful. You also have to be wary of quicksand—while you don't get swallowed up, you can sink down deep enough to need help to get out.

We kept our limit—all fine-looking males, letting the females go to lay their eggs. Some were served that evening for dinner for twenty.

Sometimes in the afternoon, we'd go scavenger hunting on the beach for interestingly shaped driftwood. We also found lots of debris from storms and also often saw baby bears eating the garbage laid out for them.

The next day, it threatened rain. Many had gone duck hunting. We ate breakfast, put on our gear, got into the cart, and, while I was thinking maybe I should stay back and read about Eddie Rickenbacker…it POURED rain. Sigh.

We got to the big bend where we could see LOTS of fish that had gotten past the commercial nets. I cast my rod. Tug. Set the hook. Jumping, playing, flipping. And that was just me. Just kidding. The fish was having a heck of a time trying to get rid of my fly.

Chuck tossed his fly in. Tug. Another one.

The next cast. Tug. Run, jump. Run…

Same for Chuck.

The next one. Oops—didn't cast where I wanted to. No tug.

Cast again. Perfect. Reel. Oops, missed the one fish—reeled too hard; slow down. Tug again (same cast). GRAB it and run! This one we kept—beautiful fresh, large fish.

Chuck cast. TUG! Jumping, running, flipping. Just as Chuck was bringing it ashore, Adrian walked up to grab it, and the fish took off. "BEAR!" Chuck cried (that's what the fish thought Adrian was). And, of course, Chuck's fish, not to be outdone by his protégé, was one pound bigger.

A few times, Chuck was just holding his rod over the water, thinking about where he was going to cast, and a fish jumped up, trying to grab the fly!

It happened once to me—it jumped, got it, and then shook it loose before I could react to the first action. What a move!

It went on like that for a while. One cast, I felt the tug, tried to set the hook, instead succeeded in pulling it out of the fish's open mouth, so started reeling it in for another cast when another fish jumped on. Very accommodating.

I teased Adrian. What is the matter? I only got fifteen fish out of sixteen casts! I made up for it with the two fish jumping on one cast.

It was fun. And exhausting! Happily.

## CHILE *in 1954 & 2001 April*

Chuck told me about the Patillo twin brothers, Buck and Bill. Chuck had done a South American Goodwill tour with them for a month in the good old days (1954). Major Chuck Yeager opened each air show (about 40) with the first aviation sonic boom in each South American country. Those shows must have been spectacular, especially for their time.

Major Yeager was also called upon to fly many dignitaries all over the world supersonic. And to dine with numerous others as well. Living history.

Many years later—50 years later—Chuck and I were invited to go to Puerto Montt, Chile, to film Chuck fishing there for an episode of an ESPN TV series.

Chuck and the show host fished from one boat and the camera crew filmed while I fished out of the other. The crew became my cheerleaders; whenever I made a great cast, they cheered. And when I didn't do so well, which was often, I wasn't even close to proficient, they encouraged me to try again—"You can do it!" Fortunately, I never hit them or their equipment with the fly or my rod.

We ate well; we love homemade potato chips and guacamole with mostly avocado. The view of the lake from the restaurant was stunning, especially with the snow-capped volcano in the background.

Several of the days, I did adventure travel instead of fishing; horseback riding, ziplining, and climbing another mountain after horseback riding halfway there. We also stayed in a yurt and had the local alcohol drink, Pisco Sour. It is deceptive. Tastes like sweet lemonade, but several minutes later; what a kick! I could sure feel the punch after just a few sips.

On another visit to Chile at a different time of year, Chuck and I encountered murtas, a red berry about the size of a medium-sized blueberry. We ate them off the vine. Our guide was horrified—the Chileans thought they were sour.

The locals picked the murtas too early and added lots of sugar for jam. When we kept picking small containers full and eating them raw, our guide reluctantly tried one. Then another. And finally, we had a convert. We brought them to the lodge chef, who made all sorts of delicious dishes with them, including crêpes murtas (a little too close to the Spanish word for death!)

Another time, Chuck told the guide he wanted to fish about 1000 yards above a waterfall just below a lake. It was fairly windy, causing casting to be quite challenging, so, to the guide's surprise, we began trolling with our fly-fishing rods. He had fished enough with General Yeager to know not to question his methods; General Yeager always caught fish.

Another time, everyone was fishing on the river. I had had my fill, so I went for a short hike, yes, in my chest waders, hence short.

I walked into the brush. Chile doesn't have any predators, so I wasn't too worried. I halted and was looking around when I saw this tiny brown deer-like creature heading my way with its head down eating brush. I wondered if it was somewhat dangerous or would be if I frightened it. So I looked back at the group and wanted to ask, but I'd have to yell, most likely scaring off the creature. I also wanted to get small but was afraid that then the small creature could overpower me and bite or claw me too easily. And if I moved at all, would it change course? Dilemma.

I stood stock still as it got within six feet of me. It then looked up and registered shock, which shocked me. For a moment, we both stood there frozen, staring at each other. Then it ran off before I had a chance to make baby deer noises to call it back or take a photo.

I described it to the lodge owner, who claimed I had seen a pudu, the smallest deer in the world—a very rare sighting.

One time, Chuck was fishing with Jason, his guide, a big, very strong young man and at the time, the son-in-law of the owner. (I was horseback riding; that's a whole other story.) Jason pushed the boat out without starting the motor. Adrift, the motor wouldn't start, so he had to do some swift rowing and steering to get out of the quick-moving current before they got to the waterfall/rapids.

According to Jason, General Yeager saved their lives—knowing currents and water, General Yeager calmly directed the rowing and steering to safety. I don't think they caught any fish.

\*\*\*

One year, our trip to Chile was full of delays. In Dallas, we approached the desk—Chuck (very observant) had noticed the cowling off the engine. Yikes!

We finally arrived in Santiago so late that we had to spend the night. The next morning, we went for a walk. We entered and sat in the back of the old church, the oldest building in Santiago. VERY high ceiling.

The services chanted in Spanish. I had meant to learn a little more Spanish before this trip, but it was November, and suddenly, it was February, and we were in Chile. How did that happen? So, rather than pick out English words with a Spanish accent, I listened to the hum of the chant and the singing.

As I was thinking all this, Chuck, with impeccable timing, turned to me and asked: "Do you know what they are saying?"

Me, smiling sheepishly: "No."

Chuck translated: "Leave all your money in the collection plate. Give the rest you have at home, too."

I laughed. Up until then, I didn't know he spoke Spanish except for "huevos rancheros con jamon (ranchero eggs with ham)." We'd been blessed enough times to carry us for at least the week, so we left. He sat on the fountain rim while I explored. Pretty architecture from the nineteenth century with its balconies and tall windows.

On the front of the City Library, an historic, nineteenth-century building with Greek columns, was the graffiti "Amor" with lots of hearts. On the bench near us was a couple taking the message very seriously.

Still exhausted from travel, we declined to walk up the steep hill to another historic building and eventually got back to our hotel. We were rewarded for going to church by being able to hire a knowledgeable driver for two hours, for not much more than it would cost to drive the twenty minutes to the airport, who drove us up that steep hill. If we had had more time, I would have lingered in the Plaza des Armes and the marketplace, where he said it is popular on Sundays because Chileans, after a big Saturday night, think eating fish is good for you.

# PART IV

# MARRIAGE & HAVING KIDS

## WEDDING & EARLY MARRIAGE

I am not good at subtle. After we got married, I looked back on the 3.5 years prior. Chuck once told me, "You can't do that after we're married." I can't even remember what it was, but I remember saying, "Well, you said you're never getting married again, so it doesn't matter," as I went off to the bedroom to get dressed.

Another time, Chuck asked me what I thought about women keeping their own names when they married. I told him what he always said, "To each his own." I told him I didn't have a strong opinion—each situation was different. If one gets married in their thirties, forties or later, it could be a business/branding thing.

As I look back, Chuck kept floating the idea of marriage up the flagpole but too subtly. I knew we were committed and exclusive to each other, so marriage wasn't particularly important to me.

In January 2003, Chuck asked me to find out how we could get married in Reno. Oddly, just as with Glennis, he never proposed. I don't remember my response, but I don't think it was committal, so he set up a trust fund for me. I made sure that if, for some crazy reason, we split, he could easily change the beneficiary. The lawyer thought I was nuts.

What I actually thought was, 'Reno?!!!! I can't get married in Reno—that's when you have to: a shotgun wedding.' I also thought about it long and hard—did he pass the live-in-a-box test, meaning if this man lived in a cardboard box and I had to be the breadwinner, would I do it? Would I stay? A resounding YES! I couldn't imagine life without him, no matter what that life presented. It would be life without my heart. As you can see from these stories—Chuck Yeager was a truly special, unique man. So, again, a resounding YES! I would do it.

Fast-forward to August 2003. Our friend, whom we affectionately called our Jewish diamond dealer friend—those are the two features with which he led when we met him—came out to visit for less than forty-eight hours. We had met Sam in the Northwest Airlines VIP lounge in Minneapolis. He had recognized General Chuck Yeager and had some questions. Chuck was amenable—we had a couple hours—I gave up my seat so Sam could sit near him. Sam proceeded to ask, as General Yeager described it, "Why, when we (Israeli pilots) take your F-15Es and put a Star of David on it, it flies better?" General Yeager replied, "You got an hour, son?" and then proceeded to tell Sam the truth. Sam's compatriots in the Israeli Air Force were obviously exaggerating. A lot.

When Sam visited to fly with Chuck, he brought his own kosher food and utensils. Thank goodness because there was nothing kosher within a hundred-mile radius or more of Grass Valley. I checked. Sam was surprised I knew much about it. When I was little, I would go to Sunday School at church on Sundays; then Dad would take the family to a great Jewish deli to pick up authentic bagels, lox, and bialys. We also lived next to one of the top rabbis in Philadelphia, whose son became one of the leading rabbis in America and still my good friend. So yeah, I know a little.

Chuck took Sam on a short flight to see if he got airsick. When he didn't, Chuck took him on a longer trip the next day, flying through the High Sierra, stopping in Bishop for lunch where Chuck's "girlfriend," a big, friendly waitress, worked. When she greeted you, she hugged you and you got lost in the size of her. Chuck told me Sam brought out his kosher sandwich—eating it a bit like a squirrel—keeping it mostly hidden in his pocket.

For some reason, while they were gone, I called Reno to find out how to get married. During that conversation, the clerk said they had a satellite office in Incline Village. Lake Tahoe! Oh! I could say I got married in Tahoe. The idea of getting married suddenly was more attractive.

I met Chuck and Sam at the Nevada County airport and we drove Sam to the Sacramento airport. Halfway there, Chuck looked in the rearview mirror and asked, "Did you find out?"

How the heck did he know? He did that a lot.

I said, "Yes. We can do it in Incline Village—Tahoe—much better."

Sam said, "Wait! What? No! You can't! I have to send the rings!"

I said, "Why don't you stay and be a witness?" How did everyone know but me?

He left as planned on his flight.

Friday, Chuck and I drove up to Incline Village and arrived at the courthouse at 11:40 a.m. It was closing at noon.

We bought our marriage license—$55. We asked, "So, are we married?"

The clerk said, "No. The judge can marry you. He's on the third floor."

We walked up to the third floor, strolled up to the clerk's desk and told her what we needed.

She asked, "Do you have any witnesses?"

We responded: "No."

Clerk: "That's okay. We can serve as witnesses. Do you have any rings?"

Chuck: "No."

Clerk: "Do you have any special program or music or…?"

Chuck: "No. No. We just want to get married."

Clerk: "Okay. That'll be $50."

Chuck paid and we went into the courtroom. The judge said the basics, then said, "I have a poem I read for people like you to earn my fifty bucks," and then pronounced us husband and wife.

We didn't know what to do with ourselves after a quick kiss, so Chuck, after the judge mentioned a mutual acquaintance, invited the judge to lunch. The judge was apoplectic; he had a prior engagement and would have to miss lunch with General Chuck Yeager on his wedding day.

And as Chuck told the story: "Twenty minutes later and $105 poorer, we were married."

We drove west along the lake and stopped at a bakery. I bought a vanilla cookie with vanilla icing. I didn't really want sugar, but it was essentially my wedding cake. A vestige of tradition; I should have kept it and frozen it.

We then made our way to the oh-so-exclusive San Francisco Fly Casting Club in Truckee, California—only twenty members at any given time, and mostly only ten use the club and fish.

We said hello to our friends who ran it and sat in the kitchen. Chuck had been a guest on a guy trip there the weekend before. They asked us if we were hungry and offered a turkey sandwich. As we chatted, although we had agreed we would keep our marriage private, it became clear to our friends that we had just gotten married. Chuck must have alluded to it the weekend before. The chef was upset; if we had only warned him, he would have made us a feast.

I assured him I loved turkey sandwiches with Swiss cheese and mayonnaise. My mother had bought hot lunches for me all through private girls' school, so sandwiches to me were a treat.

The membership invited us to the formal dining room to have fresh salmon in an hour. We were famished and preferred to be in the kitchen that visit.

After the turkey sandwiches, we drove home. Starting on that drive home, we were getting divorced for the next twenty-four to thirty-six hours. We were both freaked out at what we had just done. He said I couldn't do something anymore now that we were married. (It was so trivial; I can't remember what it was.) I replied, "Oh no, we haven't changed. I'm me; you're you."

We got over our shock the next day and lived happily ever after. If you had told me, prior to making any marriage vows, anything would be different after we made our vows, I would have pooh-poohed that notion. But I'm here to tell you, it is different. There is an unfathomable depth of love and commitment after one vows before God. Chuck felt so, too. And although he knew I would never leave before, he was now certain. He knew I took vows very seriously, which is why, although I had received many proposals, I had never been married before. There was a calmness, more profound peace, and even more depth of trust and love now, if possible.

Sam, true to his word, sent some beautiful rings. I had my choice of several. Chuck and I tried them on; he was elated to wear his. However, we both never wore them again. He had been wearing his wedding ring during his first marriage when he had his horrific NF-104 accident. They had had to saw it off. So he determined that as long as he was flying, he would not wear a wedding ring. By the same token, I did not either. I was sure I would remove it to protect it, put it down somewhere, and lose it. Also, oddly, in a plane incident, the only area I got hurt was my ring finger. If I had been wearing a ring…For a time, I wore a ring around my neck, but eventually stopped that as well. Now, I wear a necklace with a beautiful infinity symbol representing us.

A month or so after we were married, Chuck, who loved to shock or test, said to me out of the blue, "You married a professional killer."

I loved it. "Good. I feel safer. As long as we're on the same side. I'll be right behind you."

He laughed.

## DISAGREEMENTS

Chuck's and my arguments or disagreements, the ones you have in the beginning of a relationship living together when you're trying to figure out the boundaries, would last about five minutes at most. He'd have me rolling on the floor laughing, as they say. Then, while laughing, I'd be saying, "Wait, I'm angry! What was I angry about?"

But he was remarkably adaptable and had a keen intellectual curiosity, all of which kept him young. I can only remember a few times when Chuck's and my disagreements lasted more than a couple minutes.

One time, Chuck made a "joke" about my weight. I was at the top end of my okay weight, not feeling comfortable about it and did not find the "joke" at all funny. I told him making weight comments was a deal-killer and walked out the door to hike off my unfocused emotional energy. He was used to me doing this and knew I'd be back shortly. I stomped around the property, up and down the hills, tiring myself out, getting my outraged gut to calm down and figure out what really bothered me about the comment. My gut doesn't speak English.

I figured it out and then tried to figure out whether I could let it not bother me. I loved and liked this guy so much; could I find the humor and not let the past dictate my future?

Once I understood my issue, I went back to the house to find Chuck sitting on the swing on our deck. When I sat down, before I could explain, he said, "My father got very large as he got older and I don't want to do that."

I, in turn, explained my issue. "My father undermined my independent, confident, very accomplished mother's self-esteem over the years, picking away by telling her she was fat. I won't be in a relationship where someone tries that with me. Growing up in my family, anorexia was too fat. I'm not sure how I escaped all that, but…"

And Chuck never made a joke about my weight again. Bless him.

* * *

Yet another time, I told him that with his hearing loss getting worse, he absolutely needed hearing aids; new ones were much better than before. A squadron mate had started Miracle-Ear. The folks testing for the hearing aids realized Chuck was brilliant—he figured out fifty percent of the stand-alone words without lip-reading or context when he should have gotten zero.

I finally figured out what would get his attention: safety. "If I'm shouting at you, there's a fire in the house and you can't hear me, precious seconds, minutes, time is lost." He got the hearing aids. They were miserable, but better than not hearing. Many folks with hearing loss check out of the conversation and their mental acuity suffers. To his credit again, Chuck wanted to be engaged, especially after I came along (most of the time).

## ACTIONS MUST SUPPORT THE WORDS FOR A TRUE APOLOGY

I was the assistant to the (well-known in his day) ABC Sports producer, Chuck Howard, in the control room when an associate producer set up the wrong shot. Chuck Howard reamed him—without taking a breath. Finally, when he absolutely had to take a breath, the associate producer grabbed his chance and jumped in: "Sorry, Chuck, I f—ked up!"

Chuck Howard stopped short, calmer, and barked, "Okay. Don't let it happen again!"

"Yes, Sir!"

I thought, 'Wow—

Was being reamed,

Owned up,

End of incident.
No squirming and excusing.
But don't do it again.
Works for me.'

I did this ever after. And it stunned Chuck. When I was in the wrong, I'd admit it, apologize and try to make amends, the most crucial part: action supporting words. Chuck wasn't used to that—he was used to excuses—but he sure appreciated my honesty.

And he did the same. No harboring. And yes, we never went to bed angry.

## HAVING KIDS: TO HAVE OR NOT TO HAVE

When I met Chuck, I was contemplating adopting a kid. At first, I thought in-vitro, but after researching that extensively, found those drugs are not approved for in-vitro, so you are potentially shortening your life while having kids late, potentially leaving young kids without a parent. I then considered adoption.

Chuck wasn't averse to it—he wanted to be together that much and wanted me to be happy. We were staying in a friend's guesthouse when the friend's five-year-old daughter came in and chatted away a mile a minute without taking a breath.

Chuck went into the large guest bathroom to ostensibly brush his hair and called me in. "Victoria, please don't do that to me!" I assured him I didn't want to do that…to me either!

His only other comment re adoption was Chuck YEAGER-ism #135: "Get an older one so you know what you're getting." As usual, very practical.

I was very clear that what I chose to do was my decision—that if I decided not to adopt or have kids, I would never blame anyone else for my decision. So many people blame their partner and harbor resentment—he or she wouldn't let me do this or that. Very unfair.

I was always afraid that when I was past childbearing or rearing years, I would regret not having kids. I knew so many older folks who had not had kids and, with great melancholy, wished they had. Candidly, I am grateful Chuck and I did not have kids. There really wasn't room in our relationship. I think of Chuck's and my world as a target. Chuck and I were in the bullseye, the center—just us, exclusive club. The next circle was maybe close friends and/or family you choose and the farther out, the less close. Everything but the bullseye was fluid with the ebb and flow of life and friends. I realized those who were melancholy about not having kids, were imagining a perfect family with perfect kids, someone else changing the diapers, disciplining them, etc.

I enjoy kids a lot, as did Chuck; we just didn't want to raise any at our stage in life.

## THE RIGHT STUFF 20TH ANNIVERSARY PREMIERE: *June 10, 2003*

*The Right Stuff*'s twentieth-anniversary movie premiere was quite amusing. I'll never forget Barbara Hershey and Chuck's warm greeting and then posing for the photographers. Chuck told them, "Take as long as you like," with his arm around Barbara. Then he looked over at me with a wolfish, happy grin, including me in the fun.

He was also great friends with Bo Derek, who had been interested before I came along, and other beautiful women.

There was a lot of jealousy surrounding Chuck and me and some unpleasant talk. When I asked him how he felt and what I could do, including if he wanted me to split, he said, "You only have to worry about what I think, not what anyone else thinks." I added, "And what I think, too." He agreed, "That's right." Very strong.

I never worried about all these gorgeous women. My guy was all male and it was always his week for girls. And I knew with whom he was going home every night. Me. But there was one mistress I was required to treat well; otherwise, it was almost a deal breaker.

Glennis Yeager, clueing me in from the grave in a book or oral history, said she didn't have to worry about other women—his "other woman" was machinery/engines/airplanes. Same for me.

Along those lines, about the X-1, Chuck said he had faith in his machinery—it wouldn't bite him without giving him some sort of warning.

One time, I was driving, putting the gas pedal to the floor to get up a hill in my four-cylinder engine at high-density altitude, so it was gunning. Chuck was very unhappy with me, treating his "other woman," his "mistress," an engine, badly. He was right.

I learned.

And QUICKLY!

## CHUCK AS MY "FRONT SEAT DRIVER"

I generally loved driving with Chuck as my "front-seat driver." After I bee-beeped at a truck pulling out of a blind driveway in front of me and then stopping, Chuck said, "That horn ain't gonna work so well when you're sticking out of the side of the cab!" (Chuck YEAGER-ism #136.)

Another time, after some knucklehead (truck) passed the car in front of us, going eighty mph on a winding, very narrow mountain road, Chuck remarked, "Oh well, Hell ain't half full." (Chuck YEAGER-ism #137.)

## OUR VEGETABLE GARDEN

Each year, Chuck and I grew tomatoes, eggplant, and melon. Sometimes we mixed it up with corn and sunflowers. We then would have fresh tomato sandwiches for lunch and dinner with mayo on whole wheat. Or we'd bring our salt shaker to the plants, pick fresh tomatoes, throw a little salt on, and eat them. Tony did this when he visited and just loved it.

Chuck did the planting, put the six-foot fencing together and I helped, not just with the eating, but with the planting. I marvel now at how he fed the plants and went to the other farms to ask for help when the bottoms were funky. It worked. We would always end up with enough to feed an army and the "army" said they were the best—sweet tomatoes and melons.

## VIEW FROM OUR DECK: WILDLIFE

Chuck was so very wise. He knocked down trees before they fell on our house and made roads for fire breaks with our tractor.

One tree he waited. A bird had nested there and had eggs, then baby birds, then all were gone. We watched the whole show only 10 yards from our second-floor deck with a perfect bird's eye view (yes, I said bird's eye), level with the nest.. Beautiful.

One year, there was a group of fourteen baby turkeys. We watched them all spring and summer (when we were home). When they were very tiny, they could just barely fly to the roof of the pump house for the night.

Another year, there were ten baby quail—they'd come up from our creek to the house to see what leftovers we had thrown off the back deck, with the papa sitting on a tree stump as sentinel.

We had natural composting all over our ranch. We'd throw leftover food off the deck, animals would come eat it, and then distribute it wherever they felt like it. If I could train them to one spot...but we had fertile soil everywhere.

We also had/have friendly, very large bears. They would come up, eat, and disappear. Very polite bears. We actually have never seen them except on the game cameras and we have seen their scat. One time, I was talking about having to cut down a tall bush with poison berries next to the house. Literally the next day, it was destroyed. I guess the bears agreed. Earned their keep, too.

## BURNING CHICKEN PARTS IN A BUCKET

Another time, while having breakfast on the back deck, we noticed smoke that appeared to be coming from the neighbor's barn. Our great neighbors, Bill and Diane, had moved to a smaller place and so these were new neighbors. Rumor had it the city slickers had been burning chicken parts in a plastic bucket. And I thought *I* was a city slicker. They made me look like a downright legitimate country girl. We called the fire department. An hour later, we were sitting on the back deck, drinking coffee, with one foot out the front door if it got too bad, when borate bombers showed up. They kept missing—we thought we should be on the radio with them so General Yeager could tell them when to drop.

## RESCUING A BABY DEER: *2008*

"A baby deer is hung up on the rail!" cried Chuck as he rushed back inside from the front deck.

I sure didn't want to start my morning extricating a dead baby deer. As I followed Chuck out, I wondered why he came to get me—he knows I'm quite sensitive, squeamish, in fact…

As I thought about it, so is Chuck. Some hunters, like Chuck, are the most caring of animals. Chuck would only kill for meat to eat or to cull. And since I occasionally eat meat, I'm on board.

As I braced myself for the sight…I was so relieved to see a live baby deer stuck in the railing. If it had gotten through, it had a fifteen-foot drop—not sure its legs would have survived.

We approached it cautiously so as not to scare it or its Momma. As the Momma from below saw us approaching, she was racing back and forth, agitated.

I spoke calmly, softly, in that higher-pitched, babyish talk that animals and babies find soothing.

I pet the fawn's derrière softly to show her I was safe as I continued talking. As we surveyed the scene, I thought I'd need a ladder to get to her on the other side to push her back to the porch. I was concerned she was too heavy and that she may have lice, fleas, ticks, or something else unhealthy.

Chuck said: "Be careful; she might thrash and hit you with her hooves."

As Chuck and I were hovering over her baby, Momma continued running back and forth, snorting—she looked like she was considering coming up on the porch, trapping us. She could do some serious damage. Was she defensive re her mothering skills? In fact, she had done a good thing—left her baby protected on our front porch. When Chuck had first walked out of the front door, the baby had been frightened, jumped and tried to run the other way—where there was only a railing.

I looked the Momma straight in the eye and said calmly, same soothing voice: "It's okay. We'll get your baby freed."

She did stop snorting, kept alert, and seemed to give a look as if to say, "Okay…For now!"

I got a hold of the baby deer's body just in front of the hind legs, picked her up—she was surprisingly light—I was thrilled I could manage—and pulled her partially back through.

"WAaaaaah!" she screamed. Momma agitated. I calmly talked again. Everyone calmed down.

I was afraid if I let go, she'd struggle forward, rendering my effort useless.

She didn't. She then did what I do when I'm scared. She stayed stock still. Or maybe she trusted me. Or decided to—since she didn't have many options. Little thing. And her Momma seemed to be watching, not agitated now. Just alert.

I held her again farther up her body and started to bring her back farther.

I brought the baby back to her shoulders—but couldn't get them through. She stayed still again.

The baby realized she could stand and balance with most of her body unstuck. As I pondered how I was going to get her front legs back through, she realized she could help—she wiggled and squeezed her shoulders and head back out.

I sure wish I had held her a little and petted her more. She was sooooo cute. A little adorable face. But I had in the back of my mind that some animals' parents won't touch their offspring if humans have touched them. Of course, I had touched the baby to help her—but it was minimal…

She walked off a few paces, stopped, turned to look at me, and waited. I didn't want to scare her and her Momma, so didn't approach her. Instead, I said: "Go to your Momma."

She hesitated.

"Go on."

She moved off a few more paces.

"Go to Momma," I urged.

She walked off a little more. Then: Boing Boing (leap, leap). And she was off down the terraces to Momma.

Momma stood still while her baby caught up and stood next to her. She watched the baby and then me.

Then she nuzzled her baby. Was she very relieved?

They stayed there, not far from us, for a while.

Eventually, they moved off. Baby not leaving Momma's side for a second—staying within inches of her. The baby will have abandonment issues for life.

Momma stopped every few paces to look back at me. She looked alternatively just curious, then like I was an anomaly, or was she thanking me, or wondering what I would do next…or…making sure we didn't have a gun, let alone aiming at them…

That evening, I dropped a bag of rice and another of raisins for them. (Our freezer had quit, so we had to get rid of a lot of food anyway).

I hoped they'd come back. This morning, Momma was by the rice and raisins. She calmly walked off after a while. Later, she was nursing her baby—she wasn't frightened off by us at all.

I still wish I had petted the baby deer.

We saw many baby deer (fawns) on our property—one that had just been born that day—sheltering from the coyotes, bobcats, snakes, and neighbors' dogs.

## IS CHUCK YEAGER A DOG PERSON OR A CAT PERSON?

Chuck used to jokingly say, "All cats should have their tails cut off just behind their ears."

Well, here's the other side of the story. When I first moved in with Chuck, there were two feral barn cats. Eventually, over many months, they let me pet them. They were almost like dogs. If they saw me going for a hike on the property, they'd go with me. Best of both species: independent but joined up on a hike. Unfortunately, one disappeared.

Chuck started to buy cat food and feed the remaining cat. If we were going away, he'd ask Bill, our neighbor, to come over to feed the cat daily, even though that cat could hunt and feed itself. We knew this because every now and then, it brought us "gifts" (voles, moles, and the like).

Dogs, he felt, should be useful, such as huntin' dogs, and should live outside.

## VICTORIA'S TRIP TO CHINA: *2006*

Not long after I met Chuck, he said, "You leave for a month, don't come home." Frankly, he didn't need to say that; I would not have wanted to be away from him that long. Besides, I had found what I was looking for. Life was far more warm, exciting, connected, vivid, deep, meaningful, and more, with him wherever we were, whatever we were doing, than without him.

Before I met Chuck, I'd usually go to a region in the world for at least two and a half months; consult re finances, nutrition, alcohol and drug abuse prevention, education, and human trafficking; explore and volunteer. I had just returned from three months in Africa when I met Chuck. The next region was going to be China. After marriage, I thought long and hard about it and decided I better — even a shortened visit (sixteen days including four days of travel to and from); when would I ever have the chance to go again? (I haven't.) I asked Chuck if he wanted to go. He said, "Hell no. I didn't leave nothin' there." (Chuck YEAGER-ism #138.)

People have often said they didn't do something because their spouse or partner wouldn't let them. I often thought—were you tied to a tree? I was never going to put Chuck and me in that situation where I blamed him for my decision. And I never did. Nor did he vice versa. Nor would I have ever insisted he couldn't do something he wanted to do.

In 2006, I planned a trip to areas in China that weren't easy to get to—I felt if I needed to return, going to Beijing or Shanghai would be less difficult than Western China, including Tibet. When I was leaving on the plane, I turned to Chuck and, without thinking, stated my thoughts. "Why am I going? I'll miss you terribly!" Oddly, that genuine burst of thoughts made him feel happy and secure. He had been wondering the same thing.

My gut was right, though—I met an American woman teaching English in a village that took seven hours to travel by road from Lijiang, which was already far from Shanghai or Beijing, the cities into which most fly from the U.S. I was the "guest speaker" in her English class of 10-13 year olds. After I got through, all thirty of them wanted to be pilots. She, a Christian who was careful not to espouse Christianity but lived it (and was still kicked out of the village), told me I gave them the greatest gift of all: Hope. I hadn't thought in those terms but have since then.

## ONE LUNG ENGINES & CINNAMON ROLLS — NEVADA COUNTY FAIR

Chuck and I often went to the Nevada County Fair to visit the guys who run the one-lung engines and to get great cinnamon rolls from our other friends there, truth be told.

Those engines reminded Chuck of his Dad. When he was a kid, his Dad would have Chuck, not easy as a little kid, climb all the way up those hills to fill the gas tanks and keep those engines running to drill gas wells.

Helping his Dad drill gas wells is how, in part, Chuck learned about dome regulators, which were used on the X-1, and plastique explosives, which the

Allies dropped to the French Underground during World War II. After being shot down, Chuck taught the Maquis how to use the explosives. To clarify the nuances: the French Résistance was an umbrella term for all activities designed to harm the invader; the French Underground were clandestine organized resistance groups; and the Maquis were a clandestine volunteer fighting force mainly in rural areas.

After visiting the engines and their owners, we'd go to our friends' cinnamon rolls truck, go behind it and scrape off the butter and brown sugar drippings to enhance our cinnamon buns (and take some home for Chuck's honey vanilla ice cream).

## CHOICE WORDS FOR THE PODIATRIST

I remember going with Chuck to a checkup with a podiatrist. The podiatrist was a bit rough. Chuck made his point: "Doc, you ever been kicked in the teeth?" (Chuck YEAGER-ism #139.) To everyone's amusement, the podiatrist moved out of kicking distance.

## LUNCH WITH DAD, *May 2011*

I had not seen my father in a very long time, so Chuck urged me to take my father to lunch when I returned to Philadelphia for my 35th high school reunion. During lunch, my father asked me if I was happy after I'd been with Chuck 11 years, married for 8. I burst into tears (of joy) and blurted, "YES! I didn't know you could be this happy being married. You and Mom were so miserable!" He was quite taken aback, to say the least.

## DO YOU LOVE ME?

Occasionally, Chuck would play a game and ask me, "Do you love me?" I'd say, "Yes." "How much?" he'd ask.

I'd respond with "Thiiiiiiissss much," and spread my arms as far as I could.

He'd smile his beautiful smile and say, "Why?"

I'd give all sorts of accolades which were true—witty, handsome, honest, fun, loyal, faithful, caring…and end with, "because you're the greatest".

One time, I decided to see how he would respond just for the fun of it. His actions spoke far louder than words, so I was secure in knowing I was well-loved.

So I asked him, "Do you love me?" So awkward for me, especially after his answer the very first time.

He said, "Yes."

Phew. I boldly followed with, "Why?"

He gave the only real response: "Because I promised to."

Simple as that. My answers were his attributes. His was the essence. He made a vow. Love is a verb you can choose to do.

## OUT OF LOVE

I think one day in our whole marriage, I felt, 'Hmm. I'm not sure I feel in love. I love him deeply, but…Ah, maybe just wait a day, maybe this will pass.'

I don't know if he was feeling the same way, but we were usually pretty well in tune. He often read my mind.

We were sitting on the back deck with a great view of the hills, creek, pond, cows, horses, and wildlife. I walked out front to do something. I saw a sea of exquisite wildflowers, varied in color. I picked one, walked back through the house to the back deck where Charlie was sitting, and gave it to him.

His face lit up in joy with his handsome smile and expressive, twinkling eyes, and we were straight back in love.

## THANK YOU LETTER FROM FORMER SUBORDINATE: *2014*

Occasionally, we'd get really nice, interesting letters.

Got a letter Christmas 2014 from a woman born in England. It read:

"Merry Christmas and Happy New Year. In April 1957, Airman 1st Class was standing on duty on a flight line in Toul-Rosieres, France, when you (Chuck) flew in. A1C stopped you as you walked by. You so kindly listened to him as he told you his problem.

"A1C submitted paperwork to marry an English girl in November 1956. It was turned down.

"You told A1C to meet you in your office the next morning.

"Thank you. You gave us permission to marry. I am the English girl (now an American). We were married May 4, 1957, in England, about 57 years ago.

"We have three children, eight grandchildren, and our tenth great-grandchild will be born March 2015.

"So from us all, we say, 'Thank you, Sir!'

"Without your help, it may never have been."

Wonder if they named any of their brood Charles or Yeager?

This was not unusual. I've heard a few others tell me a similar story about Chuck's compassion.

## CHUCK YEAGER-ISM #140: "YOU! I'M ALWAYS CHUCK YEAGER!"

In about 2002-2003, Chuck had me take over all parts of his life: scheduling, finances, answering letters, sending out signed photos, sales, speaking engagements, etc. It was overwhelming. Previously, he had had three or four people doing those jobs. We'd get some crazy letters. People wrote and asked for pieces of his clothing, even just one shoe, donations, personal donations, guns, anything, advice re girlfriends. Several women asked if he had a twin brother who was single.

Every few months, I'd have a meltdown and just go for a looooooong hike with Chuck.

One of those meltdowns resulted in another Chuck YEAGER-ism.

One day, I was overwhelmed, doing five different jobs, tons of mail, just plain overwhelmed. So, I exclaimed in exasperation, "I'm so tired of this 'Chuck Yeager' business!" to which Chuck looked at me in astonishment and replied, "YOU!??!?!!? I'm ALWAYS Chuck Yeager!" (Chuck YEAGER-ism #140.) I burst out laughing. He had a point.

## WE WERE VERY RICH INDEED

Every now and again, especially after we were surrounded by mega financially rich folks, Chuck would say to me, "I could have gotten out of the Air Force and made a lot of money." What he was really saying was, I wish I could give/buy you more things.

That was easy. I'd remind him that every mega financially rich person we knew would rather have had Chuck's life and stature. And being with Chuck, I had all I wanted, including materially. I always said, the only thing a lot of money would do would be to give us a big jet at our beck and call instead of flying commercially. Yet, I liked flying commercially sometimes—we met some interesting folks and also, people loved seeing their hero.

Chuck's question answered, we went on with our lives together.

We were very rich indeed.

# PART V

# HIS KIDS

## MONEY

In April 2001, at a dinner in DC, which Archie, who was being honored, wanted Chuck to attend, I was seated next to Archie, who "innocently" asked me how Chuck's kids were.

I replied, "You're not fooling me, Archie. You know what's going on. Same as ever."

His lips twitched into a slight smile that he wasn't pulling one over on me. "What's their problem?"

I replied, "They think I'm after his money."

Incredulous, he exclaimed, "WHAT money?"

Me: "Thank you! If money were my goal, I'd be on Wall Street with my MBA from Columbia University. Or I'd marry a billionaire or centimillionaire with a title. Real money. I have had such offers; I used to be cute, you know!"

We laughed. And understood each other. Truthfully, I did those suitors, and mostly myself, a favor by not accepting their proposals of marriage (to my family's chagrin: "You could have been called 'Lady' or 'Princess Victoria'). Fortunately, and blessedly, I found my true handsome "prince" at 41.

## GIFTS

Chuck was a very generous guy. In addition to giving his kids millions over time and hundreds of thousands each year, every time he went on a trip, he would bring something back for his daughter and her kids, who lived nearby, and me. He also gave me a couple of signed photos.

One day, Chuck came home and asked if I was selling all his gifts on eBay. I, standing up for my rights (my brothers were always taking my things), insisted, "Well, you gave them to me, so they're mine. I can do what I want with them, no?"

He cautiously said, "Well, yes…"

I realized then—thank goodness quickly—that I was reacting to my history, but he was really asking me a different question. So I promptly said, "Come with me." I took him to the cupboard where, frankly, on one shelf, I kept my underwear and camisoles and flung open those doors. There, on the other two shelves, were all the things, along with some of my jewelry, that Chuck had given me. I said, "Every morning, I get to thank you for your generosity."

He saw I was too sentimental to ever give away anything he gave me, let alone sell it. There I was, visiting my Chuck Yeager loot every day with the signed photos he had given me staring out at us. He was stunned, ecstatic, and relieved all at the same time. He shook his head in wonder and gave his special laugh of sheer joy. (It was his daughter's friend who was selling on eBay.)

Another time re gifts, Chuck had given me one thousand lithographs to sell. He signed one hundred as a start. A few months later, he said, "Are you going to share what you make on the lithographs with me?"

I replied, "Of course. They're yours. I'm thinking 10 percent to me and 90 percent to you. You and I have been so busy traveling, I haven't had time. But honestly, I'm so sorry—I'm not good at that, so maybe you might want to ask someone else." And I showed him the lithographs—all still there.

Again, he was shocked. Others with whom he had given a few or many lithographs to sell were taking ninety to one hundred percent. Some of those others were also misappropriating memorabilia from the military and/or from nonprofits.

He sure wasn't used to someone like me.

## ACTIONS SPEAK LOUDER THAN WORDS

One of Chuck's daughters complained that Chuck never told her he loved her. I said he says it all the time in action. If I had to choose (which I didn't with Chuck), I'd rather have his actions, which speak louder than words, say "I love you" than his words.

She still complained.

So the next time Chuck wrote her a note, I asked, "Instead of just 'Dad', could you please write 'Love, Dad'?" He said, as usual, "Why?"

I said, "Because she complained you never told her you loved her, never said the words. So now she'll have it in writing and won't have that to complain about."

Another daughter was jealous and upset because her father had decided to work less now that he had someone with whom to have fun. She started yelling at me, "He's in love with you!" I don't know what she said after that because I looked at him and said, "Really? Cool." It never occurred to me one way or the other. I just knew that he had made love to me almost from the moment we met. That phrase can mean a loving act; something as simple as straightening my collar for me, a particular smile, hug, or kiss, or giving me a flower he had just picked in the field.

## BABY: 2000

Later in August, five months after we met, we went to Chuck's oldest grandson's wedding held at Chuck's son's farm. The bride's mother, frazzled, scooped me up to welcome me and tell me all the issues going on.

That evening was the rehearsal dinner, during which the bride's mother brought her other daughter's month-old baby and put her in my arms. I never tried to hold babies—always too much competition from others wanting to hold the child and I didn't care that much to hold a fragile little thing. But somehow, when this baby was in my arms, real peace came over both Chuck and me. I think the rest of the room felt it and was stunned, wondering what Chuck and I were going to do as to children.

The moments were so loving. The bride's mother returned too soon, but I didn't stop her from taking the baby. Chuck and I smiled at each other. Maybe in another life, but in this one, we were more than enough.

## GOLD DIGGER

Just after the wedding, Chuck's grandson's self-proclaimed good friend approached me and pronounced: "Why, you're not a gold digger!!!!"

Of course, since I was much younger than Chuck, people went to the obvious, boring cliché. I thanked her, stunned that she thought I looked that good. Remember, I was 41; he was 77 when we met.

I was always extremely offended, not on my own behalf but on his: they weren't insulting me—they were insulting Chuck and implying he had nothing more to offer than finances. And believe me, he had far more to offer than one can imagine. He was one of the finest people I have ever met and the greatest partner/husband I could have ever imagined.

I responded to the friend's exclamation curiously, "How can you tell?" and added faux defensively, "I'm wearing a dress!"

She said, "You don't have the big hair, and the nails, and the makeup and the fake teeth and fake big boobs…"

I replied, "I resemble (sic) that remark. I can look as good as any gold digger!" and laughed.

I think I recall as she walked away, I heard her muttering, "Well, she's not a gold digger, but she is weird…." (A compliment in our book, as you'll see later.)

I then wrote a poem entitled, "Yes, I Am a Gold Digger." I can't find it right now, but it essentially said, "Yes, I am a gold digger, but my gold is loyalty, affection, kindness, respect, love, fun, clarity, integrity, honesty, closeness," and more along those lines.

General Chuck Yeager was all that and more. Most importantly, my gold was Chuck's heart—he had a heart of gold, which I'm still receiving and cherishing.

Chuck was a meat hunter, not a trophy hunter—except, I've been told, where I was concerned—I was his trophy wife.

Yep, I can look that good, too.

## WEDDING PHOTOS

As we were eating lunch at one of the picnic tables, the family was gathering the wedding party for photos. I wondered how that would play out. If Chuck wanted me in the picture, I'd stand on the outer edge so they could cut me out if things didn't work out between Chuck and me.

The family member asked Chuck to come over while looking at me dubiously. I sat quietly. Chuck got up from the table, turned to me, and said, "I'll be right back." I breathed again. As usual, Chuck handled the delicate situation with dignity, clarity and subtlety.

## SHE INVITES US ON HUNTIN' & FISHIN' TRIPS!

Chuck's oldest son, spokesman for the kids, was asked, "Before Victoria came along, how often did you see your Dad?"

Don: "About once a year. He'd come elk hunting nearby."

"And after Victoria came along?"

Don: "About 2-3 times a year. She invited us on their fishing and hunting trips and to air shows with them." The interviewer raised his eyebrows so far they went to the back of his neck. One could see the interviewer was thinking: 'So what's the problem?'

## "YOU'RE WEIRD"

One evening, we were at Chuck's daughter's house for dinner. Her daughter, age 14, had a friend over. Chuck's granddaughter called herself a princess, aptly. The granddaughter felt her friend was getting too much attention so the granddaughter imperiously told her friend, "You're weird." Her friend started to protest until I smiled at her and said, "That's okay; we like weird around here." The friend then proudly owned being "weird".

# PART VI

# PEOPLE

## KORKY & IRENE KEVORKIAN

In July 2000, four months after Chuck and I met, we visited two more of Chuck's true friends since the 1960's: Irene and Korky Kevorkian. Korky had been an instructor pilot during World War II, a crop duster, and now was a fruit farmer. He had dropped food supplies to Chuck during Chuck's treks in the High Sierra. They had lots of fun adventures to reminisce and share.

I was sitting next to Chuck, waiting for lunch, which Irene was making. She, a great cook, had wisely declined my offer of help.

Chuck asked me something to which I responded. He had hearing loss, so asked, "What?"

Knowing a bit about hearing and hearing loss from having had my hearing tested at the Olympic Village in Georgia in 1996 (off the charts), I repeated my response but in a lower tone and a little louder. He immediately imitated me.

There was a moment when the Kevorkians held their breath, wondering how I would respond to this mocking humor. I looked at Chuck in surprise and then…burst out laughing.

The Kevorkians breathed again and joined in laughing, probably more out of relief. Chuck smiled. Passed that test, too.

We often went to the Kevorkians for Christmas. One year, we went to the Kevorkians for Korky's 80th birthday. Chuck and I went to bed early because we were getting up early to go pig huntin' on the California coast the next day. The rest of the group stayed up late drinking.

When we got up at 5am, Irene had very kindly made breakfast. Chuck asked, "How's Korky gettin' along?" Korky had a rare disease, myasthenia gravis.

Irene responded, "He was up and down all night, but he's resting peacefully now." (He was dead.)

After breakfast, Chuck went to shave, I cleaned the plates, and Irene went to check on Korky. She returned to tell me she couldn't feel a pulse. I got Chuck. We went in. Korky looked dead. But he was still warm. Irene called the neighbor, who didn't answer. At my insistence, she called 9-1-1. They asked if anyone knew CPR. I said I had read it, never done it.

The operator said to put Korky on the floor—a hard, flat surface. We got the other male visitor and Chuck and he put Korky on the floor. Chuck later on, when relating the story, would say, "When I dropped Korky's head on the floor and he didn't wake up, I knew he was dead."

The operator talked about mouth-to-mouth. Chuck and the other guy looked at each other like a bad joke, "Korky, you're gonna die." I stepped in and did it (very weird), as well as pumped his chest.

The ambulance showed up and everyone left the room to meet them except Korky and me. I looked into his one eye that seemed to have a faraway light and asked, "Korky, do you want me to try to bring you back or do you want to go?" I kept pumping because far be it from me to make that decision; there was a faint light deep in one of his eyes.

The EMTs rushed in, took over and drove him to the hospital. Chuck's and my job done, the whole family there; we got packed and left to go to the California coast as planned.

Korky lasted a day, never regained consciousness. By the next day, his brain waves were flat, so they all said goodbye and pulled the plug. The family thanked me, which confused me. One of them explained; they at least had a warm body to whom to say goodbye.

I envisioned that Korky had gotten up and down all night to go to the men's room. The last time he was headed back to bed, he was perplexed; his spirit had gotten up, but his body was still in bed. He tried to get back into his body; he didn't want to leave his family, but it just didn't fit.

This is one funeral we did attend. Chuck spoke at the event afterwards and told everyone, "Never fear—I remember all the places Korky took me to steal, or ahem, I mean, to get, free fruit."

## ROY CLARK

The first time I met Roy Clark, I had known Chuck about ten months. We attended the SCI Convention black-tie dinner in Reno when Roy was the headliner. Chuck said: "Oh, Roy's a friend of mine, come on." I thought, "Oh, these famous people, they're all 'friends'". At least he didn't say "dear friend". We went backstage to the "green room", which was just a big area behind a curtain. When we were thirty feet away, Roy looked up and yelled: "Chuck! Hi, ol' friend!!!"

I thought, 'Whoo-oops. Guess they are friends; glad I kept my thoughts to myself.'

Chuck had known Roy for decades. In the 1960s or '70s; General Yeager had been asked to fly Roy to Palm Springs from LA for a concert. And that's when they first met.

Chuck introduced us—Roy was very gracious. We chatted for a while—really, they chatted and I happily listened.

We left to let Roy get ready to perform. We had the last two seats at the President's table, which were front row for the show.

Roy and his band came out. He was excellent. In the middle, he told some jokes, then said, "This song is for my good friends Chuck Yeager and Victoria." Wow! He remembered my name, having only heard it once! I know it was a great song, but I sure don't remember which—I was still impressed by Roy's memory and generosity.

\* \* \*

We saw Roy several times—at a fly-in where Chuck and I flew in a T-6, at birthdays, various events, and at some of Roy's shows where Chuck would introduce Roy. And Roy, in turn, always told great stories about Chuck—such a wonderful, positive sense of humor.

Roy invited us to his 70th birthday party—50 years of marriage, 60 years of show business (yes, he started very young)—which was also a fundraiser for the Roy Clark Elementary School in Tulsa's Union School District.

The delicious down-home barbecue dinner was in the bright and open school cafeteria. We ate with Roy and his wife, a pleasant gal with good sense.

I noticed Roy's sharp, brilliant blue eyes. His wife agreed. Roy told me he was brought up poor in Virginia and liked to fly, hunt, and fish, so felt a kinship with Chuck.

Then the show: a *Hee Haw* reunion plus Chuck Yeager. It was fantastic!

Several people got up to talk about Roy, including *Hee Haw*'s Lulu, "the fat girl", who had lost a lot of weight so was almost unrecognizable and looking fantastic. Chuck got up and spoke about Roy flying with him in the P-51 and Roy wouldn't get out—so they went up again. And a few more stories.

When Chuck sat down, Roy called out: "Let me tell you about Chuck Yeager! His commander was complaining the Americans were not shooting down enough Germans. So Chuck said, 'How many do you need?' 'We need more aces (5 enemy aircraft shot down).' Chuck said. 'Okay,' went out, shot down five in one mission and became an ace in a day. That's Chuck!" (It's true: on October 12, 1944, Captain Yeager did shoot down five in one day and on November 12, he shot down four in a day).

That's the short version of Chuck's career by Roy Clark.

I was soooo sorry no one had taped the show. But it was fun—and the crowd loved it; raised a bit of money for the school, too.

I invited Roy to Chuck's 80th birthday party and he tried to get there—flying himself—he owned a Stearman and a modern plane (a Cessna 210), but the weather didn't cooperate. Darn!

* * *

I called Roy to see if he'd come as a guest (not necessarily to perform) to Chuck's 85th birthday party at Beale AFB (Air Force Base). And it was spectacular!

Martha and John King offered to pick Roy up in their plane, bring him to the party and then deliver him back for his show in Arizona. Roy graciously invited them to the show, too, so they spent the night there.

I had tried to keep some items as surprises for Chuck for his birthday party, but I realized that, for him, the planning is as fun as the event. Each week leading up to the party, I told him one more surprise. He loved it. He couldn't believe I was pulling all this together. Me, either.

I had asked Roy—or told him what Chuck had said: "I hope Roy plays *Malagueña*." And suggested if Roy wanted to, we'd love it.

We invited the Beale Commander at the time, who became a friend, Col Jake Polumbo, and his wife, but he was TDY (temporary duty elsewhere). His wife accepted and he asked if I would invite his vice commander and chief master sergeant. Sure. I should have asked Chuck first. Big mistake on my part. Chuck was not happy about the chief coming to his birthday. And with good reason. His experience of chief master sergeants had often not been good. I witnessed one, a non-pilot, non-maintenance guy, tell Chuck basically how to fly. I'm not kidding. Very recently, a former, highly respected Chief Master Sergeant (Chief MSgt) of the Air Force told me General Yeager was right re the attitudes of chief master sergeants during different periods in the Air Force.

Then, Col Polumbo asked if I could invite the Chief MSgt's and Vice Commander's wives. At 75 people and a sit-down lunch, we were at capacity. The Commander then realized this was not a Beale come one, come all party where each attendee paid for his/her own meal. He was embarrassed he had insisted I invite anyone.

At the party, one of the best ever (up to that point), Roy came in with his musical director, Richard, who told me the driver, who had dropped them off at the Arizona airport, had driven off with the guitar in the back. I went to the Vice Commander and said, "I need a guitar; I'll even buy one." He looked at me like I had grown two heads.

I went to the Chief MSgt. His reaction? "Okay," and left. He was back in 10 minutes with a guitar. A friend of his had just bought one. Wow. He earned his lunch invitation and my respect that day. Wish I had had room for his wife.

Roy led the 'Happy Birthday' to the relief of the Vice Commander, who was afraid he would have to do it.

After the cake and the former Oakland Raiders got up to razz Chuck (made him an honorary soul brother again), Roy's musical director, Richard, having tuned the guitar, brought it over to Roy. Roy looked up and asked, "Is it okay?" Richard, who used to do an extraordinary rendition of "Great Balls of Fire" in Roy's live shows, nodded and gave it to him. Richard, too, is one of my favorite people, and embodied the definition of great friend (to Roy).

Roy played *Malaguena*. Wow! And he was having a blast, too. I'm sure if I had asked for another, he would have. I thought, 'I'd love to hear his voice!'—especially since we're here without amplification. But I didn't want him to think that's the only reason we invited him. His enjoyment was sooo exciting—he easily brought the rest of us with him. What an exceptional birthday present for Chuck!

Later, Roy said, "I wish I'd known it was new; I would have done some hand exercises." Oops. I thought, 'I hope he didn't hurt his million-dollar hands. Yikes!'

Roy was quite happy to be a part of the whole celebration.

We often listened to Roy's CDs while driving, especially long drives to New Mexico or Colorado. Just great! And "Yesterday" gets better as we get older.

We went to Roy's concerts whenever we were in the vicinity. Chuck would step onstage at the start of the show, to the cheering crowd giving him a standing ovation, and tell a few stories about Roy. One time, I was backstage with Roy while Chuck was on stage embellishing a story about Roy while flying in the back seat of the P-51. Roy turned to anyone listening backstage and said, "That's not true," with a big smile.

As Roy got older, he became a true elder statesman. He'd let each of his musicians have a solo or two. This gave Roy a break and allowed each musician a chance to shine and showcase. Very generous and very wise, with a great sense of humor. What a marvelous fellow and great musician.

## CHUCK YEAGER COMPARES GLENNIS YEAGER TO VICTORIA

Early on, Chuck remarked on my handwriting—it was terrible. By contrast, he held up an envelope with Glennis' handwriting and said, "Glennis' was beautiful." I didn't particularly think so, but it was unimportant to me and subjective, so I didn't say anything.

Fortunately, I didn't have an ego re my handwriting. My father always complained about it. Shipley, the private girls' school I attended, taught the worst type of script.

I was the last in my third-grade class to get my fountain pen for good penmanship and used a pencil almost until the last day of school that year. I'm sure I got the pen out of pity or sympathy. Oddly, recently, I saw some old report cards from third grade and higher that say I had beautiful handwriting.

Part of the issue is I get bored writing by hand because I can't write, or write well, as fast as I think. I appreciate computers because I can almost type as fast as I think.

I was grateful Chuck had chosen something about which I truly did not care.

He liked to challenge people, including me.

He got a different response than what he was expecting: "Oh no, no, no. It's natural to compare and of course you are going to compare Glennis and me. But please don't say it out loud to me." I laughed and continued, "Especially if I'm on the wrong end."

Chuck looked at me and contemplated what I had just said.

And to put a fine point on it, I added, "You wouldn't want me to compare you to old romantic interests." What I did not say is that I was thanking God every day, literally, that none of my prior relationships had worked out, so I was footloose and fancy-free when I met Chuck. There was no comparison.

That got his attention. He raised his eyebrows in mock horror and immediately understood. I later learned he always understood immediately—never needed an additional fine point.

To his credit, he never detrimentally compared me to Glennis again.

One ammunition and gun supply retailer we knew mentioned his mother had gone to high school with Glennis. Then he looked at me. "Oh, sorry."

I said, "Why? I like hearing great stories about Glennis. She's part of Chuck's history."

The fellow said, "Well, most women in your position don't."

If I felt in competition with, or threatened by, any other woman or person, especially one no longer with us, for my guy; I wouldn't be in that relationship. I marvel at women who marry men who put them down, compare them unfavorably regarding another, cause jealousy, and the like.

Frankly, my hat's off to Glennis. She had to wash four sets of diapers (four kids) in a bathtub in a tiny two-room house in the middle of nowhere in the desert and had a husband whom she didn't know if he would come home upright, in a wheelchair or a casket each day he went to work.

Glennis and I had one thing in common—we loved to eat. In one of Glennis' letters to Chuck during World War II, Glennis stated he'd have to earn a lot of money to feed her because she liked to eat. I concur.

## SUPERB CHALK AND PENCIL DRAWING

About five years later, Chuck got a package from Australia. The note said, "I commissioned a great Australian artist, struggling to earn a living, to do a chalk-and-pencil drawing of your beautiful wife to honor her. Here it is."

Chuck opened the rest of the package to reveal a stunningly beautiful chalk-and-pencil drawing of…Glennis.

In my periphery, I could see Chuck sinking in his chair, bracing for my reaction.

I exclaimed, "Well, that looks nothing like me!!!" and laughed.

Chuck gave his usual response when I gave a very unexpected, often somewhat funny, response to life: he lightly banged his forehead with the palm of his hand as if to say, she's lost it. And, of course, he smiled broadly and laughed. Probably out of sheer relief.

## GLENNIS' ASHES: *2008*

Glennis' ashes lived with us in an urn in a cupboard for eight years. It was fine with me—growing up, we had Aunt Maude's ashes in a vase on our formal living room mantel—whoever she was.

For years, Chuck would tell folks that when he died, his ashes would be mixed with Glennis' and spread over the High Sierra. After a few years, I asked him if he would please not say that publicly—I would follow his wishes, but it made me feel like a stand-in.

He honored my request, knowing I would honor his.

About 2008, his oldest son demanded to have his mother's ashes. Chuck said, "No." Don retorted, "Well, she was my mother."

Chuck replied, "She was my wife long before she was your mother."

Chuck recounted the story to me afterward. I was impressed yet again.

Shortly after this meeting, Chuck took a friend flying and they spread Glennis' ashes in the High Sierra. When he said he was going to do this, I thought about offering to sit in the back seat and do that actual spreading while he flew, but just felt he might want to have a private moment and do that on his own.

I later thought, he might have just decided I wouldn't want to do that. One of the times I do wish I had communicated and not assumed what I thought he'd want.

## KENNY JARRETT'S VIETNAM RESCUE BY COLONEL CHUCK YEAGER

Chuck and I were at a fundraiser for conservation and hunter education. Chuck tells the story of his, now our, friend Kenny Jarrett.

Perhaps 20 to 30 years ago, at one of these fundraisers, a convention, Kenny saw, ran over, and enthusiastically introduced himself to General Chuck Yeager. Kenny, a Mensa member (extremely high IQ), wears overalls and talks like a country boy. And he is. He also never forgot where he came from. Kenny told Chuck he wanted to make him a rifle.

Chuck looked at the prices and said he couldn't afford one, but thanks.

Kenny said, "No! I want to make you a gun as a gift. When I was in Vietnam, you saved our platoon's lives.

"We were pinned down for hours by the Viet Cong who were hiding in tunnels and firing out at us and you, the cavalry in F-100s, came in and bombed them, wiping them out.

"When we saw you coming in, we were so relieved and hopeful. When you knocked 'em all out, we were so…For hours, we had thought we weren't goin' home. I want to thank you and make you a gun."

Chuck then told the story from his point of view. Chuck was leading a bombing run. He dropped his bombs. Nothing. He was sure he had been accurate. Were they duds? Did he miss? Geez. A couple long seconds later, he heard kaboom! His bombs had evidently entered a tunnel, traveled down the tunnel, hence the delay, and blew up the center.

Kenny responded: "That's right! You BLEW that mountain right off its base. You saved our lives!" and repeated, "I want to thank you and make you a gun!"

It's very nice to be genuinely appreciated with actions, not just words.

So Chuck said thank you; he'd like a 7mm rifle. Kenny tried to talk him into a bigger gun—a more expensive gift, but Chuck didn't need it, so he wouldn't accept.

Chuck had shot/culled over fifty cow elk with his Jarrett 7mm rifle with great accuracy (and I shot/culled two cow elk with great accuracy after Chuck taught me how to shoot). Chuck YEAGER-ism #120: "You can't eat the horns". Chuck and I were/are meat hunters. Bull elk meat is not as good as cow elk meat.

Our friends and neighbors appreciated the lean meat we shared with them.

## GENERAL ROBIN OLDS, AMERICAN TRIPLE FIGHTER ACE

Robin Olds, an attractive man with a dashing mustache, was a highly regarded triple ace from World War II and Vietnam. Chuck and he were well-acquainted later in life.

When General Robin Olds was enshrined into the National Aviation Hall of Fame in 2001, General Scott, Robin's good friend, introduced Robin. Generals Olds and Scott both had a penchant for much drinking and tonight was no different. General Olds shuffled up to the stage slowly, oh-so-painfully slowly, and we all held our breath, thinking, 'Oh boy. This is going to be a long night,' as we tried to get comfortable in our chairs in anticipation.

When Robin got to the podium, he said clearly and coherently, "I am honored to be inducted into the National Aviation Hall of Fame. But more than that, I am honored that so many of my friends showed up to celebrate this." General Olds then nodded and left the stage.

Wow!

That…was…one of the…best…acceptance…speeches…ever! Nice, moving, and short. Especially short.

When we arrived a little late (airplane was delayed) to a pre-party the day before, we were eating lunch at a picnic table in a hangar. Zoe Del Nutter, a lovely lady, quite a character, always dressed beautifully and extravagantly with everything matching in bright colors, often red, which is what my mother did, came up and said, "We met before. Do you remember?" I thought: "Wow. I should remember. She sure stands out (in a good way)."

But I didn't remember, so I covered, "Was I polite?"

Everyone laughed. Zoe said, "Yes." I said, "Phew!" And we continued in pleasant conversation.

We stayed with Sam Morgan, who took us to his country club for lunch. Joe Foss and Bobby Knight joined us—what fun that was.

## PANSY LEE, CHUCK YEAGER'S SISTER: *2001*

The first time I met Pansy Lee, Chuck's younger sister, she took us to Charles', as she called her older brother, and her hometowns of Hamlin and Myra, West Virginia, and showed us the sites regarding the Yeager family upbringing.

We stayed at her house for dinner and had leather britches (dried green beans with a ham hock simmered in chicken broth for days) and butterscotch pie.

Her butterscotch "pah" was to die for. I enthused that hers was even better than Charles'. While trying to hide a smile, slightly pleased she was better than her older brother at something, she couldn't just take a compliment and let a moment to scold go by. She admonished me that that wasn't nice to say in front of my husband, Charles.

Not five minutes later, Charles (Chuck) volunteered: "This is much better than mine." (Charlie, I hadn't thought I could love you more till this moment.) Win-win-win. He compliments his sister, supports his romantic partner, and is humble about his own pie. Literally.

Pansy had some great stories of her childhood with Chuck. Roy, their older brother, and Chuck used to say she couldn't go to the swimming hole; girls were not allowed because they didn't know how to swim. Pansy Lee would reason, "How can I learn to swim if I can't go to the swimming hole?"

When she was about three, her mother told the boys to do the dishes after dinner. They whined: "Why doesn't Pansy do them? She's the girl?"

Their mother said, "She's too little."

Shortly thereafter, her mother heard quite a bit of banging in the kitchen. She came in to find Pansy on several boxes the boys had piled up, trying to do the dishes.

The first time a West Virginia trooper drove us to Pansy Lee's, after we told him the menu—leather britches and butterscotch pah—we could tell he was thinking he'd be eating later after the evening was over.

After he tasted the food, he was pleasantly surprised and did not leave hungry.

After this, whenever Chuck and I would fly to West Virginia and stay with the Governor (Manchin), the West Virginia troopers would fight over who would drive us down to Pansy Lee's. Word was out—her leather britches were delicious and the butterscotch pah unmatched.

## DADDY BUSH *(President George H.W. Bush)*

Chuck and I had been together over nine months when we were having breakfast with General Norman Schwarzkopf at a Safari Club International (SCI) convention, right after a news story emerged that Daddy Bush and his friends profited from the first Gulf War. There was a lot of U.S. cash floating around in Iraq—spoils of war. I asked General Schwarzkopf how much loot did he get. He answered, "I was in every meeting about the war with President Bush and that was not an option."

I countered, "What about every phone call?" General Schwarzkopf hesitated as one could see the wheels turning, thinking. He remained silent as we continued eating. I'd love to know what he concluded. Chuck changed the subject. We knew.

Later that morning, we went to the VIP lounge and were having a snack when I noticed a bunch of large guys in suits with wires in their ears, walking in. I also noticed General Schwarzkopf. I thought, 'All that security for him?' When I saw Daddy Bush in a wheelchair (from recent hip surgery) entering, it made sense.

I told Chuck. He noted it and kept eating. Then, after a moment's thought, he asked if I'd like to meet President Bush. I had been a volunteer at a VIP reception for President Bush while he was campaigning in 1992 but hadn't formally met him, so I said, "Sure."

We went over. President Bush was thrilled to see Chuck. He shook my hand and pulled me in as if to conspiratorially tell me a secret joke that we all could hear. I have no idea what he said, but he laughed so hard his face fell on my chest. I thought, 'If I slug him, the Secret Service will have me on the floor with my hands behind my back in a nanosecond.' However, it really was his nose that hit my breastbone, so he hit nothing exciting. Certainly not any knockers.

I grabbed his shoulder, squeezed as hard as I could and put him back straight in his chair. We understood each other.

Chuck and I went back to our table to finish our snack. Daddy Bush's SCI minder came over and asked if we'd like to join President Bush for lunch. Chuck said, "Nah."

The minder was shocked—people were actively vying, offering money, for seats at this lunch. He tried to convince Chuck.

Chuck said, "We don't feel like changing."

The minder implored him, assured him, "You can come as you are."

Chuck thought for a moment, looked at me: "You want to go?"

I thought it'd be interesting, if nothing else, and if I stayed more than arm's length...I said, "Free lunch? At an expensive restaurant? Sure."

The minder wasn't sure about either one of us.

Unimpressed, Chuck's comment, after Daddy Bush's parade of minders and minions left, was, "It would take a D-5 Cat to pull Schwarzkopf's nose out of Daddy Bush's a$$."

We got to lunch at the appointed hour and found a free-for-all. There was no assigned seating, so all sorts of people grabbed seats at Daddy Bush's table. Two of those were the former President of Peru and his very thin, fake-everything, Barbie Doll, pretty, pleasant wife.

I found it interesting that the former President of Peru, though sitting next to his blonde bombshell wife, wanted only to talk to me. Someone mentioned it was his only intelligent conversation of the day.

We found a table with two empty seats. The Oak Ridge Boys found their own table of four next to us. All through lunch, Chuck was in fine form; the entire table and those at tables nearby were laughing at his humor and enjoying his stories. The Boys wished we were sitting together. Daddy Bush, about six tables over, kept looking wistfully at Chuck, the Boys, and me, I'm sure wishing he was with us, joining in the fun and laughter.

That evening, at the dinner, we were seated at the same head table with about twenty folks—a huge, long, rectangular table. Chuck saw Daddy Bush and said, "Let's go say hello." I replied, "You go right ahead. I'll wave from here."

Daddy Bush, not using the wheelchair, shook Chuck's hand, then looked for me. Chuck pointed at me across the table. I smiled and waved. Daddy Bush's expression indicated he understood full well; he smiled and waved back.

Schwarzkopf was seated diagonally across from me at a very wide head table. The blonde bombshell said hello. They shook hands and Schwarzkopf pulled her down to whisper in her ear, her hand now in his lap. Schwarzkopf saw me observing this, smiled sheepishly and shrugged.

* * *

Another year at SCI, someone invited us to attend a VIP cocktail party for President Bush before the formal SCI dinner. We told them we only had casual clothes. No problem. When we showed up, one of the apparent hosts was not happy and attempted to look down his nose at us even though he was shorter than we were. We ignored him. Chuck was commandeered by fans. I went straight to the food table and found expensive caviar with all the trimmings. I love expensive caviar with all the trimmings, blini, bits of chopped-up hard-boiled egg (and onion, but not in a crowd) because I don't have it very often. Although, when I worked in Russia in 1979, that was all I could eat. Nothing else agreed with me. It also reminded me of my childhood family Christmas cruises, stopping in St. Thomas, where Mom's friend invited us to her home and served us endless amounts of expensive caviar, blinis, trimmings and all.

At the cocktail party, two guys came up to the food table, so I politely tried to start a conversation. They were from New Jersey, so I mentioned I grew up during part of the summers on the Jersey Shore. Then I asked what they did. The one who was a classic Mafia-looking guy; broken nose, dark hair, tough-looking, pot belly, gravelly voice, said, "Who wants to know?" I wasn't sure if he was putting me on, but I wasn't going to take any chances. I quickly said, "I don't. Not me. Just making conversation. Have you tried—I mean, caviar is great," and I focused on the food.

Soon after, I was in another room listening to a story from Mary Cabela. Chuck came in. "Daddy Bush is looking for you!" I smiled. "Mary's just finishing her story, then I'll follow you." Chuck clearly agreed. Mary and Dick Cabela tried to rush me out. Mary quickly finished her story. I excused myself to go say hello to Daddy Bush. He had walked into the first room, looked around, saw Chuck at the other end and cried out, "Chuck!" After chatting for a couple minutes, Daddy Bush asked where I was.

When I shook his hand, Daddy Bush gave me a chaste peck on the cheek. He was learnin'.

The snooty host—well, suddenly, we were best friends. We continued to ignore him.

*  *  *

One year, Daddy Bush had asked that, instead of a speech, Chuck Yeager interview him. Two others horned in; so also on stage were the Executive Director at the time, who later, I was told, was kicked out for embezzling money, and the haughty, very rich host. Chuck's and Daddy Bush's questions of each other were very interesting, as were the answers. They asked each other about flying and meeting their wives; they had a great deal in common. I wonder if anyone recorded that? I wish I had written down some of the funny things Chuck said when teasing Daddy Bush.

The other two were boring, dry, and truly a drag. It was too bad anyone let them on the stage. But money talked—they bought their way on stage, I was told, to the chagrin of the audience.

*  *  *

Daddy Bush had wanted to see an airplane at the convention with Chuck.

Prior to that, I told Thomas, Daddy Bush's assistant, to tell Daddy Bush to quit calling me "Vicky"—rhymes with sticky, picky, icky, and just isn't me. He promised to do so.

We ran into Dan Quayle. He stepped right in front of us, very rude, and was talking to the later-to-be-disgraced Executive Director. I observed, "I wonder if Dan Quayle knows he stepped in front of General Chuck Yeager?"

Dan turned and stepped back briefly on my toe. "Oh, hi, Chuck!" No apology. And he still stood in front of me; no situational awareness; would not have made a good fighter pilot.

I looked down at his perfectly pressed, with a crease, fashionably faded, light-blue jeans and espied a small hole.

The devil made me do it. I quietly alerted Chuck, then said loudly, "Dan, you know you have a hole in your pants?"

He jumped, screeched and danced like a little kid, trying to find it with his hand. I was no more help. My job was done.

He turned and asked the Exec where it was. The Exec said, "Oh, it's really small and halfway down the back of your leg."

I chastised the Exec, "You're no fun—we had him going."

Chuck merely smiled. Not a good idea to step on my toes, literally.

At an airplane exhibit on the convention floor, Chuck and Daddy Bush discussed flying. Then Daddy Bush and his driver roared off in a golf cart. About fifty yards away, Daddy Bush turned, smiled and waved at me, "BYE, VICKY!!!!"

Stunned, I half smiled while the crowded floor all turned to look at me to see who was so special. I glanced, okay, glared, in jest, at Thomas, who panicked and repeated defensively, "I haven't had a chance to tell him! I haven't had a chance to tell him!"

Every time we saw Daddy Bush early on, he would somehow insinuate marriage for Chuck and me, calling me Mrs. Yeager now and again. I guess he was alerting Chuck of his approval. At least he never called me "Vicky" again.

## BARBARA BUSH, *Former U.S. First Lady*

We were invited to a Houston Astros baseball game. Daddy and Barbara Bush were there and requested we say hello. Their minders had told us we could only have two minutes with the Bushes. I thought, 'The minders obviously don't know the Bushes' relationship with Chuck and now me. You all, as usual, haven't done your research and are a little too officious, boys.'

We walked down the stadium stairs to about the third row where the Bushes were, right behind home plate.

George and Barbara's faces lit up at seeing Chuck. George introduced me to Barbara. As the minders were getting restless counting out the two minutes, George said, "Sit down, Chuck, Victoria!" and motioned to the seats directly across the aisle from them.

To the chagrin of the minders and pleasure of the Secret Service, who all loved Chuck, we watched the rest of the game with the Bushes. I noticed Barbara sneaking glances at Chuck—she adored him. We had that in common.

As we were leaving the baseball game, George said, "We're having lunch on Friday, right? Come to my office first and then we'll go over to the club."

We went to his office at the appointed hour and, while waiting for George, played a laser shooting game set up in his conference room. Chuck got one hundred percent. I got close. Chuck was starting again when George opened the door and cried, "Don't shoot!" Seeing Chuck's and my scores, his competitive nature kicked in. He had to try.

As he was shooting, he kept forgetting to reload. I've always been a great cheerleader, so I kept yelling, "Reload!" when it was time to do so.

He didn't score so well. Chuck quipped, "I'll share my food," which prompted us to remember lunch. We headed to the Houston Country Club.

It was a very pleasant day. We arrived early.

When Barbara arrived, Daddy Bush asked her what she would like to drink. She looked at my short glass full of clear liquid and her eyes lit up. She said sweetly, "I'll have what she's having. What are you having?"

I hesitated, thinking, 'This is not going to go well,' and then told the truth with a weak, ever-hopeful smile, "Water."

Barbara's face fell. I quickly became Public Enemy #1.

Daddy Bush, always bemused by me, jumped in, rescuing the situation a little, and suggested a glass of white wine. Barbara settled gruffly.

Barbara was up and down from the table, nervous, but eventually, the Bushes realized that Chuck and I were just good company and not asking for anything (except that Daddy Bush pay for lunch, I guess). Barbara introduced their son Neil, who had been playing tennis.

After, Barbara imperiously challenged me on various topics. I answered truthfully, artfully dodging taking Barbara head-on. As I've said, I went to girls' school, had three older brothers, and grew up in a very snooty, mean area. She, playing at the mean girl game, was testing me. I was passing with flying colors, but honestly, I would have rather just eaten my lunch in peace. No idea what lunch was—too busy ducking and weaving.

When it came time to order dessert, Daddy Bush asked me if I would like some. He didn't expect my answer:

I replied with my old family joke, "It's the only reason I came."

Daddy Bush, used to women who felt you can never be too thin or too rich, thus never had dessert, was taken aback but amused.

He offered ice cream. I thought, 'Seriously? Ice cream. Unless it's oh so special, homemade and the right flavor…' I wondered what else they had but decided not to push it right then.

To my relief, I didn't have to figure out how to maneuver that one. When the waiter came and Daddy Bush again suggested ice cream,

Barbara insisted she wanted to hear what else they had. She wanted the last one—coconut cake and add ice cream. Music to my ears—it was exactly what I wanted. I piped up, "Me, too, please."

I was almost back in her good graces—it was rare another woman in their circles had dessert.

After lunch, Barbara, a great chronicler, wanted photos together—a sign I had passed the tests. While posing together, I thanked Barbara for ordering that coconut cake and ice cream. It was great! She had saved the day.

Barbara retorted: "I noticed you didn't eat much of it!"

I explained: "I haven't mastered that talking and chewing thing..."

Barbara, offering her great wisdom, snapped, "And don't! Ever! You'll get fat!"

Yes, ma'am. I never forgot that. And I have yet to master that talking and chewing thing.

As we were all walking out the back way, Barbara offered to drive us home. "Georgie, I want to drive them home." The Secret Service, alarmed—Mrs. Bush had never offered that before—scrambled to figure out how to make that work.

George, realizing in addition to all the other challenges that would create—she had just consumed two glasses of wine—responded, "That's not a good idea, Barbie."

Barbie replied, "Georgie, I'd like to—it would be nice."

George reiterated, "Barbie, I think Chuck and Victoria will be fine."

They were suddenly a young, loving couple. I felt like I had stepped into someone else's romantic play and kept very quiet to see how it all played out.

Fortunately, George won that discussion. They got in their respective SUVs with several Secret Service; we got in our sedan with our driver.

## NEIL ARMSTRONG *(Astronaut, first man on the moon)*

In the first six months together, Chuck proceeded to go to several events scheduled a year ahead without inviting me. Many I didn't mind, but some

I did. Having one typical characteristic of the youngest child; I hated missing out on anything.

So, when we had been living together for about five months, in August 2000, I decided to take the bull by the horns and insisted on going to the National Air & Space Museum dinner and his talk afterward in October 2000. I was tired of being left out. Chuck was astonished but didn't say no. It took me some time to realize that he didn't invite me to travel with him because, generally, Glennis, his first wife, in the last 15 years of her life, preferred to stay home while Chuck traveled. They were still close, talking on the phone several times a day. So he just assumed I'd want to "stay home" too. Far from it. (In fact, when he wasn't home, I would also travel.)

I guess I behaved properly at that first elegant dinner on the mezzanine level with a great view of the X-1 because forever after, even when it was supposed to be a guy trip, Chuck would ask the host if I could come along.

The first time I met Neil Armstrong was that day of Chuck's talk at the National Air & Space Museum (NASM) in Washington, DC. We had walked over to the museum to visit with the then Deputy Director of NASM, a former World War II fighter pilot in China.

NASM was having a board meeting. Someone mentioned food, so we went up to the administration office to grab some of their lunch and eat in the small conference room next door.

When the Board meeting broke for lunch, a vibrant young woman came in and hugged Chuck very enthusiastically, thrilled to see him. He happily accepted a hug from an attractive, strange woman. When she announced who she was, Patty Wagstaff (a champion aerobatic pilot), an ol' friend, Chuck laughed and they hugged again. (Her hair had been frizzy, curly brown; now it was flat blond.)

We went to the big conference room; Chuck started "swimming upstream" towards…Neil Armstrong, a board member. Neil was watching Chuck warily, looking around for an escape, trying surreptitiously to avoid us, but there was no way out. It was entertaining to watch the body language. Obviously, there was some history there. I later learned why. Put simply: Chuck knew a lot about Neil Armstrong from the early days and didn't tolerate formal education arrogance. Neil had made some pilot errors after discounting Chuck's advice. He didn't challenge Chuck again.

This day, Chuck greeted him warmly and they chatted. Chuck introduced me. We said hello to others, too, and then sat down to finish our lunch with the board.

That night, as usual, the talk went well—each of the three theaters was full with standing room only. They piped Chuck's talk into the other two. Afterward, he sat down and signed one item per person.

* * *

Chuck and I saw Neil again at the 2001 National Aviation Hall of Fame induction ceremony, where he gave a speech. I later asked Neil for a copy—too many folks kept coming up to Chuck to say hello or meet him, so I had missed some of Neil's talk.

In Los Angeles, a couple years later, at a self-described "elite" club (only 10,000 members, hardly exclusive), I watched Neil decline to give an autograph so pleasantly (didn't like seeing it on eBay the next day), I tried to emulate his manner.

Many years later, in June 2012, we saw Neil at Barron Hilton's ranch. We invited Oak Ridge Boys member William Lee Golden and the Boys' road manager, Darrick Kinslow, who were thrilled to meet Neil. And Neil was delighted and gracious to meet our friends. The Oak Ridge Boys were playing nearby in the Reno area.

We (Chuck, Neil, and I) ate lunch together several times throughout the weekend. I took a photo of the two of them in the helicopter, enjoying spending time together in the back while Barron flew the helicopter with an IP (instructor pilot). That was the last time we saw Neil.

We were shocked and saddened by his passing shortly thereafter during a routine medical procedure at the young age of 82 in August 2012. Chuck is probably still razzing Neil now—Chuck YEAGER-ism #30: "You may touch, but you ain't gonna go!" (This story is in *101 Chuck YEAGER-isms: Wit & Wisdom from America's Hero, The Right Stuff* by New York Times #1 bestselling author, General Chuck Yeager, & his favorite wingman, Victoria.)

## THE P-51 & OBIE O'BRIEN, *World War II Fighter Ace*

I remember the first time Chuck showed me a P-51. We were at Edwards AFB, California, a couple days before the air show in 2000.

Chuck had me climb into the pilot's seat. If you've never climbed into a P-51—it takes some serious effort—well, the first time does. Especially if you're being careful not to touch the wrong thing—I'd hate to hit the gear controls and collapse the gear.

Seriously, that's how little I knew.

He pointed out the controls, gauges, gear, and the like. It was fascinating.

As I finally stood up in the seat and struggled to climb out (again, not easy to get in, harder to get out) onto the wing where Chuck was standing, looking about as cool as any fighter pilot could, I asked: "Wow! How did you get out of this thing after you were shot down? You wouldn't have had enough time (it was taking me forever to get out and I was pretty agile) or you would've hit the tail or wing."

With his quick wit, Chuck, observing me struggling, answered: "I didn't have to—it was falling apart in pieces all around me."

And that's what happened to him. The day after he shot down his first two German enemy aircraft over Germany (got credit for only one), to show he wasn't so Sierra Hotel (Sh--Hot!), he was shot down—March 5, 1944, near Bordeaux.

The weather was "stinkin'", so the lead bomber pilot broke protocol and silence by radioing, "We're heading to target number two", instead of simply turning east. The Germans did not know the Allied planes were there (due to the bad weather) until they heard the radio call. So just as the P-51s turned, F/O Yeager, who was flying tail-end Charlie (last in formation), head on a swivel, checked six and called, "Bandits, 6 o'clock!" (Chuck YEAGER-ism #7: "Check six!")

The Germans were behind them. The flight leader, Obie O'Brien, called, "Break!" and the P-51 formation turned into the Germans.

F/O Yeager did a head-on pass with three FW-190s. He gave 'em hell, but they got the P-51's vulnerable radiator and him, frankly—shrapnel in his legs and groin. They did miss the family jewels, fortunately.

As Chuck would say, he and his airplane parted company. As he free-fell to the ground, he waited until the last minute to open his parachute so as not to draw attention. One of the FW-190s was aiming towards F/O Yeager again to finish him off when Obie O'Brien, the flight leader, turned and shot the FW-190 down, saving his pal Chuck Yeager.

You can imagine when, three months later, Obie's pal Chuck Yeager walked into the barracks they shared in England; although thrilled, Obie exclaimed, "Charlie, don't you have enough sense? When you're shot down, you're supposed to stay down."

In fact, Obie never forgot. It was because Chuck Yeager, tail-end Charlie, had checked six and called, "Bandits, 6 o'clock!" that the rest of the flight of four was saved.

I met Obie only once. GREAT guy. He was, unfortunately, on the downhill slope of life. His mind was going a little. But when his pal Charlie showed up? Wow. He came back. Obie and Chuck sat on the couch. It was just after we had "won the war" in Iraq in twenty-six days with a loss of 103 U.S. military people.

Obie sat back, crossing his arms and ankles, and opined: "We wouldn't have lost one. Right, Charlie?"

Sue, Obie's wife, also a wonderful gal, said that Obie brightened up whenever Chuck called or visited. Real friends.

## PETE KNIGHT *(Test Pilot, Fastest Man Alive 1967)*

General Al Boyd thought it essential that another test pilot escort home the casket of a fellow pilot who had augured in. It was tough because, as Chuck said, "There you are, about the same age as their young son, and they're wondering why you are standing there in front of them and not their son." For this reason and also having lost so many good friends, especially due to war, after he retired, Chuck didn't go to too many funerals.

At Pete Knight's funeral in May 2004, which lasted too long in the church, were many politicians because Pete had made quite an impression when he was in the California State Senate. Chuck had been asked to be a pallbearer. His response was, "Hell, no! I'm not carrying that thing!" No, they wanted General Yeager to be an honorary pallbearer, which he did.

Governor Schwarzenegger, who had only known Pete briefly before his death, told a wonderful, quintessentially Pete Knight story in four minutes. Impressive. And memorable. Perfect. We should all learn from that.

Governor Schwarzenegger had been Governor only a short time when Senator Knight insisted on meeting with him in front of the state Capitol. Insisted. Governor Schwarzenegger asked, "Who is this guy?" but agreed to meet with him.

Pete insisted, "It's not a holiday tree. It's a Christmas tree. Call it what it is—a Christmas tree!" Pete, at five foot two, was so insistent and persuasive that, to Gov. Schwarzenegger's astonishment, he agreed. The Governor's story described Pete Knight to a tee. It was perfect.

The minister went on for an hour, not about Pete—which he could have; Pete was so accomplished—but like a used car salesman selling Jesus. Maybe he was looking for new congregants. The way Chuck told it, he could see the casket jumping and shaking—Pete in there kicking and screaming for the minister to stop. Gale, his widow, was furious.

* * *

I first met Pete Knight in front of a mural of Chuck Yeager, with loads of brown hair, and the X-1 on the side of a furniture store in Lancaster, California. (The mural is still there as of October 2022.) General Chuck Yeager was being inducted into the Lancaster Aerospace Walk of Honor. Pete spoke, Chuck spoke, and both had the entire audience, including me, in stitches, the kind where you can't breathe. I wish we had taped that, too.

* * *

I had asked Pete, at the time a California State Senator, if he could help with a healthcare project that would lower the cost of healthcare yet raise the standard. He said, "When I'm in Sacramento, let's meet for lunch and discuss. Call my office."

When I mentioned having lunch with Pete, Chuck was clearly against it. I asked him to come too. Still against it.

Pete would call out of the blue to be supportive of Chuck and me. I virtually always was the one to answer the phone, so he'd tell me how he handled similar challenging situations, then hang up. It was so very supportive, well-timed, and kind.

Sometime later, Pete called and asked me when we were going to have lunch.

I came clean. "Well, Pete, I'll tell ya. You're a handsome, witty, intelligent guy and Chuck is not comfortable with me having lunch with you. And I'm just not going to do that with his friends if it makes him uncomfortable. I appreciate your willingness to discuss the project, but I just can't. If you had been my childhood friend for life, that might be different, but you're his friend."

He was taken aback a little but very mature about it…and ultimately thought more highly of me.

I had to do that with one of Chuck's friend's pilots who liked to flirt at me. I was very clear. "Look, I'd hate to stop learning to fly from you, but the moment Chuck is uncomfortable, I'll find another instructor pilot." The pilot backed off. I still found another instructor pilot.

## GREAT FRIENDS — MILDRED AND DICK

Two of our favorite people lived about an hour north of New York City. They were great friends of my mother. I really got to know Mildred in Kenya during the United Nations World Conference on Women in 1985. Just after graduating from Columbia University with an MBA, I was there with my mother, who was a speaker for an NGO (non-governmental organization) on the prevention of alcoholism and drug abuse, and Mildred, who was there with *Good Housekeeping* magazine in magnificent colonial suites with high ceilings. Mildred was a major force behind the scenes in human rights, even into her early nineties. After my mother died in 1986, Mildred and Dick became like second parents to me.

B.C., Before Chuck, I would visit them fairly often, staying with them for a few days each year. Mildred and Dick, her husband, were extremely intelligent, well-read, involved, interesting, and alive.

After I met Chuck, we would travel back to New York about once a year. And we would make a point of seeing Mildred and Dick. The first time, we went to a local diner with them. Chuck was opining about how rude Northeasterners can be while three Northeasterners were perhaps considering defending themselves.

We didn't get a chance because immediately after Chuck finished his statement, a car raced out of the parking lot; the driver sat on his horn, honking at us as we made our way in the crosswalk. (Dick was using a walker.) A well-timed illustration of Chuck's observations.

Chuck truly enjoyed Mildred and Dick and hearing about their latest adventures.

So did I. Sadly, they are all gone now.

## RUSS SCHLEEH COL USAF (RET.), *World War II Bomber Pilot, Chief Test Pilot, Speedboat Champion*

Chuck was determined to see Russ. Some "friends" had lied as usual and told him Russ had had a stroke and his younger second wife had stuck him in an assisted living facility and abandoned him. They were trying to intimate that I would do the same to Chuck.

Chuck, quite naturally, had concerns about his friend, Russ.

So, in 2002, we had a reason to go to Los Angeles and we built in a visit with Russ.

It was a great reunion of the two guys. Russ was a sweetheart. When Chuck broke the sound barrier, the other test pilots were annoyed and jealous and took it as a personal affront to each of them that the most junior officer (Yeager) got assigned the best project, the X-1, and succeeded.

The only person to congratulate Chuck for breaking the sound barrier in 1947 was Russ Schleeh, who had been Chief of the Fighter Test and Bomber test divisions. As Chuck described it with great humor, Russ looked around to make sure no one was watching and then hugged Chuck and congratulated him. I'm sure, knowing Russ, he didn't care what others thought.

We entered Russ' new home. His wife had moved them from their sizeable two-story home not to assisted living, but to a one-story, nice, comfortable, accessible townhome.

We took Russ to a lunch. The host usually held a lunch with Russ once a week or more, to get him out and socializing. Because the host's assistant had unfortunately bragged that Chuck would be there, there were too many folks at breakfast, but I made sure Chuck, Russ, and Dan sat together.

When Chuck joked with Russ about shooting at Bob Hoover when they were bear huntin', Russ turned to me. "If I was shootin' at him, I woulda hit him!" Still feisty! I reassured him his prowess was intact: "I have no doubt, Russ."

Chuck told the story of when Russ had been test-flying the YB-49, a flying wing, a miserable plane to fly. Russ landed, broke his back, then saved his co-pilot's life from the incendiary cockpit and tried to prevent the fire trucks from putting out the fire. "Let the sumbit—burn!"

Russ ended up in the hospital in a full-body cast with strategic openings.

Pancho Barnes told Chuck, "C'mon! I bet he's thirsty and horny." She put on a trench coat, put a bottle of whiskey in one of her pockets, brought the best one of her girls and snuck them into Russ.

As Chuck told the story, Russ listening intently, Chuck said, "I can't remember the name of the girl– ." Russ, over 50 years later, interrupted and, with a look of sheer orgasmic ecstasy on his face, remembering, said, "Julie—her name was Julie."

## AUSTRALIA'S PIP & DICK SMITH,
*Helicopter World Record Holder: 2004*

Chuck and I visited with Dick and Pip Smith in 2004 for Dick's sixtieth birthday party in Australia, which lasted a weekend.

Afterward, Dick flew us to various places around the east coast of Australia. Dick, a restless sort, had been flying helicopters for 30 years and holds several records—such as first to fly around the world from the North to the South Pole.

We flew to the Blue Mountains in a Caravan with me in right seat. I liked that plane. It was a bit bumpy over the ridges. I held on. Dick was impressed with my straight and level flying. Pip called from the back a warning about the ridges. Dick replied that I was doing fine.

On the way back, Chuck flew right seat. And the flight was smooth as glass. Dick said even the wind listens to Chuck. It had calmed down by our return flight. "Doesn't seem fair," I said, laughing.

We flew to Echuca, middle of nowhere on the Murray River, oddly one of the few places in Australia I had been before. We got to fly PBYs (amphibious reconnaissance and bomber planes during World War II with a range of over 2500 miles) there. At dinner, Dick was the guest of honor and speaker. He told three interesting stories of his adventures, then said, "Aw, you don't want to listen to me. Wouldn't you rather hear from Chuck Yeager?"

The aviation and local audience laughed.

Dick said, "No, I'm serious."

They laughed a little less, wondering what was going on.

Dick: "Chuck, would you like to come up here and say a few words?"

The audience gasped and then burst into cheering and clapping loudly. What a treat!

As we were leaving, Chuck and I made a point of going to the kitchen and thanking those who had cooked dinner—an all-volunteer group. They were most appreciative.

The next day, one fellow, a very large fellow, a friend of Dick Smith's, picked us up by airplane to bring us to his farm, where we stayed with his wife and him for several days. The first flight, Chuck had me sit in the right seat as usual to give me more experience. The fellow's runway was hilly—when we landed, the rollout was up and down. It was a bit dicey. He had lots of land with a flat area, but he didn't see any fun in that.

For dinner, we had lamb, which I love, probably because I rarely have it. It's not Chuck's favorite because it is usually overcooked or tough. I agree. This time, though, it was perfect.

Our host fell asleep at the table, snoring a little, okay, a *lot*, having imbibed too much, apparently as usual. His wife was a little embarrassed, but when we showed no signs of caring, she relaxed. A little.

T, the wife of another couple, also guests, watched Chuck put mint jelly on his plate and eat it plain. She spoke harshly to me: "VICTORIA! Stop him! He's eating the mint jelly without anything else!"

After I got over my momentary "So what?" moment, I spoke out loud. "He's free, over 21 and can do what he wants." (This attitude Chuck and I both had is probably one reason we had a great marriage.)

As T sputtered, the slumbering, inebriated host shifted a little and grunted in his deep-toned, upper-class British accent, "Quite right, Victoria! Quite right!"

Chuck continued to enjoy his mint jelly and I continued to enjoy my second helping of lamb.

The next day, when we were leaving, Chuck told me he would be sitting right seat. If the pilot choked on those hills, Chuck could grab the controls. Thank goodness. Quite right, Charlie! Quite right!

At the Smiths' ranch near Canberra, Dick wanted to fly Chuck in his ultralight, which he had recently purchased. He hadn't had many hours in it yet. Chuck knew I had always wanted to fly in an ultralight and said, "Let Victoria go first." I'm not sure he was being considerate. I think he wanted to see how Dick flew that contraption first. And I was the guinea pig. Hmmm.

Dick and I went up. What a superb view of the ranch, all the kangaroos and other wildlife. It was quite windy, so Dick instantly decided not a good day for him to fly and we immediately came back down. That spoke volumes to Chuck—good, safe flying decisions.

The next day, Chuck went up first. I went up next. We pursued a few kangaroos in the ultralight. I remarked how wonderful it was. Dick told me the kangaroos were an overabundant pest and had to be thinned.

That was our cue. Chuck and I went out that night with a guide and took care of several. Chuck saw a large one at about 500 yards. The guide said too far. I informed him Chuck had shot an elk at over 800 meters at a 60-degree angle. The guide's eyes got wide. He stopped and they set up. Only the large head was showing. Chuck shot it in the neck, no pain. It went straight down.

We returned to Sydney from Canberra the day before we were to leave to go home, flying up the coast a little by helicopter. Pip asked if Dick would kindly do an aerial tour of Sydney Harbour for me. So beautiful. Very kind of Pip and Dick. I felt so lucky. I had been to Australia twice before, but totally different types of trips.

We flew on the north side of the harbor. Dick asked, "Chuck, would you like to fly?"

Chuck said, "Sure," so Dick handed him the controls.

Dick then told Chuck: "My daughter lives over there," as he indicated the 7:00 (left and behind a little) direction. "Chuck, could you fly over there so we can wave?"

Chuck: "Okay."

Chuck turned a sharp left—I don't know the degrees, but it felt almost horizontal—maybe sixty degrees.

Dick started hyperventilating and talking out loud to himself: "Wow…that's…gasp!…quite a bank…angle of attack…I wouldn't do that. But it's Chuck Yeager and I guess…it's…gasp…okay…he probably…knows…what…he's doing."

We straightened out, did a tremendous slow fly-by, a wave, and headed back to the center of Sydney.

Quite funny! (Because Chuck did know what he was doing! Don't try this at home.)

## BARRON HILTON, FORMER CEO, HILTON HOTELS; "I'M AN INNKEEPER, GODDAMMIT!": *June 2004*

We had flown a small, single-engine taildragger over the High Sierra to a ranch in Nevada for a fly-in and to give a talk. The runway was a bit challenging because it had a sharp left turn at the end. Odd.

Barron Hilton heard we were there, so he flew his helicopter over to invite Chuck and me to stay at his ranch a little farther south.

Chuck responded, "No, thanks, we don't have toothbrushes."

Barron: "I have plenty of extra toothbrushes."

Chuck: "Nah. We don't have any pajamas."

Barron: "I've got lots of extra pajamas."

Chuck: "We don't have…"

Exasperated, Barron interrupted: "I'm an innkeeper, goddammit. I have whatever you need."

Since Barron was speaking Chuck's language, Chuck understood clearly. Chuck then turned to ask me. "Do you want to go?"

I smiled. Barron looked doubtfully at me—he was used to women who needed bags and bags of makeup, jewelry, dressy clothes and couldn't possibly show up with just the clothes on their backs. Who could blame him? One of his stepmothers was Zsa Zsa Gabor!

Well, he would find I was very different from his norm. I replied, "Sure. Another adventure." I wasn't going to let a little thing like not having any other, let alone dinner, clothes, makeup, perfume, jewelry, or designer dogs, prevent me from another adventure with Chuck. One of the things Chuck liked about me is I traveled light and didn't slow him or us down.

We told Barron that after Chuck's talk, we'd head down. Thus began several years of several weekends a year at Barron's ranch.

Barron controlled 750,000 acres. It started out as a stagecoach stop; the building was still there and remodeled inside for the employees' living quarters.

The main ranch house had Barron's ensuite bedroom on one side, living area, bar, dining areas in the middle, kitchen and three bedrooms on the other side. In addition, there were ensuite comfortable cabins varying in size outside and beyond that.

We stayed in a cabin. In the early days, the Reno Hilton Hotel did the catering. Chuck and I quickly got wise to the considerable amount on each plate, just asked for one dinner and split it. They started adding extra to each split one until we told them to cut it out.

I told Barron I had been to his ranch before. You could see he started thinking differently of me, trying to figure out what other male had brought me. After I enjoyed letting him and others stew on that for a bit, I told him I had been to Bodie, a ghost town open to the public within the lands he managed.

He smiled at me when he realized I had been teasing him.

He wasn't used to folks like Chuck and me. He adored Chuck—the only friend who gave far more than he got, even from a billionaire. And as Chuck's favorite wingman, he appreciated me, too. I saved Barron from some bad large deals.

Barron always quickly put Chuck and me next to him. The first time he had me sit to his right, I exclaimed, "Oh, thank you! The place of honor!"

No one had ever exclaimed that—they all were "entitled" or didn't know that traditional etiquette dictated the right side was more honored than the left.

One time though, as he and I walked into the dining room first, he pondered who should sit where; he didn't want to insult anyone, especially me standing next to him. That weekend, two others, who had known Barron much longer and were much older than I, were there. "Colleen and Cleo with you would be perfect." That signaled I was fine and understood respecting them first was the right thing to do. He breathed a big sigh of relief. "Right. Right."

Barron kept looking wistfully down the table to where Chuck and I were, gales of laughter and fun, as usual.

Chuck and I were back sitting next to Barron the rest of the weekend. We also protected Barron to some degree from unwanted conversation. People asked tedious questions, trying to make conversation. I would turn the question into, or ask a question about, something I knew interested Chuck and Barron (and me), or Chuck told fascinating stories. Or we teased Barron and got him to understand our humor. I also gave him health information, which Barron very much needed.

When Barron, Chuck and I were fishing, Barron mentioned Paris Hilton, his granddaughter, about the time her sex tape came out. I said, "Well, she's having a good time, isn't she?" It was the nicest thing I could think to say that was true. Others had gushed such empty accolades as she was a great singer.

Another time, Barron was watching us fish. I asked him how his love life was—his wife had died the year before—with all the women chasing after him. (Seriously, a newly single billionaire in Bel Air??) He blushed and said he had been seated between Barbara Sinatra and Angie Dickinson at a dinner party.

I blurted: "Watch out for Barbara Sinatra; she's expensive. Frank (Sinatra) kept performing way past his voice's prime to support her expensive spending. I heard one million dollars a month or so." I had met the Sinatras at Frank's private sixtieth birthday party, with Don Rickles and Frank's best friend Jilly making us all laugh till we couldn't breathe. Ella Fitzgerald was there, too. Quite a night. Barbara was wary of me saying hello to Frank; maybe that's how she wrested him away from his prior wife. I found her thinking I was like her hilarious and, at the same time, flattering that she thought I was attractive enough to be competition.

Barron laughed, turned to Chuck and said, "I should try to find me a 45 year old that likes to hunt, fish and fly, right, Chuck?" I was 45 at that time. Chuck and I had just gotten married. Barron was subtle but not too subtle. He clearly approved. I laughed. Chuck edged closer to me protectively. A few invitations later, Barron announced for all to hear, after one very jealous guest had tried to bait me into an argument to no avail, that I was invited back any time.

Another time Paris was in hot water, I said privately, "You know, Barron, she's at a crossroads. Young girls are following her every move. She can lead them well and the right way, or she can lead them astray. She's 26; it's time to grow up and lead well." Darn if that wasn't included in the script of her

Larry King interview later that weekend.

Chuck and I flew a lot around the ranch. We were the only ones Barron, who never took passengers, would let fly his wing. We would fly down past another airport. Sometimes, after Barron turned back, Chuck and I would continue on to look at Mono Lake or Mammoth or Bodie.

Sometimes, we'd go on a recce, driving with Barron, checking on the dove and quail populations for the coming huntin' season. I'd be in the back, happy to listen to the guys converse or just be.

My go-to was usually the ocean with waves. So going into the desert mountains was new. Chuck loved it, so I decided to figure out how to enjoy it, too. It wasn't difficult—doing anything with Chuck was more interesting than not. And I got to fly a variety of airplanes.

We explored a lot—by plane or by borrowed SUV. One of the places was renamed Yeager Springs—we went out there to help mend the drinking trough fed by the springs for the wild horses. We hunted in huntin' season, fished in non-huntin' season. And Chuck taught me formation flying as we looked for wild horses from the air.

We were allowed to fly anything Barron had. But Chuck was wise. He only flew the airplane in which we flew to Barron's ranch and in which we were insured. Barron was self-insured and heaven forbid anything happened while we were flying one of his planes; we couldn't replace it. Barron wouldn't expect us to do so, but we would certainly try and it would be awkward. A few guests, who could afford it and did have accidents, replaced or paid for repairing the planes.

Barron's current and former pilots gave me flying lessons while they got formation flying lessons from Chuck.

Always with an IP (instructor pilot), by virtue of taking lessons all over the country B.C. (Before Chuck), but mostly by virtue of my relationship with Chuck Yeager, I got to fly all sorts of planes, including a Staggerwing Beech, classy-looking but claustrophobic and stuffy; an Extra; a Stearman (the one airplane Chuck didn't like, the visibility was awful and it was squirrelly); a Waco (my preferred open cockpit biplane); a Decathlon; helicopters, a Citation X, and in a glider.

At Barron's ranch, the chief (and only) pilot wanted to solo me and then do the wet t-shirt ritual. Not. Fortunately, I timely asked, "What do I do if an engine quits?"

He said, "Whoops! We haven't taught you emergency procedures yet!"

Uh, yeah. That would be a good idea. Needless to say, I did not solo there. But I did learn spins and getting out of them in Barron's Extra. Not my favorite; doing spins. Barron's pilot said, "You just did four spins and recoveries in a row! Most people can't do that!" I responded, "You told me to!" But don't try telling me to jump off the Brooklyn Bridge.

That's when I realized I had to go to a licensed CFI who taught all the time, so s/he would do all that was required to prepare me for my license—including…ahem…emergency procedures. There is no time for panic.

## HARRISON FORD, ACTOR: 2004

I often agonized over questions before I brought them to Chuck. He then would have a brilliant, simple answer and I would wonder why I had agonized.

In February 2003, the National Aviation Hall of Fame's Executive Director, Ron, asked if Chuck would ask Harrison Ford to be the emcee for the annual dinner. This year, being the 100th anniversary of the first powered flight, there would be no inductees, but they would be honoring all past inductees. Harrison had agreed to be the emcee but then called back and said he didn't think he was worthy, but if Chuck Yeager (first choice) or John Glenn would ask him, then he would do it. Ron wanted Chuck, Ron's first choice, to ask Harrison to be the emcee.

I had worked with Harrison in the movie *"Witness"* over 15 years before. There was no reason he'd remember. I was in the scene in the police precinct and offered the little boy a cookie, thereby getting the boy off his chair so he wanders the office pool area and sees the picture of the bad guy.

I replied, "I'll ask Chuck, but I won't encourage it. Harrison has already reneged. What if Chuck asks him and he reneges again?"

I asked Chuck, as promised, and his simple reply was. "No. I don't know him."

When I called Ron back, he declared, "Never mind. John Glenn did it and Harrison agreed to be the emcee."

* * *

We heard Harrison Ford was attending several aviation events, hoping to meet Chuck Yeager. Chuck Yeager had generally stopped going to these events since he now had someone to play with (me). We went to Oshkosh in 2004, seven months after pilots worldwide, inspired by General Chuck Yeager as Chairman, had exceeded the goal of giving one million kids a flight (over 1.3 million) and General Yeager had stepped aside as Chairman of the Young Eagles.

At the VIP pre-party for a Young Eagles fundraising dinner in 2004, Harrison finally succeeded in his quest and met Chuck Yeager. The first thing Harrison, his hands shaking, said to his hero, General Chuck Yeager, was (repeatedly), "I need a whiskey; you want a whiskey, Chuck?" Chuck raised his eyebrows in bemusement and declined. Someone immediately got Harrison a whiskey, which he gulped and then requested another.

## REVEREND SCHULLER, CRYSTAL CATHEDRAL, *Orange County, CA: January 2005*

The night before Chuck was to do a sermon with Reverend Schuller, the reverend's son had arranged a dinner. At that dinner, the son asked each person to stand up and explain their relationship with the church. Expecting something completely different, I was stunned when each one (except us) got up and explained how much they had made off the church. One prime example, pun intended, was the banker who loaned money for construction. I thought he'd say at zero percent interest, but no, he had made a bundle off the church. Twenty-five people said some variant of this. It was gross.

One woman made great imitation rooster crowing sounds. We suggested she go to Evian, France and give a rooster we had succeeded in teaching to crow a little better, the advanced course in crowing.

Some moments of the sermon:

Reverend Schuller: "Now you've been to 118,000 feet."

General Yeager: "That's right. By the way, I've been closer to Heaven than you have."

The Reverend persevered. "Weren't you afraid when you flew to 118,000 feet?"

General Yeager: "No, I don't have time to be afraid. I gotta fix the problem."

"Did you pray?"

General Yeager: "God can't help me. I gotta help myself. You can pray all the way down into a smokin' hole."

"You were married to Glennis for forty-five years." I took note of the Reverend's behavior.

The year before, the Reverend had wanted Chuck to give a sermon with him. He sidled up to me at a reception at the U.S. Supreme Court and asked, "How can I get Chuck to do a sermon with me—I've been asking him for years." Obviously, he was hoping he could charm me into accomplishing it. I hesitated—Chuck would have done it if he had wanted to.

The Reverend misunderstood my hesitation. "Are you a Christian?"

I thought, 'Oh, here we go,' and responded, "My relationship with God is too personal for labels." You could see the wheels turning in Reverend Schuller's brain; maybe he'd use that in his next book.

He said, "I need Jesus to get to God."

I replied something to the effect of "Whatever works."

Several months later, Chuck agreed, so we arranged for Chuck to do the sermon, two back-to-back, in fact.

So now, I was thinking, 'Reverend Schuller should be thanking me. Instead, he...negated me?'

Chuck respectfully acknowledged Glennis and then immediately respectfully talked about me. Again confirming what a classy, elegant, lovely, thoughtful real man Chuck was.

The church made a bundle that day and the following week when it aired. They had been televising for ten years and, during that time, had lost their live audience and a great deal of revenue from collection plates. But when Chuck appeared, the church was overflowing, standing room only, for both sermons.

At lunch, the Reverend talked about meeting with Qaddafi. The two retired military/law enforcement guys seated with us were disgusted. Later, I asked Chuck what he thought of that—did the Reverend honestly think he personally would bring peace? Chuck answered succinctly, "Showing off."

A week later, when the sermon aired, Reverend Schuller called us to thank us and say he agreed with our beliefs more than most knew.

## WORLD WAR II FIGHTER PILOT WHO WITHDREW FROM COMBAT

We were walking from backstage to the exit in a long, large hallway after another great speech by Chuck to a very receptive, large, standing-room-only audience at the Museum of Flight In Seattle, Washington.

I was surprised and glad no one had realized this would be our exit route. Except one guy. About chuck's age, he was walking towards us a little warily.

As he approached, Chuck greeted him warmly. The fellow was relieved. They chatted about various things, after which the fellow left, clearly lighter than when he approached.

Chuck then told me the story:

During World War II, 1944, this fellow, a member of Chuck's squadron, had returned from his second mission and flat-out said he couldn't hack it.

Admitting this was blasphemy. Many pilots were scared but didn't dare admit it, even to themselves. If you weren't, you were foolish. Certainly, no one said they wanted to go home before their sixty missions were up. Almost all the pilots shunned this guy—afraid his fear was contagious or that they would be tainted with the same brush or…

Except one.

Captain Chuck Yeager.

He appreciated that this guy was brave enough to admit his fear and his shortcomings and risk being shunned or even court-martialed. But to do otherwise, to continue to go on sorties (missions) when he couldn't hack it, could get others in his formation or group killed.

And Chuck was not afraid to stand up and say this.

This pilot didn't want to quit. He had been good enough to be selected as a fighter pilot. He just couldn't hack actual combat. He returned stateside and became a valuable instructor pilot.

And that was the guy who had warily walked towards us, wondering if, 60 years later, Chuck Yeager would look at him with disdain.

And that was the guy who, after talking to Chuck 60 years later, was light on his feet when he walked away.

## ULF MERBOLD, GERMAN ASTRONAUT

Chuck and I first met Ulf Merbold, renowned, accomplished German astronaut, around 2004 at Barron's ranch during the Barron Hilton Cup winners' week.

Hannah Reitsch, a world-renowned German pilot, suggested to Barron that he learn to fly gliders and do some gliding at his ranch—the thermals were almost always perfect for gliding in the afternoon. So Barron started the Barron Hilton Cup, an international glider competition. The winners of each region could come to Barron's ranch for a week and do lots of gliding, horseback riding, shooting, flying a variety of planes, balloon racing, exploring, and eating well.

Ulf is a keen glider pilot, owned his own glider, and had participated several times in the Barron Hilton Cup. He often attended the annual German National Gliding Conference.

Chuck and I both liked him immediately. He is intelligent, confident, kind, funny, attractive, fun, and lacking in arrogance.

Ulf was one of the first to call me after Chuck passed and wrote me not long after that, that it was a great privilege for him when Chuck took him flying in a taildragger around Barron's ranch in Nevada, flying formation with other planes, looking for wild horses, surveying a ghost town, the High Sierra, and the nearby lake.

Chuck had also been a glider pilot. Whenever anyone asked Chuck if he had ever flown a glider, he would respond, "The X-1 was a glider after I broke the sound barrier. It had just enough fuel to break the sound barrier and fly not much longer—2.5 minutes total when all four rocket chambers were lit." He had to get rid of the fuel before landing; otherwise, he would be landing a bomb of liquid oxygen for which the gear was not stressed.

## SCOTTY CROSSFIELD

People tried to make a big deal out of Crossfield going Mach 2 first just days before the fiftieth anniversary of the Wright brothers' first powered flight. But Mach 2 didn't advance aviation and, oddly, they said the margin of error was plus or minus .05, which meant below Mach 2. The D-558 was not stressed for Mach 2. I would have thought since they were fudging numbers, they would have said Crossfield went 2.05 Mach so that the margin of error would not factor in.

One day, several TPS (Test Pilot School) alumni instructors and commandants were speaking to the students. Everyone walked into the seminar except Scotty and me, who were stragglers. Scotty admired me, his female pilot friend had told me. Chuck was much happier than Scotty had ever seen him and attributed it to me. Plus, I was always courteous with Scotty. I had grown up with arrogant folks and Northeasterners, so was used to them.

Out of the blue, Scotty said to me, "Maybe I didn't go Mach 2," looking me straight in the eye, and then went inside.

I thought, 'Why do people always tell me?' And Scotty's story would make a great TV movie—he knows he didn't do it, but his bosses say he did. If he disputes his bosses, he'd never find work again as a test pilot. What a dilemma. So he keeps quiet and never brags or mentions it. Fascinating. Regardless, Scotty still was the fastest guy alive for a very short while in 1953.

Just three weeks later and before the 50th anniversary of the Wright brothers' first powered flight, Major Chuck Yeager flew Mach 2.44. With this feat, the USAF stole the Navy's thunder. And Major Yeager did advance aviation by experiencing/discovering inertia coupling, which discovery would help with design to prevent it. What caused it, in simple terms, was too small a tail.

(Note: Spaceshipone had serious problems due to too small a tail. General Yeager was annoyed that modern scientists were repeating mistakes learned, many of which had cost lives, apparently in vain, over 50 years before. This was but one example.)

## HUMPY MONDAY — *Mayor of Hamlin, West Virginia*

Chuck and I used to visit Hamlin, West Virginia, at least once a year. Often we'd have lunch with Humpy Monday, a couple years older than Chuck, who had been mayor for 17 years and knew the history of all the generations, including those who had inhabited each house there. (Unfortunately, that history was lost because some folks did not keep their promise to get an oral history from Humpy.)

Humpy took us up to Maul Rock, so named because of its shape. We would visit every year, even after Humpy passed away. It was very muddy that last year we visited Hamlin, West Virginia (2019), and the only passage was on the edge of a slippery cliff since a tree had fallen and blocked the rest of the road.

One of our friends warned: if Victoria and/or Chuck Yeager invite you for a meal or an outing, bring fishing gear, raingear, sports gear, bathing suit, and clothes for anything; be prepared for all sorts of weather and conditions… you never know what you'll end up doing. She wasn't kidding.

## STEVE FOSSETT DISAPPEARS: *September 2007*

Steve Fossett was enamored of and admired Chuck Yeager. We first met Steve at the Explorers Club annual black-tie dinner in about 2003. Chuck was the keynote speaker at that event. Steve ran over everyone, pushing people out of the way, to get to Chuck. It was so interesting to watch. We met Steve again later when Chuck advised him about fuel for his round-the-world distance record. Steve didn't follow Chuck's advice and landed short of his previous record.

Steve's tires also blew. Chuck teased him the next time he saw him—landed a little hard, didn't you? Steve said his guys told him the fueling advice wouldn't work (it somehow worked in the X-1 and other airplanes). "His guys" also told him that the tires blew because they were frozen from being at altitude. Chuck replied his usual "Sheeeee-it" when he heard absurd tall tales.

* * *

Steve presented to a bunch of VIP types at Barron's ranch an NF-104 project that several folks had owned and to which they had tried unsuccessfully to get Chuck Yeager to lend his name; some even tried to sneak in Chuck Yeager's name. The F-104 project was to put the plane on wheels and drive well past Mach 1 on land to regain the speed record. Chuck said to Steve after the presentation, "Did you feel the door hit you in the a$$ as you walked out after you bought the project?" This is an expression signifying you were dumb and taken. Doing a presentation to raise money (when you're already a billionaire) at a private dinner was…gauche.

Steve Fossett would say he did these records to show that an ordinary guy could do anything. He neglected to mention an ordinary billionaire who could afford these boondoggles and experts to actually do the work.

Once, we were sitting on Barron's right in the place of honor; Steve and his wife were sitting opposite. Not known for their witty repartee, I asked Steve, "If you were stranded on an island, what two books would you like to have?"

He responded, "Oh. Uh. That's a good question. Um."

His wife, Peggy, also responded but sharply, as was her wont to do, "Why do you want to know THAT?"

I smiled. I noticed out of the corner of my eye Barron smirking a little and Chuck looking at me curiously; how was I going to respond to this attack?

I said, "I learn something—new books that may be interesting to read and I get to know someone better."

Steve perked up and got momentarily smart: "What two books would you bring?"

Everyone at the table couldn't help but hear Peggy, so all eyes were on me now.

Me: "*Yeager, An Autobiography* and *Press On*, of course," both written by Chuck Yeager.

Everyone laughed.

\* \* \*

On Labor Day, September 2007, Chuck and I were in Alaska fishing on the Tsiu River when the lodge owner asked us, "Don't you know Steve Fossett?"

Chuck, "Yes."

"It's in the newspaper (the owner had flown to Cordova that day) that Steve Fossett has gone missing from Barron Hilton's ranch in Nevada."

We had intermittent email, so when I could one evening, I emailed the two folks I knew might know more.

From Barron's much younger former secretary, J, who had married Barron's lawyer after his wife died, we heard that Steve had taken off in one of Barron's planes—the Decathlon—and not returned. Steve's Australian Citation X pilot, whose girlfriend said had no experience flying anything but the Citation X which he had just learned to fly six months prior and no experience in such a search, was directing the search operation.

Chuck sent suggestions. Barron's pilot, who also had no experience in search and rescue, told us they knew what they were doing. They didn't and mocked the Civil Air Patrol, who was trying to help.

J, who had Barron's ear, told us to keep sending suggestions; Barron is implementing them. They were all excited to have such an important mission and each person was sure they'd be the one to find Steve and become the "hero" and rich! (There was a reward at that time.)

All sorts of folks showed up at Barron's ranch—many who would never have had the chance to be invited. Rumors abounded—Steve had a 44 year old girlfriend and was just ditching his wife; and/or he had run out of money, and all his projects were too expensive, so he was ditching his life. He landed the airplane somewhere, maybe on a road, and someone picked him up so he could get a new identity. Steve left his new, shiny, expensive watch, that could have located him, behind. We heard them all. The 44 year old girlfriend rumor, frankly, explained why Steve's wife had been congenial to me the first few times we met, then turned on every younger female at Barron's ranch—I was 44 at the time. And definitely not a threat.

Chuck and I thoroughly enjoyed our time in Alaska as usual: fishing. We did, however, check in every couple of days for the latest news on Steve. J reprimanded me, "If you two had been here, you (Victoria) would have been flying the Decathlon and Steve would not have gone missing!" Story of my life.

Fortunately, oddly, Carroll Shelby's wife had lost control of the Decathlon about three or four months earlier and crashed into the fence. Fortunately, because she wasn't hurt—maybe her ego was—and the Decathlon had been overhauled, everything brand new and tested very recently, so on the surface, they couldn't blame the airplane re liability.

Chuck had long before told Barron his pilot needed to check folks out in airplanes before just giving them the keys on their word. And he needed to find out where people intended to fly. They started all this after Steve went missing.

When we got home from Alaska, I emailed, "We are perfectly happy not to come to the ranch with you being filled to the gills, but if Barron wants us there to help, as friends, we will."

To our relief, we got word that we didn't need to come, but please keep sending advice.

After two weeks of searching, including Civil Air Patrol and all sorts of pilots flying around, Chuck called Barron and said, "You're not going to find him. Someone hiking a year from now will find him."

Barron, while enjoying the activity, ended the search staged from his ranch. It was costing a fortune with no results. Some people erroneously admired Steve's pilot because he was flying, searching from dawn till dusk. I suggested that was not very bright—no one can focus one hundred percent that long, so he missed vast tracts.

A week or two later, when the crowd had left, we flew over for the weekend.

Barron's pilot, who took lots of liberties and, he said, lots of huge tips from guests wanting to be invited again, had invited a group, former Haliburton guys, that had a new detection device they wanted to try out. Part of this group was a current USAF pilot about to retire who said he was borrowing the device (legally?) from the USAF. It kept malfunctioning.

This group, led by a guy nicknamed "Psycho", was eager to meet Chuck.

Chuck was not eager to meet them and managed to avoid meeting them the entire weekend.

J commandeered me to do something at the airfield. She just wanted to get photos with these boys. I was in a couple photos but was very uncomfortable, although that's when I learned about the device from the USAF pilot—he grew up near where I (and the actor Will Smith) had in Philadelphia.

Chuck told Barron, "Barron, these guys are mercenaries. You have a lot of money. We are out in the desert in the middle of nowhere. I suggest, for your safety (and ours), you invite these guys to leave."

Barron followed Chuck's advice once again.

Shortly after that, in October 2007, we drove from California to Colorado to hunt elk. Every airfield we passed, and there were many, especially small ones with small airplanes; Chuck instructed, "Check to see if there's a Decathlon." It was hilarious. We never did see one.

A year to the day, when Chuck said it would happen, a hiker found Steve's wallet and, about a mile from the crash, a human thigh bone. No kidding. They then found the plane.

Theories abounded. Steve had walked to where the thigh bone was found but died of malnutrition. He had survived worse, but maybe he had hypothermia. Chuck dispelled that crisply—an animal ate him in his airplane (his five-point seatbelt was still connected).

Barron mused he must have flown there to see where his father and he had hiked a lot when Steve was a kid. Barron's former pilot went by plane to investigate. He concluded that Steve, unused to such high-density altitude, had lost lift flying close to a mountain. "But," the former pilot said, "all Steve had to do was turn to the right and glide down a sloping valley and he would have been fine."

## GOVERNOR JOE MANCHIN

One year, when we were staying with Governor (later Senator) Joe Manchin at the West Virginia Governor's mansion. Chuck offered the Governor that Pansy Lee make him leather britches and butterscotch pah for dinner since he had never had either.

He was dubious but reluctantly game. He could always get the chef to feed him something after the guests left…

The Governor's Mansion chef was thrilled to be cooking for Chuck, yet not cooking. Having no familiarity with leather britches and to make sure we all didn't starve just in case, the chef made a delicious, loaded salad as a side dish that would have sufficed as a meal.

There was one hitch: Pansy did not have enough beans to make leather britches for seven. So we sent her some a friend had dried. She turned up her nose at those and cooked them separately.

She came to the mansion with her daughter, son-in-law, and granddaughter. Her grandson was in college and couldn't get away. Upon meeting the Governor, Pansy Lee announced: "This is a first; I'm invited to dinner, but I have to bring the dinner!"

Governor Joe graciously replied, "Thank you! I'm looking forward to tasting leather britches and butterscotch pah."

We ate outside on the porch on a pleasant evening. Governor Joe and everyone took some of each batch of leather britches.

Pansy's impolitic son-in-law asked, "Well, Governor, which batch of leather britches do you like better?"

I jumped in with lightning speed: "Governor, these on the right are Pansy Lee's; she is sitting to your left. The ones on the left are Gus'. He is not here."

I guess I wasn't as clear as I thought. The Governor answered, "I like these," pointing to the left.

Me: "Governor, perhaps I wasn't clear enough," and I repeated which beans were whose.

Chuck, being much wiser, diverted attention with his story about flying around the gold Capitol next to the mansion and then flying under the Southside Bridge not far from the mansion.

We talked about several things. About fifteen minutes later, Governor Joe said: "You know, I said I like these, but I keep going back to the ones on the right for seconds and thirds."

Pansy Lee, without a moment's hesitation and with typical Yeager humor, quipped, "Too late. You lost my vote!"

Governor Joe wasn't used to the Yeagers' irreverence. He was enjoying himself immensely.

Next, we had the butterscotch pah. That caused great quiet to descend on the party—and that is saying something considering we had a politician in our midst (who had to regain one vote) as well as some very chatty people—as everyone thoroughly enjoyed this delicious dessert.

The chef put the two extra pieces of pah in our guest apartment. I learned later that the Governor had searched in vain for those for a midnight snack.

The following year, we visited during the Christmas season. Governor Joe invited Pansy Lee and her family to the mansion with us for dinner (which the Governor's chef cooked this time!) The Christmas decorations were enchanting and put one in the spirit.

After dinner, the Governor gave Pansy a Proclamation—Pansy is the first person (not hired for the job) to cook for the Governor at the mansion. What fun! She loved it.

## EDWARDS AFB, ANNIVERSARY FLIGHT & DINING IN: *September 2007*

Edwards AFB celebrated the seventieth anniversary of the USAF and of breaking the sound barrier with a flight of four, each carrying a pilot of note. In the first plane, General Carl Bedke, Commandant at the time, had General Chuck Yeager as his IP (Instructor Pilot).

Then-Governor Joe Manchin came out for the event and got a great tour of Edwards AFB, especially all things Chuck Yeager. Governor Joe then met us on the flight line to watch Chuck get in the F-15E and General Bedke start the engines and taxi out. So very cool.

We were a bit naïve and very glad the maintainers knew it. They warned us not to walk in front of the F-15E engines, putting a fine point on it by describing the guy who had been sucked up into it and out the other end in pieces, although one guy was sucked in and out whole. Yikes! I didn't want to test which fate Governor Joe or I would have.

There's nothing like watching the prep for flight in an F-15E or F-16, especially when General Chuck Yeager is flying. Driving nearby or ahead of the planes, then waiting in the "run-up" area is a close second.

Magical.

Governor Joe watched the sonic booms and the fly-bys with me, then sat at the table with us for the Dining In dinner.

The Secretary of the Air Force proceeded to give a speech that lasted three days. Okay, maybe in reality, only forty minutes.

Governor Joe insisted on speaking. He and I had a serious talk (okay, I gave him the serious talk) about brevity, which would make people remember a politician better. We just didn't need more speeches; we wanted to visit with folks and, most importantly, have dessert. I told him my Dad always rated a sermon by length. He would take his gold watch out of his waistcoat and time the sermon. His favorite was the first minister at St. Asaph's outside Philadelphia, Pennsylvania; sixteen-minute sermons that said all one needed to know each Sunday.

Under four minutes later, Governor Manchin was done. And had given one of the best speeches I've ever heard anyone (other than Chuck Yeager)—let alone a politician—give, illustrating the highlights of Chuck Yeager.

The moment Governor Joe sat down, he smiled impishly at me but still checked: "Too long? Okay?"

I smiled. "Didn't time it exactly; felt like seconds, it was so good, but I'm pretty sure under four minutes. Perfect." He was pleased. More importantly, so was Chuck.

The Secretary did have class. He quietly picked up our lodging and dining bill. The only one who has ever done that in all the years we've gone to Edwards when General Chuck Yeager did so much for the USAF. And the Secretary did it discreetly—we were completely unaware till after the Secretary had left base and we had gone to pay. Thank you, Secretary. I forgive you your long speech.

## JOHNNY MYERS—TEST PILOT/FRIEND:
*October 2007*

Johnny Myers, 12 years older than Chuck, had followed in his father's footsteps and become a lawyer. About age 30, the story goes, he told his father he didn't like practicing law and wanted to be a test pilot. His father, a prominent Los Angeles attorney and judge, encouraged his son to follow his passion.

Johnny was an attractive guy. As a young man, Chuck had looked up to and admired Johnny, a great test pilot.

We'd see Johnny at least once a year at Oshkosh Air Venture and sometimes in Los Angeles. He had invited us to his ranch, not far from where we lived, but he passed before we could get there.

As soon as Barron Hilton invited Chuck and me to his eightieth birthday party, I asked Johnny if we could stay with him in his Beverly Hills, California home that weekend—a resounding YES!

Johnny was beginning to have a little dementia, but as soon as we arrived and Chuck and he started talking, he perked up and was all there. I asked the first question and they were off and running. Chuck and Johnny went through Johnny's aviation pictures on his wall. They traded stories—it was great being a "fly on the wall". Chuck talked about how he admired Johnny's handling of a particularly dangerous plane. Johnny merely laughed in appreciation that his hero, Chuck Yeager, was praising him, Johnny Myers.

*\*　\*　\**

Johnny's assistant told me to drive Johnny's 1950s yellow Bentley. I replied, "If we even have a ding, we'd have to mortgage our house to pay for it." She told me not to worry about it; they would take care of it. With that, Chuck and I went for a drive to the ocean, had lunch in Malibu watching the waves, and then stopped at a grocery store on the way back. I just prayed nothing would happen to that car on our watch. It didn't. Phew.

I had the good fortune to drive several expensive cars without having to own them. Barron let us use his top-of-the-line Mercedes; Tilley, another acquaintance, his top-of-the-line Jaguar from his collection of 10 or more—on Los Angeles' terrible roads.

Johnny's married assistant, who, I was told, apparently later somehow ended up with a lot of Johnny's estate, including the yellow Bentley, told me I would be driving Johnny, Chuck, and myself to Johnny's date's house, pick her up, then go on to the Bel Air Country Club for Barron's birthday party.

I hadn't been to the club in 20 years, so wasn't sure I could find it. The assistant said Johnny knew how to get to Betty's house and Betty could direct me to the Bel Air Country Club.

With me driving, Johnny in the front passenger seat, Chuck in the back, we pulled out of the driveway. I asked Johnny the way to Betty's house. He had no clue. Alrighty then. I drove down the street, turned left, and he started to remember. We made it to Betty's house. I asked Chuck if he would please go to the door and collect Betty for Johnny.

Chuck and Betty got in the backseat. I asked Betty how to get to the Bel Air Country Club. She had no clue. This was becoming a theme.

As I cleared the cobwebs, I headed in the direction I vaguely remembered. After a few blocks, Johnny said, "Are we going to pick up Betty?"

I asked conspiratorially in a stage whisper, "Johnny, we have a gal named Betty sitting in the back; do you think she'll mind if we pick up another gal named Betty? I mean, seriously, two dates? Wow! You da man!"

He understood exactly what had happened, smiled, and appreciated my coverup, making light of it.

When we got well into Bel Air, Johnny piped up and told me to turn right. We fairly quickly realized it was the wrong direction. Johnny started to look embarrassed and annoyed with himself. I wouldn't let him. I calmly and cheerfully thanked Johnny for showing me that area of Bel Air I had always wanted to see and turned around. We chuckled. We both knew.

After a few minutes, we found the club. I thanked Johnny for his help. We were now best buds.

It was an entertaining adventure. The birthday party was fine. So many toasts from folks who talked about how much money they made with Barron. We were sitting at the table of one of Barron's sons. Chuck remarked, "No one is talking about Barron's flying, fishing, and huntin'." The son said, "Why don't you do a toast?" Chuck declined. "I'm not a braggart." As we were leaving, Barron said to Chuck, "You're my only true friend here." He was right. Chuck (and I) did far more by a considerable amount for Barron than vice versa and made no money from it, although we learned later that Barron did.

## JIM NABORS (GOMER PYLE); DR. JOHN SMITH; BEN CASSIDAY, USAF GENERAL (RET.)

Chuck and Jim Nabors first met at the Indy 500 in 1986 and 1988 when Chuck drove the pace car. I was lucky enough to meet Jim Nabors December 7, 2006. What a stellar fellow. He sang and Chuck spoke on Ford Island near the Pacific Aviation Museum at the commemoration of Pearl Harbor Day. Two non-Navy guys headlining the event. Chuck joked, "The Navy brass were glowering at me."

Our friend, USAF General Ben Cassiday, World War II fighter pilot and an heir to the righthand man, a Caucasian, to King Kamehamehamehameha—joined us. Goodness! I never know when I'm finished saying that name!

To reward the righthand man for his great help, King Kameha-etc. gave him faraway lands...now called Diamond Head.

General Cassiday had great poise, elegance and manners and was very kind and generous.

*  *  *

Frank, a Pacific Aviation Museum Board member, flew us in his Navajo to Lanai. When we took off, he played the *Star Wars* theme—very apropos. We stayed on Lanai for two days, just Chuck and me. We explored and dined tête-à-tête overlooking the luscious gardens. Very romantic. Once I acknowledged that most of Hawaii is not a watersport kind of place—too much lava—I figured out how to enjoy it more.

On that trip, we also stayed with Dr. John Smith, a legendary orthopedic surgeon with whom Chuck had gone huntin' for axis deer on Molokai fairly often. John had all sorts of animals that wandered in and around the house on Molokai, but not the guest house where we stayed, the only clean area.

The first morning, as I emerged from the guest house, I yelled, "Hey, come here, ya big fat pig!" It was very satisfying.

Chuck came out worried—we were in the middle of nowhere and sure didn't want to upset our hosts. He asked very quietly but half expecting to either be amused or have to cover, "Who're you callin' a big fat pig?" I pointed and said, "The big fat pig," which by this time was waddling (I mean, it was "as big as Adeline" big) over to see what was up. I petted the pig, who was clearly enjoying it. It struggled to get down on its knees and roll over so I could rub its tummy. I made sure I stayed out of the way—if that pig rolled over on me, I was sunk.

This happened every morning. John marveled at it—she never did any of that, running over, rolling over, for anyone before. He wasn't so sure each time the pig would be able to get back up again, but each time, she managed.

We toured part of the island—half of it we couldn't get to due to the rain and a major mudslide. Chuck went fishing. I declined—just the thought of being on that size boat in the ocean made me ill. I had hoped to go scuba diving, but the water was too muddy.

* * *

We returned to Hawaii a few years later.

We found out how to contact Jim Nabors and his friend of thirty-eight years, later husband, Stan. Jim invited us to lunch. When we arrived at his house, Jim was warm and welcoming, especially to his great friend Chuck Yeager.

Jim's neighbors and Stan, a quiet, caring, friendly fellow, were already there. We then found out we were going to a hotel with a view of the water for lunch. I recognized the role of the "neighbors." They had moved there to befriend Jim and try to take over his life, money, and assets as he aged. I'd seen this before with John Carradine (family friend and great character actor, father of David and Keith Carradine) and others. Fortunately, Jim had Stan, whom he later married when it became legal in the state of Washington. Stan did a great job of quietly protecting Jim. The LGBTQ community wanted Jim to be a spokesperson for them. Being very discreet, Jim declined—he kept his private life private. I admired him even more for this.

What I also liked about Jim Nabors—he never minded when someone wanted him to say his trademarks, "Gollollollollolleeeee!" and "Shazam!" He said he was able to buy nice things from those trademarks and did not begrudge being identified by them. He was kind to all who approached, loved kids, loved people.

At lunch, Jim said, "Chuck, why don't you come sit by me." Chuck responded, "I don't know, Jim, this is my week for girls," and smiled. Jim laughed and then suggested I sit next to him. Only Chuck could get away with saying that in that setting.

As lunch progressed, I asked Jim a little about his origins. He enjoyed telling me. He had started out by just going to the local club in Alabama and telling stories, including about a character he created, Gomer Pyle. After a few weeks of this at the local club, which the audience loved, the club owner told him to borrow some records of Mario Lanza, the great American tenor, and learn to sing. And that is how Jim developed his magnificent voice—by imitating Mario Lanza. Wow.

I recently listened to Jim Nabors, as Gomer Pyle, singing "To Dream the Impossible Dream." Chills.

Jim felt so comfortable and enjoyed the luncheon so much that he exclaimed when it was time to go, "We'll have to do this again before you leave." I was looking forward to it.

He also invited us to his plantation on the island of Maui near Hana, another town to which I had always wanted to go for some reason. Jim's plantation was stunning—a mile of oceanfront...lava. But the groves of macadamia nuts and the processing were fascinating. Of course, there were all sorts of jokes about how to market the nuts using Jim's name.

Frank, who had flown Chuck and me over to Hana, had wild expectations of Chuck and me. He thought we would stay up with him getting drunk on whiskey. Neither Chuck nor I drank and preferred going to bed together fairly early. Frank was on his own. So, the next day, he gave me the keys to the rental car and told me he was going back to Oahu and would return that evening. I suggested that Chuck would probably prefer to fly with Frank than sightsee and I would be fine sightseeing on my own.

It became apparent that Frank flew back to Oahu to pick up a drinking buddy. So, the day worked out well, as did dinner and the evening. Chuck and I retired to our room for the evening; Frank and his buddy stayed up drinking. And Chuck flew right seat back the next day.

Before leaving Hawaii, we had dinner with Jim and Stan again, this time without the neighbors. I loved listening to Jim and Chuck—an incredibly special friendship indeed. Jim reminded me of a teacher/librarian who was like family growing up: attractive, great storyteller, colorful, inspiring, witty, kind, knowledgeable, old-school manners and elegance. The family friend was also a descendant of American Revolution General Anthony Wayne.

Sadly, we never got a chance to see Jim again before he died. He lived a remarkable life, a shining example of quietly, discreetly living his private life while generously sharing his extraordinary talent, kindness and friendship with the rest of us.

## DINNER IN OAHU: *True Gentlemen, Admiral Ron Hays & General Ben Cassiday, to the Rescue*

We were invited to dinner by a high-end Italian restaurant owner in Hawaii, a friend of food supplier Frank, and asked us to invite others. So we invited the highly respected, and deservedly so, Admiral Ron Hays and his wife, USAF General (retired) Ben Cassiday, Frank, Jim Nabors, Stan, and a couple other folks. A pretty gal invited herself. Jim and Stan couldn't make it, which the host confided made him more comfortable. I found that odd because the host historically hosted male-only dinners at least one to two times a week and, to this dinner, he did not invite his wife and his friends' wives.

The host did all the ordering, including very expensive wine, drinks, and food. It was lavish and delicious. Chuck and I did not drink anything but water. When the dinner was somewhat winding down before dessert, the host, seated on my left, turned to me and said he would give me a 10 percent discount on the dinner.

I. Was. Flabbergasted. To say the least. I started trying to add what this would cost (well over $3000) and determine how to handle it without upsetting the other guests. I looked at Frank, our host for our trip to Hawaii, and I think the look was not lost on others. I asked to speak to Frank privately. Outside the room, I reiterated what had happened. Admiral Hays and General Cassiday materialized and said to Frank, "We'd like to split the cost of the dinner." I about kissed them. What incredible and honorable gentlemen stepping in to save me (and Chuck, of course)! Not many of those men left (including them—sadly, they have since passed). It was decided. I was all for telling the host he could just pay for it himself since he had invited all of us, did all the ordering, and was showing off General Yeager to friends, but these gentlemen preferred their elegant solution.

To give an idea of how this host handled money, this host and Frank were betting $20,000/game for televised football games while we were in Hawaii. Frank was up $40,000. General Yeager told him to keep the money and quit betting, but the next day, Frank lost it all due to one bad call in the last few seconds of the game. General Yeager told Frank that he was nuts.

We all went back into the private dining room when in walked the woman who had essentially invited herself. She was not wearing much and, honestly, looked very pretty in her slinky outfit. She looked a little self-conscious, not sure of how she'd be received, so I welcomed her, introduced her all around and suggested she sit between the (now persona non grata to me) host and me.

That sealed it. The host was happy and he took care of the bill. I silently thanked her. Frank bought a signed lithograph, which we sent to the host. Apparently, the host was ecstatic and bragging about the dinner, the lithograph and how great we were. The host has invited us to various things since. Needless to say…we've been busy.

## VIKTOR BELENKO, *Russian Fighter Pilot Defector/Friend*

In 2008, I was posting on Myspace daily—sorry I lost all that—about each flying lesson, the good, the bad, the ugly, so that others could learn from my experiences.

Viktor Belenko, a Russian defector whose story is captivating, called twice during my training. Once, I had forgotten to put the mixture all the way in (full rich) on final after leaning it out for cruising and, on the runway, the engine quit. Chuck thought not much of the plane if it would do that. I got it started again and taxied back to its tie-down. This happened, sorry to admit it, twice. I could swear that a poltergeist had removed it from the checklist. Apparently, several others had done this in this plane but could not get it started again, stuck on the runway. So, oddly, my instructor was impressed.

Viktor called and said, "Victoria! Don't have any flame-outs!" and hung up. I guess he wasn't one for talking too long.

After I passed my check ride and got my license, Viktor called, "VICTORIA!"

I enthusiastically said, "Hi, Viktor!"

He said, "How'd you know it was me?" in his charming, thick Russian accent.

I thought, *'Well, we don't have too many Russian defectors calling us. In fact, only one.'*

I merely laughed, thinking he was in on the joke.

"Congratulations! Now don't let any jet jockeys pull one over on you—much harder to fly a prop plane," he said and hung up. Yep. Confirmed. Not much of a chatterbox on the phone. But I took what he said to heart and observed.

Chuck agreed with him.

Several years later, we invited Viktor to the Cal-Ore Fish Derby. He regaled everyone with stories. He was a virtual wind-up doll—just say go and he was off speaking at warp speed, having everyone in stitches, as much at his energy as at what he said.

Those kinds of antics put Chuck off if they went on too long, say more than two minutes. For people with hearing loss, those are just annoying sounds. They're annoying to some without hearing loss.

At one point, Viktor was riding in the back of our car. I said to him, "Viktor, you can relax with us and be calm. We like you for you, not your entertainment." He was somewhat in awe of and intimidated by Chuck, but once I said that to him, he relaxed.

And all was right with the world. Chuck couldn't believe it.

## THE CLIFFORDS IN TONOPAH
*Stone Cabin Ranch, Nevada*

We got a call from the Oak Ridge Boys' Road Manager, DK, in December 2012. "You'all coming to Vegas for the show?"

We had never been to Vegas for their show, but it seemed like a good idea.

Chuck had been wanting to visit Stone Cabin Ranch near Tonopah, Nevada for a while and it's a little more than halfway, so we started thinking of driving in that direction. Then someone said it was the Boys' best Christmas show ever. That clinched it. Hate to miss that.

It was a glorious day for driving. The mountains and valleys with the late fall light are impressive. I'm always reminded of how magnificent the United States of America is when I go driving out west.

I had tried calling the Cliffords at Stone Cabin Ranch. Either the subscriber was unavailable or the number was disconnected. The ranch, the oldest continuously running ranch in Nevada, was still intact. So we figured we'd stop in.

Stone Cabin Ranch: Chuck was stationed in Tonopah for flight training from March to May 1943. His buddy Mac McKee and he decided to take a jeep and go hare huntin'.

They also decided to drop in on one of the ranches they had been buzzing.

Pa Clifford came out and invited them in for some food. Luckily for the 357th FG, the Cliffords were most appreciative of these boys going off to fight for their country. The Cliffords found it rather exciting to be buzzed.

They set up a system. Whenever the boys buzzed, Ma or Pa Clifford would wave a white sheet to let them know they could come for Sunday dinner. If no sheet, don't come.

Ma would have a long kitchen dining table, "sagging in the middle from being loaded down with homemade pies, cakes, all sorts of food," as Chuck said later in life. There would be fifteen guys from the base.

One time, Pa or Pops was murmuring about the tree needing to be cropped. F/O Yeager said he'd do it.

Next flight out, here comes Yeager on a very low buzz (eight feet above the ground). He cropped that tree very neatly. When he returned to base, his maintenance guy asked what happened.

F/O Yeager said, "I hit a bird."

Maintenance: "Must have been carrying a pretty big nest!"

We saw the tree, a type of weeping willow—you can see where it had been trimmed. But it is huge again now.

Stone Cabin got its name from the cabins being built of stone and into the stone outcroppings very near a creek. Sort of reminded F/O Yeager of Grandpa Yeager's home—storing food in the caves to keep it cold.

So F/O Yeager and I drove to Tonopah. (Of course, he was then a retired general. But as memories filled the car, we were transported back in time.)

We passed by Mina as F/O Yeager told me of the time the 357th FG guys went to check out the girls there. The boys had gotten bored of Taxine's and her girls in Tonopah.

After a while of rowdiness, the sheriff in Mina threw them out. Now, if you've ever driven through Mina, you'd agree with me: That must have been some serious rowdiness, so bad I can't even imagine, for Mina to throw you out.

The next day, the water tower at Mina was shot up by a P-39. They could never figure out who had done it.

And, of course, the 357th boys never went back. As Chuck joked, "Nah. The girls were too dirty—no water to take a bath. Heh heh."

We stopped at the Mispah, now a hotel, but in F/O Yeager's day, a bar, or the bar. It's an interesting, historic hotel. Reminiscent of the Wild West in style but with fairly modern amenities. I could just imagine the guys hanging out at the long bar.

Chuck was reminded of his pals in the 357th FG and told this story to the hotel owner: One guy, eating his soup, was so tired his head fell into his soup. Blub blub, blowing bubbles with his face partly submerged. The way Chuck tells and mimes it just cracked us up, bending over double.

The next morning, after breakfast, we headed out to Stone Cabin Ranch. There, we found Roy, the grandson of Ma and Pop Clifford, and his mother, Doris. We joined them for coffee and water. Chuck reminisced, as did they.

Doris told us that whenever they heard/saw Chuck Yeager coming, they all hit the dirt. This particular time, they were on the road. All yelled: "Hit the dirt!" but Doris couldn't—she was nine months pregnant and so just leaned against the car, bracing herself.

I asked if that child had grown up to not like loud noises. Or was s/he a nervous type? She pointed at Roy, one of the most relaxed people I've ever seen. We laughed.

Roy talked about his grandfather refusing to "hit the dirt" by getting off his horse. By golly, after that buzzing, he never tried to stay on his horse again.

They were all good-natured memories of a time gone by.

We then walked around the ranch—saw the spring behind the house in which Ma and Pa Clifford lived. Delicious drinking water. That cup has been there since perhaps the late thirties.

Chuck reminisced about the kitchen table some more. The house had been a bar for the local miners and had been moved to the ranch. Another building had been a schoolhouse.

We then walked to where the horses were—wild stallions would try to come steal the mares. Nothing's changed.

And we looked at the buildings built into the rock. A horse had fallen through the roof and its bridle only had gotten caught on a meat hook. They were able to get her loose and get out of the way as, once freed from this panic, she took off.

We visited with Gladys, Ma and Pa's daughter-in-law, and with a few more grandkids. Gladys was a pleasant woman, just a few months younger than Chuck, on whom she exhibited a serious crush. After a few pistachio nuts, photo viewing, and reminiscing, we headed out.

We saw the air base. Three hangars were still standing. Barely. And the old entrance was still there.

We stopped at the museum in Tonopah—saw a photo of Taxine and her girls. We also saw the remains of a torn-up P-39 that was four feet under—just the prop tips sticking out of the ground when they found it.

After a brief visit, we were on our way to Las Vegas. From 1943 to 2012.

To see the Oak Ridge Boys. Just a quick note: The Las Vegas hotel where the Boys were staying put us up in a two-story suite. That was wild. The second story was an extravagant loft you could access by the next floor up or by the stairs from the living room. It all looked out on the city and night sky with remote control for the shades and all sorts of fun things. Wild.

## BABY BUSH *(President George W. Bush)—No Ties! 2009*

When we were invited to dinner with George W. "Baby" Bush and approximately thirty others at SCI after he left office in 2009, we again told the minders that what they saw us in, was what we had—nice button-down shirts, light jackets, jeans, hiking shoes.

The minders said, "President Bush said, 'No tie. You can wear a coat if you want.'"

Everyone got to the dinner before George W. and were all dressed in coats and ties or nice dresses…except the Yeagers.

When George W. entered the room, he was wearing a coat, no tie, unbuttoned collar. And made a beeline for the Yeagers—his kind of people by the way they were dressed. I'm half-kidding. He made a beeline for his hero, Chuck Yeager. When we had our photo taken with him, Baby Bush, as we affectionately referred to him, told me to take off my name tag. As I did so, I laughed, "I guess you've done this before." Only a million times.

## GRANDPA (MARION GENERAL) & GRANDMA (ADELINE) YEAGER: *2010*

I had returned to the Hamlin area to find Grandpa and Grandma Yeager's house while Chuck was on an all-male fishing trip with Barron Hilton in Alaska. I had asked the researchers to find it—and they couldn't. The trip prior, we had driven up the holler, saw a white clapboard house and kept going. The researcher said much later she thought that might have been it. When I asked why didn't she speak up at the time, she had no answer. Had she done so, we could have gotten the professional crew, such as they were, to film it in its best shape to date.

So I did what I had told the researchers to do but which they hadn't done: I went to the county recorder's office and asked them to research land in a particular area in the 1930s, early '40s, under the name Marion General Yeager. Within forty-five minutes, the recorder called me and asked if it could be under the name Adeline Yeager. Bingo. That was Grandma Yeager's name.

When Chuck and I returned in October for the West Virginia One Shot Doe Hunt, we made a trip in a four-wheel drive truck up the creek, literally, to Grandpa and Grandma Yeager's house.

I often imagine young Charles, as he was known, roaming the hollers, either swimming in the Guyan(dotte) River or Mud River, or swinging from branch to branch in the trees or visiting Grandpa up the creek…literally, or fishin', or huntin', or riding his bike, using his ingenuity. All of this helped him later in life, especially after he was shot down.

Charles often roamed by himself, lost in his own thoughts and dreams (one of his nicknames was Aristotle, the thinker), and other times, since he was quite popular, he roamed with friends. Another nickname was Charlie Main, after Charlemagne, the great conqueror — an apt nickname.

When we visited Panther Branch, Chuck sometimes mused about Grandpa

Yeager: "I was watching a fleet of snake doctors today. That's what we called dragonflies as kids. Reminded me of my grandfather: Grandpa Yeager. He could fix anything. I used to hike from Myra, then later, when we moved, from Hamlin—quite a long way—to visit Grandpa Yeager. He literally lived up a creek. Mom would supply me with an onion—I'd eat the whole thing, peelin's and all, on the way.

"Even today, some of the walls of Grandpa and Grandma Yeager's house are still standing. You can see where the go-down was—there's still some broken glass there.

"And where the crapper was. On the creek.

"Downstream, of course.

"You can also see where the 'refrigerator' was—a little cave above the creek that stayed cool even in the summer.

"The gas well is still there, too.

"Grandma Yeager was the barometer of big. If someone was describing someone as big, the response was always, 'As big as Adeline?'

"She used to carry a pipe in her garter. She'd take it out and smoke.

"Grandpa Yeager was skinny. He had a glass eye he would take out and put in upside-down, making us kids laugh."

## INDIAN FIGHTER PILOT CALL: *September 28, 2010*

We got an email from someone who said he had been a fighter pilot for India in the 1971 Pakistan-Indian War; he was visiting his family in the United States and would like to talk to General Chuck Yeager.

Well. Let's think about this. Chuck was the American military attaché assisting the Pakistanis in their war with India in 1971.

One of his jobs was to pick up downed Indian pilots and interview them. Over the years, we got several nasty emails and social media attacks that General Yeager was aiding Pakistan's coverup; that Pakistan was still holding Indian pilots as prisoners 30 years later. (He wasn't. They weren't.)

We've had a couple of emails from Indian military who were still fighting against Pakistan in the Kashmir region, which weren't particularly friendly. Or unfriendly.

So we asked this man to call us. He did. I chatted with him and, frankly, gave him a bit of a gentle third-degree while I looked for Chuck.

What a wonderful gentleman! And I do mean gentleman. Respectful. Gracious. Kind. He told me, without my asking, that the Pakistanis had not treated the Indian prisoners very badly; but after Chuck interviewed the Indian prisoners, the Pakistanis treated the prisoners very, very well.

So you see, Chuck is admired for much more than just one historic flight that changed aviation over 76 years ago. Occurrences like this—and there were many—keep him in high esteem, even, and especially noteworthy, with a former enemy combatant.

I told Chuck who was on the phone and he motioned me to give it to him. "Yeager!"

They conversed about the war, about talking in the prison. Chuck had flown all the Russian planes the Indians were flying, so they had much to discuss. The Indian pilots were amazed.

Chuck mentioned that it was a shame—some Indian pilots had shot down a humanitarian plane—the Pakistanis were airlifting wounded Indian POWs to the hospital. The two fighter pilots agreed. No words could express... "That's war."

They talked some more—this time about fishing in Alaska, flying, traveling.

The gentleman said he is a farmer now and promised he would stay in contact.

I hope so.

# CORINNE MENTZELOPOULOS, OWNER,
*Château Margaux: October 2010*

I had known the owner of Château Margaux in the 1980s and stayed there in 1986, which is quite a story for another book. By 2010, that owner had died and her daughter Corinne had taken over. I had met Corinne 30 years before, at a Château Margaux wine tasting, and then a couple days later on a movie set, both guests of the director, Francis Ford Coppola.

In October 2010, since Chuck and I were going to be where he had been shot down, which was within two hours of Château Margaux, I contacted Corinne to see if we could visit her at the château. We were promptly invited for lunch during the vendange, the grape picking.

When we got there, we were led to the back veranda of the château and given champagne. I hadn't had alcohol in about eight years and rarely before that. Not particularly fond of champagne, this one was different, too delicious, with tiny bubbles tickling the tongue. Yes, I know wine-tasting language. I drank the whole small flute, which wasn't much, really, except it was for me. I had to wait a bit before standing up, or I should say, before trying to stand up and going to where lunch was being served for the one hundred or more grape pickers and us.

Corinne, a delightful, energetic, strong, smart woman, half Greek, half French, joined us for lunch. We conversed and, at one point, I started to say; "Chuck—" She jumped in again with her enchanting French accent, "Chuck? (sounding like "Shook") Shook? Shook? Who is this Shook?"

I laughed, indicated my husband, and explained. I thought her staff had already filled her in; I had sent them a synopsis of his history.

Corinne was processing this as she gave us a tour. As we were leaving, I asked if she would like a signed lithograph and explained what that was. She said, "Sure," and started walking us to our car.

As we were crossing part of the driveway, a group of Americans were coming in for a tour. One, and then all, recognized their hero, Chuck Yeager. They could not believe it. Of all places. ...

The Americans surrounded General Yeager, asked for photos and completely ignored Corinne, which rarely happens because she, in her own right and circle, is a well-known, commanding presence.

Corinne quickly and finally understood with whom she had been having lunch and whom she had been regaling with stories and her history.

## TOKYO SEXWALE — *Nelson Mandela's Righthand Man in Prison*

Chuck talked to the South African Air Force and some of the honorary colonels. They could not believe that someone of his stature would visit them. They took a lot of photos.

I stayed out of the photos until one older, very attractive, black, honorary colonel, standing with Chuck and about thirty pilots in uniform, called out with a huge grin: "MRS. Chuck! Come get in this photo!"

How could I resist a summons like that from a handsome colonel?

I jumped in happily. And I like his moniker for me, Mrs. Chuck, especially with the colonel's accent. Kinda formal-ish but not too formal. And with the South African Air Force, that is who I am; "Mrs. Chuck".

At lunch, we were sitting next to the handsome honorary colonel, Col Sexwale. He was thrilled. General Chuck Yeager is one of his heroes. As I tried to address him, I looked dubious, so he explained; it's pronounced: Say-qwhall-ay. Sort of. Or the "xw" is more like the Mexican pronunciation of the "j" in Jose, only harder, or the French "r", or as if you're (if American English is your first language) going to do a hacking cough. He said it was from Arabic.

I knew he must be someone of some importance since he was seated on General Yeager's right. I wasn't bold (or rude) enough to say, "Who (the heck) are you?" so I asked what I thought was innocuous. "Do you have kids?"

Tokyo responded, "Yes. But I got started late because I was in prison so long."

Wow. That's a pretty good icebreaker. No one would ever admit that right off the bat in the U.S. Quite forthright. So I decided to be as well.

Tokyo Sexwale was an anti-apartheid activist in prison with Nelson Mandela for fifteen years. Tokyo has the same approach, as far as I could tell. He is all about forgiveness and helping his country and the people of his country, whatever race or tribe they may be. I have to find some books about him—but I think he told me he took up arms with the rebel anti-apartheid group, the African National Congress, as a teenager.

Some people had tried to engineer an introduction between General Chuck Yeager and President Mandela, but it was not to be. President Mandela, true to his priorities, wanted to spend his remaining days with his family. I can't help but think had he known it would be just Chuck Yeager and me (Mrs. Chuck), no entourage, he might have met us and even introduced his family to us. However, President Mandela probably, quite rightly, knew there would be many intermediaries and interlopers trying to horn in.

However, I was thrilled to meet Tokyo. What a role model from what I have seen. And a bundle of enthusiasm and positive energy for life. Prison sure didn't break him. Thank goodness. And imagine, General Chuck Yeager, one of his heroes. Who would have put that together?

## MR. TERRY & MRS. TERRI (SMITH), PILOTS

We were shocked to hear about the plane crash that killed Senator Stevens. The pilot, Terry Smith, and his wife, Terri Smith, were our friends. We had flown a lot in the Grumman Goose with Terry to go fishing; I had learned a great deal about safety from Terry.

Early on, before taking flying lessons, I noticed Terry saying the checklist out loud before taking off. Keenly interested in learning to fly, I paid close attention to these things. I wondered if Terry was saying the checklist out loud because he hadn't flown this plane much, so I asked him how long he had been flying it.

Terry responded, "This particular plane? Over 20 years."

Me: "I notice you say the checklist out loud."

Terry: "Yes. I've been doing that since the beginning. If I say it out loud, it's easier to make sure I do everything on the list and don't miss anything."

Terry had about 38,000 hours flying time when he said this. I considered him one of the safest pilots I knew. He had nearly 39,000 hours flying time when he was killed.

So, when I started learning to fly officially, I said the checklist out loud. And I still do it. Terry was right. One notices more easily if one has missed something. Also, if I have passengers, it makes them a part of the experience and much more comfortable. More so if they are pilots; they can check my checking the checklist.

We called Mrs. Terri soon after we got to Alaska to give her our condolences and spend some time with her if she wanted. We sure didn't want to impose—people's reactions to the death of a loved one are all over the place and all valid. She left me a message to stop by if I wished. So I did just that. We sat on her deck overlooking the lake, reminisced, chatted, cried and even laughed. Their pets, a dog and a cat, joined us.

Their cat decided my lap was comfortable, so lay there as I petted her behind the ears and her derrière. As I petted her derrière, Mrs. Terri said, "Terry always said not to worry; if something happened to him, he'd come back as one of our pets."

I immediately stopped petting the cat's derrière and apologized. We both burst into laughter. It was a good release.

Chuck and I had seen both Mr. Terry and Mrs. Terri the prior September when they had invited us for dinner. A delicious, amusing dinner in their attractive home. We were looking forward to seeing them again this trip.

No one can figure out what caused the crash yet. If ever. Very bewildering. The thought was maybe he had had a stroke.

It is all very, very sad.

Later, we met some of the surviving passengers who claimed Terry had saved the life of his co-pilot, a young boy, by turning just before the moment of impact. Wow.

## PRINCE MALIK ATTA MUHAMMAD KHAN:
*Pakistan 2012*

We hadn't had much sleep—going sometimes forty hours without it—visiting the troops in Afghanistan, Kuwait, and Qatar. Our flight from Kuwait to Pakistan left at 10:30 p.m. and arrived at 4:30 a.m. (two hours difference).

Chuck was able to sleep some on the flight. I was very glad we had upgraded to Business Class. Economy was a free-for-all and we might have been knocked down or treated badly.

Too late, the USAF told us they could have snuck us across the border from Afghanistan, which would have taken us two to four hours. Although the border was officially closed, in reality, it was not. Instead, we had to fly to Qatar, then Kuwait and back up to Islamabad, then a four-hour drive to Prince Malik's palace. I vowed if we ever "visited the troops" again, I'd get more involved in the DoD (Department of Defense) planning.

We got off the plane in darkness and were guided to a special bus that took us to a different entrance. As I got off the bus, amidst all the darkness and dark-clothed men, was a man in traditional tribal dress, high white turban, white trousers, white shirt, and black vest. Imagine Aladdin. I had seen him many times in photos. Prince Malik Ata Muhammad Khan.

As I was first off the bus, I turned to Chuck and said, "He's here." I now felt safe in this new land with much turmoil. Chuck saw him and grinned.

Prince Malik enthusiastically welcomed us, thrilled and honored to see the general after almost 40 years. And happy to meet me.

He gathered us up and put us in his car—which also had character. His men would get our luggage and bring it later.

We set out to the palace, stopping for gas and bottled water. One and a half hours later, we were driving through the gates of the very large, white palace with magnificent columns. We fell into our bed and slept until noon.

Prince Malik had been up all night, too, waiting for us, so he got a bit of a sleep-in as well.

At noon, a retired colonel and his son, both professional polo players, came for lunch. We sat outside on the veranda to have a soda before lunch.

The son was off to England the next day to start playing polo professionally again there. A fascinating fellow, the colonel had a good grasp of history and politics and a different perspective. He also was a hunter and a doctor, educated in England, and still hunted along the border and into the Himalayas. He told us that the Pakistanis knew Osama bin Laden had died—several years earlier than the time the U.S. had purportedly taken him out—of kidney disease.

We went to lunch in the grand dining room of the palace. The table was set as though 20 guests might show up at any time to enjoy a grand feast. How welcoming.

On the mantel was a photo of General Chuck Yeager, U.S. Ambassador to Pakistan/Mrs. McFarland, Prince Malik's father, and Mumtaz, Prince Malik's aunt's husband, from 1973, signed by Chuck Yeager to Mumtaz. Mumtaz, who died a long time ago, is the one with whom Chuck went hunting most often in 1971–73.

At lunch, the colonel was careful what he ate—I should have taken note. He was a city person, so was careful in the country. He didn't drink water, only soft drinks with no ice.

Chuck regaled us with the tales about Prince Malik, which he also relates in his book, *Yeager, An Autobiography*. Prince Malik had come to dinner. Chuck's first wife, Glennis, had complained that one of the servants was lazy and was stealing sugar. Whereupon Prince Malik leapt from the table, gun drawn, saying: "Point him out, I will kill him. I will give you servants who won't steal and who will die for you!"

I think Glennis replied with something like: "Did I say steal? I meant takes or tastes or…"

Also, Prince Malik would bring a friend to Chuck's house and say: "General Saab, make a bullet." General Yeager had his loading equipment there and would make a bullet for Prince Malik, who thought that ability was incredible!

That afternoon, we raced back to Islamabad to see the tent-pegging contest—General Yeager in the left front seat next to the driver. (They drive on the right in Pakistan. Usually.) Prince Malik and I were in the backseat. General Yeager insisted the driver slow down. It was a bit harrowing—several close calls, passing everything in tight situations. At one point, we were driving down the middle of the two-way road with cars approaching us head-on, then going on either side to avoid hitting us.

We passed big trucks—what colorful designs were on these trucks. If we did such artistry on ours, what prettier sights they would be.

We made it to the tent-pegging contest in time to see some pageantry.

The teams will trot, prance or jog by in all their finest, colorful regalia on both the riders and the horses. The horses always seemed feisty, ready to take off at a gallop.

At the starting point, someone calls out to start and the jockey kicks his horse into a gallop. As he nears the tent peg, he reaches down and…spears it. Or not. If he doesn't, he doesn't go onto the second round. If he does, he does a second round—and this time, speed counts. The fastest jockeys that spear the peg in the second-round win.

The purpose is to keep up the skills should one tribe need to fight another or should a skirmish or war arise. In a surprise attack, the tent pegger would spear and lift the tent peg, thus causing the tent to collapse on their enemies and have the advantage while the enemy is squirming or trampled, caught in the tent.

I busily took photos of this new sport, the general, Prince Malik, and the prancing horses. I realized I was the only female. I crossed the track a few times to take photos—had to be careful—at one point, horses were prancing in all directions.

We decided to get in the car just in time after General Yeager pointed out the dark clouds.

We drove back to Prince Malik's village and sat down in the palace's large dining room for dinner. We had traditional food and halvah with gold leaf, Chuck's favorite dessert from when he was the Defense Representative in Pakistan in 1971-73 for its war with India.

We went to bed early, still needing to catch up on much-needed sleep.

While we were visiting, Malik took us to the horse races. They were his horses, his track, and he somehow knew which horse would win. I wanted to bet—talk about a sure bet—and he was surprised. But I didn't have Pakistani money and didn't push it.

One day, we went to a funeral. The men were sitting outside a traditional building, the women inside. Malik insisted I stay outside with the men, General Yeager and him, probably to watch over me and protect me. It was a pleasant exchange—the men all thrilled to see General Chuck Yeager. I rather wished to go inside to see the women's customs, but it was not to be.

As we were leaving, Malik told me the women had food inside. That's when I was truly bummed.

As we drove back to the palace—chauffeur/security and Chuck in front, Malik and me in back—Malik, about 10 to 15 years younger than Chuck, grabbed my hand and caressed it. He said it was a shame I had not gotten more involved in the horse world when I lived in England aged 22 to 23; then he would have met me first and we could have been married (and me absconded to Pakistan, never to be heard from again). 'Not in a million years,' I thought and 'What number wife would I have been?'

Some folks thought that I, being much younger than General Yeager, must be a player. Nothing could have been further from the truth and they each learned that very quickly.

Thinking as fast as I could how to handle this without offending—in a lawless land as the guest of essentially the dictator of the region—I smiled, pulled my hand back, leaned forward to General Yeager, massaged his shoulders, and asked him, addressing him as Charlie, how he was doing. Malik got the message loud and clear with no animosity, thank goodness.

One day, he sent me to a big town with the driver and bodyguard to buy form-fitting long dresses to take home. Clearly, he didn't know me. I purchased several scarves to give as gifts when we returned to the States. He was somewhat disappointed.

Another day, we went to another tent-pegging contest. Very exciting and fun. Beautiful horses all decked out in colorful finery. I was the only adult female at this event, too. Sitting with Prince Malik, sovereign of the province, legendary Tent Pegging World Champion, and the village elders, with me on Chuck's right, Chuck noticed the young girls and boys looking at me furtively and somewhat flirting. I smiled at them; they smiled back. They probably thought I was a very, very important person to be female and sitting with the leaders, all male. I tried to look and act the part with warmth. They were adorable.

Another day, we went to town and Malik showed us the house where Chuck had lived from 1971-1973. We wanted to pass by it again, but there were police everywhere and Malik didn't want to chance it.

We then went to the colonel's house. To get in, we had to pass through several armed gates. What a way to live! Some of the former Pakistani Air Force were there and were very excited to see General Yeager. I told them that General Yeager had said they were the best pilots in the world because they flew the most. Malik, seeing the former fighter pilots' thrilled and proud reaction, later told me he was impressed with me for telling these pilots that. I merely responded it was the truth.

Two younger married folks were there—they, Christians, were trying to find things for the kids on the Afghanistan/Pakistan border to do—to prevent boredom and joining the Taliban. When this couple was on the border, some Taliban Muslims challenged them. The married couple responded, "We are the same. We are of the book" (the "book" is the Bible). Fascinating. The problem is worldwide—bored teens getting into trouble.

The next day was exciting.

## BULL RACES IN PAKISTAN— TWO-YEAR-OLD BULLS

Prince Malik, a direct descendant of Alexander the Great's best general, gathered us in the truck to go to the bull races, putting General Yeager in the seat of honor in the truck's cab with the driver. After climbing a ladder to get in the open air back of the truck, I sat there with Prince Malik and four of his men, all armed to protect us.

It was quite a wild ride—I decided to stand up, holding on for dear life—but it gave me a great view over the walls of people's courtyards and the schools.

I had much ducking to do unless I wanted to wear some branches. One time, I was watching a schoolyard when one of the guards called, "Memsaab!" I ducked just in time. Those branches could be prickly. I could get used to having very loyal, skilled guards protecting General Yeager and me wherever we went. I also kinda like being called "Memsaab", at least the way they said it.

At the race grounds, we drove carefully through the gathering crowd, across the levee and onto the field next to the racetrack. Such as it was. It was merely a very long, plowed dirt field.

We got the best seats in the house. Many people wanted to be near us, so they tried to sit right in front of us or park next to us, thus blocking the general's view.

The surrounding spectators cleared them out to honor the prince and his foreign visitors, especially the revered honorable General Chuck Yeager, who had helped the Pakistanis in 1971-73, and his wife. Frankly, there was no need for the others to park so close; there were other areas with good views as well. And having others so close could have been dangerous. Crowds in a panic (with bulls chasing) are perhaps a good place in which *not* to be.

On this first day, the two-year-olds were racing. They put a yoke on two bulls. Two ropes went to what looked like an upside-down trashcan lid without the usual handle. A third rope went from the yoke to the jockey's hand. The jockey stood on the upside-down lid and held the rope and a spear. The spear was to jab one or other of the bulls in the derrière to keep them running straight…ish…on the track.

There was a crowd at the start with trucks or enclosed trailers with bulls. Some people walked their bulls to the races.

Suddenly, a raucous shout and, out of the crowd of people and bulls, a jockey on his upside-down, colorful trashcan lid would erupt, driving two bulls with someone on either side of the bulls holding on, trying to keep up, trying to keep the bulls running straight on the track.

If the bulls left the straight dirt track or finished without a jockey, they were disqualified.

This happened often.

The crowd was good—if the bulls looked like they were veering off—some would wave at the bulls to deflect their direction back on the track.

What was pretty funny was the bulls often veered right where the judges, moments before, had been sitting. It was funny to see the judges diving for cover. It seemed the perfect place to be, as many bull teams veered right there. I wondered if this was the bulls' opinion of the judges.

More often than not, the bulls would veer within twenty yards of the start, turn back towards the starting crowd and then often veer to the side and keep running for dear life, trailing an empty, bouncing, upside-down, colorful trashcan lid. The jockey had long before jumped off.

From the truck, we could see the various sets of errant bulls.

Prince Malik said: "They are running home." Indeed, it did seem so.

We watched as various bulls made it to the finish line amongst great cheers. One fellow skipped down the racetrack after his bull did well, shouting joyfully, "My bull did well! Look at my bull!" in Pashtun. Prince Malik translated for me. While this fellow was taking credit, Prince Malik added, "But the women are the ones who care for these bulls at home."

When I mentioned to the prince that I thought I was the only female there, he confirmed it and added, amongst 30,000 men or more. I was even more grateful for Prince Malik and our armed guards.

Many people came up to the truck to say hello to Prince Malik. Each would take his hand between theirs and bow. Or just bow. I like this custom—no bone-crunching handshakes, just gently touching hands; better yet, not touching, just bowing.

I looked at all the colorful turbans—many in dark blue and red, all wound above their heads.

Many looked over to see who we were, especially since Caucasians are rare here, as well as the tribal chief, Prince Malik, and his guards.

I took several photos. At one point, one of the men with us served me tea. Afternoon tea at the bull races. How civilized.

My mother always said hot tea in the hot summer cooled her down; something to do with body temperature compared to outside temperature…or just because.

I had to put down my umbrella (for the sun) to handle the tea and the camera. Such a dilemma. Kidding.

I was drinking my tea out of my cup; no, no little finger raised when we noticed the bulls running in our direction…and not veering. I had the tea in one hand and the camera in the other, trying to position it while not spilling the tea. But no hand to hold on should the bulls bang the truck.

I put the camera down to have two hands to put the tea down. Where to put it so that it wouldn't spill should we get banged...?

Finally, as time was running out for me to make decisions, and the bulls—having already dispersed the crowd in front of us, people flying, diving, leaping everywhere out of the way—were not deviating from their head-on collision course with us, I just put the tea down, grabbed my camera to take a photo, and decided I best just hold on, when at the last second, the bulls diverted.

Geez, if I had known that, I could have taken the photo, gotten a great shot, and kept holding onto my tea. No savoir faire, here.

The bulls took off for home.

Prince Malik had suggested earlier I try being a jockey behind one of these sets of baby bulls. I considered it; very tempting –a few years earlier or more, I might have tried it and probably done okay. I used to be pretty good at balance, having waterskied and skied since I was 12 and 3, respectively, and having taken ballet and dance from age 3 to 10. And if all else failed, I was good at tucking and rolling.

But the hospital was a few hours away and, fortunately, I had not thought to bring along my riding helmet and jumping vest and no one, including, or especially, me, mentioned it again.

Also, there was not just my well-being to think about...Chuck put a fine point on it; he had heard Malik and, after Chuck gave me time to consider and no answer was forthcoming, he gave his opinion in no uncertain terms. I guess he wanted me around for a while longer.

It might have been then that Prince Malik commented: "This is not very interesting—the bulls aren't tossing anyone in the air. It's because the ground is too wet, slowing them down."

And you wanted me to go race?!?!?! Thanks a lot.

I laughed—he may have forgotten that I live with General Yeager, who can be known to say things for shock value or for a laugh, so his statement was comparatively benign.

For a moment, I thought Prince Malik might be serious about the uninteresting bull races when another set of bulls dove into the crowds just beyond us and headed for the "snack bar," an overhead tent under which were open fires cooking food.

The presumable owner stood in front, waving at the bulls to divert them. He should have known better. They took him and his snack bar out. What was he thinkin'?

I glanced at the prince to see if the bull races had now become more interesting. Instead, Prince Malik was looking at the man on the ground, quite concerned. The laughter at the silly idea of the man trying to stop the bulls head on by standing in front, became a shock of concern that the man didn't dive out of the way at the last second when it became clear the bulls weren't going to heed the man's commands to stop.

I noticed those successful at diverting the bulls waved at them from a little to the side, with big gestures or cloth just as the bulls were thinking of turning. Timing was everything. Once they had turned, it was a bit late to keep them on the track. On the racecourse—a big name for a wide, long, dirt track that was straight—not an oval, men and boys would jump up and wave pieces of cloth, their unwound turbans, to get the bulls to stay straight or get back to going straight down the track.

Once, the bulls went off the track and somehow surprisingly came back on the track with the jockey still on (lots of ridges and mini hills to go over once one is off the track) and finished the race. I think they were already disqualified due to the detour, though. Au contraire, I think extra points should have been in order.

While many tried to grab the bulls' harnesses to stop the bulls, the men and boys often got tossed or overrun. But one young man had the timing down perfectly. He caught one set of bulls and just steered them in a circle until they stopped. That's how I used to stop horses that were trying to run off with me. I had been racing along with wild animals in Africa and the new horse I was riding showed no signs of heeding my signals to stop.

One of the guys with whom I was racing had played polo and told me to just turn the horse in a circle. I thought, "Great, now the horse and I will start spinning and I will surely come off." I can do straight (and in a plane, I'm fairly good at straight and level), but the potential danger of an off-balance turn...However, I did as he suggested and voila, the horse came to a stop.

That's what this young man at the bull races did. And it worked within seconds. Even Prince Malik was impressed.

I watched the enormous crowds of men—over 30,000 as mentioned, which were only one one-hundredth of the usual crowds because it was wheat harvesting time—the bulls all decked out in glittering refinery, the various bright, busy designs of the trashcan lids, the "snack bars". What a glorious day!

Dark clouds started forming, though, so the driver decided it was time to go. But the truck's battery was dead. The men got out and tried pushing, rocking, anything—heavy truck. A few of the crowd tried to help. That truck wasn't going anywhere.

A guy in a small tractor came over—he was going to save the day for the prince and his distinguished guests. He pushed and pushed. It wasn't working. The idea, of course, was to pop the gear into starting. So several men from the crowd helped the tractor push the truck backward to get it up, yes, up, the hill a little with a running start. Then, the tractor and the men rocked the truck. And voilà!—it started. Phew.

As the truck turned around, I shouted, "Thank you!" with a wave. The men all smiled back, happy that we were delighted, waving back as we drove off, exultant in their mission accomplished for the prince and his VIP guests.

As we drove out, my bird's-eye view was wonderful. I could see what they were cooking in the snack bars—a man squatting in front of the large bowl on the fire, stirring it occasionally. I had already not had a great reaction to the water and some food, so thought fleetingly: 'It would be interesting to try,' followed quickly by, 'Probably too spicy for me,' and 'Probably wouldn't last long in my stomach.'

We threaded our way through the crowds and onto the levee—unfortunately, a narrow-ish one—so people had to move off. The levee, though, was at the end of the race. If those bulls didn't stop after the finish line, all these people would be diving. A funny but exhilarating place to watch the races, if you like the threat of being run over or tossed by a bull.

We started to race home, but General Yeager suggested to the driver that we, in fact, did want to get home safely intact, so slow down. We passed several farms where the women were working while the men were playing.

The two-year-old bull races were good training for the bulls and for the younger jockeys trying to get experience.

Another fascinating day in the life of Prince Malik Ata Muhammad Khan in Pakistan.

## HORSEBACK RIDING WITH PRINCE MALIK ATA MUHAMMAD KHAN

While on this trip, I was to ride very early every morning with Prince Malik, the chief of Kot Fateh Khan, in Attock District of Northwestern Punjab, Pakistan. By email, I had asked for a Western saddle. Although I had grown up riding English, I liked the idea of the horn on the Western saddle to grab if a horse unfamiliar to me thought I should be off his back.

The first day after our arrival, Prince Malik said an English saddle was more suitable; Western saddles are too heavy. So, he put me on a horse with an English saddle to see how I could ride. I introduced myself to the horse first, blew into his nostrils (how horses check each other out), and discussed safety with the horse. I should have been more thorough.

We were inside the high brick wall that encompassed the inner oblong palace grounds. Once I was on his back and situated, the pure white horse took off—zoomed around the mile long track just inside the walls. I held on okay, but at the corners were trees in wells that appeared like cliffs to me and, as such, had my attention. That horse was almost ninety degrees to the ground as he raced around each corner. I prayed each time we hit those turns that I did not smack the tree or that the horse did not slip or have a hoof miss and fall down that hole with me on him. As the horse straightened out, racing down the straightaways, I thought, 'I'm okay, but what do I do to stop?' The horse did not care about the reins, the bit in his mouth, leaning back or anything. It reminded me of skiing and sandboarding (Swakopmund, Namibia)—I'm okay going; it's the stopping or trying to stop that causes trouble. I tried just to enjoy the ride and *Que sera sera.*

I thought I would try to stop on the long stretch. As I was fast approaching Prince Malik, we were not stopping. My stirrups were somewhere, but I had always been taught to hold on with my knees anyway.

Suddenly, the horse appeared to respond to my commands and signals and stopped. Almost suddenly, but I stayed on. I felt pretty good about my skills. Un-huh. Nope. The horse had to poop.

We sauntered in slowly after that. Prince Malik, Chuck and, frankly, I were impressed.

I realized that all the "gardeners" around the enclosure were, in fact, Prince Malik's elite guards. They had fought in the various wars with India, including the 1971 war with India when Chuck was there, had met General Yeager, then, and had protected Malik and maybe his grandfather. They were quite seasoned, absolutely loyal and strategically placed along the mile-long elliptical route, should I need help. Nice. These guards adored General Yeager, as did Prince Malik, and respected him greatly—so pleased he was visiting, and, by virtue of that, respected, were kind to, and protective of, me, General Yeager's wife, as well.

So, it was arranged.

The following morning, one of the manservants brought tea and knocked on our door very, very early. Quite a genteel "wake up call". I got up, got dressed to ride, and drank the tea left just outside the door. General Yeager must have clued them in on how to get me up early.

I left Chuck sleeping—best he could with the "guards" making a racket on the roof of the palace. The guards were peacocks—best guards there are. Better than guard dogs. But hard to keep quiet.

By the time I was dressed and ready, Prince Malik and the groomsman had arrived on horses. I had to go up about eight steps at the palace to get on the tall horse. But first, I went to the new horse (different from the day before), again introduced myself, blew into his nostrils gently, and had a chat with him about safety. This time, Prince Malik asked me what I was doing. He was not used to someone like me—talks to horses, is independent, does not just get on a horse she doesn't know. I told him. He merely observed, didn't say a word or voice an opinion.

It took me ten minutes of riding to get the horse to calm down after the groomsman had been riding it. They rode with a very tight rein, keeping the horse's chin tucked in.

My horse tripped or stumbled a lot. I figured out much later that it probably had poor eyesight.

Each morning before it got too hot, Prince Malik and I would ride for a couple of hours in different parts of his kingdom. It was like what I imagined medieval England to be. The people rented land from him and paid in crops. Wheat.

His subjects brought their troubles to him; he was judge and jury, solving problems. A benign and generous dictator.

While we rode, people would come up, bow or hold his hand in both theirs and convey their problems. He would tell each one to bring their issues to Court for his men and him to handle, unless it was something simple to handle right then. "Court", I observed later, was the prince chopping wood for exercise, with his men, ever vigilant but appearing nonchalant, as each person(s) having a dispute was brought up to the pile and pled his case or asked. No women.

I observed all this. After presenting one case, two men walked away appearing very sullen. Prince Malik translated what had transpired; the two men had wanted to use some of the water from his lake for their crops and he had agreed to do so. I asked why so sullen. He replied, "No, they're fine." That was their happy face?

Prince Malik told me that he was at Disney once and a little kid came up to talk to "the genie from *Aladdin*." This is how Prince Malik dressed—in traditional garb. His ancestor, the righthand man of Alexander the Great, had received vast areas of land in India and now Pakistan. When the British carved up the countries, Prince Malik's lands were reduced to just those in Pakistan. His grandfather sent him to Oxford to study law to protect his land and people from the government of Pakistan. Prince Malik had joined the government as a representative but left because he kept asking, "What are you (the government) doing for the people of Pakistan?" Nothing. And no one else cared.

It was beautiful countryside full of fields of wheat about to be harvested, small houses, bulls, and people who seemed happy.

Prince Malik chastised me—too kind to my horse and that is why the horse kept stumbling, not tight enough on the reins. Then Prince Malik's horse tripped to his knees. Perfectly timed.

I had a tough time getting my horse to stop or not run up on Prince Malik's horse when we were galloping, so Prince Malik had me go first—he didn't want me to get kicked. Then, I couldn't get my horse to do more than canter—he did not want to gallop ahead of his leader. At the last, he tripped. I was glad we weren't galloping. It was then that I realized the horse's eyesight was probably not good, so it felt more comfortable right behind another horse. It never tripped behind Prince Malik's horse.

I had contemplated asking for another horse but was concerned the next one would be less suitable or too fast or…

All in all, it was great fun.

By the time I returned each day, around 8 a.m., Chuck was up and having breakfast. I would alight from my horse on the step outside the guard house and would walk to the palace to join Chuck for breakfast.

Prince Malik wanted me to wear a turban instead of my top-of-the-line (safety) riding helmet. He said a turban would protect me and be more suitable. He also said I did not need my green safety vest.

I asked Chuck what he thought. We inspected the turban. While vaguely sturdy, it didn't light a candle to my safety helmet. Chuck said in no uncertain terms to wear my helmet, not a turban, and the safety vest, which I did. In Pakistan, coming from General Yeager, defying Prince Malik's request was far more acceptable and honored.

What was interesting is that Prince Malik often wore a green vest as part of his uniform and so, with my green safety vest, I looked like I was part of the royal party when we rode.

One time, as I was dismounting, the groomsman decided to hold onto the stirrup so that when I dismounted on the other side, the saddle would not slide. However, he made several mistakes, which I figured out later.

I was descending and could not find the step. I was going down and down, trying to feel it with my right foot, my left foot still in the stirrup. I kept going farther and farther down, stretching my legs almost beyond their ability. Where was that step? I ended up going down to the ground, scraping the side of the step because we were not close enough for me to step on it.

This scraping sound and the groomsman spooked the horse, which took off a few steps, me holding on for dear life. As soon as we were clear of the step, I catapulted myself off so I wouldn't be dragged in the stirrup. I rolled back from the catapult and gently tapped my head (in the helmet, not a turban, thank goodness) on the brick-and-stone wall. No factor due to the helmet.

The horse reared away from the groomsman and somewhat stepped on my foot as I rolled. The horse realized it was me, which frightened/horrified him even more, got off my foot immediately and raced away.

The groomsman chased after him, which is about the worst thing you can do to catch a runaway horse. Prince Malik was first concerned with me. I told him I was okay. He yelled at his men to stop chasing the horse.

As I got up and dusted myself off, Prince Malik told me to go back to the palace. After again making sure I was okay, Prince Malik attended to getting the runaway horse back. I wanted to go get the horse because I did know how to do so and the horse trusted me, not the groomsmen, but Prince Malik told me not to worry. I realized later he was upset, but not about anything I had done. Interestingly, it seemed the horse stopped, turned around almost as if to see if I was okay and headed towards me. But the groomsmen, somewhat between the horse and me, kept frantically running after the horse, scaring it even more, causing it to turn again and run farther away. I would have run farther away from the groomsmen, too.

When I arrived at the palace, there was no ice, so we looked in the freezer. I borrowed a frozen orange soda and held it to the foot on which the horse had trod. Nothing broken but ice is the wonder "drug" to prevent bruising, swelling and resulting pain. The faster you put it on, the better. It works.

At first, I thought I had messed up and despondently told Chuck this, that I had no business riding. But at lunch later, when I apologized to Prince Malik, he protested, "No, it was not your fault. Not at all." I could see Chuck was somewhat relieved. As was I. But I wasn't yet convinced.

I still chose not to ride the next day—take a day off and contemplate. Chuck was even more relieved.

I started reconstructing what had happened. The groomsman, who must have been very new, had pulled on the stirrup so hard that he had moved the horse away from the step. Thus, I could not find it. This was about the tenth day. Every day before this, I had had no problem. Why he chose to hold the stirrup on this day...I don't know. Prince Malik was right: it was not my fault. And I was grateful I listened to Chuck's advice. The turban would not have protected my head. And an injury, even a cut, in this part of the world could be disastrous/fatal. My helmet made my head tap a non-issue.

I relayed my analysis to Chuck.

And I felt confident enough to resume riding each morning with Prince Malik. I did take a lot more control of what the groomsman was doing. The horse had somewhat protected me, so we were quite fine.

Addendum: After we left Pakistan, we often heard from Prince Malik—he'd send us a Christmas ecard each year. He had been great friends with Princess Diana and apparently had a huge place in England. He could not get a visa into the U.S., though. He declined our help and we never saw him again. He died in February 2020 at the age of 82.

## RUSS SCHLEEH, COL USAF *(World War II Bomber Pilot)*, CARROLL SHELBY *(Race Car Champion)*

Immediately prior to going to Pakistan, we were in Los Angeles for some emergency tests for what we later learned was a mistake in the results of lab tests done at Travis AFB. It turned out to be nothing, thank goodness.

We had the chance, though, to have lunch with Russ Schleeh at a mutual friend's. We could see that Russ was truly aging—he had fallen and broken his femur, so was now in a wheelchair. There were too many at lunch—about eight—all talking, not respecting that Russ wanted to spend time with and speak with only Chuck. Russ fell asleep in his chair at all the chatter. But when Chuck spoke, Russ would wake up, perk up and be quite present, smiling at Chuck. I'm quite grateful that we took the time to visit with Russ.

And we had the chance to see Carroll Shelby in the hospital at UCLA. We walked in, Chuck said hello to one of Carroll's sons and Carroll woke up—he had been sleeping for many days. The son would not stop talking, so I told the son we were there to see Carroll and moved with Chuck over to Carroll's bedside. Chuck, on the way, quietly asked what he should say. I said anything; tell stories, talk about flying, combat…And Chuck did just that. Carroll couldn't speak—he may have been intubated—I can't remember.

We didn't want to tire him out and Chuck correctly assessed it was time to go. As we left, I looked at Carroll to say goodbye. Carroll mouthed a very grateful, heartfelt "Thank you!" to me.

He started getting well, recovering from pneumonia, but mysteriously died a week or so later while we were in Pakistan. I'm grateful we got to see him before he went. He admired Chuck greatly, was always kind to me and gave me good advice.

On our way back from Pakistan, we stopped outside London for an overnight rest. I checked messages on our home phone. We had a frantic call and email that Russ Schleeh was in hospice, but no telephone number to call. I emailed back for the number, no response. We went for a walk along the Thames River, watching the water overflow the locks—it had rained hard. It reminded me of when I was nine. My childhood family had come to England and towards the end of the trip, Dad had rented a boat on which we traveled the Thames, going through locks. It was quite an adventure.

As soon as Chuck and I got home the next day—it was 10:30 p.m.—we called anyway and spoke to Russ. His nurse put the phone to his ear. He could hear us but couldn't speak. He was thrilled to hear from his good friends Chuck and Victoria. The nurse told us later, he was grinning from ear to ear the whole time. Whenever we called, he was always positive and grateful.

We hung up, glad we had gotten a chance to talk to him.

He died the next day. What a lovely guy. A great soul. GREAT, great soul.

## DAVID "TEX" HILL, BRIG GEN USAF, FLYING TIGER

Several years prior (2007), we had had a similar experience regarding General Tex Hill (former Flying Tiger during World War II). Although Tex, a member of the American Volunteer Group that fought in China during World War II before the U.S. entered the war, and a big hero fighter pilot to the likes of F/O Yeager, was a big admirer of Chuck. I remember one dinner; I was sitting between these two old friends; Tex mentioned his granddaughter was writing a biography on Tex. Chuck's response was, "Are you going to tell the truth?"

Tex said, "Aw, hell. Chuck, nobody wants to hear the truth. You didn't tell it all."

I interjected, "I do! I do!"

In 2007, we had called Tex while driving to hunt elk in New Mexico. Maizie, his wife, a beautiful, strong soul, told us that while Tex couldn't speak, he was smiling and nodding, so happy we called. Maizie, a special woman, was forever grateful.

## WARREN BEATTY, JOE MONTANA, & ANNETTE BENING, *California Hall of Fame: 2013*

We attended a couple of California Hall of Fame Inductions, including the one where they inducted Warren Beatty and San Francisco 49ers quarterback Joe Montana.

We arrived in the VIP pre-party lounge. Annette Bening was regaling a table full of well-known folks, Warren Beatty, Joe Montana, and others. Annette was holding her wineglass; I think with her pinky up.

No one turned, noticed us, or invited us to join them, so we sat at the empty table next door. I alternatively watched the body language at the table next door and the crowd passing by outside the little enclave. A gal came by and asked if she could sit at our table. I truly wanted to say, "Depends. Are you interesting? Will you be annoying?" but I just said, "Sure."

As soon as she sat down, she said, "Oh MY God! Do you see who's at the next table?"

I replied, "Do you see who's at your table?" She looked at me, then looked more closely at Chuck and we could see it slowly dawning on her.

She then became very loud, telling anyone who passed. More and more people were coming in to say hello to Chuck Yeager, causing a bit of a ruckus and grabbing total focus from Annette to her utter dismay. To find out who was stealing her thunder, with her wine glass still raised, pinky still up, still talking, she looked up at the paintings, eyes moved across the paintings to above us, down the paintings, and landed looking straight into my eyes. Whoops. Busted. I smiled.

When we all got up to go start the program, Warren Beatty recognized me (we had met a few times ages before), came over, big smile, and said hello. I introduced him to Chuck. Annette, wondering who I was and not to be outdone, immediately introduced herself to me.

## MIKE CUSACK — PLASTIC SURGEON/ ALASKA FISHING LODGE OWNER

We visited an old friend Chuck had not seen in over ten years, Mike. I started to ask the receptionist — the man standing there turned and did a double take. Chuck and Mike greeted each other warmly. We went into one of the appointment rooms and chatted for a while. Mike was a plastic surgeon, who also used to own a lodge where Chuck had fished and flown Beavers on floats a lot. Mike introduced us to his very attractive, all-female staff; they were his advertisement. He had patients waiting, so we left just in time. I was afraid he might try to start sculpting me. Lost cause.

## THE MONDAVIS

Chuck and I met Marc Mondavi at the Cal-Ore Fish Derby over the course of several years. We all had such a good time, great camaraderie, all for a good cause: fish habitat. And Marc was very generous at this charity's auction.

One year, we were going to be in Napa to see the Oak Ridge Boys, so we invited the Mondavis. The Mondavis, in turn, invited us to their company Christmas party. Charles Krug Winery, the oldest in Napa Valley, was purchased by Marc's grandparents.

At the Christmas party, Chuck and I sat with Peter Mondavi, Marc's father, and Janice, Marc's wife. Oak Ridge Boy William Lee Golden and the Boys' road manager, Darrick, sat at another table. One of my most favorite photos is of Peter Mondavi and Chuck Yeager enjoying a huge belly laugh together, sheer joy and delight. I'm quite confident Chuck had said something to set them off. William Lee Golden, an avid photographer, took the photo.

Another time, we went to lunch; Peter, Marc, his wonderful wife, Janice, a couple others, Chuck and me. After a delightful lunch, as we were all leaving, Peter quietly came up to me and asked me whom he had to thank for the delicious meal. Such class, elegance, kindness, and style. I will never forget Peter Mondavi, Sr.

Marc and Janice continue that elegance, kindness, and generosity. Over the years, Marc joined Chuck and me and other friends at a few sporting events; the San Francisco Giants, the 49ers—always an adventure, always great company.

## LARRY BOCHKAY, SON OF WORLD WAR II FIGHTER ACE, DON BOCHKAY

In 2010, I got to meet Larry and Louise Bochkay. Larry was the son of Don Bochkay, triple Fighter Ace and great friend of Chuck from World War II's 363rd Squadron, 357th Fighter Group (FG).

They visited us for lunch and brought some of Bochkay's old photos, newspapers and the like. Fascinating, wonderful historical information. I was so glad to see that Larry and Louise were honoring Don Bochkay's memory and as interested in preserving history as I.

Chuck said Larry is the spitting image of his father in looks, demeanor, and character. It was exciting to meet someone who was so much like Bochkay, about whom Chuck often spoke fondly. Bochkay's mother and aunt had been actresses and the good looks were being passed down.

One interesting fact that came out: Larry asked Chuck: "Did anyone ever figure out what happened to the barracks door?"

Chuck answered, "No," then explained to me that they had marked a swastika into the door every time any of the four guys in their Nissen hut had shot down an enemy aircraft. Shame it is lost.

Bochkay had returned to Leiston Air Base before he died (1981) and said the farmers and motorhome park had wiped out the area where the 363rd Squadron had been. What a shame.

Chuck reminisced about going to Bochkay's house in Hollywood—where Bochkay was staying with his parents. Bochkay was a motorcycle racer and maintenance guy before he enlisted. It sure helped in learning to fly.

Bochkay joined the Army Air Corps at age 25 in 1941 and was called "Pops" because, by 1943, he was the ol' man in the group (at 27!).

Bochkay was an excellent artist. In his scrapbook were some great drawings. He painted Alice in Wonderland on his own airplane during World War II. He died in Pahrump, Nevada, age 65, in 1981.

Chuck delighted in telling the story that Larry and Chuck dumped Bochkay's body in the San Francisco Bay after he died. (It was more like they spread his ashes there, but that's not as interesting a story.)

I love hearing stories about Don Bochkay and Chuck Yeager.

# PART VII

# HUNTIN'

*Chuck YEAGER-ism #132:
"Where'd you go to school?
You ought to get your money back.
It's huntin', not huntinG."*

## RELOADING

Chuck Yeager was from Lincoln County, West Virginia. I was from the big city of Philadelphia, Pennsylvania. Chuck Yeager taught me how to hunt, fish, but not just fish; how to fly fish; and how to fly; not just fly but fly taildraggers (much more difficult.) And, most importantly, he taught me West Virginian. "It's Kanaw-uh, not Kanaw WHA-," for Kanawha River, West Virginia. And it's "go down" (pantry) and "paper poke" (paper bag), and more.

One day, I returned to the house after errands, looked all over, found Chuck downstairs reloading ammunition for our huntin' trip, and bounded in to give him a big hug and a kiss, very excited to see him. "HI, CHARLIE!"

That stern look and putting up his hands to stop me, halted me in my tracks, silenced me and dissipated my energy to sheer calm. He educated me: "An inaccurate load can be deadly." Say no more. He then used my help to reload. Fascinating. Fortunately, after we finished and went upstairs, he clearly showed he forgave me my enthusiasm and ignorance.

## CELEBRITY QUAIL HUNT FUNDRAISER:
*Abilene, Texas, February 2011*

For many years, we participated in the Celebrity Quail Hunt fundraiser for Down syndrome folks in Abilene, Texas. Chuck had attended 23 years' worth. Doug English, the professional football player, was a close second—he missed half of one. We teased him one year: we got there on Wednesday, a day early, just to ensure we stayed ahead of Doug.

One year, I took a photo of Doug while he was talking to Chuck. He looked at me quite perplexed, "What are you doing?" I had raised my hands up high over my head with the camera in them. I wanted a photo of Doug from a level with his face—not looking up at him as he must have always gotten. He's a tall, attractive, ex-professional football player who has stayed in great shape, a proud father and husband who truly admired Chuck, so he's okay in my book.

It's interesting, after seeing many of the people here for ten years, you start to feel rather like a kind of "family," all supporting Disability Resources for Down syndrome, brain injury, or autistic adults. The Down syndrome folks loved seeing Chuck (and apparently me, too) each year and we sure enjoyed visiting with them. The folks would come out to one of the ranches for lunch during the hunt. They used to sit at their own table over the years until I came along. Chuck and I sat down with the folks instead of with the hunters and encouraged the hunters to do the same. The folks were very surprised and delighted by this as we laughed and smiled through lunch. It was very sweet.

I was talking with Von Faulkner, also a former football player, and his wife. Von had just gotten his pilot's license. I was imparting to him some of the bon mots or concepts I had learned from Chuck Yeager. I could see why everyone from whom I ask advice re flying is so helpful—Von's excitement as a new pilot was infectious.

Fly safe, Von!

* * *

One of the days on my first trip in 2001, I went on the all-female spouse outing. One spouse, prolific, successful writer Karol Ladd, had a fun, great sense of humor. The rest…not so much.

So the next day, I went out huntin' with Chuck. Daddy Bush always had trouble huntin' because the ranch owner, not the manager who knew the ranch intimately, would insist on driving Daddy Bush around. It was never as successful as if the ranch manager had.

The same thing happened this day. I sat in the front of the truck between the owner and Chuck, who was riding shotgun.

The two non-celebrity hunters, donors, were in the back.

At one point, the owner, telling a story just before he got out to open a gate, concluded in disgust, "And then he wanted to know how many acres I had!!!"

After he was out of earshot, I asked, "What's wrong with asking how many acres he has on his ranch? I'd do that."

One of the two guys, both from New Jersey, explained: "That's like asking how much we have in our bank account."

Me: "Oh…How much do you have in your bank account?" We all laughed. They never did answer the question, though.

We drove around, didn't see any quail. Then we came upon six trucks. One hunter from each was walking towards a branched-out tree. The two hunters in the back said, "It's your turn, General."

Chuck assessed the situation and declined. "Nah, you guys go." Naïvely, for a moment, I thought he just wanted to stay in the truck to protect me.

One of the hunters went towards the tree about a quarter mile away.

And then I saw what Chuck had seen developing.

The hunters, I kid you not, stood in a semi-circle to shoot at the tree when the birds were flushed. The birds were flushed, lots of noise from shooting: bam bam bam bam bam bam bam!

Not one bird dropped. The hunters had all missed. And fortunately, had all missed each other, too.

## HUNTIN' PIGS, VICTORIA'S FIRST TIME

One of my first huntin' experiences was as follows: Chuck was huntin' pigs in Texas at a friend's ranch. I went along. The pigs were destroying the food for the deer. The friend had limited ammunition but wanted the pigs eradicated. Chuck shot one; it flipped upside down, waving its legs. I shouted, "It's still alive, Chuck! Shoot it, it's suffering."

Chuck, to his credit, then would shoot it so it stopped waving its legs even though we had limited ammunition. I think he'd rather me be upset than cold. Eventually, I was able to understand and get used to the fact that the legs waving didn't mean it could feel anything and that it was essentially dead. That pig fed a lot of poor people.

## ELK HUNTIN'

In November 2000, we drove to Montana to hunt elk. At the Safari Club International convention for several years, anyone who bought a lifetime membership had his/her name put in a hat to win an elk hunt with General Chuck Yeager in Montana at Madame Prophet's.

We drove halfway and stayed in a motel in Nevada; oddly one I had stayed in before on my first trip out west with a school friend, both age 19. I wasn't comfortable then and would not have felt comfortable this time if Chuck had not been there. Earlier, I had bought some pine nuts as Chuck looked on. When he saw me trying to figure them out, he said, "I wondered how you were going to eat them." I continued to be a source of great amusement for him.

After we arrived at Mme Prophet's, the guide drove us all over, never seeing one elk, let alone a yearling cow elk (best eatin').

The next morning, again, we saw nothing except all the elk in the town or Yellowstone—both places where they were protected—thumbing their noses at us. While driving around, the guide was militant and extreme about the government trying to take his guns. I could feel Chuck sit up straighter in the front seat. I wasn't sure if it was because I was there (guns in Philadelphia meant gangs) or whether Chuck was becoming wary of this guy. Crazy talk. As I got to know Chuck, it was the second choice; this guide was creepy.

Blocking our way into lunch at the last turn were three trucks and a couple of folks looking up at the very high hill. There were plenty of elk up there. Chuck got out and asked them if they were going to shoot or stand around gabbing.

The first hunter complained, "They're too far away!"

Chuck said, "Well, I'll shoot," and started setting up, checking the distance and altitude: over eight hundred meters away and sixty degrees higher.

The first hunter, Ron, not wanting to feel emasculated, said, well, yes, he would shoot.

I got out of the truck to take a photo the moment Chuck shot, but I wasn't fast enough.

Kaboom. Ron shot. That percussion ran right through my body.

Kaboom immediately followed. Chuck shot—and I heard the thwack—definite hit and the elk was down, dead in one shot. Chuck later said he held over eleven feet above the neck where he was shooting, intuitively calculating the accurate descent of the bullet to its target.

I thought they were done, but Ron shot three more times; one could hear a ricochet or two, and Chuck shot a second time. Ron had missed three times and wounded it on the fourth. Chuck got fed up and put the hunter's wounded elk out of its misery in one shot.

We drove to the base of the hill. Chuck and I started walking up. It was so steep that side by side, my head was the height of his derrière. The guides couldn't believe how quickly we ascended the hill. Chuck's nickname in Pakistan, where he had stationed and hunted a lot, was "mountain goat". Turned out there was a spike behind the cow elk, so Chuck had killed two elk with one shot.

The guides started gutting the elk. I watched. Chuck watched me. Turn green. Not wanting to watch me puke my breakfast out and carry me down, he walked a little away and called out to me: "Victoria! Look at the view!"

It took me about six years to be able to watch the animal's dressing without feeling nauseous or faint. Even my best acting skills weren't helping.

We took the gutted elk by the "handles" on the legs and started dragging it down the hill, but it was so steep it began to get ahead of us. We left it for the guides and hiked down.

Since this was my first big-game hunt, I didn't realize this was a remarkable feat—shooting an elk at such a distance and height, let alone shooting two with one bullet.

We took the elk to the butcher's, an ol' pal of Chuck's, Bryan Wells. The game warden separated Chuck and me to ask what happened. I enthusiastically said, "Wow! What a shot! Killed the cow instantly and it went through the cow and hit the spike, which you could not see at all from where we were. At over eight hundred meters! At sixty degrees above us! That was so cool." I didn't see anyone waving their hands, signaling, "Be quiet!!!"

Chuck helped Bryan skin the elk and cut up the meat. Sally, Bryan's wife, a Renaissance woman extraordinaire, great cook, great gardener, great artist, and a great friend of Chuck's and mine, gave us a beautiful bronze of Chuck she had made herself, which I still have and cherish.

## SQUIRREL'S BRAINS — A DELICACY:
### New Year's Eve 2001-2002

Chuck and I took his son and grandson, Kip, huntin' in Jawbone Canyon, where Chuck used to hunt when he was stationed at Edwards AFB (1940s, '50s, '60s) and near where Pancho Barnes had her last home. The boys drove from Colorado and we drove Chuck's motorhome from Grass Valley, California. The boys slept in sleeping bags outside. We slept in the motorhome. Chuck cooked halibut one night using an old fishing guide buddy's recipe; tasted like a poor man's lobster. Delicious.

We were huntin' chukar and dove. Chuck's grandson was waiting to turn eighteen to go into the Marines in about eight months. On this hunt, he would shoot and shoot. He might get two in two, but he could never find that second bird. So, Chuck told him: "Aim, shoot, and pick up that bird. Focus. Concentrate. Don't waste a shot or an animal."

This grandson went on to become a top sniper in the Marines. Because of Grandpa's training and quick thinking, Kip saved men's lives during door-to-door combat in Fallujah. Kip received a Bronze Star, similar to Grandpa. Chuck received his Bronze Star with a "V" for Valor for carrying a wounded airman over the Pyrénées in three feet of snow.

While huntin' in Jawbone, Chuck saw a gray squirrel and told his grandson to shoot it. Kip looked at him questioningly. Chuck confirmed the request, "Haven't you ever eaten squirrel?"

"No," said his grandson, unsure if Grandpa was kidding or not. Kip had been duped before — that time it was cow tipping, so now he was rightfully dubious of anything anyone told him.

"They're delicious. Especially the brains," continued Chuck.

His grandson was even more unsure.

"I used to hunt them as a kid before school, drop them off at home and race to school usually a little late. I brought my gun with me in case I saw anything on the way to school or after school. I'd hang it up in the back of the schoolroom. All the kids did."

Kip was sure Grandpa was pulling his leg—a gun to school? Unheard of today.

"Mom would skin 'em and cook 'em for supper. She always gave me the brains, the choice part, a delicacy, because I had shot it. There's another one—shoot it!"

Kip hesitated. I smiled and suggested to Kip, "Why don't you ask your grandfather when he last had squirrel?"

Kip dutifully complied. "Grandpa, when's the last time you had squirrel's brains?"

Chuck considered this. "Ohhhhh. About 1950."

I smiled at his grandson. He understood—maybe not that delicious if one has not had it in fifty-something years.

(Chuck's and my neighbor made squirrel for us several years later. Tastes like chicken. Except the brains. Chuck made sure I tasted the brains, the choicest part. I bit down, not thinking. Once I got used to the texture—pâté—they tasted fine; like whatever seasoning was put in. What were they like? Haven't had them since.)

* * *

About a year later, Chuck spoke at Kip's graduation. Then we took Kip, any Yeager family that showed up, and Kip's girlfriend out to lunch. Kip drank a gallon of coffee. The drill sergeant was unreasonable; he would not allow them coffee, water, or food for hours and hours. Very unhealthy. One or two of the kids died in the heat, no water, no food. Kip's father, Chuck's son, called the drill sergeant on the carpet. The drill sergeant challenged Chuck's son: "You don't know how to train these kids. You've never been in battle or the military!"

Chuck's son, who had fought in Vietnam and had also received some medals, was one of the advance team waiting until they could smell garlic on the enemy's breath—that close—before they blew up the enemy bridges.

With this background, Chuck's son educated the subpar drill sergeant. That sergeant's eyes got wide and he was speechless. Chuck spoke to the top brass. The next classes were in less danger in training because of these three.

## CHUCK YEAGER-ISM #141: "THE PIGS AREN'T SHOOTING BACK AT YOU."

Chuck and I were huntin' pigs out of a helicopter in Texas. I was the spotter perched in the co-pilot's seat. Bob, an excellent pilot, had flown helicopters in the Vietnam War. Chuck said Bob was so good, Chuck didn't even have to lead the pigs when shooting; Bob was pacing them perfectly. The back door was removed. His feet resting on the skids, Chuck, wearing a harness, leaned out to shoot the pigs. He shot fifty-nine pigs with fifty-five shots in fifty-nine minutes!

I naively exclaimed during a lull, "This is so cool! Just like war."

Chuck replied, "Except the pigs aren't shooting back at you!"

I felt suitably silly, naïve, and chagrined with these two awe-inspiring combat pilots who had been shot at, risked life and limb, and rescued others. Again, I was the source of great amusement for Chuck. Fortunately, they both saw it that way. The pigs Chuck shot fed a lot of poor folks.

## HUNTIN' WITH BARRON HILTON

Chuck hunted ducks and pigs in the winter at Barron's duck huntin' club on Venice Island in the Sacramento Delta, California. For several years running, Chuck and I hunted dove in September and quail and chukker in October at Barron Hilton's ranch, Flying M, in Nevada.

The first few years, I was Chuck's "retriever". Shooting those quail and chukker– they were fast little rascals.

Chuck would shoot the chukker and I'd scamper up the hill and find them better than the huntin' dogs. I was born in the Year of the Dog. (So was Chuck, actually.) The other hunters with dogs noticed, so they'd call out, "Victoria, did you see where my bird went?"

I'd also flush them well-timed.

Once I got comfortable, I hunted as well. I even hit a chukker, which are faster and wilier than quail.

One time, when Chuck and I were huntin' alone with Barron, Chuck had me carry his shotgun. He turned to me and asked, "Is that gun loaded?"

I hesitated—Chuck could read me so well—then replied, "Yes."

He looked at me, knew I hadn't checked it, just took it from him when he handed it to me, trusting him. He tested me. "How do you know?"

Barron, who seemed to have eyes and ears everywhere and also knew I had not checked the gun, was keenly watching and listening, wondering how I was going to handle this one.

I replied, "Because all guns are loaded."

I could see both men unable to hide a slight grin. That was close. Chuck was pleased, especially in front of others, and I think Barron was particularly impressed—he wasn't used to huntin' with women, let alone one who was safe and, well…quick and canny. (Next time, though, I did check the gun!)

* * *

When we hunted dove with Barron, often he would get his limit in the morning or include ours in his limit, so Chuck and I would hunt alone in the afternoon. The first day, Barron suggested we take his dog, Dusty, who we had noticed that morning was still learnin'. Generally, I would pick up Chuck's birds and Dusty would pick up Barron's.

That afternoon, we would shoot a bird and Dusty might decide to go get it. Sometimes, she'd pick it up and then drop it right where she picked it up while wagging her tail. If she did bring it, she'd bring it to about five feet away—out of reach, get bored and wander off. We tried training her a little bit and she got a tiny bit better.

When we got back, after getting our limit, Barron asked us, "How did Dusty do?"

I started to reply, "Pretty good. She could use a little more—"

Barron interrupted me, "Great, I bet. She's a great hunter."

Me: "Yes, sir." I didn't want to be sent to my room without my supper.

* * *

Another time, after shooting our limits, Barron, Chuck, and I dutifully followed Dusty to pick up three of Barron's she had missed.

She couldn't find any of them.

I pointed to where I thought one was, but Dusty wouldn't follow and Barron decided if Dusty couldn't find it, a mere human, especially a female one, couldn't either.

He said, "Let's go." Chuck and he walked towards the car with their dove.

I stayed behind, found all three, and caught up to the guys at the car. By the time I arrived, they had unlimbered their guns, as Chuck would say, and placed the dove they had in the car.

I took out one dove, to Barron's astonishment. Then, the second. Then, the third.

His eyes grew wide, wider, widest. Chuck knew me, so wasn't surprised at all but thought it hilarious and delighted in my success.

I merely said, "Found 'em," and smiled.

So, when we went out the following morning, Barron, having lost sight of where one of his birds had dropped, yelled to me, "Victoria, did you see where that bird dropped?"

Several times, I could answer him accurately. One time, I had to tell him I was sorry, but I was watching Chuck's bird drop.

Sometimes, Dusty would grab Chuck's bird and bring it back to Barron. We thought that was fine because Barron would "limit out" and we could keep huntin'.

One evening at supper, Chuck told Barron, "I'm going to get a piece of raw meat and, every time I shoot a bird, throw the meat out for Dusty so Victoria can get to my bird first!"

Barron chuckled.

One time, unbelievably, I had gotten to Barron's bird before Dusty. As I picked it up, I heard, as TV production crews called it, the "Voice of God" (voice out of nowhere)—"Put the bird down!" It was Barron. He was serious, so I dropped it like a hot potato for Dusty to pick up.

* * *

The new cook at Barron's ranch was not good. I thought, 'All that money and he can't find someone to cook delicious, healthy food?' Fortunately, Chuck, a great chef, told her how to cook the dove and quail; wrap the breast in bacon. For the first time, all the guests enjoyed the dove and quail and ate it all.

Heavy hors d'oeuvres were at the bar at 6 p.m. Having had nothing since lunch at noon, which finished by 1 p.m. at the latest, we all gorged. Dinner (which was superfluous then) was always 7 p.m. and we usually finished by 8 p.m. Chuck would look at his watch and say, "Barron, it's 8 o'clock," and the three of us would get up to go; Barron to his room, Chuck and I to our cabin. The rest would stay and drink late into the night.

## HUNTIN' TAHR: *2009*

I had won a raffle, huntin' in New Zealand. I was excited that we had a free trip to New Zealand for two. Chuck educated me, "Oh no, you don't. You have to pay for airfare." The raffle was merely the hunt, transfers to and from the New Zealand airport, lodging, food during the hunt, and the guide. It didn't include getting to New Zealand, trophy fees, shipping, etc.

Chuck had already culled many tahr in New Zealand. The New Zealand government had been considering eradicating the tahr because they weren't native, weren't good eatin', and ate all the feed for the farmers' sheep. The hunting community told the government and farmers, we'll make it profitable to keep the tahr by selling hunting trips and at the end of the season, we'll manage the numbers of tahr.

I almost gave the hunt away because I had never hunted big game before. I had only watched Chuck hunt. He was so good; he killed it instantly on the first shot.

I eventually decided to go. Chuck's response was, "I didn't leave nothin' there," so I went on my own. I was a little nervous. I was good at target practice with Chuck, but this was my first large animal and my concern was wounding it, not killing it instantly as Chuck did. I told Chuck, "I may not shoot." Chuck said, "You have a good shot and you don't take it, that's just fine."

He sure knew how to take the pressure off.

At the conservation and hunting convention, Chuck had told the guide, "No add-ons." I didn't know what that meant but figured it out after I successfully culled a tahr. The excitement of success tends to inspire one to want to cull more and add on more animals to shoot, which can get expensive.

I shot the tahr, killed it instantly, although I thought I had merely wounded it and frantically, desperately cried, "Shoot it again!" The guide said, "I can't! You have the gun!"

We called Chuck the moment we got to a phone. Chuck was quite pleased or relieved. Perhaps more pleased because I was pleased.

## OUR FIRST TIME HUNTIN' IN AFRICA: *2010*

We were often asked if this was General Yeager's first time in Africa. His usual response was, "Other than bombing Libya, yes." (Yeager won top individual honors and led teams to victories at gunnery meets in Libya in the 1950s.)

Our first morning in South Africa, we were whisked away to an hour outside Cape Town. Only an hour and you had the most beautiful open fields running up the side of the mountains. It was raining, but our PH (Professional Hunter—guide) had thought of everything, including bringing proper huntin' raincoats for us.

We had some coffee and tea at the lodge—and then set off to sight in the gun. Chuck shot a couple of times at the paper target set one hundred meters away. Right in the sweet spot. Then he got a feel for the sticks as a rest.

My turn. I shot one shot—is it on the target? Cirdri said yes. Then I shot a second time. Cirdri walked out to check the shots.

As he walked back, he said: "You've shot before."

I nodded. "A couple times." (And I do mean only a couple of times!)

My second shot nicked the hole of the first shot, about an inch to the right of the bullseye. As luck would have it, as good as my teacher, General Yeager, that time. Everyone was so surprised that they forgot to give me a chance to get a feel for the sticks (essentially a tripod with a sling holding the three legs together).

Chuck, who is a far better shot, especially when it counts, smiled—again proud of his protégé.

We ditched the open-air game viewing truck for the enclosed, warm one. We saw springbok, red hartebeest, wildebeest, and bontebok.

A lynx! The truck stopped. Chuck told me to go, so I jumped out and followed the tracker and PH. I wasn't sure I wanted to shoot. I sure wasn't sure I wanted to shoot a lynx, pretty cat. I was thinking all this as we tracked this creature.

Really, when you see a lynx, you'd best be ready to shoot! Otherwise, it's long gone in a matter of seconds. The PH started telling me how much havoc a lynx wreaks on livestock—they kill a lamb a day.

Oh. Alrighty then. Where's that gun and where's that lynx? The tracker checked a few potential hiding spots. No go. We went back to the truck and drove a bit farther.

A few Bontebok weren't too far away. Bontebok are unique to not only this area of the world but also this area of South Africa. Chuck told me to go shoot.

Oh dear. What if it runs before I've set up? What if I miss? Worse—what if I merely wound it?

The PH set up the sticks. These had a sling between the sticks. I put the gun on it and it moved too easily—wasn't steady. The PH told me which animal to shoot. As the gun barrel moved around on that sling, I tried to gauge when it would come around to the right spot on the animal.

Squeeze…thwack! I hit it. But where?

PH: "He's hit."

Got him in one. Phew. We walked up to the Bontebok, an older male who had seen his share of fights, definitely about to start dying of wasting disease. A mercy shot. While he was the one they wanted culled, it turned out he was also one for the record books. I silently said a prayer of thanks over him.

Chuck and I took some photos. He was rather impressed. Frankly, so was I.

We then drove to the neighboring concession and picked up the concession manager, Steve. He's been the conservationist there for 26 years. Loves his work. A knowledgeable, kind, gentle man.

We couldn't get close to any of the animals.

The wildebeest were pretty funny—called the clowns of the Cape. They will hightail it in one direction, perhaps away from you, then turn around and head straight back at you.

It was fascinating to see all these beautiful animals, red hartebeest, springbok, and an impala that had an identity crisis as it was the only one in a herd of springbok. There were many, many young ones. Sooo cute. The fastest animals in South Africa—they leapt and ran—and leapt—over nothing in particular.

Lots of birds, red-winged blackbirds, plovers, eagles, blue cranes…

Lots of flowers—blue, purple, yellow, the national flower, which looks a bit like thistle, but its stem and leaves are very, very soft. Another plant looked like small cotton—and was also very soft. Loved those flowers.

Towards the end of the day, we were headed home when the PH got me out of the truck to stalk a male springbok in the next draw (or dam for a reservoir). We crouched down and scuddled over rocks, almost tripping a few times.

And then we crawled behind a mound and inched our way up. There was not one, but SEVEN bucks. All lying down. Can't shoot them.

We tried to set up for when they might get up and walk out of the draw. But we daren't risk standing up with the sticks. Cirdri put the gun's legs down—still not tall enough. So he put a camera cover under one leg and a binocular under the other and held them. I held steady on where I hoped they would walk out.

Cirdri said: "They know something's up. But they'll walk up to the ridge and stop."

After all this, again, I hoped I could get a good shot off—one that killed the springbok instantly.

The springbok started trotting up the hill. I waited. They weren't moving fast. I considered a shot on the run. I considered standing up and trying freehand—I knew what to do in theory.

I decided I'd just wait. None of the seven ever stopped, so as they started disappearing into the brush, I decided not to take a shot. The PH was disappointed (that there was no good shot) and agreed General Yeager had taught me well.

Then it was Chuck's turn. He hiked a bit downwind of some hartebeest. The game manager told him which one needed to be culled. Chuck set up and shot. Thwack! The hartebeest was killed instantly. No overanalyzing like his wife! Just get the job done.

We loaded it up and set out again. On the way back to leave this ranch, we saw some springbok. While Chuck was setting up, the springbok took off. Chuck shot one on the run at 300 yards. Actually, he shot it when it leapt on the run—the only time we could see it through the tall grass. Again. Perfect shot. Due to the tall grass, we couldn't see where it landed. The PH and I moved in that direction.

The PH is a lot taller, giving him a better view for finding game. I have a pretty good eye for where game is headed and this day was no different. At a certain point, we thought we'd lost it, so we started walking in concentric circles. On the first turn…there it was.

We had three animals—lots of food for the local tribes. They were pleased. And we took animals that would have died of wasting disease or starvation or being kicked out of the herd or killed by a younger bull. So the game manager was pleased, too.

## CULLING ANIMALS — MEAT FOR LOCAL SCHOOLCHILDREN: *Namibia, Africa 2013*

I felt a little hand in mine. I looked down. It belonged to a five-year-old child, beautiful black skin, wearing a colorful red sweater and orange hat with curlicue hair. She wasn't letting go. She wanted to say hello to Chuck and thank him.

She wanted a photo. But wouldn't give me back my hand to take it. She eventually let go and took Chuck's hand, hoping Chuck might take her home with us. Her little boyfriend in yellow and blue came up to join us as we all watched the pot (which did boil) full of the meat from the very large blue wildebeest Chuck had shot the day before.

The government of Namibia gives schoolchildren maize daily. Meat is a treat.

We talked to the older kids. They danced and sang for us—in beautiful harmony. We thanked them.

Then lunch for younger kids was first: Chuck Yeager's wildebeest went a looooooong way! The teacher at the school was thrilled to meet General Chuck Yeager and get her picture taken with him. We were, too.

We've donated books and a DVD documentary to the school libraries in Namibia. The principal told us of some of the successes and some of the challenges.

We enjoyed our visit; eventually taking leave to go hunt some more meat for the kids.

## BABY ELAND—LESS THAN A WEEK OLD:
*Namibia 2013*

We went back to the watering hole where we had seen so many birds early in the morning. It was after 9 a.m., so most of the birds were gone.

However, we were rewarded with a beautiful sight. A little eland—less than a week old. So young, it already had been taught by its mom what to do about potential predators.

It stood stock still with its knock knees. We watched him watching us, watching him watching us, watching him…

Eventually, his A.D.D. kicked in faster than ours and he just turned his head slightly and looked at his mom—What now, Mom? I can't remember. Can I eat and play?

We looked where he looked. Mom was partially covered under the shade of the voluminous bush/tree. Being beige/gray, she blended in easily with the background. Until her baby gave her away.

Mom decided since they were now exposed, they'd better go. She trotted away from us with her front flap flapping, keeping her cool. Some signal we couldn't see was conveyed. Baby followed her immediately. All legs; not quite sure about this trotting thing.

Beautiful as they trotted off into the sun. (Just like the deer on our property at home.)

## SOUTH AFRICA: *2013*

In South Africa, we went to a game park and were driven around with others for a few hours looking at African animals, including a honey badger ultimately, surprisingly successfully, defending itself against a lion. Thirsty, we headed towards the restaurant/bar for refreshments. On the way, the jeep driver stopped at a vacant watering hole except for two hornless rhinoceros who left within a few minutes. The driver dove into an extremely lengthy sermon against poachers and needing money. The area is enclosed, so how did the poachers get in?

I had forgotten Chuck's hearing aids so happily he could not hear a thing the driver was saying and could observe the rhinos, watering hole, foliage, and nature in peace. It was times like this that I could see the silver lining in Chuck's hearing loss. The driver kept addressing Chuck, who ignored him. Finally, the driver gave up, mistakenly and naively thinking that Chuck wasn't all there. Although I suppose, in a sense, he wasn't; he was mentally 50-100 yards away with the rhinos, as were most of us in the truck. The rest of us just didn't have the volume control required to completely tune out the driver.

As we approached the bar, there were several other trucks and tourists and employees milling about. In one truck, though, was a couple going at it. Everyone's attention was focused on them when suddenly Chuck yelled out, "GET A ROOM!"

That stunned the driver—clearly this "elderly man" was very with it, including expressions and humor.

The rest of us burst out laughing.

## MISSED! OR DID HE?

We drove to Stonewall for the West Virginia Governor's One-Shot Doe hunt. A West Virginia Natural Resources Police captain picked us up there and took us to sight in the gun. General Yeager examined the new rifle, sat down, aimed and shot. No one could see the bullet hole. He had missed!

General Yeager, matter-of-factly: "No, I didn't."

Everyone was looking at the target at one hundred yards. He had shot at the two-hundred-yard target.

Governor Joe shot and hit three-quarters of an inch to the right of the bullseye of the lefthand one-hundred-yard target. General Yeager shot at the same lefthand one-hundred-yard target and hit a half inch to the left of the bullseye.

The Governor shot again—at the righthand target. About two inches high and two inches wide.

They asked General Yeager to shoot at a fresh target—for the auction. He hit next to the bullseye again.

I asked for the target with the two shots—and showed it to Chuck—his shot being closer to the bullseye.

Chuck smiled and said, "Second guy doesn't have a chance!" (Chuck YEAGER-ism #142.) (Subtle joke as in since I got the target, I identified the best shot as Chuck's).

## PART VIII

## FLYING

## HEARING WAIVER

Once, Chuck had to do a flight test for a hearing loss waiver. The examiner, Richard Conte, called to set it up. I answered the phone and detected a slight accent in his deep, booming voice. He was from Haiti; his accent was Caribbean French. I was a little concerned that Chuck might have trouble with the accent as I gave Chuck the phone.

The two talked for a little bit and arranged the flight.

Chuck flew down to Sacramento International in a taildragger. Richard got in and away they went. When they returned and got out, Richard handed Chuck the already filled-out waiver.

Chuck was astonished. "You had it already filled out?"

Richard replied, "You understood everything I said on the phone. What's the difference?"

## BIG ISLAND, HAWAII: *2001*

A friend offered us his condo and jeep on the big island of Hawaii as a thank-you for a charity appearance.

On the plane, some friends boarded. The wife was ecstatic that Chuck was on board—she felt we'd all be safe now; as though there would be time for him to run up to the cockpit and take over if there were any problems. We met them for dinner several times at various restaurants for the lofty goal of determining which one had the best chocolate souffle. Superb mission. Great fun. And delicious.

I wanted to take a tourist helicopter flight. Chuck, not fond of helicopters and less so of most helicopter pilots who hung out in the dead man's curve, reluctantly came along. We were seated together in the left front seat. The helicopter pilot, a Vietnam vet, took off and tilted down. I was not comfortable—we were staring straight at the ground instead of the horizon. Tony in Alaska never took off like that, neither did Bob in

Texas—the two helicopter pilots Chuck trusted.

After we landed on the other side of the island, Chuck, every bit the General, got out and waved to the pilot, "Come here, Son." General Yeager took him behind the building (proverbial "woodshed"). I think I heard thwack thwack. Maybe verbally. Whichever it was, it hit the mark because our next takeoff was much smoother without the dangerous tilting down.

About six years later, we met the owner of that company. I started to mention the incident. The owner said, "Yes, we heard about that. He's no longer with the company." End of that story.

The only way to impress Chuck when flying was to be safe. Period. Chuck YEAGER-ism #83: "There's nothing you can do with an airplane that hasn't been done before, including a smokin' hole in the ground."

\* \* \*

On one of our hikes along the small cliff around the beach, we also ran into a football coach from Penn State whom Chuck knew. He invited us to their beach party that evening. Nike had invited the top thirty college football coaches for a week of fun.

Free food. That's where you can often find me. We went by, got some food, sat down and listened to the karaoke they had set up. They kept urging Chuck to participate. He declined while he was eating. Eventually, he agreed. He and another guy sang "American Pie." Fortunately, Chuck had a beautiful, melodic, deep voice. I was standing next to Phil Knight, CEO of Nike at the time. He, thoroughly enjoying watching Chuck, turned to me. "You're invited to all and any of our events here."

I responded, "We don't have the right shoes!"

Phil laughed. "We can take care of that."

After Chuck finished, we learned that the karaoke machine was broken, so no words were showing the entire song, just music. In other words, Chuck had sung that long song marvelously from memory! Wow. Talk about singing for one's supper!

## CHUCK YEAGER TEACHES VICTORIA TO FLY FORMATION: *July 4, 2002*

I learned to fly formation with Chuck Yeager before I learned to land.

One just never knows when one will be called on to fly formation…

Although, in all those '70s airplane disaster movies, I don't remember in the ensuing panic on the plane in distress, anyone ever yelling: "Can anyone fly formation?" It was always: "Is there a doctor?" or "Can anyone fly the plane to land it?"

We had been invited to a huge July 4th party in 2002 on Lake "Owl Manure." My imagination ran wild as to why that name. Chuck shook his head, greatly amused by me. Again. And he spelled it for me: Lake Almanor. Oh.

Four people were going, so we flew in two small two-seater airplanes. Chuck thought it a good idea to use this flight to start teaching me to fly formation.

After Chuck and I took off first, Chuck "jumped" our friend who had taken off second (which was always just…so cool!) and we flew our friend's wing.

Before handing me the stick, Chuck set us up in perfect formation on our friend's wing about five to ten yards away and instructed: "Now, keep the wingtip lined up with the spinner."

All I had to do was just hold the airplane where he had set it up in relation to the other plane. Mmm-hmm.

I did. However, apparently there was a catch.

Chuck exclaimed: "You're getting out of position!"

Me: "No, I'm not. I've got the wingtip lined up on the spinner."

Chuck: "Yeah, but you're five MILES out."

If I had been more savvy, I would have covered: "He gave the signal to spread out." (That signal is moving one's airplane's tail back and forth.)

But the truth was, at five to ten yards, not very close for an experienced formation pilot like Chuck, was very tight for a newbie—which I was…even though I knew Chuck was on top of it—he would have grabbed the stick if I had headed toward danger.

Chuck set me up again. This time, I stayed pretty tight, but altitude maintenance became an issue:

Me: "Gosh. I wish he'd fly straight and level. He's all over the place!" (meaning constant altitude changes). (The lead pilot had never flown formation either.)

Chuck replied: "*He's* not."

Of course, it was me overreacting to the lead's slight changes.

I slowly got the hang of it; even small corrections—a bit like sailboat racing, which I grew up doing—can be huge. (Ultimately, others, including Chuck, said I became a very good formation pilot leading or on the wing.)

## FLYING IN A P-51 WITH CHUCK YEAGER: *July 2002*

Not long after sitting in the static P-51 display, I got to fly with Chuck in a P-51 for the first time. Soooo lucky!

We took off on a guy's wing with permission. That guy was fairly scared, though—he kept looking at us instead of ahead.

Up in the sky—here I was, sitting behind Chuck Yeager in a P-51. How cool is that?

He did one positive G (gravity) roll. I watched his head framed by the sky, the scattered clouds amidst the blue sky, the ground and the blue sky with puffy clouds. WOW!

We flew some more, explored some more. Dodged clouds. I imagined we were flying escort to Germany. And then he did another positive G roll. Quadruple wow! Oh boy! I fantasized we were dodging Germans in a dogfight.

Along the way, Chuck gave me a lesson re clouds and turbulence.

We came in for a landing. I still cannot believe it. Over too quickly. It was so exciting!

I don't think I slept for a week. While visions of P-51s danced in my head.

## CHUCK YEAGER-ISM #143: "JUST FLY YOUR AIRPLANE: MAKE YOUR AIRPLANE GO WHERE YOU WANT IT TO GO."

The ATIS (Automatic Terminal Information Service), AWOS (Automated Weather Observing Systems) or windsock—"That's yesterday's news. Just fly your airplane."

When I was getting lessons from a licensed CFI (certified flight instructor) required for a private pilot's license, I never got any crosswind training. I got lots of verbal instruction, but we never found good crosswinds with which to practice.

The verbal instructions had me skittish.

One CFI, stunned that the crosswind didn't seem to worry me, said, "Do you realize you just landed with a crosswind? I sat back; you didn't seem concerned, so I let you just do it."

Oddly, that CFI called attention to it, gave me verbal instruction, defined it, and, you guessed it, made me skittish.

On one wheel?

AAAAAAAAHHHHH!

Could flip?

AAAAAAAHHHHH!

Could ground loop?

AAAAAAAAHHHHH!

And by the way: What is a ground loop? (It's when your plane swings around so it's going in the opposite direction—sometimes catching a wing tip or prop, which can be very expensive.)

A BIG flip?

AAAAAAAAHHHHH!

So, if there was any crosswind, I didn't fly.

Finally, I got the final word from Chuck Yeager.

"Just fly your airplane."

and

"Make your airplane go where you want it to."

I threw away the mechanical verbal instructions from the CFIs—if the wind picks up your wing from the left, put in left aileron. Well, that takes too long to think through, act, and be safe.

Chuck Yeager's wisdom is for those who know how to do coordinated turns and have the basics.

I just started flying my airplane, making it go where I wanted it to, and, for a time, I was doing landings in 40 degrees off the nose, 12 kt crosswinds. And frankly, I didn't consciously notice.

I just flew my airplane, made it go where I wanted, landed and…oh.

I'm here.

And then took off again.

I kept it straight for landing and, before now, was afraid I might not know what to do if I landed on one wheel. Well, it happened; I just "flew my airplane" and naturally, eventually, put the wheel down.

Fun!

I flew with a variety of CFIs. Several of our friends had private planes and pilots who were CFIs.

One time, coming in for a landing, I kept being indecisive. Take the controls. No, I'm fine. Take the controls. The CFI was screaming in the front—wanting me to have an authentic experience of what could happen if I needed to take the controls and land the plane from the back seat. The problem was I suddenly had to go to the ladies' room. I found when I was concentrating, I was fine. But then I was worried I wasn't concentrating enough on holding it. After we landed and were safely rolling out, I explained my predicament. The CFI burst out laughing.

Another time, I had overcompensated turning base to final, expected the CFI to correct it, but he didn't, so I had to do so and, in realizing this, exclaimed, "Oh!" After we landed and put the plane to bed, the CFI said to me: "'Oh' is okay. 'Oh sh--' is not."

So many different CFIs with so many different ways of how to fly and land.

Another said we would flip on our back at altitude so he could show me what to do if that were to happen when I'm alone so I wouldn't be scared.

General Yeager, quite rightly, nixed that crazy idea.

The same CFI had me diving straight at the ground from altitude. Just before, he said, "We're going to do something very scary, but I want you to get used to it so you're not scared in case it happens when you're on your own." We did it. The guy asked if I was scared. I said, "No." He attributed it to my being used to flying with Chuck Yeager.

Chuck got rid of him.

Another showed me what it was like to go careening down the runway tilted high on one wheel. It was frightening.

Chuck got rid of him, too. We had to be very careful—some CFIs were trying to show off for General Yeager, which antics would have put me in danger.

Another said I'd have a trick of the eye landing at night. I didn't. I, or rather my plane, was about to kiss the ground when the CFI screamed. I lifted up, afraid I was about to hit something he saw and I didn't. No, it was the CFI whose eyesight was having a trick of the eye.

CFIs can make things so complicated.

Finally, after several years of ad hoc lessons, no license, and frankly, Martha King (King Schools) asking me every time I saw her if I had gotten my license yet, I went to Chuck and said, "I want to learn how to fly and I want you to support me in this." (I thought it would be some kind of stupid if I outlived Chuck Yeager and didn't know how to fly.)

Bless his heart; he did, even though he was concerned; learning to fly is the most dangerous time flying. He nixed the first four or more CFIs. And he was right. They were not safe. One was a kid who said that soon I'd be texting while on final. Next.

But when we finally found one that was somewhat adequate, Chuck came out to every lesson and watched. Thank goodness he was there to answer all my questions the CFI couldn't and to correct the CFI when we were driving home.

Towards the end of my training, nearing the time for the check ride, I was having trouble with short field landings. My very first landing with this CFI had been one of my best ever and a great short-field landing, but it was too good for the CFI, so he sped up my approach speed.

After I finished practicing with the CFI and was still having issues, we landed and taxied in. Chuck said to the CFI, "You have her approach about three to four knots too fast." You could have knocked the CFI over with a feather. To put this in perspective, that's like being one hundred yards from a speeding car saying you were going 63.3 to 64.4 miles an hour instead of 60 mph—impossible to detect if you're outside the vehicle or cockpit and difficult to detect even inside unless you look at the speed indicator.

The CFI, who knew who my husband was, asked me later, "How did he know? He was absolutely right!"

The only response was: "Let me introduce you—this is General Chuck Yeager, greatest aviator who ever lived."

## CHUCK YEAGER-ISM #144: "YES, SIR, BUT I DON'T RECOMMEND IT."

I never got sick flying with Chuck.

Before, I always felt or got sick in small airplanes. Even sometimes when I was the pilot in command when I was 22.

One time was with my father, stepmother, and others. I was the youngest, about 30.

Dad had chartered a plane to present the gift of a stained-glass window for a client to The George School in Rhode Island for their chapel.

I was on the back bench. We were all sharing the Sunday paper. Or they were and, when finished, passed it to me. I was genuinely feeling ill. I carefully took off my pearls and set them aside. I got out the classified and got rid of breakfast. Very quietly. Very proud of myself that it was no big deal. I felt better, had put my pearls back on when my stepmother, who never quite rose to the behavior of elegance, shouted, "Ewww. Tori got sick!"

I did what anyone would do when a silly stepmother draws attention to something one had so quietly handled; I offered her the classifieds and asked if she wanted to read them.

Chuck's squadron mate, Andy, was flying a 414 badly. I grabbed a bag and lost lunch. Chuck started laughing. I was momentarily incensed at his insensitivity to my embarrassment. I quickly realized that his was the best response. Ever. He didn't think I should be embarrassed at all. Just that realization made my body calm down and I was able to regain my composure. That, and there was nothing left in my stomach. What a gift Chuck gave me!

Another time, not long after 9/11, we were flying into New Jersey by private plane but were ordered to stay low, where it was very turbulent. I had just eaten fresh strawberries. And it became quickly apparent that eating them was unnecessary and a waste—they came right back out. At least it was so immediate; they tasted the same.

Chuck just started laughing. This time, so did I, in between getting rid of the strawberries.

For those who don't know, Chuck, the greatest aviator of them all, got sick his first few flights right after he applied for pilot training. But fortunately for him and mankind, he wasn't a quitter. In fact, one time, he showed up to fly and puked in front of his CO (commanding officer), prompting the CO to query, "Can you fly like that?"

Yeager replied: "Yes, Sir, but I don't recommend it." (Chuck YEAGER-ism #144.)

## CHUCK YEAGER-ISM #145: "YOU'RE NOT FIGHTIN' A WAR!"

I was taking my time deliberating whether it was too windy to fly. Clearly, Chuck thought it was too windy for me and was letting me know I didn't *have* to fly that day and merely gave me a hint as to the correct answer; "You're not fightin' a war!" Neither the Eighth Air Force nor any commanding officer was ordering me to do so.

And to the contrary, one day in 2008, Chuck and I planned to fly the rental plane (in which I had finally gotten my pilot's license), but it was swelteringly hot and the bubble canopy didn't help. I told Chuck I wanted to postpone a couple days.

I think he had looked at the closed bubble canopy cooking the seats. He said: "Good!" Then chastised me good-naturedly: "You can't fight a war like this."

Can you imagine during World War II: Oh, I don't think I want to stop the enemy today—it's too hot. I thanked Chuck again for all he has done, so I now have (among other things) the choice not to fly when it's so hot.

## CHUCK YEAGER-ISM #146: "WHEN FLYING, ESPECIALLY VFR, ALWAYS KNOW WHERE YOU WILL LAND IN CASE OF AN EMERGENCY."

*This is a subset of another Chuck YEAGER-ism #17: "Always leave yourself a way out."*

The California 2008 1,100 fires, mostly from lightning strikes, created dangerous, blinding smoke, which delayed my flight training for two to three months. However, one day, before I had my license but had soloed, Chuck and I decided to fly to Willows for lunch, about an hour's flight. Visibility was four miles, exceeding the VFR (visual flight rules) minimum of three miles.

We took off from Nevada County Airport, but as soon as we got up in the air, we could not see the airport or much else, which can be somewhat disorienting…especially in the mountains where just snippets of pictures of the terrain don't look familiar. I was sure glad Chuck was flying.

Even Chuck's response was to return to the airport: "We'll just practice slow flight by the airport and touch and go's. You can practice approaches."

Two days later, the visibility was better—seven miles. We proceeded over the ridge to have lunch at Nancy's at Willows Airport, known for their homemade pies.

After we cleared the ridge and flew into the valley, I looked around, did a personal assessment, and thought, 'Hmmm. I actually feel comfortable even though only seven miles visibility. Now, do I feel comfortable because Chuck

Yeager is flying, or would I feel comfortable on my own? Hmm…Yes, I'd be comfortable flying solo…But why? There was still plenty of smoke and haze.'

As I was trying to figure out why I was comfortable at seven miles visibility and not four, Chuck said, "As soon as we don't see the ground, we're turning back."

OH! That's why.

Uncanny how he knows what I'm thinking. And what a great lesson! He knew at any given moment where he would land if we had engine failure or fire.

Got it.

I passed my check ride with flying colors in part because of learning that.

When we got to Willows, it was so windy that we flew down the runway to the end where Nancy's restaurant was, as Chuck said later, "Pacing the police car driving on the taxiway." Just as I thought we'd gone too far; if I were flying, I'd have to commence a go-around; Chuck landed almost like a helicopter. So lucky to have so many experiences flying with Chuck.

## TRIMMING THE PLANE WITH MY FOOT

I'm so grateful Chuck Yeager taught me how to fly. I fly about two to five times a week when I can. I always feel Chuck with me.

I remember when Chuck had me flying from the back seat in a tail dragger and, with my seatbelt on, I couldn't reach the trim with my hand. Aircraft trim holds control surfaces (rudder, elevator, or ailerons) in a specific position, requiring less manual input from the pilot to maintain a desired flight attitude. So, I learned to trim the trim wheel with my foot. At first, I always trimmed too much because I didn't want to have to keep lifting my foot and balancing. Slowly I learned and eventually did pretty well. Sometimes, Chuck took the controls and seriously trimmed it much better, then gave the controls back to me. Whenever he gave me the controls, I didn't need to do anything, including hold onto the stick; he had trimmed it so perfectly. As we flew along and used up fuel, naturally, the plane became lighter and I had to re-trim.

I could also hold altitude and speed even though I couldn't see all the gauges from the back seat. I could see speed, so I figured out if the speed increased, we were descending, and if it decreased, we were ascending. Thus, I tried to keep the speed constant. It was hard to tell altitude changes from looking at the terrain because we generally flew in mountainous terrain.

Lots of people try/tried to compete with Chuck Yeager (to no avail, useless endeavor). I never tried to compete with Chuck—I tried to be as good as I could be, so competed with myself and was inspired by Chuck Yeager. By golly, if Chuck could trim the plane perfectly, I would try to do so as well. I quickly learned tiny adjustments were required and took a little more, no, a lot more, patience. And with my foot! Like Fred Astaire getting all the kudos, but Ginger Rogers was dancing backwards and in heels!

## CHUCK YEAGER: "PUT ME ON FINAL AT NEVADA COUNTY AIRPORT."

The Sierra Buttes, the smallest mountain range in the world, are a great landmark—rising out of nowhere on the valley floor. Chuck's squadron and he used it a lot heading back to Oroville AB (air base, now a civilian airport) when he was training for war and where he met the original Glamorous Glennis. The Buttes were especially good in inclement weather and at night.

Another time, eight years before I got my license, we were in Reedley, California, heading home from a visit with his friends, the Kevorkians. (since 1963).

He said, "Put me on final at Nevada County Airport," handed me the controls perfectly trimmed, and promptly fell asleep.

I wasn't too worried; I knew if the plane jerked or moved too much, he would be awake and on the controls.

I could sit up and glance over his shoulder now and again and could see the compass.

About one hour twenty minutes later, we were near Auburn. Chuck woke up, looked at the instruments and where we were and said, "Wow. You hold altitude and direction better than I do." (I think he was really just thinking out loud.)

His competitive nature took over and he said, "I'll take it from here."

From behind him, I said, "Just a minute," as I unpeeled my very stiff, tense fingers, one by one, off the control stick.

And another time, he gave me the controls and said, "Put me on final at Nevada County." I did, but we were below the runway (canyon). Well, in my defense, he didn't say what altitude.

He grabbed the controls and quickly sped us up to a safe altitude to approach the runway and land.

Another time, we were flying to visit Jerry in Sierraville, just over the High Sierra ridges.

I remember the first time it was a little—no, it was a lot—bumpy. I had the controls in the back seat and we were going over some of the High Sierra. We were bouncing all over the place. It had my attention. I noticed Chuck wasn't concerned in the least, wasn't grabbing the controls, so I held on and kept us straight and level—every time the wind tried to pick us up, I straightened it.

When we came out on the other side, it was smooth again; talk about confidence-building.

Looking back, I think Chuck was testing me again—seeing if I panicked or…Yet, when he said he'd take the controls so we could buzz Jerry et al. to let them know to pick us up at the deserted airport and to do the landing, I said, "Just a minute," as again I peeled my fingers off the stick and shook them out. Whew.

I gladly did some horseback riding into the hills while Chuck and Jerry visited.

After our visit, Chuck did the takeoff and then did a spiral to the opening in the clouds to get out on top. There is no one else in the world with whom I would have flown that day or trusted to get us through. There's a bad nickname for that: Sucker hole. Very few pilots understand weather and often get caught trying to fly VFR through a hole in the clouds.

One time, flying back from Barron Hilton's, just as we were coming into view of the south side of Lake Tahoe, we dropped precipitously a colossal amount. Thank goodness Chuck was at the controls. He did not react; we just dropped and kept going.

About 10 minutes later, he said, "Well, that was quite a drop."

I said, "About how much of a drop?"

He replied, "Oh—about 10 feet."

That's a whole story in a little plane.

"Wow" was the only extensive vocabulary that came to mind.

## FORMATION FLYING LESSONS IN P-51: *Fall 2004*

The P-51 Chuck often flew lived on the East Coast and the owner and his keepers, extremely dishonorable, were not good at keeping up maintenance. I endeavored to find a P-51 near us.

At the local airport air show, there were five P-51s. I told the first person I approached I was there picking up Chuck Yeager and would he like to meet Chuck Yeager.

The P-51 owner, clearly skeptical, said, "Chuck Yeager? Sure."

Chuck landed Barron Hilton's aircraft and got out, as did the others. I said hello to all, including fellow West Virginian and basketball great, Jerry West. After we got Chuck's bag and his frozen fish, I asked if Chuck would like to meet the owner of a P-51.

Chuck was curious. "Sure." Then he was very observant.

The owner and Chuck chatted as the owner showed Chuck the airplane. As we were leaving, the owner asked Chuck if he would like to fly the P-51; the owner could fly it up to where we were. Chuck said, "We'll see." I held my breath and my tongue, thinking, "Whaaa —? What did he see that I didn't?"

Then, "No, we'll drive down to you."

I breathed, stunned, but still kept quiet. That drive was a four-and-a-half-hour drive versus a forty-minute drive to this airport.

Before we went to the owner's place, Chuck had not flown a P-51 in a year, so he went to a commercial civilian instructor pilot to get checked out. This is why all the maintainers thought the world of Chuck Yeager. He never jumped in a plane he had never flown before without asking the crew chief or former pilot to check him out. He did this even if the new plane was the exact same year, make and model of the plane he had flown just an hour before.

As usual, his landing was like butter and he taught the outfit a thing or two. When they struggled to find something, they could only think of one thing: engine longevity. Chuck explained what they did in the war and why. Oh. And that was that.

Later, by telephone, we arranged a time and day.

As we drove down, I said, "If he offers to have me fly with you, please don't say no!"

Chuck: "You arranged this so you could fly with me in a P-51 again?"

Me: "Busted. Of course." I smiled. "Wellllllllll, that was part of it."

A few weeks later, we drove down, spent a night in a hotel and were ready the following morning. Chuck inspected the hangar. The lightbulb went off. Chuck wanted to see the P-51 owner's maintenance and plane environment. The hangar was spotless, organized. The owner was clearly someone who took taking care of his planes seriously and had enough money to do so.

He offered General Yeager to fly me in his back seat when he flew the P-51. I tried my best stoic look, but inside, I was mentally dancing and yelling, "SAY YES! YAY! Woo hoo!" or some such excited words.

The owner explained he was going to fly his T-28, a friend was going to fly his own P-51; did Chuck mind if they flew his wing?

Chuck sized them up and consented. He asked the owner to check him out in this P-51. After they finished (I listened in discreetly), I got in the backseat, overjoyed. So excited!

We took off and flew over a restricted air base with permission. There were a few stray airplanes not invited, but a bit of a nuisance. Once they were clear and we were past the air base, Chuck educated us all about what to do when we got in a new plane, "Okay, give me some room; I want to test the stall on this plane."

Our wingmen gave us LOTS of room; it almost looked like they were chasing after the other interlopers.

One couldn't tell we were stalling. Chuck said, "This has a clean stall.

Good." Straight, doesn't lean to one side. I often noticed and marveled that Chuck sounded more like Chuck Yeager when he was on the radio flying an aircraft than at any other time. Seriously! Was Chuck Yeager imitating Chuck Yeager?

A few weeks later, the owner asked Chuck to speak at a formation flying clinic at Castle Air Base. We flew formation, us in the P-51, the owner in his Corsair (T-28) and his friend in his P-51.

We hadn't gotten twenty minutes out from the originating airport when we heard a loud pop and the lead airplane, the T-28, started spewing smoke and lots of it.

The T-28 pilot cut his engine, declared an emergency, turned and headed for the fields. There were two perfectly good-looking fields for an emergency landing.

And a road. No wires.

We kept circling and watching over him.

The T-28 landed on the road. But a truck was moving on a crossroad and…barely stopped in time.

As Chuck told it, the T-28 missed the truck by about twelve inches. We wondered why the truck driver had not stopped sooner or reversed.

We continued to circle to make sure the owner was all right and that the citizenry was not going to come out and pitchfork him to death, as they sometimes had done in Germany in World War II.

When we saw that he was okay and help was on the way, he radioed us to continue on and he'd meet us at Castle AFB in another plane later that day. We continued on our course. After we landed at Castle, I asked the friend why he had shot the T-28 down.

The owner arrived sometime later in his modern airplane. They had put the T-28 on a trailer, closed part of the highway and towed it back to the airport from whence we had started that morning. Quite a sight to see for the cars stopped on the highway.

The T-28 owner spoke that evening about what he might have done better, perhaps not cut the engine. Chuck thought he did a good job—safe. He could walk away from the airplane.

When Chuck attended the briefing for the formation flying clinic, those running it obviously did not have military experience and what they did know was allegedly from the Navy. A lot of hand signals, so Chuck gave them a one-finger hand signal, then laughed. Only he could get away with that and have everyone laughing.

In the USAAF (U.S. Army Air Forces) in World War II, no speaking, no hand signals, just signals through the airplane's movement. On March 5, 1944, during World War II, the lead bomber pilot talking over the radio unnecessarily is what alerted the Germans that the bombers were above the clouds near Bordeaux. They came up and shot down several planes, including that of Yeager.

Formation flying nonverbal signals: What certain airplane movements In formation flying mean: Wiggling the tail means spread out. Porpoising means "get in trail". Waggling wings means "get closer". Dipping a wing quickly means "move to the other side" (the side of the dip).

It was great fun.

## BALLOON COMPETITION AT BARRON HILTON'S NEVADA RANCH

At least one weekend a year, Barron would have a balloon competition. Chuck and I flew one morning with Bruno, a very experienced balloonist from Germany. Barron flew in his balloon named Paris.

You got points for throwing your bean bag closest to the flag near the other end of the airfield and then more points for a splash and dash, touching down in one of the little ponds and taking off again for a decent landing on dry land.

This morning, we made it to within 10 feet of the flag. I exclaimed, "No, let's go touch it!" Everyone pooh-poohed me because no one had ever come even remotely this close. Someone threw the very heavy bean bag out –. It landed within five feet of the flag.

Well, doggone it if Barron, for the first and only time in his 50 years of conducting these contests, didn't land right on top of the flag, essentially holding on to it! He was so pleased.

We had to get some points! However, after our successful splash and dash, we ended up in the trees on the other side of the East Walker River.

Chuck and I climbed down the tree per Bruno's instructions while he blew more air into the balloon to lift off and then land in the alfalfa field.

Before lunch, we put branches sticking out of our hair and clothes, walked into lunch and said, "Thanks a lot, Barron! Because you hit the flag, we had to attempt a splash and dash and ended up in the trees!"

A couple times, Barron's balloon ended up across the East Walker River, past the pasture, and up the hill near Black Rock.

The whole glider winner and support group—about one hundred, drove over and hiked up the hill to rescue Barron, his passengers, the balloon and basket (which weighed a ton or more). As we got there, Barron was walking carefully down the very rocky, gravelly hill. Chuck joined him in the truck to go back to the house, while I stayed to help.

A few years later, Barron became ill with a degenerative illness. Chuck and I suggested some supplements and advised him to see a doctor regarding some issues we were the first to observe and quietly mention. It was confirmed. Although 4 years younger than Chuck, and although he said the ranch would be kept in perpetuity with special weekends, he died over a year before Chuck. The ranch was sold. Sadly, an era was over.

## STOP AND GOs—MORE FLYING INSTRUCTION FROM CHUCK YEAGER

I hadn't flown in about a month, so I needed to practice takeoffs and landings. Chuck said he would rate my landings. I did two touch-and-go's and one full-stop landing. After my second touch, I checked the trim and cockpit and took off again. I sorted out my pattern, came in at a nice slow speed, flared well, did a three-point landing by kissing the ground and staying down. I stopped in time to turn off at the first turnoff.

Chuck asked me how I did. He was really asking how I felt I did. I said, "First two not so good, last one just right."

He said, "Your second one was a good three-pointer."

Me: "Until the gust got me."

Chuck smiled. We both knew—I corrected, what's my worry?

# MEXICO

We met Barron in Mexico because while fishing in Chile, Barron had precipitously changed the dates for the fishing trip, so we had to go directly from Chile. The change was due to Socorro's airstrip renovation, so they had to go on the boat to Socorro from Cabo, which would take twenty-two hours at full speed.

We flew to Cabo—it felt like it took days—and spent two extra romantic nights together. It was quite peaceful sitting on the veranda overlooking the expansive ocean.

We met Barron at the boat. I helped Chuck get situated in his cabin. Barron was in such a hurry that they almost took off with me on board. Yikes. I'm fine, but I prefer not to hear all that goes on in male locker rooms. Frankly, Chuck wasn't keen on it either. Each day, Barron would assign a different person to fish with him. Chuck preferred fishing with Barron—the others constantly talked about the stock market, money, and the like, none of which was to the like of Chuck.

Each morning, Chuck would be ready to fish at 6 a.m., knowing full well that the assigned person would not be ready in time. Most of them were there to say they had been on Socorro with Barron Hilton. Chuck was there to fish with his friend Barron.

Invariably, Barron, not known for patience, would ask Chuck to join him instead, and off they'd go. Both were perfectly content to fish in peace and quiet with their own thoughts, enjoying the day. Chuck did try to fish upwind of Barron because Barron usually had a cigar in his mouth. That's also why Chuck liked flying, fishing, or huntin' with me. I also was not a chatterbox while doing those endeavors and I didn't smoke, just peacefully enjoying the outdoors with Chuck.

One year, I asked Barron if I could fly with the group from Los Angeles to Cabo and then back when they returned from the fishing trip.

Barron said fine. A few days later, he confirmed that I was indeed getting off the plane at Cabo and not intending to go fishing with the men's group. Definitely all correct. Even so, Barron was quite relieved when I got in a loaner car, drove off my way, and not to the boat.

I enjoyed four days driving around Cabo myself—learning to surf, going to Margaritaville, having delicious lobster tacos at a local taco stand, and parasailing, where I kept one eye on the beautiful view and one eye on the one tiny little knot that was the only thing keeping me tethered to the boat on an extremely windy day.

I met the group at the airport when it was time to leave. After we dropped everyone off in Van Nuys, Barron, as he was wont to do, asked Chuck if he had made that landing because it was smooth, wherein you almost couldn't tell you had landed. Barron's pilot usually did a clunker landing.

On the last leg of our trip, Chuck put me in the right seat. Barron's pilot had me do the taxiing and the takeoff. Pretty smooth.

It was a pretty clear, smooth day flying from Los Angeles to Sacramento.

Guided by ATC (Air Traffic Control), we ended up right downwind for 16 Right. Sacramento has parallel runways north to south. We were on downwind, turned right base for the right runway. After a few seconds, I asked, "Should we turn final?"

Barron's pilot said, "No, not yet."

There was a United plane on final for the left runway.

I asked again, "Should we turn final?"

Barron's pilot again said, "No, not yet." His head was down—I wasn't sure what he was looking for or at; I was focused on flying and that United airplane.

Thinking gee, we were getting awfully close, I asked one more time, "Shouldn't we turn final? That—"

I was cut off. "No!"

Chuck shouted from the back, "You gonna fly that United 737's wing?"

Well, when Chuck speaks, people, especially pilots, listen. Barron's pilot's head snapped up, saw the United plane and said, "Yes—TURN!"

Interesting, I wasn't nervous. Of course, I wasn't by myself either. We came in, I flared, and flew a little—and clunked down just a little—the last two feet. Not too bad for a first landing in a Citation V.

But I can do better.

Chuck made a joke about our formation flying and my landing. And smiled. "It was a good landing."

With feigned indignation, I retorted, "It was an excellent landing. Barron's pilot can fly it again right now, let alone the next day."

Chuck smiled at me: "You're learnin'." (Chuck YEAGER-ism #152.) And, "Good landing: you can walk away. Excellent landing: you can walk away AND use the plane the next day." (Chuck YEAGER-ism #29.)

Wow! What a thrilling day!

* * *

I'll never forget one time—I thought our wings were going to come off and we were a goner. A pilot—with whom we had flown a dozen times without incident but who, it turns out, had been wildly overstating his experience—was flying us in a private jet to West Virginia when the air became extremely turbulent. The pilot panicked. General Yeager, from the back, was yelling (to be heard) advice: "SLOW DOWN! GET TO A DIFFERENT ALTITUDE!" The pilot could not function.

I made my way to the cockpit and calmly repeated what Chuck was saying. The pilot was belligerent and doing everything wrong but finally followed directions in the nick of time. We made it to safety with Chuck again, saving our lives. Needless to say, Chuck refused to fly with that pilot again.

## VICTORIA & CHUCK YEAGER — FLYING FORMATION TO WILLOWS FOR LUNCH

I had to go to Oroville to drop something off. I was going to take our neighbor, Bill, as promised. Chuck said, "You'll have a lot of extra weight." Chuck then decided to fly the taildragger and take our neighbor's cousin.

Chuck took off first. I asked the guys to turn the rental plane around for us. One of them did but positioned it to perfectly blast everyone in the hangar when I started it.

Bill and I got in.

Bill: "Should I take off my coat?"

Me: "Yes. It will get hot; you'll be nervous with me flying."

We laughed.

I was going through the checklist after starting the engine; the wing was really bouncy and I thought. 'I don't remember it being that windy. Hmm, too windy?'

I looked out—K, who had moved the plane, was trying to get my attention—to move on out since I was blasting everyone.

Bill: "I wondered why he didn't point it on a diagonal."

We taxied on out. Chuck was already in the sky.

I did my checklists out loud, as usual. Bill was an ex-airline and private pilot. His wife hates flying but was a trooper when they owned a Mooney years ago.

Bill sure appreciated my doing the checklist out loud so he could know what was going on.

We took off and Chuck jumped us.

Chuck: "Change freq."

We changed.

Chuck: "Check in."

Me: "Rog!"

He then took the lead for a while. I locked right in. He waggled us to the right. Woo hoo!

Then to the left. Fun!

Then he put me in the lead. Well. I forgot to find out the runway numbers so I called Chuck's backseat pilot to look in their black book.

Bill: "Where is Oroville airport in relation to the lake?"

Me: "West. West of the city."

He was looking for it.

Me: "I have the toughest time finding airports. Usually, I find them when I'm just overhead or on a perfect downwind. Funny."

I pointed to what were probably hangars and said so.

Bill looked: "Ah, yes."

I turned out to be correct. We did have GPS, but we had agreed to practice our dead reckoning—more fun since we were flying VFR.

As we approached Oroville, I heard someone in the pattern was going to land on 3-0. I asked for the runway numbers from him.

I listened to the ASOS (Automated Surface Observing Systems). Winds variable. As I was on a downwind for 120, I chose…120.

Getting onto downwind, Chuck was on my left, so I flipped Chuck to my right.

I realized I hadn't landed at an airport other than Grass Valley in a while. Hmm. Wonder if I'll have to do a go-around.

Bill and I discussed the water near the airport—usually lots of birds. Of course, bird strikes were on every pilot's mind since the Hudson River landing. Everything went right for Sully and his co-pilot did everything right. Had there not been a river handy that was smooth without boats…

Well, I did the checklist, got down low-ish, and had to power on a bit because…you guessed it—we were sinking faster than I was used to with the extra weight. True to form, Chuck had thought ahead, knew the extent of my experience, had alerted me and now I was prepared. (Chuck YEAGER-ism #73: "How can I bust my butt? How can I prevent it?") We leveled off and I kept it off, but those last two inches clunked down on the numbers.

Bill was thrilled. I looked at him and said: "I can do better."

He was stunned: "THAT was great."

I think he would have kissed the ground if he could have.

Me: "Aren't you glad you took off your coat?"

He laughed: "Yes."

It was a beautiful, sunny, clear day. Warm—not too warm, though.

I didn't know if Chuck had landed in formation, but I doubted it—yet needed to know for certain so I could freely turn right (the rental plane has poor visibility to check six, look behind)—just then, he called final again; as usual, reading my mind. I turned right off the runway and called to the guy poised to get on runway 3-0, "Number 2 is landing, Number 1 is clearing, clear the runway."

As we taxied, we were trying to figure out how to get to the buildings when Bill said, "There's a helicopter in there (the hangars to our right) taking off." He had seen it when we were landing. I aspire to be more observant but am still concentrating on landing.

I stopped just as the helicopter flew low out from between the hangars and would have hit us. They called then that they were going across the field and had traffic in sight. They flew just behind the other plane, then lifted up a bit. Unnecessarily close.

I asked them how to get to the buildings—they said follow them.

Bill pointed out flaps. Oops. I needed to stop and clean up the airplane. Flaps up, landing light off. Fuel pump off.

We crossed the runway and followed them. Chuck: "Bob's truck is at 1 o'clock."

I headed to 11 o'clock, where I had been eyeing a truck. I have a dyslexic clock in my head. I explained this challenge to Bill and that Chuck is used to me by now.

After two days flying and fishing with us, even Tony, our helicopter pilot friend, when I called out a bald eagle 9 o'clock, immediately looked to 3 o'clock, and he was correct!

Actually, this time, I got it right, though. Chuck was heading down the taxiway; I was crossing the runway—so his 1 o'clock WAS my 11 o'clock.

Bob was waiting for us with coffee. We went into the office and returned the item we had bought from Bob's store. When Bob gave Chuck the money, Chuck quipped: "Hey, this doesn't cover the airfreight!"

Remember, this is where Chuck was stationed before the war and where he met and spent time with Glennis, his first wife. There were all sorts of photos of Chuck and different airplanes. Also, there was a photo signed to Jimmy Doolittle from Chuck Yeager. VERY cool.

We decided we were hungry, so we planned to go to Nancy's at Willows Airport.

Chuck: "Which runway are you going to use?"

Me: "3-0?"

Chuck: "1-2 and turn right."

Me: "Got it."

Most efficient, except I taxied to the very end of the runway, so not as efficient as it could have been. Bill and I weren't exactly sure how far to taxi. Where we turned, the end of the runway had weeds growing out of the cement. As we were moving past the weeds, before I powered up, I did my checklist—flaps, fuel pump.

Me: "Ready to go?"

Bill: "Yes."

As we passed the threshold, I powered up and we took off.

I led the whole way to Willows. A formidable two-ship. A beautiful day.

Bill called out a plane ahead of us going across the nose (one mile out). No factor.

We looked for the airport. I kept thinking we should see it sooner than we did—but then we were low for that.

Bill: "Probably in that patch of green."

I couldn't figure out..."Oh, you mean that triangle."

Bill: "Yes."

Me: "I think you're right."

I was about to call overhead when we heard another plane call overhead at 2750 feet. I was at TPA (traffic pattern altitude)—1000 feet. So I called in. I couldn't see the other plane.

I called downwind. The other plane asked altitude. I repeated, "One thousand feet." I called downwind, base.

A gal called in—"Left or right traffic?"

Me: "Left traffic."

Gal: "Are you white?"

The other plane: "Yellow."

I responded: "3 Delta Charlie. I am white. My #2 is yellow. I am on base turning final, #2 on downwind."

A collective: "AH. Traffic in sight."

I saw them too—high. VERY high and still about midfield overhead—they had called somewhat early.

This runway is far shorter than Oroville. Would I have to do a go-around—never landed here myself—would be messy with all those bandits (enemies).

Me: "Okay. Fly the airplane."

I focused on the task at hand.

We got down on the numbers. That last two inches—we clunked down. Argh.

Me: "I can do better!"

Bill: "Any landing you can walk away from. ..."

We taxied to the other end, where the restaurant is, and then onto the parking area. We had to pull past some planes. One guy about had a heart attack. I had asked them if I could fit. They said yes. But two feet was too close. I was watching the shadows—we were fine.

We went in to eat.

Chuck asked me why I hadn't pointed out the bandit. Did I see it?

Me: "Yes. Bill saw it. It wasn't a factor."

Bill's cousin raised his eyebrows—he doesn't fly much anymore, so he knows a lot.

Chuck (smiling): "A quarter mile out."

Sometimes he exaggerates with me, but I got his point.

Bill backed me up.

I was looking down to sort out the mixture. I did look up sooner than would have been a problem, but I have to practice that a bit—that triple focus. Chuck was watching me—he saw I got his point. He was having fun with his student. He'd make a great fighter pilot out of me yet.

I had told Bill that seeing airplanes and airports…I still needed some practice. And I had told him no free lunch—if he's flying with me, he's paying attention! He loved it.

After lunch, which wasn't very good, Chuck took off first. Then I did. I put on the power to catch up. Suddenly, I was about to overtake him and FAST. I was wide enough that I wouldn't touch him, just in case I couldn't slow up fast enough.

Me: "Whoa!"

I slowed that baby up—with pitch after pulling back the power. And didn't go past. But it was close. We were flying at sixty-five kts (knots). Our angle of attack or attitude was quite high, but we held flying Chuck's wing. It did take me quite a while to settle in.

Me: "Whoops, too fast, wow, can't quite...hmm."

Me: "Wait! I was looking at my mixture and checklist. Did he flip his wing or was it turbulence? (slight)."

Bill: "I think just turbulence."

I tried to do the mixture. I also tried to get myself to untense my legs on the rudders. When I focused elsewhere, I backed off or up. Then I had to sort myself out again.

Chuck flipped us to the left. Flying on his left is harder for me. Bill was very encouraging.

Me: "He wants my wingtip to be in line with his propeller blade tip. I'm not ready for that."

Bill (perhaps nervously—just kidding): "Just go as close as you are comfortable and practice till you get more comfortable."

Several minutes went by.

Me: "Lots of concentration."

Bill: "Yes."

Me: "Bandit at 12 o'clock!" as a plane flew by high. I wanted to show I was learnin'.

Chuck: "That's a bogey."

Me to Bill: "What's the difference?"

(We learned later—bandit is enemy; bogey is unknown.)

As we got over the ridge, Chuck flipped me to the right. Then he put me in trail and did some lazy s turns. I kept up. Boy was that fun!

The whole time I was chattering:

"Whoa—left side. Weeee. Oops. In trail. Whoops, too fast—gotta swing out a bit. Whoops, now swing to the left…Woo hoo!"

Chuck waggled me in and flipped me to the right. This time, I tried not to power on full and zoom past him.

I was taking some time inching up, so he waggled me in again.

Me (although he couldn't hear me): "I'm coming. I'm coming."

I pointed out Grass Valley airport to Bill. He wasn't familiar with the white line (that's all it looked like at that point).

Chuck had me take the lead. I turned crosswind with Chuck to my left. I flipped him to the right and turned downwind.

On final, we had that lift over the reservoir. We were still low enough I had to power on a bit. We…floated a bit and…the last two inches clunked down and settled in. I kept the plane from sinking on the nose gear. Each of the three landings, we heard the stall warning sound for…ever, it seemed.

We heard Chuck on final.

Guess I should brake to turn here….

We exited the runway, cleaned up the airplane, and taxied on down.

As we were putting the airplane away, Bill's cousin dropped off Chuck.

Chuck said: "You like to do the best you can, don't you?"

Me (using Chuck's expression): "Well, sure! Might as well."

As we were driving home, Bill was telling us his wife was visiting a friend in Southern California with a few girlfriends.

Me: "Whatever she was doing this weekend, we won."

Bill laughed: "That's right. We won."

It was a splendid day. Another fun adventure.

## FLYING A NEW TAILDRAGGER

Chuck and I checked out a new taildragger for a friend. What fun!
Chuck insisted I fly the front seat, with the airplane owner in the back.

He put a stick in the back just in case. The plane had massive tundra tires—I mean, I literally had to climb in like a MAC truck. While the pilot made a personal pit stop, I studied the gauges.

We did some touch and go's and then taxied in to where Chuck was with our other two friends.

Chuck asked the pilot: "Did Victoria do that first landing?"

Pilot: "Yes. Without any help from me." (Gracious and truthful of him.)

Chuck: "I thought so. She heads straight for the numbers, then flares just in time."

Our friend on the ground said: "Yeah, after your perfect three-point landing, Chuck said: 'That's Victoria!'"

Glad I did a good one!

Chuck was pretty happy. So was I.

## Q&A AFTER SPEAKING AT A RENO, NEVADA HIGH SCHOOL

One day, we spoke at a school in Reno. The tenth-to-twelfth graders, some flight students of all ages, teachers, parents, and the community were there. They loved hearing him talk. So do I.

After playing the inspiring documentary of his life and twenty minutes of talking, General Yeager opened it up to questions. That was my cue. I came on stage with him (and, in this case, in front of the room). My job is to repeat the question—or find the question within the statements and repeat that for General Yeager. I also answer some and you'll see why in a minute.

Me: "Any questions?"

The usual silence—no one wants to be first. Too bad because, by the end, they will have a question and we won't have time for all of them.

To inspire the crowd, I said: "You get extra credit if you ask an intelligent question."

A few adult hands rose. They knew the drill. Some of the usual questions: What is your favorite airplane? Which one is the best to fight a war today?

General Yeager: "F-15E."

One from the back: "Did any literature and poetry inspire you?"

I said: "You must be the literature teacher?"

Laughter. Yes, he was. I smiled, knowing the teacher shouldn't ask that sort of question in this sort of setting unless s/he knew the answer would be helpful. And I knew this pending answer would not be beneficial. I repeated the question: "Did any literature and poetry inspire you?"

General Yeager: "Nah."

Laughter.

General Yeager: "I didn't know until the third grade that 'A' didn't mean awful and 'F' didn't mean 'fine.'"

The audience relaxed, realizing it wasn't so bad to ask a question and many hands went up.

One was: "Did you want to be an astronaut?"

General Yeager: "No, I trained all of them."

Someone once told me: "My late husband revered this man. He said that Yeager was asked to man a spacecraft and refused, saying if he could not be the pilot, he would not go."

General Yeager went on to explain about the ARPS (Aeronautical Research Pilot School, the precursor to the test pilot school) and why NASA took over the space program (and probably slowed down the progress).

Then he ended that answer with: "And I didn't want to wipe the monkey crap off the seat before I sat down." (Chuck YEAGER-ism #93.)

I added that General Yeager was an astronaut, having flown above 118,000 feet and seen the curvature of the earth. However, in 1959, the Fédération Aéronautique Internationale, along with Russia and the U.S., decided solely for security purposes that beyond fifty miles was space. The reason for this decision was to declare that each country owns its own air space up to fifty miles. Thus, no one could fly over a country closer than fifty miles without permission from that country. Obviously, fifty miles was an arbitrary number having to do with security and ownership, not the official definition of space.

At one time, in an interview, General Yeager did say: "Sure, I would have liked to sit in a capsule and look at the earth from one hundred and sixty miles away, but I've flown some great airplanes and had a great military career being in the right place at the right time."

Before the next question, I said: "Actually, unless it was the shuttle landing, where you can actually fly the plane, I know General Yeager; he would have been bored sitting in a capsule."

A few more questions, then: "What words of wisdom would you give these kids sitting here today?"

Again, I smiled, knowing the answer would not be what they wanted, as I repeated it for the audience and General Yeager.

General Yeager: "None. No one ever gave me advice about my career. Those who do it on their own are the best." (Chuck YEAGER-ism #22.)

I think the adults were hoping for some wisdom for themselves. I added: "General Yeager always says, figure out something you like to do, and make your lifestyle fit your income. Not the other way around." (Chuck YEAGER-ism #9.)

Another question: "Describe the differences between test work in the early days and today."

General Yeager: "Four people were working on the X-1 once I was flying it: Jack Ridley, outstanding engineer; Dick Frost, who flew chase; Jack Russell, my crew chief, and me. Today, there's a big committee."

I added: "...And congressmen who say you have to put on a gun package you don't need (because it's manufactured in their backyard), and if you don't, I won't vote to finance the military." (True story re the F-22 which Chuck Yeager didn't like and which was outdated by the time it was operational.)

Another question or two...and then I returned to the words of wisdom.

I said: "General Yeager is constantly thinking, 'How can I bust my butt, how can I prevent that?' (Chuck YEAGER-ism #73.) He had to eject fuel from the X-1 or he was landing a bomb. And he only had the electrical system..."

General Yeager grabbed the microphone—I was messing it up. (I do that willingly so that he does take the microphone and tell the story instead of me.)

General Yeager: "If my electrical systems went out, I couldn't eject the fuel. The gear was not stressed for landing with a full load of fuel. So I added a JATO (Jet Assisted Take Off) bottle," (and he explained it—I still can't, but it was a redundancy system to eject the fuel.)

The very next flight, he needed it—the electrical system went out as soon as the X-1 was dropped from the B-29. To test if his backup was working, he stalled the airplane at well over 250 mph or more indicated. Then, a few thousand feet lower, he stalled again; the stall speed was slower. It was working—he was ejecting fuel.

There were more questions—several from students.

I had some more words of wisdom from General Yeager: "During World War II, when others went on leave, they went on a drunken binge in Leiston, Yoxford, or London. General Yeager often stayed behind to practice. He wanted to stay on top of his game to stay alive. Twenty-one of the thirty that went over with General Yeager got shot down or killed. Captain Yeager practiced. General Yeager says. 'The most experienced pilot is the best. They've lived through their mistakes. You aren't born a great pilot.' So practice, practice, practice." (Chuck YEAGER-isms #34 & #32.)

I didn't tell the part that he usually claimed: the main reason was that he was the head of maintenance, so he had to fly all the airplanes to figure out the problems and ensure they were fixed. He wasn't against a little leave time to go party to unwind.

More questions. After General Yeager finished answering questions, we thanked the group for inviting us. They gave another standing ovation; we shook some hands and left the gym-turned-auditorium.

One of the F-86 pilots in General Yeager's wing came up to say hello. We invited him and his friend to join us for lunch.

Delighted.

After lunch, Barron Hilton's pilot landed the Citation to pick up the General and me. The pilot started taxiing till he spied the General ready to guide him to "park" him—giving him hand and arm signals. The signals became rather funny. Finally, General Yeager shook his finger at him to stop, then drew a finger across his throat to signal cut the engine.

I got the copilot seat. Chuck ordered, "Now, no flying Southwest's wing this time!"

Even so, from Reno, the jet ride was a little turbulent, and on final, we were crabbing at a forty-five-degree, sometimes sixty-degree angle. The pilot talked me through his approach and landing.

We were left of the runway and struggling to stay straight down the runway. I've never seen such a crab, especially in a jet. Wow.

"We'll keep the aileron down (as we floated, no, not in a jet, flew! down the runway…)

"Touch down on the right wheel first," (hefty crosswind from the right or west)

"…then left

"…wheel, then nose, keep aileron in. Right?"

(With the approach and touchdown a bit almost too exciting and us touching down at about halfway, all I could think was, 'Whatever you say, Kemosabe.') I don't think I responded out loud—sure didn't want to distract the pilot! And frankly didn't realize he had a question mark until…

And there we were careening down the runway on our "roll out"…reverse thrusters…and brakes…and…do we have enough time to stop…do we have enough power and runway to take off again if we can't stop…oh yeah, it's just desert, the plane may get hurt, but we'll be okay…

We stopped…before the end of the tarmac.

I breathed again and said, "What would you have done if the crosswind had been stronger?"

The pilot burst out laughing. "Holding your breath? I would have tried Yerington or Carson City."

That was something.

In fact, that was pretty darn cool! Learned a LOT. I was grateful to General Yeager, who had let me have the right seat to get more experience and learn. Or maybe so he didn't have to see that landing up front and personal. Just kidding.

The passengers in the back—Chuck included, were…quiet.

However, the next day, Chuck was flying with this pilot to pick up another friend in the same airplane. When we got to the plane, Chuck crawled under the wing to inspect the wheel, tire, and wheel well, under the wing.

I watched. After he crawled back out, I said: "Okay. So I can learn. What are we looking for?"

"Well, it was quite a landing, just checking everything out."

He proceeded to check the other tire, wheel, and wheel well.

No leaks, tires not too worn, no cracks…not sure what else, but he was satisfied it was not only flyable, but it was also safely land-able.

Since the plane could be used the next day, our friend's gusty, strong crosswind landing was not just good; it was…excellent.

## FLYING TO PLACERVILLE ON A RECCE WITH CHUCK YEAGER

I went flying with Chuck to check out Placerville airport. From its publicity—it sounds like a nightmare to land and take off. My instructor from a few years earlier told me to shoot some touch-and-go's there—confident I could do it. I figured I could check it out and didn't have to do any landings if I felt uncomfortable. I had enough fuel to go there and back a few times.

I got on downwind and asked Chuck what he thought about my landing there. It was a bit hot and there was no sign of a restaurant or deli.

Chuck said: "No, it's better practice at Nevada County. But do what you want to." I can't imagine not taking Chuck Yeager's advice, especially when it comes to flying. Nevada County has a canyon on one end of the runway, trees lining one side of the runway, and steel posts closer to the runway to warn you there are big trees—I guess in case you can't see the trees.

But as Chuck asked me one time: "Would you rather land in trees or hit a steel post?"

Since I knew that on their first date, Bob and Colleen Hoover went flying and ended up in a tree and that didn't deter her from marrying him, I picked "trees." (The farmer, who owned the tree, came out with a pitchfork and yelled at them: "Get down from there, you S.O.B.!" I guess he wasn't too happy.)

I thought about landing but decided Chuck was right. We headed back. We could see Folsom Lake, so pointed north/northeast of that.

We got to Nevada County—a bit windy. I longed for Placerville, which had had no wind!

The first landing—wow, what a float. Chuck did that shift-in-his-seat thing that experienced pilots do when another is landing and he might have to take over.

We floated, started to land, ballooned. I thought we had enough lift to just land and seemed to…but suddenly, the lift dropped out, so I put on a little power, but we still did a clunky landing (clunky for me).

Chuck breathed again.

And we took off.

We came around again—junky winds, but again, we got down okay. Took off.

And the last time around, I was grateful. Did I say the winds were junky? So I certainly wasn't greasing it on near the near end of the runway!

On final, as we got close, we got pushed around a little. We eventually landed and taxied in. After shutting down the plane, I remarked that those were definitely not my best landings.

Chuck said: "It's funny," and then hesitated to see if I was ready to hear a critique. I was ready—plane was secured.

Chuck: "You tend to land on the left side of the center line. Concentrate and stay in the center." He's quite right—and I told him so. (And I still do sometimes—if a line weren't there, I'm convinced I'd land right in the center.)

I once did an advanced eye test at the Olympic Village in 1996. Very few people see the center line where it is. Very few see horizontal or vertical lines where they are. I see horizontal lines where they are, but vertical lines—I place them to the left. Hence, in trying to stay on it, I go left a little.

I sure love flying with Chuck!

## BEAUTIFUL, GLORIOUS DAY PLANTING GOLDEN TROUT IN THE HIGH SIERRA

Having traveled all over the world all my life to many beautiful places, I'm often reminded of how magnificent and diverse the United States of America is.

Today, Chuck and I helped plant fish in the High Sierra. We did two of the three flights—each lasting 1.5 to 3,5 hours.

It gave me a feel for when Chuck planted fish in New Mexico so his commanding officer could fish for golden trout after he retired.

We saw rivers pouring over cliffs and…well…infinity lakes. We flew around the lakes, figuring out safe plans of attack and egress flight.

We had to:

Fly over the ridge,

drop down low,

lower one to three of the tanks full of tiny golden trout,

slow waaaaaaaay down just over each lake and,

just at the right moment, press the button that would drop 1000 fry: tiny golden trout,

then immediately pull up or turn to fly down a valley so as not to slam into the side of the mountains.

Sometimes we could turn and watch the little fish reach the lake, glistening little sparklets of white light.

I had visions of little fish screaming as they were dropped from the plane: "WAIT! I'm not evolved! Not a bird yet—no wings! Hey! Aaaaaaaaaah!"

And others screaming: "FREEEEEEEDOM from the bonds of the hatchery…weeeeeee!"

And at the last minute, holding their little noses as they dropped into the lake.

If we missed, we'd have left lots of little golden trout petroglyphs and fossils.

We figured the very few (one-three) left in the tanks in the plane; we could make petites fritures poissons (small fried fish with them—one eats the whole thing, crunchy, tasty, moist)—one of Chuck's favorite dishes from his days near Arcachon, France in the 1950s.

The pilots made it look easy, but this was altitude flying, close to the mountain cliffs, so waves of wind, gaining and losing altitude—as much as 500 to 1000 feet, sometimes with turbulence.

Mono Lake, Half Dome, Tahoe, Emerald Bay, glaciers, John Muir Trail; so many, many lakes tucked away hidden just around or over the ridges. Some were brilliant blue, some dark blue, others light blue, some a combination.

Chuck gave us a running commentary from his years of fishing and huntin' in the High Sierra starting in 1945. Each year, he'd spend thirty days walking across the High Sierra.

One of the most stunning commentaries was Chuck's landing tests of the C-130 on a tiny mesa.

The pilots (who are good pilots) and I were lost in our thoughts, trying to envision landing that huge plane on a postage stamp. And taking off! Even more challenging. The pilots were all wonderful—clearly enjoying their work. They worked well together, were fun and very kind to us.

I flew some—heavier aircraft than I am used to—and much faster—so had to make smaller corrections to stay on top of the direction and altitude.

Sierraville, Downieville, Mammoth…we covered a lot of ground and planted a massive population of fish.

As he looked out at the fish reaching the lake, Chuck observed: "Do you notice all the bears trailing us? Waving for us to come back?"

## LEARNING APPROACH & LANDING WITH CHUCK YEAGER

My first time in this plane. I was in the back seat—General Chuck in the front. We taxied up to the run-up area, did the run-up, waited for the plane that called, "Runway 7 garblegarblegarble."

Ah. There he was, having landed and was…turning off.

General Chuck called, "Taking the active," and taking off as we did so.

The other plane had cleared.

And we were off very quickly.

As soon as we were up, General Chuck gave me the controls. Soon after, he asked: "Where are you going to take us?"

Home. Just wanted to "buzz" our neighbors. One was battling an illness. Me buzzing is like the jets that go by so high they are merely a speck one can only pinpoint by their contrails—I was not comfortable getting low.

We saw our property and their property and headed back.

General Chuck told me to do the approach and follow along lightly on the landing.

Okay.

I called downwind and traffic in sight.

He asked me if I could see the speed.

Yes. I got the hint and slowed down.

I gradually descended as we turned base and final. On turning base, I suggested he take it—I felt a bit off.

By the time he heard me, I had recovered my confidence and continued on. I said to myself, 'What if you had to land it?'

Right. I can do this.

General Chuck put in the flaps for me.

As we got close, I was still afraid I was high and finally said: "Okay, please take it."

He did.

As we got closer, it got bumpy. Boy, did we float.

He landed. Beautiful. Then GUST. I mean, wow!

Chuck immediately put in left aileron, left rudder.

I, on the other hand, was a second behind in thought—a second that can nail you. In that second, I knew I wasn't ready to be signed off on a taildragger. I was still wondering what I would do after I saw General Chuck immediately put the stick to the left, flying the plane, making the plane go where he wanted it to.

And he decided to take off again.

This time he decided to keep the controls. I didn't blame him—it's quite a task to recover from someone else's setup.

We landed—greaser.

And off again. Gen Chuck gave me the controls this time again.

I stayed lower in the pattern. The setup was pretty good.

He took the controls. Again the wind tried to carry us. He patiently waited—flew the airplane, made it go where he wanted and when the wind was right, he greased it on. Again.

One day, I'll be able to do that!

Later, General Chuck said: "Good. That last one was a good pattern."

Smile. Okay; BIG smile.

* * *

One time, as we were about to touch down, the wind picked us up and headed us straight for the trees. I thought, 'I wonder if this is going to hurt?' Chuck had put full aileron and rudder in, to no avail. Chuck then cobbed it (sped up) and we were heading faster towards the trees. I thought, 'Oh, that's not good. That's going to hurt more!'

As pilots would know, Chuck was getting more lift and authority by cobbing it. He calmly brought the plane back to the middle of the runway and greased it on.

About forty-five minutes later, after we had put the airplane to bed and were driving home, Chuck nonchalantly said, "I ran out of aileron."

## FLYING FORMATION AGAIN WITH CHUCK YEAGER

I hadn't flown the solo in almost two months—a different kind of confidence. I dropped Chuck off at his borrowed taildragger airplane and drove on down to my rental plane. I had learned how to save money on an airplane rental—call ATIS (weather) first before you get in the airplane. Winds calm. Not so sure about that. I did the pre-flight, got in, followed the checklist and taxied on out. Comfortable.

At the 2-5 end of the runway, off to the side, there was a fire, so I called in—someone was clearing brush and doing controlled burning. No one was there and it was a pretty high fire—next to the run-up area, so I stayed on the taxiway. When finished, I took the runway and took off. Calm. I mean me. I was scanning more easily and was comfortable. Until—

General Chuck Yeager "jumped" me. Good thing he didn't have any guns and I wasn't the enemy. He was on my wing. Then he motioned for me to fly his wing. He waggled me in. I did. Fun! I didn't get too close because I was still sorting out my speed, getting back used to the plane without the added formation flying. I was fine.

Then he put me in trail and turned left. This was cool. I knew what to do and was doing it.

He then told me to take the lead to do a touch-and-go as they were doing a full stop.

I did as told. Called downwind. Then all heck broke loose. Everyone was in the pattern. Someone called out on a forty-five, then downwind. He eventually mentioned me. Then, EVENTUALLY asked if Chuck's plane was going ahead of him.

Chuck, of course, said: "No, I'll go behind you," and put himself in a position to watch this unsafe pilot. That got my ears up. I turned early so I could see the guy and just did a go-around—I didn't trust him behind me.

## MOUNTAIN FLYING—WHERE'S QUINCY?

Chuck and I flew to Quincy, California, in a rental plane. I had asked about Quincy because the book *The $100 Hamburger* described a restaurant there that seemed almost worth the $100 hamburger. (The reference is the cost of the airplane fuel to get there.)

I had heard high-density altitude and ridges obscuring the runway when you are on downwind. And you have to take off in only one direction, no matter the wind, in order to gain enough altitude to clear the ridges.

I had wanted to go with Chuck first and waited till he got home from his trip. The original plan was to fly formation, but the taildragger was on vacation with its owner.

As usual, I learned a lot. It was mountain flying, hot summer, high-density, and more.

First off, I did a weather briefing on the drive to the airport. The weather briefer was very patient. When I put the Quincy identifier in the GPS, it would not take. After several attempts, motor running, we decided dead reckoning would be fine.

When we got to the run-up area, Chuck asked me: "What heading are you going to use?"

Me: "Without wind, it would be four degrees."

Chuck: "Allllll right."

So we headed north. The weather briefer had said the winds were out of the Northwest. But Chuck (I was in left seat) kept making motions with his hand to indicate the wind was coming from the east and pushing us a bit.

I pointed out the lakes on the map. I should be a bit to the east of that lake. Hmmm.

We had tracking on the GPS, so could see the MOA. Chuck expounded: "It hasn't been active for years."

Oh. I had avoided it a lot.

We had trouble seeing Quincy. Chuck: "We can always go to Lake Almanor (which is north of Quincy). That's easy to see."

Me: "Okay."

We flew a little farther. I showed Chuck the map and where we were.

We flew a little farther.

Chuck: "Well, there's Lake Almanor."

Hmm. Oh! Hint hint is what he was really saying.

Me: "IT IS?"

OH.

I flew a little east and looked over the ridge. Nestled in the mountains was a little town—didn't look like the shape on the chart but close…ish… little ish…

Me: "That looks like it…could be Quincy."

Chuck looked—from his side, he couldn't see the runway I could see. He was questioning.

Me: "Now, if the FAA Chairman had just taken my suggestion and implemented it—how easy it would be if the airport, location and frequency were painted on the airport for me to read."

Chuck: (ever the pragmatist) "Well, she didn't."

Me: "Close enough—I think that's it. We'll try it."

I called in—its official name was Gansner. Now, if that isn't a mouthful! Wonder who Mr. or Ms. Gansner was?

I turned a little steeper and showed Chuck the runway. He felt better re my judgment when he saw there, in fact, was a runway.

We had to lose 6,500 feet of altitude. So we circled down. While doing this, I cautioned Chuck I needed a sterile cockpit while in the pattern.

Chuck: "I won't say ANYTHING."

Me: "Well, no! (Yikes!) I WANT you to please jump in if there's danger or potential danger and I do want your help."

I realized I was still freaked out about the P-51 incident a couple days before (it was on the wrong frequency and was doing a fly-by right at me as I was trying to land) and being distracted. I guess it was still distracting me.

I chose runway 6 and was too uncomfortable getting on downwind behind the ridge where you couldn't see the runway. So I was still 900 feet high when I turned base too early—the mountains aren't that close, but I still can't judge distance too well. And you hear of people losing lift and the ability to turn around when they fly up canyons—I still haven't sorted out the edge of that envelope.

I tried to slip the plane while on final. It appeared we weren't going to land until at least halfway down the runway—we might have had three hundred to five hundred feet to spare. Might have. I did a go-around.

Chuck, I could tell, was itching to say something. Heck, I was itching to say something!

After I chose to go around, he made a suggestion. Instead of going all the way around, since there was no (zip, none) traffic set up for 2-4.

So I looped around.

I still couldn't get myself down enough, so we did a 360 at slow flight, getting lower and lower.

I realized I'm not comfortable these days doing slow flight low to the ground. As a result, I have zoomed to the final and then tried to slow down. Doesn't work.

I still headed for the runway, a little bit high but much lower and a little hot at the end. But we floated and landed fairly smoothly.

Chuck breathed a huge sigh of relief. It wasn't loud, but I could feel it.

We walked in the 107-degree heat to the restaurant in town. After we had each had a fresh-squeezed lemonade, he said: "You need to get lower on final."

Me: "Yes."

AND: "I saw you slowed it up to lose altitude, but when you pitched up, you gained two hundred feet."

Me: "Ah. Okay."

AND: "You could have landed it but would have needed some heavy braking—and would have stopped before the end."

Me: "Oh, good. I *thought* so, but I didn't need to wear out the brakes, didn't *have* to land—that's why I went around."

We ate a superb lunch—unusual sandwiches.

And walked back to the airport with a lot more energy.

As we were walking back, Chuck said: "Take off to the west."

I looked at the terrain – he may be able to do so and get enough altitude, but…how do I…Well, it's not contradicting; it's telling him I'm not as capable as he. Wait a minute, he's testing me!

By the time we got to the airport, there was a light breeze suggesting we take off the other way. I mentioned this.

He grinned and said: "Okay."

Testing.

I asked the guy in the first hangar about the code and the GPS. I had forgotten something, if I had ever known it: no "K" for an airport without an IFR approach. So I should have just inputted 2-O-1—not K2O1. Got it.

As we taxied out, Chuck said: "Now start at the very end of the runway, hold your brakes while you bring the power all the way up and when it's up, let your brakes off."

I started toward the end and he said: "The end!"

I understood completely just as he said: "Where the pavement touches the grass."

I straightened out, held the brakes, powered up, let go the brakes and we started our roll.

I think I would not have thought of that. We needed all the climb we could get to get over the ridge. This morning, I had checked the length we needed for the density altitude, temperature, etc. and knew the runway at Gansner Airport in Quincy (where we were) was long enough by fifty to seventy-five percent.

I'll be remembering to start at the end and hold brakes while powering up from now on—I have Chuck in my head.

We took off, slowly gaining altitude up the valley. After a short time, Chuck asked: "Where's Grass Valley?"

Testing. Hint. Hint.

I pointed to my right.

He told me to turn toward the ridge—I had enough time and distance to clear it.

I headed that way. Had I been alone, I would have gained more altitude. So this was a GREAT learning experience.

I kept heading.

Chuck: "Where are you going?"

Me: "Toward the saddle."

Chuck: "That one is closer."

I headed for it.

Chuck: "Climbing at one thousand feet a minute."

Hint. I was so pleased with myself—I had already noted that.

We'll make it. But if I were alone...I could keep heading this way, not in trouble yet—still room to turn and then gain some altitude. Didn't have to do my Plan B, of course—we cleared it with plenty of altitude to spare. Got it.

Headed home.

Got back to Grass Valley—and got on downwind. Slow flight, losing altitude slowly. Then base. Slowly. Final. On target, low and slow, but still safe.

We landed beautifully. Still a little bit fast on short final. But just a little bit and we could use the plane the next day.

We loved these great adventures.

# QUINCY—TAKE TWO

"If you have to do more than one approach, I'm not flying with you to Quincy no more!" For me, good food is always a great incentive.

I decided I had better get myself low enough. And if I have to go around, resign myself that Chuck will not be flying with me to Quincy again. Or not in the near future—even though we go there for some GREAT sandwiches. Little did I know that Chuck loved going to Quincy enough that he would give me extra coaching, which I treasured.

I checked with weather briefing—sky clear, smooth, great day for flying. Some fires northwest not a factor. TFRs (temporary flight rules) at Beale—not a factor.

This time I had learned to just put in 2O1—NOT K-2-O-1.

We pre-flighted, got in—now I have to tell you, getting in that rental plane takes some doing, no matter how old you are. Getting out is even harder. Especially if you are male and over twenty. Chuck did it...carefully, but he is unusual.

We climbed to 9,500 feet. It was hazy and so I asked: "Do you think the visibility is good enough to go to Quincy?"

Chuck: "You always have the option to turn around if there are fires in the area—but you have at least fifteen miles of vis."

I can't get used to realizing that before I get to the area I can't see, I'll be able to see it. Hard to explain—but if I can't see the sixteenth mile, then I think—better turn around because that's where vis(ibility) is zero. Instead, vis may still be fifteen miles there. And if it's not, I'll know before I get there.

So we continued on—some mild turbulence that gave a gentle wag of the plane.

And distance is not my best talent either. Chuck: "Let down before you are over the airport." (Last time, we were doing dead reckoning, so weren't sure we were there till we were right there.)

And: "Head a little east so you can reverse course from the way we left (gaining altitude down the valley—so now lose altitude down the valley)."

Me: "Is it just over this ridge or the next one?"

Chuck: "Next one."

When we got down to 500 feet, I called in long final.

And we got down just past the numbers. However, I had misunderstood what Chuck had said before and so we lost lift about two feet up, so certainly didn't grease it. I put some power on and smoothed it out. I was too slow at the last bit—overcompensating for being too hot and high before.

We taxied in, parked. I called the FBO where I had rented the plane—they have their own flight following. We walked into town. A mile is an exceedingly long walk when one is hungry.

While waiting for our food, Chuck said: "We hit kinda hard, didn't we?"

Me: "Yes. Why?"

Chuck: "You lost lift. You need to either come in flatter or with more speed and flare. You know how high you are above the runway."

I looked perplexed.

Chuck, watching me: "Understand?"

Me: "I understand the words. But a while back, you had said get the attitude, I thought on final, and then land."

Chuck: "No." He reiterated what he had said and then: "You get a downdraft and you are going to land even harder and hurt your airplane and yourself."

Me: "I think I was overcompensating for being too high and too fast last time."

Chuck: "Well, watch your airspeed. And you could have been lower on final."

After lunch, Chuck headed back while I did a detour to check out Quincy—nice town, lots of interesting places to eat—wish we had those where we lived. And the city hall and museum area—nice and open. The façades along the main street—that old western feel which has its own beauty. I headed back to the airport jogging to catch up to Chuck.

At the airport is the Visitors Center. I asked the woman there (Casey) if we might be able to get a ride into town next time—it's a long way in when we're hungry.

Johnny was talking to Chuck—gave Chuck a book about himself. It was often thus—people wanted to meet Chuck, to tell him about themselves. Can you imagine 1000s of people doing this? Casey came out to get an autograph for her husband, whose birthday was the next day and who thinks the world of Chuck Yeager.

Chuck wanted to take off in the opposite direction from the "recommended" direction to show me how to handle rising terrain and valleys and how to judge if there's enough room to climb.

I asked Johnny about it. He said, "There's no wind—we recommend 6." He assessed the situation (that Chuck wanted to take off on 2-4), checked the wind and said, "You'll be fine; the wind is coming from the south in the valley as usual, so you'll have some updrafts if you stay to the north side. Remember, you never fly down the middle of a valley because you may not have room to turn around, and if you turn downwind, you'll have to turn steeply, and that's where you get in trouble; you'll lose too much lift."

After we were alone, Chuck to me: "You'll be one thousand feet above the ridges before you get to them."

I reminded Chuck that I ask others because sometimes they tell me or remind me of things that Chuck assumes I remember. I don't *ever* ask others because I don't believe Chuck.

We talked a little while longer and then headed to our plane. Another plane was just coming in—a family of four (two little girls).

While getting in, I said "Hello" to one daughter staring at me from just outside their plane.

I realize more than ever, now that I am a pilot, that it is especially important not to talk about anything else while prepping to fly. And by the same token, I am going to try to remember not to approach anyone as they are preparing to fly.

Chuck doesn't want anyone coming up to him an hour before he's to fly a complex plane, especially one he hasn't flown in a while.

We taxied down to the other end, did the run-up and Chuck was pleased—well, I was!—that I remembered to go to the very edge.

Me: "Ready?"

Chuck: "Yes. Now remember, turn slightly to the right once you're airborne."

Me: "Okay."

I held the brakes, slowly pushed the throttle up to full power, let go the brakes and we were off.

We climbed quickly. We turned slightly right.

Chuck: "See? Plenty of time to get above the ridges!"

Me: (The eloquent one) "Yep!"

We were getting all sorts of updrafts and lift.

Chuck: "This is a much better way to go—more on track to Grass Valley."

He was right.

We headed home. We had some moderate turbulence now and again, but it was a little less hazy. About twenty miles out, I saw the airport.

Chuck: "Now remember, don't go so slow when you land; you lose lift."

Me: "Okay." (Gulp. I knew my timing was off.) There was some more turbulence and I thought—oh sure, and now there's crosswind too!

I did the pattern and came in about the right height, but we were sinking. As I put on power, Chuck mimed putting on power. Great minds…I wish!

As we got to the numbers, I pulled the power, but again, we were sinking too fast, so I put some on and waited till we were just about touching and pulled the power and we…yikes!…greased it on.

Woo hooo! And Phew!

Another great adventure with Chuck!

## HEALTHY FEAR

*"Slow down so you can get there faster." – Victoria YEAGER-ism #1.*

Chuck Yeager often said he knew he could die. He used this fear productively: "I was always afraid of dying. Always. It was my fear that made me learn everything I could about my airplane and my emergency equipment and kept me flying respectful of my machine and always alert in the cockpit."

I remember being on the flight line with Chuck. He was like a herd of llamas with which I once hiked—alert; aware danger might be close. He was listening intently. I stopped in my tracks and watched him. I knew I'd learn something important if I just waited.

After the plane had taken off and you could hear human speech, he said: "Why does he abuse that engine? Just ramming that throttle to full speed."

And he mimed shoving the throttle with a scowl on his face.

He cared about and for his engines. And he advised, if you do care, they won't bite you.

Chuck has always instructed me to gently, smoothly push the throttle to full speed. Save your engine. And I think you'll also feel any problems with the engine sooner.

He often reminded me when I felt I was in a hurry to get an errand done and was running out the door: Don't power down on the gas pedal while the car is still cold going up that hill.

I really appreciated his reminders—they make me slow down so I can get there faster. (Victoria YEAGER-ism #1.)

## "I KNEW YOU WOULD BE A GOOD PILOT!"
*Chuck Yeager to Victoria: December 2011*

After quite a hiatus, I got to fly again. What a relief. I hadn't flown a plane, takeoff and landing, in a long time. I organized to fly with a CFI to get recurrent.

We flew to the practice area and after executing various maneuvers well, we headed back to the airport.

First landing: the CFI said: "Great short-field landing."

Comes from flying a taildragger.

Chuck said afterwards: "First landing A+. Right on the numbers. And great tight pattern."

The second one, the CFI suggested I wait a little longer to add the second set of flaps—so if engine out, I had time. So I landed a little longer. Chuck gave me an A.

The third one was a little long as well—intentionally. It was a practice engine out. The CFI had said if I have to add power, don't worry—this is a practice. Well, I didn't have to add power. Woo hoo. And the landing was a kiss.

We took off and decided to go all the way around and land the opposite direction—it has its own challenges—a big downdraft usually at the end of the runway—and it's uphill.

We landed no problem—another kiss-the-ground and we still could slow down enough to turn off at the midsection. We taxied in.

I was pretty thrilled—I could still fly. I appreciated the pointers, too. My CFI enjoyed flying with a keen student and commented: "It shows that you fly a lot with Chuck, one of the best stick-and-rudder pilots. He's obviously keeping you in shape and teaching you a lot."

And Chuck said later in private: "I knew you would be a good pilot."

Wow.

## SPREADING DICK'S ASHES

I liked Dick. He was very kind to me and a great chef. One time, when dropping off Chuck for an all-male fishing weekend at the San Francisco Fly Casting Club, where Dick was the chef, I was invited to stay for lunch before I left. The San Francisco Fly Casting Club has only twenty members, only ten of whom fish. It was started by some rich fellows out of San Francisco naturally. A train used to run from the bay area to Truckee and had a stop across the river from the club, where there used to be a bridge. Each year, the club stocks the Truckee River in front of the club. Chuck and I have participated in that. Dick's wife, Anne, was the manager.

Dick always made Chuck's favorite for him; escargots smothered in butter and garlic. He asked Chuck if he wanted his usual double order. Yes. Dick then said he didn't have many this time but saved the double order for Chuck. He asked me if I wanted any. I said, "No, thank you." Then he went and asked the members. There was only one more request. As I watched Dick cook in the large kitchen, I quietly asked, "Just in case, do you have enough escargots for one more order?" Dick studied me, "Yes."

"Then do you think I could have some, please? I love butter and garlic with some escargots and Chuck says you prepare it the best." Dick stopped short what he was doing, contemplated this, and realized I was merely being considerate when I had said no, thank you before. We smiled and ever after, he was even more kind to me, if that is possible. The more Dick got to know me, Dick once told me, he could see Chuck had made an excellent choice.

A few years later, Dick died of lung cancer. Chuck offered to spread his ashes during the memorial at the club. His wife was most appreciative.

To practice, Chuck put some flour in a gallon-sized baggie and zipped it closed. After we got the plane out, he handed the bag to me. When we got up to altitude over the Sierra, he told me to cut a tiny hole in the bottom corner with my trusty penknife he had given me. (He always carried a small one, which did come in handy.)

Then he opened the door of the taildragger, flew very slowly and told me to hold onto the hole till I was ready, get the bag down real low and behind the door. I did and let go of the hole but held on tightly to the bag. Success. None came in the cockpit.

Chuck had had a bad experience with his friend Gus when they had tried to spread Jackie Cochran's husband's, Floyd Odlum's, ashes for Jackie. Gus goofed and all of Floyd's ashes ended up in the cockpit. Jackie was furious. Gus had to clean it up. Hard to get ashes out of crevices.

So when we flew up to Truckee, landed, went to the club, quickly visited, got the ashes (except what Dick's wife wanted to spread by their boat and other places), got back to the plane and took off; I was ready. We had put the ashes in a gallon-size baggie, and after we were aloft, I carefully cut a tiny hole. As we flew down the river very slowly, Chuck opened the door. I leaned out and let loose. The huge crowd, everyone loved Dick, at the club was outside and watching.

A couple of fishermen on the river called in that a plane on fire had just flown by. Fortunately, all the firefighters and a fire truck were at the club paying respects to Dick, so knew that was us. The group said it was perfect as the ashes streamed behind us. This time, I got low enough, so none got on the fuselage. I quietly said a little prayer and goodbye to Dick as the last of the ashes streamed out of the bag.

The bag empty, staying true to form that Chuck rarely went to funerals or memorials; we continued on to Barron Hilton's ranch.

## CHUCK YEAGER & THE BAD RADIO INTERVIEWER

Chuck got tired of journalists who had not done their homework. He was quite good at interviewing himself, but why bother? Thus, when a journalist asked for an interview, our first response was: Have you read *Yeager*? If they hadn't done their homework, the answer re an interview was no.

He did a radio interview once where the interviewer who had flown a single-engine plane once said arrogantly to Chuck, "Now, General, we have a lot in common."

To this, Chuck replied, "Son, the only thing you and I have in common is that we're on the same planet!"

During this interview, it came out that Captain Yeager, after he broke the sound barrier, said, "I'm still wearing my ears and nothin' else fell off neither."

The interviewer asked about flying slower aircraft like the P-51 or another modern taildragger. Chuck responded: "You're not going faster than the speed of sound; you just sound faster than you're going."

# PART IX

# MILITARY

## OUT OF RETIREMENT: *April 2000*

In April 2000, right after I met him, Chuck went to Edwards Air Force Base for his required annual Class I flight physical.

Chuck relayed this conversation to me:

"General Reynolds, the Commander of Edwards AFB, ordered me, I mean, ahem, invited me, into his office and said, 'Now, Chuck, I'd like you to open the air show this October.'

"I said: 'General, thank you, but I retired in 1997 after the fiftieth anniversary (of breaking the sound barrier) air show.'

"General Reynolds, a two-star (general), pointedly said: 'You're not listening!'

"Me: (a one-star general): 'Yes, Sir'" as Chuck mimed saluting.

And that's how Chuck came out of his second retirement from military flying.

## EDWARDS AFB OPEN HOUSE AIR SHOW: *October 14, 2000*

For the Edwards AFB, California Open House Air Show, Chuck went down almost a week before I did for re-training in an F-15. When I arrived in Lancaster, Chuck, so happy to see me, picked me up and took me to Edwards. He said his IP (instructor pilot in the U.S. Air Force) was smart, beautiful, talented, and more. And he had just spent a whole week flying with her!

His enthusiasm made me wonder if I suddenly had competition (not really, but it was funny). He asked Dawn to show me around the cockpit of the F-15. I got in the static airplane and looked around. She explained a few things, then asked if I had any questions.

I had one—how difficult was it to take a plane out of autopilot and manually fly it? She responded, "That's a good question. I've never gotten it before."

I thought to myself, beautiful, talented, accomplished, and diplomatic, too. I'm in trouble. I think I hate her. (Kidding.)

It's always exciting to see Chuck Yeager fly, with another on his wing, break the sound barrier, and then do another fly-by, razor turn and ultimately land. Chuck Yeager gets out, climbs down the ladder, and salutes the commanding officer. Wow.

That year was fairly cold and windy, so, rather than carry General Chuck Yeager's heavy military jacket with the insignia on it, I wore it. As he left to go fly, Chuck admonished me for impersonating an officer; I could be arrested and thrown off the base. I took him seriously for a moment, then laughed when I thought it through—NO one would mistake me for a general, let alone for General Chuck Yeager.

## DINING IN — MANY MASKS

Before my first Dining In, which was at Edwards AFB, I was in the bathroom putting on makeup. When I was fourteen, Mom started me on makeup. My friends at school started at twelve. I wore a bit of color around my eyes—it looked good but made me look too much older—eighteen or so. And taking it off was a nightmare.

By the time I was seventeen, I wasn't wearing much, especially after reading about Zsa Zsa Gabor getting up an hour early to put on her makeup so she didn't scare her lover or husband. I love sleep and was not about to cater to some man by getting up an hour earlier just because my face au natural might frighten him, let alone he just might not like my real face.

An Indonesian Member of Parliament, a friend of my mother's, told me that we all wear many layers of masks, and that, as we get to know people, those masks fall away or change. I guess others figure I'm brave to start without wearing the top, the first, mask.

Even when I got my first laugh line, my mother remarked, "FINALLY. You're finally getting some character in your face." Thank you, Mom!

The result of not wearing much makeup after age 17 was I looked 17 from about age 12 to 30, frozen in time. Mom didn't like this new trend in me one bit and till the day she died (okay, until about six weeks before), she was constantly suggesting I put a little makeup on. Again, it wasn't the putting on; it was the taking off that was the challenge.

For the Dining In, I had put a little, seriously a very little, blush on and a little bit of color above my eyes, as well as mascara and some soft-towards-red lipstick.

Chuck walked in, saw me, and let out a small shriek. "Don't like the makeup?" I queried. "NO!" he replied. I immediately thought, "I *love* this man," as I wiped it off.

## FOUR HOURS IS MY LIMIT

At my first, never forget one's first, dining in, the speeches were far too long and getting old. Many attendees were now drunk and tedious. So I turned to Chuck and said, "You know…I can only be nice for about four hours."

He raised his eyebrows. "Does that include me?"

I smiled. "Yep."

He said, "Let's go!"

That became our insider cue to get out of situations. All I had to say was, "You know…" in a certain tone.

## 9/11

Chuck and I would have been oblivious for perhaps a day or two as we didn't always turn on the television. But a friend called me within minutes, very early, at o-dark-thirty in California. "Turn on your TV."

Chuck and I got up and watched the plane fly into New York City's Twin Towers. I was sorry she had called. We didn't need to get up to watch this. Nothing we could do. Not knowing until much later would have been fine with us.

Our reaction was far different from most.

Chuck's reaction was twofold:

"There was no difference between Pearl Harbor and 9/11. In both cases, we let our guard down badly. Complacency will kill you."

And:

"Now they (people today) know what we were faced with in World War II, " referring to Germany and Japan. The Japanese had a name for theirs: kamikaze pilots. I found many people who fought in World War II had similar reactions. Having been in precarious situations in some dicey places in the world, I had a fairly similar reaction.

# 9/11 MEMORIAL

I wondered what he would say. We had been invited to Clovis, south of Fresno, California, to participate in a tribute to the New York firemen and women and the NY police regarding 9/11. It was December 2001, three months after the 9/11 attacks on our country.

A company had flown 1200 of the NYPD and NYFD to Clovis on private jets. Local farmers had given them each big goodie bags of local fruit (San Joaquin Valley supplies a lot of the rest of the country and world with Halos and other fruit).

On the day of the ceremony, we arrived by private airplane and were taken to the corporation's headquarters. Our first encounter with the CEO was him coming out of his office yelling to his assistant: "Tell Governor Davis he can call me PERSONALLY!" (Apparently, Governor Davis' aide was calling. The Governor had turned down the CEO months prior; hadn't thought the event was a big deal until that very day — after he heard General Chuck Yeager was going to be there.) Impressive response. Chuck liked the CEO immediately.

Introductions were made. We chatted a little, then went to have a bite to eat before the ceremony. On the way there, an over-made-up woman materialized and said to me, walking a few paces behind the General, in a sickly sweet, overbearing voice: "We've got to get the General in for his makeup."

I warned her: "He doesn't want any makeup. Thank you."

She insisted, "Oh, but he must!"

Me: "No, he mustn't and won't."

Ignoring me and my warning, she caught up to Chuck from behind, put her hands on his shoulders—sort of a hug from behind—big oops. Don't ever grab a war veteran from behind. You'll be on the floor with a foot to your neck pretty quickly.

She was lucky…this time.

As she grabbed Chuck, she repeated in her over-pleasant, sickeningly syrupy, sweet voice, "Let's just go put on some makeup, General, to make you look good for the TV."

He instantly jerked away, assessed the situation quickly so the woman remained standing, and said, "NO."

She wouldn't let go.

Chuck continued jerking away more forcefully and made it clear: "BS! No!"

She stuttered, looked at me, saw I was supporting his decision one hundred percent, and melted away.

At the lunchroom, we met Bubba from the TV series *"In the Heat of the Night"*. NICE guy. Now, he was Mayor of Fresno and apparently doing a great job. Mayor Alan Autry.

He still had the tissues around his collar so as not to get the very thick makeup on his shirt. He asked Chuck: "Aren't you going to get some makeup? We're going to start pretty soon."

Chuck replied: "I never wear makeup."

I chimed in: "And he always looks great. Men generally don't need it on TV. You don't need it. Just get good lighting."

Bubba regarded Chuck and thought he looked pretty darn good, which got Bubba thinkin': "Yeahhhhhh. I don't like it. Next time, I'm not going to wear it. Hmmm." Now, he was disappointed with the threat of getting it all over his clothes.

Alan, perfectly happy to be called Bubba, was so thrilled Chuck watched reruns of his show. I think he would have let us call him anything. Bubba, unlike many actors who bemoan their career highlight was only one role, was happy to have a role and an income.

Outside, in front and center, were 403 empty chairs lined up in several rows, each with a rose and a photo in them. Each represented one of the men or women who lost their lives trying to save others' lives at the World Trade Center on 9/11.

Governor Davis showed up late. Not knowing what had been said, Governor Davis was repetitive and too long. A quick one to two minute statement in tribute would have been sooooo much more effective.

We were outside, so the "green room" was visible. I looked at Chuck, who was clearly unhappy, making faces while the CEO was speaking. I was perplexed—I thought he had liked the CEO. I leaned over to see next to what or whom he was standing. It suddenly all made sense: Governor Gray Davis. Just like Chuck's dad glaring at President Truman when Chuck received the Collier Trophy from President Truman in 1948 for breaking the sound barrier in 1947, Chuck was not so fond of most Democrats, especially this one (who was later successfully recalled). I laughed to myself.

It was General Chuck Yeager's turn. He sauntered up to the podium, pointed at the empty chairs, and admonished, "These chairs may seem empty. But they're not. They're full of memories. And don't you ever forget!"

I still tear up when I remember those words from General Chuck Yeager. How so very, very true and so very, very helpful. I used them at Chuck's memorial while in tears.

The men and women of the NYFP and NYPD—I can't remember if they cheered or were silent, but the response was loud. After the ceremony, everyone wanted to say hello to General Yeager, to thank him, to be a part of him. That's what happens when someone speaks transformative words. Truth with a capital "T" from a man who has also risked his life to defend America and save lives.

## "SHOOT IT!" – CHUCK YEAGER, EDWARDS AFB:
*September 2001*

The Edwards AFB, California annual Open House Air Show was canceled due to the 9/11 attacks on the World Trade Center and the Pentagon. A couple weeks later, General Yeager and I were still invited to visit Edwards AFB. They had rolled out the red carpet. Literally. They had painted a red carpet on the flight line. It was very cool.

We had just landed at Edwards AFB in a small two-seater taildragger and a coyote was running ahead of us about to cross the runway. Chuck cried, "SHOOT it!"

Call me silly, but I just didn't think it would be wise to land on a U.S. air base and start shooting just two weeks after 9/11.

## DISCUSSING NF-104 INCIDENT AT AUCTION DINNER WITH CHUCK YEAGER

In about 2001, an acquaintance of Chuck's had auctioned off for charity dinner with Chuck Yeager for six others.

At the table, they asked the usual questions. I was hesitant to speak up but did anyway because the questions were too…juvenile and dull. I asked Chuck: "After you had your incident in the NF-104, did you all learn anything?"

He responded, "The Air Force changed the oxygen from 100% to ambient air composition." NASA didn't listen. The Grissom accident would have been prevented if they had.

I felt a little self-conscious jumping in, but Chuck later reassured me that he appreciated it very much; no one had ever asked it and it was the only intelligent, interesting question that evening.

## 357TH FIGHTER GROUP REUNION: *2001*

At a 357th Fighter Group reunion dinner in 2001, some "friends" of the group tried to hog Chuck's time. I knew he was there to see his buddies from the war, not these strangers. So I made sure he sat with some of his buddies, to the dismay of these: not wannabees but "wish they had-beens".

As Chuck would say: "These people don't know what it's like to be shot at, to be in a real dogfight."

Several of these hotshots would say: "I wished I had lived then; I would have been a great fighter pilot."

Chuck's response is more realistic. Of the thirty in his group that went over to fight the Germans, twenty-one didn't come back—shot down or killed. One comes to mind: Fletcher Adams, who bailed out and turned himself over to the German military.

But this German military was two off-duty soldiers who wanted their free time, so they turned him over to the police chief in the town. The police chief, along with his wife and a few friends, proceeded to beat the young pilot to near death. Then, they half marched, half dragged Fletcher off to the woods and shot him.

Just before this mission, Fletcher had had a letter and photo from his wife of their first child, their son.

In 2010, Chuck and I attended the 357th Fighter Group Museum opening in Ida, Louisiana, where Fletcher grew up and where his son, who never knew him, and his wife still live.

At the reunion dinner, I arranged for Chuck to sit with some of the maintenance guys from the 357th in World War II. They were ecstatic and thrilled. They didn't realize through the noise of the "friends" of the 357th that Chuck wanted to visit with them more than the "friends," many of whom were there for free autographs or to make money off these veterans.

However, unlike some of these "friends," I truly am in extreme awe and a state of gratitude.

And I don't have illusions I would have been a great fighter pilot ace who survived.

I asked the one maintenance guy, "Tell me something about Chuck that's not in his book."

The maintenance guy said admiringly still, "Whenever we couldn't figure something out, we went straight to Chuck. He always figured it out quickly. I remember one time we couldn't figure out where the whine was coming from on the airplane, so we got Chuck. As soon as he got to the plane, he knew. It was the antenna. He fixed it right away. Anything, an engine, the cowling, he knew."

During that weekend, Chuck was going to fly a P-51. He had warned me pretty soon after we first met: Do NOT talk to him at least an hour before he's going to fly, especially a P-51. I understood.

The first time Chuck flew a P-51 after World War II, about 30 years later, in the 1970s, he marveled, "When I get back in a P-51 now, I think, 'How did I ever fly this goddamn thing?' It's yawing all over the sky and you have to be on top of it all the time." Imagine. The world's hottest pilot admitting that he gets rusty in a plane in which he has so many hours!

By the 1970s, aviation had advanced so much beyond the P-51 in technology and aviation: jets, space, on the verge of stealth...

A P-51 has all sorts of challenges; including a lot of torque on takeoff, so if you don't stay on top of it, you can easily flip, especially on a go-around. Also, the radiator door on automatic can make the engine overheat and freeze on, or just after, takeoff, and more.

As we were walking out to the P-51 at Wright Patterson AFB, a young man was trying to catch up to Chuck. I blocked him and said in no uncertain terms, "General Yeager does not want to be disturbed before he's going to fly."

The young man hesitated but kept walking with me behind General Yeager. Finally, he got up enough courage to say, "I'm his escort to the plane." Oops. Never mind.

Well, at least Chuck knew I took his words seriously.

# AN OFFICER OF THE LEGION OF HONOR (LEGION D'HONNEUR), *Féternes, France: July 2003*

What a great day! Sunny. Bright. Very unusual. You could see Mont Blanc (Switzerland) in one direction and Lake Geneva (France/Switzerland) in the other from the beautiful bluff of Féternes, France, where a bomber had bellied in during World War II.

It was July 2003, the 100th anniversary year of the celebrated first powered flight, the 56th anniversary year of Chuck being the first to fly faster than the speed of sound, and the 50th anniversary year of Chuck Yeager zooming past Mach 2 (Mach 2.44) and holding his title of fastest man alive.

Members of the French Resistance told us the following about the bomber that had bellied in during the war:

It was the bomber crew's second mission and the pilot's first. They all had civvies with them—appearing as though they planned not to return. When they landed, the Maquis were there within minutes. The crew was trying to burn the plane, saying they had been shot down. However, this bluff was the wrong direction from their mission. The Maquis fought with the crew, telling the crew that the Maquis had the Germans halted at the bridge several miles away and that the Maquis needed the fuel and the parts from the crippled plane.

The Maquis also asked the crew to stay and fight because the Allies and the Maquis were winning—the Americans were only one hundred miles away.

The crew said, but we are in Switzerland and free. The Maquis told them, no, you are in France. One member of the Maquis told me they almost got into fisticuffs over this.

The crew insisted on being taken to Switzerland twenty miles away. The Maquis tried to dissuade the crew—the Swiss will intern you. The Americans are no more than a few weeks away. Stay and fight with us—or we will hide you, no problem.

But the crew demanded they be taken to Switzerland, where they thought they had landed to avoid the war, so eventually, the Maquis drove them to

Switzerland and just as the Maquis had warned, the Swiss interned the crew for many months. One surviving crew member, the navigator, of all people, told us he had been interned for four and a half months, at which point he heard the Americans were near, so he walked out of the camp (apparently, no one stopped him) and joined up with the Americans.

We saw the exhibit—and photos—several of the Maquis were still alive. They would point to their pictures. There were several photos of the plane on the plain on the bluff in Féternes. There was no evidence of the airplane having been shot or disabled.

One gal, who had been instrumental in the Maquis, told us she missed the Americans' parade after they liberated the town. She was 30 years old and having her first child. But in typical southern, country French humor, she said, but it was okay; the crowd's cheers drowned out her screams of labor. She developed a crush on Chuck as she served us tastings of different cheeses in her cheese shop.

While in the area, we visited the folks at a high-end watchmaker in Geneva. They gave us chocolates. Then we visited the CEO of Nestlé—he had flown in a P-51 with Chuck the summer before. I suggested that he needed to give us watches since the watch manufacturer had given us chocolates.

Ten thousand villagers from all over were there to see the knighting of General Chuck Yeager and two others. The French Air Force band played *La Marseillaise* (the French National Anthem) and then *The Star-Spangled Banner*.

Our host led us to six chairs. Three men were being honored. Two were becoming Chevaliers, Knights. General Yeager was becoming an Officier (Officer), the highest honor a non-French citizen could receive.

The American Air Attaché to the American Embassy in Paris and his son were in attendance. The son had piercings all over his face. General Yeager told the boy he was a disgrace and then asked the Colonel why he allowed his son to do that to himself. The Colonel's only response was: "Oh, you know kids today, General."

General Yeager shook his head. I wonder if he was thinking what I was, "Oh no—we know parents today."

Also in attendance were some luminaries of the region, including one of

President Roosevelt's grand-nephews and his French wife. The French wife expressed her opinion, which was apt: "So you let your child mutilate his body; that is your choice. But you do not bring him to an event like this of great decorum to represent the U.S. government."

I started trailing behind a little, taking in the whole scene: the green field that the town of Féternes had bought so that no one could put a mall on this spot, beautiful blue sky, bright sun, snow-covered Mont Blanc, calm Lake Geneva or Lake Leman, as the French call it, handsome General Chuck Yeager, the French military band, who had played the night before, there to honor General Chuck Yeager.

The two soon-to-be knights and their wives sat down, as did General Yeager, taking up five of the only six chairs on the field.

I walked over to take my seat but found it occupied by President Roosevelt's grandnephew, clearly feeling entitled for doing…what? Oh, being a grand nephew of someone. He had not even acted as a gentleman, had not offered (my) the seat even to his wife. She took her place behind him.

I contemplated the situation—heck, I had removed (politely but insistently) the likes of Andy Warhol from his (my) seat when I was 21. This day, though, I decided I'd probably rather walk around a little anyway.

Yet, I missed a great opportunity—it would have been interesting to see his reaction if I had confronted him and asked him to give me my seat.

Some of the organizers made short speeches. Chuck said he'd like to speak. Oddly, they had not expected this. Everyone was thrilled. None of the other honorees were interested in speaking. Frankly, thank goodness.

Remember, this was in 2003, just after the Iraq War, and the coalition was still there in Iraq. "France" had appeared to be unsupportive.

When we told people in the U.S. we were going to France, anti-French sentiments ran high. Chuck's response was always: "They saved my life," as indeed some French had after the Germans shot him down during World War II.

And I would always respond: "Have you only been to Paris, the Riviera, or Biarritz? I ask because some Parisians can be, not always, a bit snooty, a bit dismissive, or controlling/commanding/judgmental, rude and/or unpleasant—a bit like some New Yorkers." I would tell the U.S. person that if s/

he traveled in the countryside, s/he might have a different opinion of the "French." They can be very amusing, playful, fun, warm, entertaining, kind, brave. Like any group of people, there are all kinds.

And one can find anti-American sentiments within different groups as well.

So, as General Yeager walked across part of the field to the podium, I wondered what he was going to say. And wondered if I should go with him to translate into French.

Chuck led with: "Let's forget our governments!"

Ten thousand cheers went up and the ice was broken as only Chuck could do. No translation needed. When Chuck spoke to foreigners, he spoke more slowly and precisely.

He then continued on to relate how he had been shot down, worked with the Maquis as they saved his life and got him to the Pyrénées, over which he, carrying a wounded airman in three feet of snow, escaped the Nazis and eventually returned to combat.

The French Air Force band played while the minders positioned General Yeager and the others to be knighted. A retired French General (the equivalent military level as General Yeager is why this man) had the honors.

The French General pulled his sword out of its scabbard and tapped General Yeager with it, first on one shoulder, then the other, then returned it, he thought, to his scabbard, kissed General Yeager on either cheek (traditional French greeting and goodbye), congratulated and welcomed him as a new Officer of the Legion of Honor (Officier; Légion d'Honneur), and then moved on to the next honoree.

General Yeager quietly bent down, picked up the sword from the grass, and handed it to the French General (who had missed the scabbard). The French General quietly received it and moved on to knight the remaining two honorees.

The French band played some more — they were outstanding. We had attended a concert by them the night before. All the honorees had been invited. All were quite tired and the concert was a bit late given the events of the day and the next day.

Chuck and I knew it would be extremely impolite not to go, even if we only went for a short time. The others didn't care. This difference in character may be why they were only becoming knights and General Yeager an officer.

We arrived at the hall; everyone was very pleasantly surprised and thrilled. It took a while for the concert to start—it was about an hour late.

I turned to our host, a high-level politician, and said in French: "Much as we are enjoying this wonderful extravaganza, at the first break or intermission, we plan to sneak out—it's a bit late for us. I hope no one will mind or think it rude and hope they and you will excuse us."

He turned to me and said, "We certainly understand and are most honored you made the effort to come at all. I will sneak out with—I mean—escort you out."

We laughed.

The concert was outstanding: innovative and very entertaining. I really didn't want to leave, but if we didn't, we (or I—Chuck's stamina when needed was outstanding—even at 80) might sleep through the next day's ceremonies even if we attended (asleep with our eyes open).

After the honorees were knighted and the band finished playing for the ceremony, the attendees made their way to the tent where the refreshments were. Seriously delicious food. This was France, near Evian, where the bottled water is sourced.

The French General approached us—he was amazed that an American, a member of the military, had been so elegant and demur in saving the French General from the embarrassment of fumbling for his missing sword. I was translating this to Chuck.

French General: "I hadn't realized the sword had missed my scabbard when I was putting it back in."

General Yeager responded: "I couldn't help but notice when it was sticking out of my foot."

As I translated, I could see the French General's shock and rethinking his assessment of Americans and the American General. I double-checked my French to ensure I had translated correctly and had not said something offensive.

Ah, but then he saw Chuck and I were laughing, teasing him. He slowly and, at first reluctantly, joined in.

Others approached us. I tried to get the great-looking food as the servers passed by, but by the time we reached the dessert table, it was all gone. Misery!

After the event, as we were driving, we saw a gathering of folks in someone's courtyard and stopped in, to the great delight of the retired French general and the others.

Later that evening, Chuck gave a talk to the pilots. They had combined this day's ceremony with an air show which the organizers creatively called Air Poche One, a play on "Air Force One," and "poche" means "pocket" in English.

Chuck had asked me to translate. I had last spoken French 4 to 6 years before in Cambodia and Laos; before that, perhaps only once in 17 years. There was an American there who said he was fluent in both languages, so I asked for his help.

The first thing Chuck said was: "I was born so fer (far) up a holla' (holler—a small, sheltered valley), they had to pipe daylight in."

I told him: "Heck, I can't even translate that into English, let alone French!"

Neither could the self-proclaimed bilingual American. Turned out he wasn't as bilingual as he suggested.

So, I continued translating.

When we got to breaking the sound barrier, I was translating literally—the flying tail. (The key to breaking the sound barrier was having a method of changing the angle of the entire horizontal stabilizer instead of just the elevator to control pitch, otherwise known as the flying tail.)

The French pilots were giving slight looks of confusion. Except one. Relieved, I asked him to translate. I listened carefully so I would know how to say it all in French in future.

Well, dang, if he didn't say exactly what I had said. I mean, he used the exact same French words and phrases. I wondered if the difference was that they had now heard it for the third time and now realized that I had meant what I was saying or whether they trusted the Frenchman or because his accent was far better than mine. Ha ha.

Again, relieved and happy to sit down and just listen to Chuck and the translation, I put it to the audience: "Would you prefer he translate? I'd be happy to sit down."

They replied: "No, no! You're funny. We prefer you."

Thank you.

I think.

## OPENING SONIC BOOM AT EDWARDS AFB OPEN HOUSE AIR SHOW: *2003*

One year, to shake it up a little, Chuck decided to fly the P-51 for the Edwards AFB Air Show, but that P-51 was not maintained well and had engine trouble, so Chuck didn't fly that year. The person who was supposed to do the sonic boom also didn't show, so the commander, a general, decided to do it in his F-15E.

Chuck pulled him aside—they had known each other a long time—and generously and courteously told him it was a perfect day with a certain type of clouds to see the shockwave that causes the sonic boom. The best way to ensure this is to punch it to at least Mach 1.4. WOW! See a shock wave! I was looking forward to that.

Although he had never done an air show or purposefully placed a sonic boom for the audience to see a shockwave, the commander nevertheless responded impatiently and arrogantly: "You don't have to tell me—I know how to do it. I've exceeded Mach 1 a few times."

Well. It's just not a good idea to say that to Chuck when he's offering his help.

"Be my guest" was Chuck's usual response to knucklehead behavior. (Chuck YEAGER-ism #31.)

Since the P-51 hadn't shown up, Chuck and I sat in the VIP area with his great friend, Pete Knight, a former test pilot and California State Senator and his wife. Pete was the fastest man alive in 1967 when he went 6.7 Mach. When he landed his plane, the X-15, it was on fire.

Pete was a very witty guy. Between Chuck and him, we'd all be laughing so hard we couldn't breathe.

A little while later, after the other general had taken off, while Chuck and I were chatting with Pete and Gail Knight, I heard a slight whisper—like a Pfffffff-t.

We all looked around. It took a moment for all of us to realize what it was... Was that the "sonic boom" to open the air show?

Chuck, of course, recognized the situation immediately and created levity, exclaiming, "Hell! I can hear a gnat fart louder than that!"

The commander's wife laughed. "His job security for retirement just went down the tubes," meaning he won't be asked to open the air show again.

Needless to say, no one heard a sonic boom or saw the shockwaves through the stratus, which was very disappointing.

Later, the commander was disappointed and a little embarrassed, especially around Chuck (as he should have been).

Much later, at dinner, the commander said his people had heard a boom in the housing area and said it was loud.

I replied, "Of course they did. They work for you. The public and VIPs don't."

## GERMAN AMERICAN GLIDER CLUB 50TH ANNIVERSARY: *Traben-Trarbach, Germany, 2004*

Often, military folks say they've traveled when they've been stationed outside the U.S. But many of them mostly stayed on base. By contrast, wherever Chuck was stationed, he'd always go out and become friends with the locals. In keeping with this tradition, Chuck started the German American Glider Club as soon as he arrived in Germany for the first time on the ground in 1954. He also learned that to hunt in Germany, you had to have permission from a landowner; there were no public huntin' grounds. He met Herr Melzheimer, became great friends with his sons, and became a gamekeeper for Herr Melzheimer, allowing Chuck to hunt.

In 2004, the German American Glider Club in Traben-Trarbach invited Chuck and me to their fiftieth anniversary. To their amazement, we said we'd come if they took care of our first-class travel.

We stayed in a vacation rental owned by the mother of one of the members. It was stocked with great food. The problem was—just as in Houston—they fed us so much otherwise; we couldn't eat it. In fact, they had hams, bratwurst, and cheeses almost every meal, but they were quite thin as I gained five pounds. I asked them how they stayed so thin eating all this. They replied they don't normally eat like this—just on special occasions. I thanked them and said, "Let's stop and please eat healthy except every morning; a bakery left hot rolls on our doorstep. Let's not stop those."

We'd sit on the deck overlooking the Mosul River, eat our hot rolls, and drink coffee and tea. Very civilized.

They had bikes, too. I hadn't ridden one in ages. Neither had Chuck. We each took a turn. I thought about riding downriver (which made it slightly downhill) to Trier and taking the ferry back, but there was no time and a group wanted to go by car.

A lot of history in Trier. Chuck happily sat at a café drinking espresso with our new friend while I explored the cathedral and the square. I had been there before, age 12 or 15.

Another day, the Club took us in a powered glider. Good thing it was powered, so we didn't need the field's powered tow rope or the jeep to catapult us into the air. It was quite hot and muggy that day, especially inside that glider. Over the mesas and around the river, I got a bit queasy. Fortunately, we were not up for long.

The fellow who flew us had been a young boy during World War II. He remembered Chuck from when Chuck had been stationed there in 1954. I asked him what he and the rest of the townsfolk thought of the Americans as they "liberated" their town in 1945.

He said they welcomed the Americans; the townsfolk were sick of war, shortages, and fear. The Americans brought prosperity and freedom. That was nice to hear, frankly.

We visited Herr Melzheimer's house—the current owners were not related but gladly showed us the public rooms of their house and the gardens. They had added myriads of Buddhas of all sizes. Fascinating to watch Chuck remember the rooms while he tried to obliterate the Buddhas crowding his memory.

He loved the sweet wine they made there at quite an angle on the extremely steep hillsides. We brought some home and gave most of it away.

The two-day glider air show was a great success. Chuck spoke both days.

People came for miles around and saw that what they had was priceless. Other towns had built shopping centers on their mesas and were making a bundle. As one can imagine, some townsfolk also wanted to make a bundle, so they were against the airfield and were pro-development. But after this weekend with General Chuck Yeager, they changed their tune and the airfield was saved.

## CHUCK YEAGER FLYING P-51 BESTS THE F-22 AT EDWARDS AFB OPEN HOUSE AIR SHOW

In 2005, General Chuck Yeager decided he'd rather just fly the P-51 in the Edwards AFB Open House Air Show that year instead of a fighter jet breaking the sound barrier to open the show.

So, the powers that be had the bright idea to have him fly alongside an F-22 to show off the remarkable capabilities of our modern warplanes and how far the U.S. had advanced versus the old P-51, a great plane "in its day".

Yet, they didn't want Chuck to fly the F-22's wing. Chuck pointed out that he had more formation flying time than all the Edwards pilots and then some put together.

So, the P-51 flew the wing of the F-22. First, they did slow flight, showing how a jet could be as slow as a propeller airplane. Then, they were to cob it (full power) and show how fast the F-22 is compared to the P-51.

However, Chuck Yeager knew something none of them considered; when they cobbed it, the P-51 took off and was far ahead of the F-22 in front of the crowd.

You see, a jet engine needs time to spool up. General Yeager knew this and delighted in following the "plan," showing what he, in his P-51, could do. "It's not the plane, it's the pilot" or "It's not the machine, it's the man." (Chuck YEAGER-ism #55.)

"Scope", flying the F-22, loved it, too.

The powers that be…not so much.

Maj. Sean "Scope" Borror, F-22 Test Pilot flying in formation with General Yeager, wrote, "I had the great pleasure of flying with General Yeager at the Edwards airshow," adding that it was "truly one of the highlights of my flying career."

## AUSTRALIAN INTERNATIONAL AIR SHOW, AVALON AIRPORT: *2007*

At the same time as the Australian International Air Show at the Avalon Airport, Victoria, Australia held a conference of all the Air Chiefs around the world. They were ecstatic to meet General Chuck Yeager. The Pakistani Air Chief invited us to Pakistan. He had been a young PAF pilot when General Yeager was stationed there, so he, as a grown man and air chief, was downright giddy to talk with General Yeager. The first time, he was far too nervous to enjoy it. Fortunately, over the course of a few days, he relaxed and had the time of his life. He invited us to Pakistan in late 2007, but two days before we were to leave, he postponed our trip. I was very disappointed. However, we learned the former Prime Minister and over twenty others were killed in a suicide bombing right where and when we would have been.

I spoke with the Iraqi Air Chief who said they had a joke in Iraq: General Tommy Franks, the American General in charge in Iraq, had taken the cotton out of their mouths that Saddam Hussein had put there, but now Franks has put that cotton in his ears.

I found this often to be true. Some countries will rush in to help, but they don't listen to the locals who can best direct the help to be most effective. Are these countries there to really help or really there to help themselves?

The Iraqi Air Chief said he was in opposition to Saddam—enough so that he had sent one of his children to Australia, the other to America during Saddam's regime, to get them out of harm's (Saddam's) way. So, this chief clearly was not an Iraqi spy or insurgent.

He said, "The Americans didn't win in twenty-six days. We cleared the path and let you in—we needed the Americans to get rid of Saddam. We could have told the Americans who would be loyal to the Americans and who would undermine them out of loyalty to Saddam."

I espied the U.S. Ambassador and suggested, "You should talk with the Iraqi Air Chief—he has some great insights." Instead, the U.S. Ambassador got very nervous and did everything he could to *avoid* the Iraqi Air Chief.

During the air show, a powerful, wealthy man, who had a trucking business in Australia, invited us into his tent. He told me he had tried to expand to America but said our unions were too formidable and scary. I thought, 'Wow, if you found them dangerous...I mean, this trucking company owner was one tough dude.'

I asked the trucking magnate what he would have done regarding Iraq. He said, "If you're going to pick a fight, you have to punch the other guy in the nose so hard that he can't get up. Then you negotiate."

Pretty clear to me. Glad this guy liked us.

Australia probably had the first nighttime air show, which has now caught on around the world. We watched it with a flight doctor we knew from Beale AFB, temporarily stationed in Australia.

After the air show, Dick Smith took us around the southern part of Australia, including Tasmania, where we went fishing in a little boat and visited the former Prime Minister, also fishing, enjoying a quiet life; remote Kangaroo Island, where we ate great fish, wish I could remember the name, and Ayers Rock. I had it in mind to get up very early and hike Ayers Rock, but fortunately, it was too windy to climb, and I went back to sleep. We flew around it before we left, so we saw plenty.

## VISITING EDWARDS AFB WITH CHUCK YEAGER

It's always a blast to visit Edwards AFB with Chuck Yeager. As we approached, we could see Rogers Dry Lake had water in it from a very rainy winter and early spring. Prehistoric shrimp that lie dormant below the lakebed had a chance to surface and lay their eggs. Then the lake was pink.

Chuck pointed out the areas where he had lived with Glennis when he was TDY (temporary duty)—one at the edge of the lakebed—and the base commander's house a colonel had built on a hillock. Even though Chuck was full-time at Edwards, he was marked as TDY for the first few years, which was challenging—they couldn't use base services or shops. It cost $400 to have their third child off base—a lot of money in 1948 (almost two months' pay).

On the way, we had stopped in Reedley and picked up seasonal fruit from Chuck's fruit farmer friends. They, through Chuck, have been gifting fruit to the folks at Edwards AFB for over 40 years.

After checking in to the VOQ (visiting officers' quarters), we headed over to the commander's house to drop off the fruit.

The following morning started early enough—breakfast at 8 a.m. with the base commander, his wife, his aide and a few others of the staff, a few briefings of various programs, and a visit with one of General Yeager's old friends: Dr. Jim Young, Chief Historian, Air Force Flight Test Center, Edwards AFB. Dr. Young had been there thirty years.

I teased everyone, saying Jim knew more about Chuck Yeager than Chuck Yeager. If I didn't know something from listening to Chuck, I would go to Jim first when a question came up re Chuck, especially from folks who said their family member had flown with him. Then I'd ask Chuck. The truth is I did both because Jim often had the data at his fingertips that we didn't have re others, such as Form Vs (flight logs). Or at least had good suggestions of where to look up information. I did educate him on a few things—about which he had always wondered, such as the Budweiser rocket ship, which had been driven past MACH 1 on Roger's Dry Lake at Edwards AFB once. It didn't hold an official record because the administrators of official records had determined it had to be driven twice, not once, past the speed of sound. Thus, others who did it twice hold that record.

At lunch with Jim, the General and his wife, and a few colonels on base, I asked the one to my right, "What do you do?"

He gave me his title and rank. I looked around the table and said: "Okay. But what do you do?" Everyone burst out laughing. We all understood.

After lunch, we went to the Test Pilot School, the best in the world.

General Yeager had been Commandant of the precursor to the Test Pilot School, the Aeronautical Research Pilot School, from 1962 to 1966, training twenty-six of the astronauts: most, if not all, of the early Air Force astronauts.

The auditorium was packed. The audience really appreciated and enjoyed Chuck's presentation. Standing ovation.

Then a gathering—with burgers. Long day. But very enjoyable.

## CONGRESSIONAL MEDAL OF HONOR SOCIETY DINNERS: *2009-2010*

In 2009, Chuck went on an annual fishing trip with Barron Hilton near Socorro, Mexico, where the tuna thrived. As it was a "boy" trip, I was not invited and instead attended the Medal of Honor Association dinner at the President Reagan Library near Los Angeles.

I was invited to the VIP pre-party with Nancy Reagan, former First Lady of the United States.

Nancy Reagan had written me a letter of condolence after my mother died in 1986. It was heartwarming and thrilling to know someone of her stature was aware and appreciative of all my mother; who had been a world-renowned authority on, and great advocate of, preventing alcoholism, drug abuse, and addictions; had done.

When I met Nancy Reagan for the second time, she was very gracious as always, very calm and elegant, and remembered my mother.

I saw Tom Selleck and his wife, Jillie, in the elevator on the way to the VIP pre-party. Tom mentioned we had met before, wondering if I remembered.

I smiled: "I do." And that's all I said. I remembered all three times. Once, at a convention, he stepped in front of me to speak to Chuck. Another time, Tom and a CEO, who had been fired for skimming, were whispering and pointing like schoolchildren, as I recall. A third time, at an event with Jillie, Tom kept turning his back on my blond bombshell friend merely wanting to say hello.

I reminded Jillie that I had met her when she was very pregnant many years ago, about to pop—at the 100th episode party for *Magnum, P.I.* She appreciated that I particularly remembered her since she does not normally get the attention her husband does.

Luckily, I got to spend a bit of time with Mrs. Petraeus. What a wonderful woman; intelligent, down to earth. She also was thrilled to talk to Mrs. Yeager, one degree of separation from her hero.

I also met Gary Sinise with his attractive wife, whom I had met about 15 years prior. She had been ill, so I asked how she was. She was so appreciative that I remembered. Afterward, I saw her whispering to Gary and pointing at me. They, at least, were smiling enthusiastically.

I went to my table. Sitting down and eating—the only one doing so in the huge room; everyone else was schmoozing—was Mrs. Milken. Michael Milken introduced himself and then his wife.

She said almost sheepishly, "I was hungry." I jumped in: "My kinda gal. I'm going to join you." And I did. She liked me a whole lot then. I teased Michael: "I have a bone to pick with you! I was about to get a job with your outfit."

You could see Michael curious and wary as to what I was going to say. After all, that outfit didn't end well—he, the king of junk bonds, ended up in Club Fed (Federal prison) for twenty-two months and a $500 million fine for securities fraud and bilking senior citizens out of their retirement funds.

Me: (continuing)..."When all heck broke loose. I coulda been somebody. I needed a good mentor."

Relieved (sort of), he laughed.

I continued: "Before that, Carl Icahn was going to teach a class at business school (Columbia University), but he got in trouble, so they canceled it and

I obviously didn't get to take it." (What would it have been—how to make billions by skirting the law?)

The Milkens gave me the impression that they want to do good in the world these days. Very delicate, caring, broken, and sweet.

Gary Sinise gave a talk, a fairly lengthy talk, which he or someone had written, and he stumbled over the words several times. I turned to Mrs. Milken, surprised: "He's an actor! Why didn't he memorize it and act it?" Mrs. Milken laughed and agreed.

Charles Durning received a special award for actors (they are so never recognized—kidding) for his courage in war or something. I recall the video claimed that Durning was there on D-Day, had been mortally wounded—three to five times, but each time, he got back in the fight. And he was captured behind enemy lines and escaped a few times. It was incredible. And I do mean that literally.

I met some humble Medal of Honor recipients just outside the restrooms. You know, the ones who say they merely represent their mates. We were all hiding out from our formal tables and the endless speeches. I inquired as to who they were. When they responded, I thanked them. They each said, "I didn't do anything; my men did" or "The other guy deserves it more" or "The whole squadron did" or…The common denominator being each hero was very humble.

They then asked me who I was. When I told them I was Victoria Yeager, General Chuck Yeager's wife, they perked up excitedly, "Is he here?" as they looked around and beyond me for him, a real hero.

I was getting used to this. Truthfully, I was always happy to see people excited to want to see Chuck and agreed wholeheartedly with the sentiment. I replied, "No, sorry, ya got chopped liver!" We all laughed. I told them he was fishing in the best place to fish for tuna, off Socorro, Mexico. We all agreed he had his priorities right. I told them I would try to bring General Yeager next year, but it depended on his fishing schedule. They sure understood; but we all hoped…

These Medal of Honor recipients are so…can't think of the words—accomplished and heroes themselves—but Chuck Yeager is their hero. Imagine. The hero's hero. These guys went beyond the call of duty, risking their necks to save so many others (as did Chuck) and still so humble that they look up to someone else. Impressive.

I truly missed Chuck that night. I mused about Chuck's reaction when he unpacked his bag on the boat and found my warm little love note nestled in amongst his clothes.

*  *  *

The following year, it so happened that the dinner was the day Chuck returned from that annual Mexico fishing trip. This time, former Mexico President Vicente Fox joined them on that fishing trip, which made for interesting stories.

So, I convinced Chuck, grumbling, to go to the dinner.

When we arrived at the Reagan Library, the Medal of Honor recipients lined up in two lines, creating an aisle for us to walk down to meet General Chuck Yeager. He was quite moved by this. I told one: I kept my promise and he's here. He smiled broadly and nodded, speechless. Chuck talked to each one as only those who have been in the midst of battle fighting for their lives, their men's lives, and their country can understand what it was truly like.

I was glad to be able to bring them together.

During dinner, Gary Sinise came over to our table, excited, repeating, "How did I not know Chuck Yeager was here?" He was so excited to meet the General. When he announced General Chuck Yeager was in the audience, the crowd cheered and gave a standing ovation for a very long time. Not bad for a staid Hollywood-type black-tie crowd.

Chuck greatly appreciated that evening, but the most enjoyable was talking with the veterans and recipients.

I have always felt, and continue to feel, blessed that I could be a "fly on the wall," able to listen and just be with these great, brave, accomplished, amazing, yet humble veterans.

Note: General Chuck Yeager was awarded a Medal of Honor by a special act of Congress (making it one of the rare true Congressional Medals of Honor), presented to him by President Ford in 1976, a year after he retired from the Air Force as a Brigadier General and 29 years after the act with which he earned it: breaking the sound barrier.

## BEALE AFB AIR SHOW: *2009*

I must go meet the new ATC (Air Traffic Control) at the local air base. I used to tell them if they see my plane coming in without me calling in, bring out the ambulance and fire trucks; I'm in trouble and I've got precious, priceless cargo. They laughed, saw I was pretty darn serious, and agreed. I told them I'd be too focused on landing to try to figure out their frequency.

I do hold a record: the shortest amount of time between getting my private pilot's license to opening an air show with a fly-by leading a two-ship formation with General Chuck Yeager on my wing. How cool is that?

Leading was last minute. Chuck was going to lead but, once up in the air, told me to lead. Flying wing takes more precision skill. He was amused that I didn't know military aviation language. As we were coming in, ATC said, "Check initial."

I just assumed that meant when I was on downwind.

No, it meant when I was heading in on final—I didn't need to do downwind and base.

But I did. ATC went with it, as did Chuck, since I was the lead.

Several years prior, I had flown a T-6 from the backseat. We were flying lead for a three-ship of two P-51s and us. In those 2 P-51s were Chuck Yeager and another WWII vet. My front seat pilot later told everyone I was like autopilot; I flew so straight and level, with steady turns. When he asked for the controls back to get set up for landing, I did my customary "Just a minute" and peeled my hand off the stick.

As I mentioned, I learned how to sail as a kid; that helped me understand wind a little and how to keep steady. Many have told me flying straight and level is the hardest thing to do. I think landing a taildragger is.

After we landed and parked our airplanes, General Yeager and I went to the VIP tent. It was a scorcher of a day. I recalled a couple years earlier,

Nicole "Fifi" Malachowski, the first female Thunderbird, graciously, respectfully, and enthusiastically had come over to say hello to her hero, General Chuck Yeager.

I went out to look at displays and saw people in their lawn chairs leaning against our planes' fuselages and on and under the wings. I told them all to go elsewhere.

I asked the minders for help. "Please get some security around these planes."

"Yes, ma'am."

Fifteen minutes passed. Nothing. I asked, "What's happening? I really don't need to spend the day shooing people away." No response, so I continued: "Do I need to talk to the Colonel (Vice Commander) to get this done?"

That got their attention. "We'll talk to him!" One of the two minders ran off. He returned fairly quickly: "They're on their way."

At thirty minutes, I said, "Do I need to go ask the General (base commander) to get this done?"

Their eyes got wide. One left and came back, said, "Fifteen minutes."

A young woman with two kids, coming out of the shade under the wing, reached up to hold the wing so she didn't bump her head, but stopped herself before she touched it. Impressive.

I said, "I'm sorry—we're not allowing anyone near the plane."

She exclaimed, "I didn't touch it!!"

I said, "Yes, I watched. Very impressive. The problem is if you are there, others will gather. I'm sorry."

She left. Her boyfriend came running back and asked me, "Did you tell her to leave because she is black?"

I replied, "She is?" and continued, "Absolutely not. For forty minutes, I've been shooing folks away—I have not noticed what color, ethnic group, tattoos, piercings, I don't care. We're flying in a couple hours—can't have these planes damaged. However, she was impressive and careful. If she would like to shoo others, she is welcome to sit under the wing, not touching anything."

He said, "Okay," and took off to catch up to her.

At first, I was stunned, but then I was glad he asked since that thought had crossed their minds.

After forty-five minutes, the security detail showed up with ropes and stanchions and put them around each airplane.

Finally.

I went back in and thanked the colonel for getting it done.

He laughed and said, "They came in and said, 'Mrs. Yeager is a little upset.' I said, 'No, Mrs. Yeager is either very, very, very upset, or she's fine. Which is it?'"

We laughed. He made it clear, though, that he agreed when I was upset, I was right: safety concerns, as well as other concerns such as integrity and competence, not unlike General Yeager. I said, "Could you please tell the next person taking over your position?"

"No, it'll be more fun learning it as he goes along."

## CHUCK YEAGER ROAD, BEALE AFB: *November 2010*

It was a long time coming, but Monday, November 29, 2010, the road from Beale AFB to Route 20 and Grass Valley, California, had been repaired, repaved and renamed. Since World War II, 1945, all they had ever done prior to this was patchwork—one big pothole. It would take us forty-five minutes to drive it. Until now.

Getting it done took over eight years from the time the money was raised and allocated by Yuba County and the Federal government (Feds). Five government agencies had to sign off on it. A curve in it had to be straightened—at least one airman a year was killed on that curve. Yes, probably driving too fast.

Every time Congressman Wally Herger—and all the many such politicians before him and since—wanted a photo op with General Yeager, General Yeager said, "NO, not until you fix the egress systems from Beale AFB," (specifically, the eight miles of road at the Grass Valley gate—very dangerous).

Wally had gotten some money from the Feds, but it had to be matched by the county as required, and soon, or the money designation would expire.

John Nicoletti, a county supervisor at the time, emailed one day: "Could

General Yeager please attend a meeting (the next day) regarding the road from Beale AFB to Grass Valley?"

We had never met him before, but he happened to catch us at home and available, which was highly unusual on such short notice. Chuck said, "Yes."

Everyone was there—representatives from five government agencies, the Vice Commander of Beale, John, General Chuck Yeager, and me.

General Yeager told the group what he had been saying for several years: if Yuba County doesn't fix Beale AFB's egress systems, Beale should be and will be closed. The Air Force, when it assigns missions, was very interested in egress systems, roads, access, and more. "You've got to protect the airmen and military and treat them well." General Yeager was always looking out for the men and women of the Air Force and their safety.

The others spoke about...I don't know what. Nothing pertinent or interesting, just politicians.

I hesitated because I had not exactly been invited to the meeting, but I couldn't stand the waste of time and words, so I jumped in. "I'm Mrs. Yeager. I'm a little slow, so please help me out here. I wanted to know: What is the very next step to get this done?"

Someone answered. Then, before anyone else could speak, I asked, "And when do you expect that to get done? How long will that take?" Again, I got a concrete answer: two weeks.

Then, several jumped in with nothing useful or on point. You know, politicians and government employees—just have to speak even though not useful.

Thank goodness the Vice Commander then jumped in, following my lead. "What is the second step that has to happen to get this done?"

Then she asked, "How long will that take?"

The others would answer and then go off on tangents.

The Vice Commander would bring them back. "And the third step?" and after the answer, "How long will that take?"

And so on.

The meeting adjourned.

After ten days, I emailed John Nicoletti and said, "The two weeks are almost up. Are they finished with the first step or on track to finish within four days?"

The next meeting, same thing. I interjected: "Remember, I'm a little slow. What's the very next step that has to happen to get this done?"

One guy spoke up; he had to give his finished report to the guy at the end of the table.

I waited.

And after what seemed like an interminably long time, I offered, "Shall I give it to him for you?"

It was…no words…

I learned later that John Nicoletti would forward my emails saying, "Mrs. Yeager wants to know…" and somehow, that got people to straighten up and fly right. And the road was finished, in record time, ten months once John Nicoletti got the ball rolling with General Yeager. Instead of celebrating, the five agencies grumbled and forever after called the road project, "The Yeager way of doing things." Right, efficient, done well.

When it was nearing completion, John asked me to ask the general, "Could we name the road after you?"

Chuck, truly humble, it ain't an act, queried, "Why?"

I had to explain to Chuck that he was a hero and this was a small way of recognizing his large contributions to the world, risking his life to do so and finally getting this road done to protect the troops.

Beale AFB and Yuba County had a naming ceremony. General McGillicuddy (love that name—trips off the tongue, although it must have been difficult with all the forms one has to fill out in life)—spoke first.

It was not open to the public. We weren't sure we could make it—but we did and so did some friends of ours. It was a nice ceremony: short, to the point, and just wonderful.

General McGillicuddy had known about Chuck Yeager since he was 10 years old! General Yeager talked about doing boot camp at Beale. It was Camp Beale, an army base, during World War II. The Air Force was part of the U.S. Army until September 1947. Chuck still doesn't understand why a fighter pilot needed to practice crawling under barbed wire while they shot over him. (And he sure didn't need to do that in France after he was shot down and worked with the Maquis before escaping into Spain. However, he did have to crawl under a bed.)

General Yeager said he was honored, but mostly, he was pleased that the airmen, who have to use the road, now have a safe route.

County Supervisor John Nicoletti gave General Yeager a piece of artwork—a bomb stuck in a portion of a road—suggesting that may be why the road had so many potholes—bombing practice.

Then he said, "Many of you don't know this, but General Yeager used to bring tomatoes he grew in his garden as gifts to the people on base. By the time he got to base on this road, it was salsa. Now the tomatoes will make it intact."

John extolled General Yeager's contribution globally and locally. And concluded with, "To me, Chuck Yeager is the sound of freedom."

Chuck Yeager Road. What an honor! Thank you to all those who worked so hard to get it done!

Chuck and I liked the new Chuck Yeager Road so much we were finding all sorts of excuses to go to Beale AFB—I think three times in the first week.

Each time we returned, we saw a new Chuck Yeager Road sign (people wanted one, so they stole it; one right after the other for a while). Very funny. I never noticed how many hills and valleys and curves the road had—we used to have to go so slowly because of the potholes.

Now you can just fly over those hills…Just kidding.

Took us ten to fifteen minutes instead of the usual forty-five before the re-do. What a pleasure.

And just plain cool to see the sign as we drove by, and as I drive by now, at the intersection: CHUCK YEAGER ROAD.

Woo hoo!

We have learned that since they fixed the road, including straightening out a curve, there have been virtually no accidents.

Thank you, General Yeager!

## RETIRING FROM FLYING WARBIRDS AND TALKING TO MAINTAINERS AT EDWARDS AFB

This event was, in part, one of several that started Chuck thinking about retiring from flying warbirds. At 87, he just did not want to have to jump out of an old airplane—most were 70 years old and then some. Some planes we had flown were not well-maintained and because of that, one almost killed us. Only Chuck's remarkable flying skills saved us. Even in a well-maintained aircraft, one can throw a rod that requires an emergency landing, as happened to the T-28, and there are not always good places to land.

They never did find out what caused the rod to break and hit the engine in the T-28 whose wing we were flying in 2005. Can you imagine all the things that could go wrong, forcing one to have to ditch a plane in enemy territory during war? That's also why Chuck always appreciated his crew chief and maintenance guys—they (and he) kept his plane running well, which kept him safe.

That is also why he wouldn't let anyone else work on the X-1 when he was flying it to break the sound barrier.

When I contemplate this, I genuinely admire, thank, and respect our veterans over and over and over again.

This was also why we did a talk and Q&A for all the maintainers and the entire Edwards team, as well as the pilots, when we visited Edwards AFB in 2007. The commandant said that's okay, you can just speak to the pilots at the test pilot school, but we insisted on talking to the maintainers, too. In fact, we had signed some photos, which we had taken with the maintainers a couple years before—the ones who helped us when we flew in and took off three days later in the P-51 and T-28. They were speechless and thrilled when we called them to the stage. Worth the effort!

## SOUTH AFRICA: *2010*

Friends invited us for an action-packed trip to South Africa. We culled animals, the meat of which was fed to the tribes, went on safaris, and flew many flights, mostly with the South African Air Force, to several South African Air Bases, to Stellenbosch, the rooibos tea plantation, Cape Town, Johannesburg, Kruger National Park, where we saw a herd of thousands of water buffalo, tons of elephant, lion, among other wild animals.

We also flew a Kitfox airplane looking for lost elephants.

One landing by one of the two young pilots of the South African Air Force was a bit rough. Having the greatest aviator in the world on their plane, they burst out laughing in embarrassment. As General Yeager disembarked, they were a bit concerned about what he would say and if they would be reprimanded. General Yeager stopped at the cockpit and reminded the two young lads that it was an excellent landing—we could use the plane the next day. They giggled nervously but with relief. Chuck could be quite kind and generous if the situation warranted it. He'd had his share of imperfect landings; in fact, three without an airplane.

## FLYING INTO BEALE AFB AIR SHOW: *May 1, 2011*

I was talked out, listened out and my ears hurt; not the best time to be at a public function as the wife of an honoree. We had gotten in late Saturday night. And we had gotten up early Sunday to fly into the Beale Air Show.

It was a bit windy for me as I was pre-flighting the airplane. I had checked: "10 kts gusting up to 25 and then becoming calm." But that's at altitude. I hoped the winds would become calm for our return flight and landing. I said to Chuck, "I'm not so sure about me flying with this wind."

He said: "What wind?" Here's a guy who, on my birthday in 2000, flew his grandson's entire football team, 22 kids, one at a time, in a light taildragger, in fifteen-knot winds gusting to twenty-two knots (kts) at Nevada County airport with the trees causing winds to be squirrelly and only one runway. I helped by showing the kids how to get in and ensuring they were strapped in properly. There was one black kid on the whole team—he had moved from the San Francisco Bay area to our area as a foster kid. The others told Chuck the kid was quite scared while callously laughing at the kid. I let the kid know he was all right in my book as I helped him strap in. And Chuck, in his special way—let's just say after that flight, the kid walked a little taller and with confidence after he got out of the plane.

As we drove home (after picking up a birthday cake, of course), Chuck casually remarked, "It was a bit windy." It was so windy that no one else was flying that day.

On this day nine years later, I smiled and indicated I was serious and concerned. He replied: "If it's a crosswind, the runway at Beale is wide enough that you can just land across the runway."

I smiled—he was probably right. Or at least HE could land across the runway and stop in time. He had done it in an F-15E. He agreed if I was or became uncomfortable, he would fly. I was flying because the plane was one I could fly and Chuck wanted me to continue to gain all the experience I could. We got in the airplane—no easy chore.

I always get a little concerned starting this plane cold—especially when the shop is closed, so no available battery backup. However, today, I primed it just the right amount and with a few attempts, got it started right up.

Chuck breathed again.

I followed the checklist and started moving to get us away from the other planes—we were parked pretty close to one—and checked my brakes. Chuck checked his.

And off we were taxiing. We listened to the AWOS (weather).

Chuck: "Take off on 7."

Usually, we're supposed to take off on 2-5, but today the winds were ten kts at ninety degrees—almost straight down 7 and I didn't fancy doing a downwind takeoff. What can happen is you think you are going fast enough to lift off—and you aren't, so you may lose lift or not have enough lift and land badly out of control.

Did the run-up, took the runway and took off. No problems, so once we had enough altitude—which was fast, we did a 180 and headed to Beale.

Chuck: "You don't have to gain any more altitude." Our airport was at 3150 feet and Beale was about 3000 feet less.

Fairly quickly, I switched frequencies to Beale Tower: "Beale Tower, XX-3 Delta Charlie."

Beale came straight back with winds, pressure setting, squawk numbers. Then –I stated my position and intention. (My intentions; I so wanted to say, "My intentions are honorable.")

Beale asked me to identify the type of aircraft. For a nanosecond, I wondered if I had missed saying it on my first and second calls. No, I hadn't. I re-stated the type.

Beale asked me to identify again and also asked my position. I was the only one in the sky at that point. Chuck, who understood far more than I, simplified it for all of us: "Tell him you're white and you're little."

I repeated this: "I'm white and I'm little." (Probably the littlest coming in that day).

After a pause, Tower: "Got you. Check initial at sixteen hundred feet."

I repeated this.

It was a glorious day for flying—you could see forever and it was a little cool, so good density altitude. I started for downwind out of habit. The general said: "Head for initial."

This time, I knew what that meant—head directly for the numbers of the runway on which you are going to land.

Chuck reminded me: "You'll have to lose a lot of altitude."

Me: "Roger."

We got on initial. Chuck: "Break at the second taxiway."

How extremely lucky I was—a novice with the most experienced pilot giving me instructions, guiding me!

I broke as instructed. I marveled at how comfortable I was becoming doing safe, steep turns. On downwind, I checked my checklist. I had never turned off the fuel pump because I was never "cruising". I had been climbing or descending.

On final, Chuck said: "Tell them; 'Gear down and welded.'"
Me: "Tower, xx-3 Delta Charlie. Gear down and welded."

We got down low over the runway with a little power on—the wind had picked up a bit—but we had over 10,000 feet of runway and lots of taxiing if I landed on the numbers. When it felt okay to land, I let her down the final couple of feet. Chuck breathed again.

We taxied almost as much as we flew. I was on the right side of the runway—Chuck was about to tell me to get in the middle till he saw that we didn't need to waste the fuel to go back to the middle just to turn right within the next fifty feet.

So he corrected: "You're fine."

Tower told us which taxiways to exit and then cleared us to call Ground.
Me: "Beale Ground, xx-3 Delta Charlie."
Ground: "Taxi mumble mumble mumble Follow Me."
Fortunately, Chuck knew what the intent was and guided me.

We taxied in, saw the "Follow Me" sign and followed him until we saw the fellow standing in front of our parking space guiding us with arm signals.

Shut down the aircraft. The maintenance fellow and General Yeager knew each other, so a warm greeting. We knew our escort, whom we hadn't seen in a while, so another warm greeting.

And away we went to get some coffee and to look at all the static displays.

Little did we know this was going to be a very big day for the United States and all the families around the world who had had members lost in wars.

General Yeager talked with several pilots and others along the way.

And then we went to sit in the VIP tent.

And that's when I realized I was peopled out. However, I knew this was a time to dig deep and smile. Several people approached me: "I don't want to bother the general, but..."

I smiled. Whenever someone said that, I often felt like joking with them and saying, "Why is it okay to bother me?"...but truly, none of these people are ever a bother. And I find them most interesting. How can I not? They admire General Yeager.

We got in the golf cart and went through the crowds to the van, on top of which was the air show commentator. General Yeager went on top. Not much room up there so I stayed below as the show "opened" with a parachutist jumping out of the airplane with a United States of America flag and someone singing the National Anthem over the loudspeaker system. When it was General Yeager's turn to speak, and after he finished, the crowd cheered.

After he climbed back down the ladder, someone remarked: "Did you see him go up that ladder? He was like a Billy goat! He's 88 years old!" A few kids at the fence asked if they could meet General Yeager and take his photo. I said I'd try, but please don't ask for autographs; please go to the website. So after Chuck got down, I asked—he walked over, shook a few hands and stood for a few photos. They were all thrilled.

While sitting at the table eating lunch, someone kept talking at me, asking questions right after I took a bite.

I explained I just needed some fuel and then could possibly answer his questions. He understood and realized just sitting with us might be enough. And he was, he said later, rewarded: After having a bite to eat, General Yeager started commenting on the planes. Fascinating!

We saw the general who commands Beale AFB. He looked very alert. We found out why later that night—May 1, Sunday night. (The President announced Osama Bin Laden, the mastermind and financier of the attack on the World Trade Center towers and the Pentagon, had been eliminated despite some Pakistanis maintaining Bin Laden had died years before of kidney disease.)

We toured the static displays again. A very cool morning turned into a very warm day and lots of people were camped out under the wings of the cargo plane. What a sight! The plane has more uses than we thought.

We went over to where the Thunderbirds were starting their engines (F-16s)—even that is part of the show. Very crisp maintenance fellows, all in sync. We headed back and waited for their show, after which we were going to leave. And waited. And waited. We learned later that a life flight was flying through the air space, delaying the Thunderbirds.

They did their usual routine, including the four-ship fly-by where it looks like they are going to collide.

After this, we headed to our plane in a restricted area. I noticed some serious guns on the guards. Very serious. More than usual. Someone else had noticed the more than usual serious guns on the security forces roaming the crowd, too. Little did we know why until the President's announcement as stated above.

Our escort (G) pulled our plane out. I did the exterior pre-flight while Chuck talked more with G. Again, with effort, we got in, and I did the interior checklist. Again, I was concerned about startup, but it was fine. Chuck and I both breathed a sigh of relief this time.

We called Ground. Several times.

Ground eventually: "Mumble, mumble, mumble."

Me: "This is xx-3 Delta Charlie. Say again?"

Ground: "Take this, this this…"

Me: "Could you guide me?"

Ground: "Take a left then…"

Eventually, we got cleared to follow the flight of six F-15s. I kept my distance and thought, 'This is going to be interesting. I will have to take off before their takeoff spot but won't be able to climb like them, so will have to turn to try to stay out of their wash…oh boy.'

Ground: "Can you do a mid-field takeoff?"

I didn't understand a word he said, but Chuck did. "Tell him, 'Yes.'"

Me: "Affirmative."

Ground told me to turn right at this taxiway to the runway and cleared me to contact Tower.

Tower cleared me for takeoff.

I gained the runway, took off, and turned east.

I wasn't sure of the exact direction, but knew I'd get my bearings soon.

Tower asked if I needed flight following. Chuck said: "Negative."

I repeated to Tower: "Negative."

Chuck pointed out a few landmarks—we were headed toward our airport. Chuck said not to go any higher. I smiled and told him that's how I'll find our airport—get really, really high and…

Chuck did his funny mock scowl at me.

And as I gained some (not a lot) altitude, there it was. We were heading straight for it.

A few minutes later, Tower handed me off to flight following. I thought I said "Negative."

So I called in—it had been a while since I had had to call any "Approach," but I still remembered the language. However, I was out of practice understanding these guys.

Approach: "Mumble (at Mach speed)."

Me: "Say again?"

Approach gave me the numbers for flight following. I punched them in.

Approach: "Ident(ify)."

I was pleased I remembered all this. I pushed Ident.

By this time, we had the airport in sight. Approach asked me another question I didn't understand. Chuck did: "Negative."

I repeated to Approach: "Negative." So Approach handed me off to VFR and our airport.

We checked AWOS. Winds were now ten kts at 270 for our 2-5 runway. From Beale, we were already on that downwind path. We called in.

A bit choppy around our airport.

We called final. Very choppy, so I kept a little power on. And I forgot my second set of flaps, which is just as well in turbulent air.

An airplane was about to take the runway after all my calls, including final. But then he stopped just short.

I decided we probably could land with plenty of runway, but maybe none to spare and I was concerned about that other airplane, so I called a go-around.

I came around again—no one on the runway; one plane called in behind me.

I got low enough, kept a little power on.

We were bounced around on final and I heard Chuck's voice in my head: "Just fly your airplane."

Chuck said: "Crab."

I did.

As we got low enough, I just flew a few feet over the runway with a little power. The wind died down for a little bit, so I chopped power and landed.

The plane wasn't sure it wanted to stay landed, but we stayed on the ground and taxied off the second exit.

Me: "Three Delta Charlie—clear the runway."

I cleaned up the airplane and we taxied to the parking spot.

After we shut down the aircraft and got out, Chuck pointed out I was nowhere near the center of the white line for parking.

He was testing me. I pointed to the other planes—had I been in the center, I would have hit one of them.

He smiled.

We closed up the airplane, put away the keys, and left. The plane was able to be used the next day.

Two excellent landings today.

## GENERAL CHUCK YEAGER, GRAND MARSHAL, SACRAMENTO VETERANS DAY PARADE, *11/11/11 at 11 a.m.*

*General Chuck YEAGER-ism #147: "You know what's causing that, don't you?"*

John, a flight instructor, picked us up, put me in the left seat, Chuck in the cozy seats in back and flew to Sacramento Executive. I did the approach and landing. We had quite a sink rate, so added a little power. John, the flight instructor, helped a little bit, okay, a lot, more the last five seconds and we did a kiss-the-ground landing. Wowser.

Jim, our chauffeur for the day, including in the parade, picked us up at the airport. John and he had brought coffee and breakfast muffins, breads, scones, so we liked them very much right away. Seriously—nice folks. We got in the vintage convertible Cadillac and he took us to the Crocker Museum, the staging ground for the parade, where we met our contact: Vincene, an extraordinary woman, very energetic, very talented, very giving, bright, funny.

Chuck commented on how great the clutch was. Jim has about eight antique Cadillacs and about the same number of other antique cars.

Kinda fun.

We helped Jim open the convertible top. Everything is manual—cars didn't start having power gears, steering, and windows until after World War II. For my entire childhood till he died, my father had a black 1949 Cadillac convertible, red interior—very elegant and stylish—all power; windows, convertible white top, gears, except the steering.

Jim had gotten a flag with one star and draped it with a few flags on the front. One of Vincene's volunteers put signs on the car, "General Chuck Yeager, Grand Marshal." John delighted in riding shotgun, protecting us. Jim had had the foresight to bring blankets for our legs. The car and we were dressed and ready.

Many people approached the car to get a photo with General Chuck Yeager or to shake his hand. Lots of parents brought their kids. Lots of veterans came out.

The guys from the Aerospace Museum said hello from Roxanne, who heads it, and mentioned they were having a Veterans Day celebration there—free hot dogs. I turned to John—hmmm. Free hot dogs. He smiled, in on the joke, and said yes, sounds good—we could hop over there in the plane…Free.

Of course, with the cost of fuel, it would have been a hundred-dollar hot dog! But at least the hot dog was free.

We drove down Capitol Mall. People were waving hands or flags and calling out: "Thank you, Chuck!"

It was heartwarming. Chuck and I waved at people. I was able to look into almost everyone's eyes. Anyone who seemed to be a veteran, I thanked. Those who weren't I thanked for coming out and waved to them all. They were thrilled to see their hero and mine, General Chuck Yeager—kids, adults, all.

After we got to the end of the Mall, we drove on a back road to the stage and watched the rest of the parade—bands, Corvettes, an airplane from the Aerospace Museum of California, an army vehicle, a Boy Scout troop, a Cub Scout troop—those little kids were "too cool" to smile back at me—funny!

We met Congresswoman Doris Matsui. What a powerhouse! Bright, well-spoken. Then we met several of the local Tuskegee Airmen. They were thrilled to meet General Yeager. And Chuck was happy to meet fellow World War II fighter pilots.

I asked if they wanted some coffee. As we weren't close to a restroom, some opted out. Vincene had had a station set up for the VIPs for coffee. I got the coffee for the two who wanted it—handed it off to a volunteer to give the Congresswoman and the Tuskegee Airman—and did a recce. When I came back, I grabbed some fruit from the VIP stand. Someone said, "Those are for VIPs." I didn't pay attention. The woman repeated it. I suddenly realized she was talking to me and looked up.

I smiled: "I'm Mrs. Yeager—"

Oh. She apologized: "You're fine," and tried to explain. I said: "You're doing a great job! Thanks! I would have done the same."

Now she was smiling in wonder.

I went back to the stage and informed Chuck of the restrooms nearby—so he decided the coffee would be fine and would warm him up.

We chatted with people on the street. One of the volunteers had not eaten yet at all that day, so I pulled out one of the cakes from the back of the Cadillac. He was most appreciative—but saved some for later.

I went back to the stage and suggested they get started before the crowd dissipated. I gave up my seat to Congresswoman Matsui so she could sit next to General Yeager.

Dana Howard, a former local newscaster, introduced Yvette Gauff, who sang "The Star-Spangled Banner." Outstanding.

I helped one of the Tuskegee Airmen to his feet.

Congresswoman Doris Matsui gave an inspiring talk thanking veterans. She then said, "I have the great honor of introducing General Chuck Yeager."

They gave a warm hug and General Chuck Yeager took the podium. He gave a brief review of his history and then said, "I am honored to represent veterans today as the Grand Marshal of the Sacramento Veterans Day Parade. Thank you!"

He shared the attention on him and made the day about veterans. It was perfect and most appreciated by the veterans and the Tuskegee Airmen present.

Several other veterans spoke: one Army, one Navy—both of whom had fought in Iraq and Afghanistan. One said it was interesting to be bombed on New Year's Eve.

Dana clarified—he meant literally!

One of the Tuskegee Airmen told me that they needed help to get back to their cars or they could get a taxi. I said I'd handle it—and found Vincene. She said: "Already done."

Me: "I knew that!" And smiled.

Vincene pointed: "See that bus?"

Me: "Got it."

I returned to the stage and reassured the Airmen.

The program ended with Yvette singing "God Bless the U.S.A." First, though, she talked about how much she appreciates veterans and how she hoped she got through the song without tearing up as she usually does.

Halfway through, she invited us to sing along. I kept tearing up the whole day, including during the song, as I was singing. (And only partially due to my own singing. Kidding.)

After this, we said hello and goodbye to everyone on the stage. One of the Tuskegee Airmen told me he flew the P-51. When I said, "Of course! Very cool!" he replied—"Not like your husband, though!" We both smiled.

Chuck stayed and took photos with all the veterans who wanted one.

After the photo with a family of eleven kids, Chuck pulled the father and mother aside, referred to the kids, and said: "You know what's causing that, right?" (General Chuck YEAGER-ism #147.) We all laughed.

Vincene turned to the father and ordered, "STOP. Just stop," re having kids, as only she could do.

Several more photos with more people and groups, and we were finished, just as the rain was threatening. John had checked the aviation weather and had suggested to Jim he put the roof on the convertible just in time. A few drops of rain were starting as we got in the now-covered car.

John and Jim talked about the people they headed off—ones who looked like "stalker" material.

We decided we were hungry—as I used to tell Chuck whenever he'd ask if

I was hungry, "I'm *always* hungry." I had seen some interesting restaurants on our way from the airport. Jim suggested a few places. First one was closed. Second one—pizza—was open and good.

Some people listened in to our conversation and thanked Chuck for his service. We watched a little kid (under sixteen months, for sure) dancing to the music. First with his arms—then he decided he needed a little leg action, so he bounced to the music. *Dancing With the Stars* is probably next.

Jim drove us to the airport. John put me in the left seat again and, after we took the active, gave me the controls.

John gave me climb speed, altitudes, and direction. I followed his guidance.

We got on upwind for 7, crosswind, downwind, base, final…had to add power—downdrafts and heavy nose…pointed the nose at the numbers, kept pointing, then flared and floated. John helped, thank goodness, and we got down with another kissing-the-ground landing. Super!

I had to get us back from the left side to the center line; which I did without problem.

As we cleared the runway, John took the controls, taxied in, parked, and shut down the plane.

We exited, gave John a signed photo and a big thank you. A good day was had by all.

## U.S. AIR FORCE ACADEMY LEADERSHIP SEMINAR: *2012*

The U.S. Air Force Academy has a leadership seminar each year. Around 2012, General Chuck Yeager was the keynote speaker. It was the first time the Academy had a full house, standing room only, let alone anyone at all in the balcony.

General Yeager was excellent, as usual. I handled the Q&A portion. The questions were pretty good. Sometimes I'd add to the answer. General Yeager couldn't say he had the best eyes, or was the best aviator, or…but I could.

One question was: "What do you think about unmanned vehicles?"

I said *sub voce*: "You're not going to like the answer."

General Yeager responded with Chuck YEAGER-ism #62: "Anytime a pilot doesn't have to bleed, it's a good thing!"

The fighter jock wannabes were very disappointed.

I asked our minders, who were supposed to be the crème de la crème, if they liked the talk. "Oh, YES."

I asked, "What did you learn?"

"Uh. It was funny."

Sigh. After learning their goals, I tried again. "Did you learn that to become a great fighter pilot, you should know your maintenance and egress systems better than those who manufactured them?"

One piped up, "I fly a 172 with my father's friend and I check the oil."

I gave up. They might have an epiphany later. One black gal who seemed the brightest of the bunch told me she was considering transferring. I supported that. "General Yeager says it's better to do ROTC at a great school. He had to train officers from the Academy how to communicate with enlisted men and women."

The next day, while eating a buffet breakfast, a woman came up to me, thanked me and asked me to thank General Yeager profusely. Her husband, a USAF Academy graduate, had been in deep despair over the Obamacare debacle. They had lost their insurance due to Obamacare and had a child, age 30, who had Down syndrome, now with no coverage. After listening to Chuck, he had hope for the first time in a year. I said, "I'm very glad to hear that." Then I asked her, "Do you think any of the kids got it? Three to whom we spoke didn't seem to…"

She said, "Oh yes."

I have learned that sometimes people can't hear you right away, but sometimes, it does hit them later. Let's hope. But I could see Chuck had positively, deeply touched at least two people.

## NEAR-FATAL CRASH IN AFGHANISTAN; CHUCK YEAGER SAVES LIVES AGAIN: *2012*

It took me 11 years to convince the Department of Defense (DoD) that the troops in Afghanistan and Iraq would love to see General Chuck Yeager. We received several emails from the troops asking why General Yeager was not visiting. I tried with such luminaries as Gary Sinise, who wouldn't help, and various politicians who all always wanted something from General Chuck Yeager, but giving? None of them, including those who called him "a dear friend", helped.

Finally, the DoD organized a trip with Robin Williams and us around Christmas 2011, but Robin got a job, so it was canceled at the last minute.

Eventually, a trip was planned for April 2012. The DoD still didn't think anyone would be interested, so they added two "pot smokin' gittar players" (PSGP), as Chuck called them. In fact, they were somewhat respectful (more so after General Yeager and I schooled them) young men, energetic, talented, naive.

The DoD then sent out the proposal to all the bases in Afghanistan and Kuwait. Every single one came back and said they would support us visiting. They must agree to put us up, feed us, provide transport, etc.

The DoD representative called me and asked if Chuck, age 89, could do sixteen-hour days. I replied, "Better than you or I. And by the way, you owe the troops and him an apology for those eleven years."

We arrived in Kuwait, got off the airplane first, and got to customs, only to be told we needed a visa. The DoD had neglected to mention this, let alone arrange it, and there was no one to meet us. So, we went upstairs as directed. I was apprehensive since we had no Kuwaiti money and no telephone number or name to help us. Fortunately, the guys there told us there was no charge and we could get a visa right then, but it would take some time. During the over two hours we waited after the exceedingly long flight from Europe, I was able to get on email gratis, so emailed everyone I could find from the DoD and said, "Hello? Anyone here to meet us?"

I considered our options. Was it safe to go to a hotel in Kuwait City? Do we just grab a cab? Is that safe?

By the time we got our visas and exited the control area with our bags (about 3 hours later), the ex-Haliburton group was there to meet us. They drove us thirty minutes to the Army base and dumped us off at our room, letting us know that they would pick us up at 8 a.m. the following morning. They also said it was still too windy to travel by helicopter, so we had to travel by SUV; thus, travel time would be much longer. We walked down to the BX (base exchange), a mile away, bought some food and walked back to the room. The building was locked. So, we walked back towards the BX, found an open building and a Lt Col (lieutenant colonel) in an office and asked for his help.

He, disgusted that General Yeager had never been properly greeted or accommodated, let us in. That night, the PSGP boys showed up. The next morning, we walked the mile down to the BX to find out it had closed at 7:30 am. So I asked Chuck to stay there and I ran/walked back to the sleeping quarters. Oddly but fortunately, I had brought Cheerios with us from the U.S. and the day before we had bought milk. I told the driver who showed up at the sleeping quarters at 8 a.m. that we were going to pick up General Yeager, bring him back to the room, and he was going to eat some breakfast; I did not care if we got a late start. I also let them have it as to the disrespect to General Yeager—no one waiting for us at the airport, no one greeting us at the base, no keys to the building, no food.

We picked up General Yeager, brought him back to the room, had breakfast, and got back in the SUV.

I asked the driver for some details and reiterated how they all were going to behave toward General Yeager and me. Just then, one of the PSGP boys popped up from behind the back seat. There were two SUVs—one for General Yeager and me and the other for the boys, but this lead singer/player thought it would be funny to sneak into ours. Then he was afraid to make himself known, given that he might become a target for his disrespect. I did let the driver and the PSGP guy know invading our privacy was unacceptable. This was not fun and games time. There was a war going on. No such pranks ever happened again.

We went to several bases. General Yeager gave several talks. I emceed the Q&A (question and answer session). The audience emptied before the boys played. So, the leader was not dumb. He said, "I think we should open for the general." I smiled. "As long as the troops don't come to see General Yeager, only have a few minutes, and have to leave before they can see him."

At one point, we did a pit stop on the side of the road. As I looked around, Chuck said exactly what I was thinking, observing our civilian "bodyguards" and drivers: "We run into trouble; we're on our own."

We had arrived in Kuwait just after the vacation season, where everyone camps out, leaves a lot of trash, and lets the whipping winds blow the trash to the next country. So very odd. One of the strangest concepts/traditions I had ever heard or seen. And having traveled all over the world, I have seen some very strange things indeed.

The head of the Air Force base told us that several were out on maneuvers or maintaining planes so could not make it and were heartbroken. We said that we would try to stop back on our way back from Pakistan (where we were going to visit General Yeager's friend Prince Malik after we visited Afghanistan).

We returned to our barracks at about 10:30 p.m. The boys had been given passes to the DFAC (Dining Facility Administration Center), so we went with them to eat. We were told we were leaving, so be packed and ready by 1:30 a.m. to go to the airport to fly to Kabul, Afghanistan.

I packed and told the minders driving us to store about two bags—we did not need them in Afghanistan but would in Pakistan.

The minders drove us down to the airport and told us to wait in a room. It was 1:50 a.m. We waited. And waited. The chairs were exceedingly uncomfortable. I asked for what were we waiting. "The pilots," was the answer. "They're arriving at 4:30 a.m." I asked why they had brought us down so early. They said they had hoped the pilots might be able to get there early. I let them have it for their continued disrespect to General Yeager. It turned out the pilots had arrived earlier than we—they were in the next room, but our minders never checked and the pilots never looked around!

We loaded up in a C-130—General Yeager and I on the bench in the rear of the cockpit; the PSGP and DoD minder (representative) in the cargo seats down below.

Seven hours later, we landed in K-a-n-d-a-h-a-r.

I kept thinking: 'Ka-...Ka-...Ka-...that's not Kabul!'

We unloaded and went to get a bite to eat. We wanted to go to the DFAC, but the PSGP boys wanted to try TGI Fridays. Very strange going to a TGI Fridays in Afghanistan (and worse—paying triple out of our own pockets for something basic). The PSGP boys remarked how they had never eaten in a restaurant in the U.S. with so many guards armed with AK-47s. Being on a military base in a country at war and having traveled to dicey places, I didn't even notice.

Our DoD minder made several phone calls and by 2:30 p.m., we were loading onto another cargo plane. This time, a C-141. Two U.S. Air National Guard pilots were in the pilot and co-pilot seats, General Yeager in the navigator seat, me on the back bench and the PSGP boys and DoD minder in the cargo seats below again.

After we took off, General Yeager asked, "Where are we going?" We had not slept in over thirty-two hours.

The two pilots looked at each other, obviously thinking disrespectfully this older man, poor fellow.

I saw that look and anyone who knows me, knows this is true: I about came out of my shoes to knock their heads together. Instead, I pointedly said, "No one has told us where we are going. Last time, they said, 'Kabul' and I know you do not spell Kabul, K-A-N-D-A-H-A-R. We figure you would know right now. That may change, but right now, where are we going?"

They bowed their heads with some shame and muttered, "Sorry, Sir, sorry, Ma'am. We're going to Mazar-i-Sharif" (which means Tomb of the Prince.)

Another thirty minutes went by and General Yeager cried out, "Break!"

The pilots turned back to him (neither one looking where we were going), "Whaaat?"

"Break!"

Pilots: "Which way?"

General Yeager: "Any way, it's coming right at you!"

The pilot did a giant wing-over, quickly moving us to a new path. We looked over; right where we had been was another plane going the opposite direction. I wondered/hoped the PSGP and DoD minder down below in the back had been strapped in.

After twenty minutes or so, when the pilots had somewhat settled down, General Yeager calmly asked, "Don't you guys look out the window?" (Chuck YEAGER-ism #148.)

We were in a war zone, a no-radar zone. Thank goodness General Yeager's eyesight was as good as ever. With no sleep for over thirty-two hours, he saw that plane when it was a speck and was tracking it the whole time. Thank goodness!!! I told him, "Honey, I don't care how little sleep you have had; when we are flying here, you are sitting in that (navigator) seat!"

Those pilots owed General Yeager an even bigger apology. I can see why the USAF pilots are not impressed with these weekend warriors—the "National Guard weenies," as General Yeager would say. You can't fly these planes so little and expect to be proficient.

After we landed, the Base Commander asked General Yeager, although he had not slept in over thirty-six hours, if he would please still be willing to talk that evening to the men who had been waiting for days and months since they heard.

Ever the professional, and knowing our mission, that's why he had come, General Yeager said, "Sure."

The two PSGPs traveling with us had been shaking their heads vigorously in the background, indicating adamantly we should say no, but when General Yeager, at age 89, said yes, they, age 35 or so, couldn't very well pass.

They gave us forty-five minutes for a nap/rest and we were off and running again.

We had some dinner and then General Yeager spoke a bit about his history, especially about his time in Pakistan and Afghanistan in 1971-73.

The airmen were very kind and very thrilled to meet and hear General Yeager. We did a Q&A for fifteen minutes and then…we slept very well that night, a very welcome sleep.

## MAZAR-I-SHARIF: *Afghanistan 2012*

Afghanistan is a beautiful country. We got a birds-eye view as Chuck pointed out areas where he had hunted oriel as well as other animals in 1971-1973. I remember hues of red and yellow in the canyons in the morning light as we flew over mountains and valleys with small villages. Each house was surrounded by a mud wall with an interior courtyard.

No roads—lots of tracks.

We visited several areas. I'd love to go back sometime. Many visiting U.S. politicians visit the lakes and especially beautiful areas. As much as I would have liked to do so, we did not—we were there to visit the troops.

At Mazar-i-Sharif, the next morning, we had elected to go to the German commissary. I surprised a few with my German: "Wie Gehts?" Which means: "How's it goin'?"

If they said more than "Gut, danke" (Good, thank you), I was sunk.

General Yeager had been adamant that we visit a forward base because no one had visited his base in England during World War II. And we were going to visit a forward base out of Mazar-i-Sharif but we were told there were transportation problems due to a civilian outside contractor issue and we could not. That was a big letdown.

## SHINDAND & AFGHANI PILOTS-IN-TRAINING

After Mazar-i-Sharif, we went to Shindig. Okay, it's really Shindand. Used to be a Russian base. One of the buildings left standing, the nicest one there, or least rough, was nicknamed the Hilton Hotel. One of the airmen gave up his room for us. Nice of him. It continued to be weird to require a guard escort to go to the restroom or to the shower in a trailer outside.

We had the opportunity to talk with some young Afghanis (male and female) in flight training who were first learning English, the international language of flight. Whenever we saw them at a meal, we invited them to sit with us, to the surprise of the American officers. I encouraged the young Afghanis to talk—practice their English. Attractive people. Smart, too. Good questions. One promised me if I went to Kabul off base, I would be quite safe. I smiled at him in doubt and said, "Maybe with you as an escort." His eyes intrigued me—I felt certain that he would be a leader one day and hoped he'd be a benign, good leader. And that he would remember we had been kind to him!

What I noticed was the U.S. officer in charge of the young Afghanis would talk to them like they were five-year-olds and stupid. He seemed to not be able to distinguish that they were uneducated, not stupid. And they could be very clever, like my new Kabul friend.

One always hopes that good personal communication helps international relations. In the 1970's, when the Russians had invaded Afghanistan, I remember hearing that captured Russians were mortally afraid; they had heard that Americans eat Russian babies. I have no idea if the Russians, in fact, did believe that, but I like to think that if one has good personal relationships/communication, it would be harder to fight. Somewhat true, but naïve when facing determined warmongers who get rich off of war.

When I worked in TV sports in Russia in 1979, my Russian KGB interpreter exclaimed when we were outside, "But I'm not supposed to like you!" The Russians were having their eyes opened by our American TV group. Under the severe duress imposed by the Russians (just business, not physical, so hardly worth mentioning), we still argued, had fun, laughed, got things done, and on very little sleep. Several drank too much, including the head of the KGB assigned to us, to alleviate the man-made stress.

At least I wasn't quite as naïve as the PSGP, who wanted to sleep with the troops out on the "front lines." We had to remind them: this isn't a game; this is a war zone. The troops don't need to babysit you and get killed doing so because you want to play at war.

That evening, General Yeager gave a talk; the hall was jam-packed, as usual. Outside was a brilliant sunset. I took a couple photos and was accosted by a hyper soldier on edge wanting to know what I was doing, who I was. I understood – they had just fought against the spring offensive; danger lurked in this war zone. I introduced myself, apologized, and went inside.

Just the day before, at Bagram, as I was escorted from the latrine, a soldier, who had just come in from combat, was frantic because he was afraid he had missed General Yeager's talk. All the while fighting, that's what was on his mind. He had missed the talk, but I took him to meet his hero personally.

## IMPRESSIVE LT COLONEL AT MILITARY BASE IN AFGHANISTAN

I was very impressed with the Army Lt Col in charge; wish I could remember his name. He told me what had happened the last few days. The Taliban had stormed a Pakistani prison on the border—500 inmates were freed. This base was the home of another major prison. As soon as he heard about the Pakistani break, the Lt Col went to the Governor, or tribal chief, and asked him what he wanted to do. The Governor sent his own elite guards to play soccer in front of the prison there. No breakout. No problems.

I was quite impressed that this Lt Col had established such a great rapport with the Governor and asked the Lt Col how long he had been here. He replied, "A month." What? The Lt Col had been stationed in Chad—but before he went there, he had studied the culture. He had done the same with Afghanistan. The first thing he did when he took over this base was go to the Governor and say, "We need to work together. What improvements can we make?" The Governor was stunned—and expressed that no one had ever talked to him, let alone asked his opinion. Seems so obvious to do. The Lt Col continued, "We're going to have lunch every week to discuss the situation and how to improve it. And you're buying." That base was building schools for girls.

General Yeager and I had security there that were ten feet tall, it seemed, wore 150 pounds of armor and surrounded General Yeager (and me as I stayed very close). By contrast, General Yeager and I each had fifty pounds of armor. I sure wouldn't be able to run fast in that gear. I told the Lt Col I wish we could visit the school. He said we could have with a little more notice. Darn.

## RESPECTFUL GENERAL IN QATAR

We then flew to Kabul and had but a few hours there before we were flown to Qatar. In Kabul, we were taken to the general's office. He promptly showed us footage of an A-10 taking out the Taliban on a building's second floor during the spring offensive the day before. I asked who was flying the plane. He tried to look demur and humble but wasn't cutting it when he said he was. I thought that so odd to risk a general and wondered how much flying time he had. It was also improper that he was showing off, showing footage of himself obliterating the enemy.

That evening, that same general was on our flight to Qatar and instead of offering General Yeager the bunk for sleeping, took it himself. I was unaware there were bunks until he emerged after we landed. I would have rearranged the seating, as it were. I wish I remembered that officer's name, too.

We waited in Qatar for transport to Kuwait…all night long. There were some beds that General Yeager and I took. I gave mine up after a couple hours to one of the boys. We ran into Anthony Anderson from *Law & Order*, who was thrilled to meet General Yeager—they were on their way in to visit the troops.

We couldn't leave that area of the base because we didn't have visas for Qatar.

When the USAF General in charge of that base arrived the next morning, he was angry. No one had told him General Yeager was there, let alone arriving. He would have certainly been there to greet General Yeager and then send him on his way to Kuwait right away. "I have twenty-seven aircraft here; surely you could have used one to get General Yeager to where he needs to go." And he ordered his own jet to take General Yeager and me to Kuwait immediately. Fortunately for the boys and the DoD minder, there was just enough room for them and their gear.

Note: I recently met this general again happily and heard his version of this story, which was about the same; he was truly angry but also remembered some nice things I had done that I hadn't remembered. Glad to hear.

## GRAND MARSHAL, NATIONAL MEMORIAL DAY PARADE: *Washington DC, 2012*

In May, 2012, we had just returned from visiting the troops in Afghanistan, Kuwait, Qatar, and visiting Pakistan, France, Spain, and England. We had to turn around and go to Washington, DC, because General Yeager was Grand Marshal for the National Memorial Day Parade there. He saw it as representing and honoring veterans and he, in turn, was honored to do so.

I had never been to Mount Vernon, George Washington's home, so the day before, we met some friends and received a VIP tour. It was hooooot.

At George Washington's grave, Chuck gave a small speech honoring George Washington and veterans. The families there were so excited to (unexpectedly) see General Chuck Yeager and hear him speak.

Fascinating tour of our history.

Before the parade, we met Joe Montegna from T.V.'s *Criminal Minds*. He waxed poetic about an episode coming up the following year about his Vietnam days. I asked: "Are you a Vietnam vet?"

Joe: "Yes." (Then, after seeing my impressed reaction, came clean): "No, my T.V. character is." I was speechless, but I think my expression said it all and his chagrined one showed he understood his gross error.

He wanted Chuck Yeager on the show, but it never happened.

Many of the military in the parade came up to shake General Yeager's hand or to get a photo with him—they were so honored.

Just before the parade, there were speeches in front of the VIP viewing stand. They wanted Chuck to speak for five to ten minutes. But several politicians who had heard Chuck Yeager was going to be there demanded to speak, so the ten minutes became nine, then eight, then seven...then -10, -15.

Finally, it was General Yeager's turn. As he stood in front of the crowd of over 250,000 people and who knows how many millions on T.V. and radio, he conspiratorially, pseudo-quietly said: "Now don't tell anyone, keep this a secret...but I've flown down this avenue at treetop level. Big No No.

"After General Eisenhower died, Mamie Eisenhower asked if I could plan, lead and execute a fly-by during his funeral procession.

"I responded: 'Yes, ma'am!'

"I called the Pentagon and Andrews to set it up. A two-star said: 'You aren't allowed to fly down Pennsylvania Avenue, so you will not be doing so.'

"Me: 'Yes, Sir.'

"Just in case, though, I led a flight of eight F-4s from Seymour Johnson to Andrews AFB, ready to do the fly-by down Pennsylvania Avenue for General Eisenhower.

"However, on the day of the funeral, March 31, 1969, probably reflecting how we all felt about General Eisenhower's passing, the weather was stinkin'—foggy. The two-star general made it clear: we were not allowed to fly down Pennsylvania Avenue.

"I got a call there: 'Yeager, this is General McConnell.'

"Me: 'Yes, sir.'

"Gen McC: 'Do you think you can fly down Pennsylvania Avenue today?'

"Me: 'Sir, can you see the Capitol Dome?'

"Gen McC: 'Just barely.'

"Me: 'Then yes, sir, I think I can.'

"Gen McC: 'Good. Then do it.'

"Me: 'Sir, there's a two-star general here that tells me we can't do the flight.'

"Gen McC: 'Yeager, do you know who I am?'

"Me: 'Yes, sir. General McConnell.'

"Gen McC: 'Right. And do you know what I do?'

"Me: 'Yes, sir. Chief of Staff of the Air Force.'

"Gen McC: 'Then fly down Pennsylvania Avenue.'

"Me: 'Yes, sir.'

"The two-star was very, very unhappy, to say the least.

"I'll never forget as we were flying down, I was leading two flights of four. The second flight was stacked down. The leader of the second flight called in: 'Colonel, we're awfully close to the tops of these trees.'

"I told him: 'It ain't the trees you need to worry about; it's the Capitol Dome that will wipe you out!'

"That's how Mamie Eisenhower got a formation fly-by to honor her deserving, well-respected husband: General Eisenhower."

After this short speech, General Yeager was escorted to the lead parade car. I caught up with him sitting on the back, waiting to make the turn and start the parade. I had been invited to ride with Chuck but declined. I realized that the last time I did that, I had blocked the view of General Yeager from participants on one side of the parade.

Chuck and I chatted, then they turned the corner and the parade commenced. I followed him a little. Or tried to.

I ran along just inside of the barriers to take video of the turn and the start of the parade. I got about ten feet on the parade trail when a woman blocked me and told me to get on the other side of the barrier. I started to explain who I was and why I was there when a very, very large woman proudly strutting her size—which was considerable—bigger than Adeline considerable, one big step and I'd be squashed considerable—materialized to help complete the linebacker line and block me. She was itching to do a tackle.

I stepped back out of squashing and fist-swinging range and explained, "I'm Mrs. Chuck Yeager. I'm trying to take video of my husband, the Grand Marshal. Please let me by."

The larger woman cackled in a nasally high pitch—the wicked witch of the west had nothin' on her!—"HAH, HAH, HAH, she thinks she's Mrs. Chuck Yeager!"

I started laughing.

Fortunately, one of our minders came back in time from putting my dangerously dehydrated Dad in an ambulance.

I looked at the barrier and the security guy. Even though the minder, now standing next to the security guy, had seen the exchange, he did nothing. I remembered Chuck's words in Afghanistan, "We're on our own," after he sized up our security.

The head security fellow on the other side of the fence snorted: "That woman says she's Mrs. Chuck Yeager." The minder was remarkably tongue-tied till I literally had to order him to tell the security guy that I was indeed Mrs. Yeager.

There was a collective gasp. The head security fellow sputtered an apology and gave me an all-area pass.

He added: "You were pretty polite about it all," as the second woman grabbed me and said GO! catapulting me like a football in the direction Chuck's car had gone. When I got my feet under me, I turned around to see the linebackers, the blockers. They had unbelievably melted away and were nowhere to be found. It was better than any magic trick. How'd they do that?

By then, it was too late; the video opportunity was gone. I saw Chuck get out of the car up ahead and go into a stand. I got there just as he was leaving the stand. He told me, "Dumb interviewer," and got back in the car.

The crowd loved seeing Chuck Yeager—one could tell where he was by the cheer in the crowd. A wonderful sound!

## FLYING F-15E WITH 65TH AGGRESSOR SQUADRON, NELLIS AFB

### 65th anniversary of Breaking Mach 1: October 14, 2012

What an amazing day! Started at 6 a.m. The day before, Michael, a friend, had picked us up in a Citation X and flown us through the Sierra to Nellis AFB. I had brought sandwiches, so we checked into the VOQ (Visiting Officers Quarters), chowed down, had a short rest, and went off to the Flight Surgeon for a check. Very informed and informative flight doctors. Next were egress systems. Without being cheeky, Chuck might have taught them a thing or two. The active-duty pilot checked General Yeager out in the cockpit. After studying the cockpit by himself—General Yeager is very observant and having never flown in the backseat, always the front—General Yeager queried, "Has this always been in there?" The pilot, who had been flying this airplane for a long time but clearly not in the backseat, didn't know.

This attention to detail is one of the many reasons General Yeager is held in high esteem by the maintenance guys and gals and most of the rest of us. Even if he has flown the same type and model before, if it's a different airplane, he'll ask them to check him out. Lots of pilots will just jump in and go fly. Not a good idea. Each plane has its own idiosyncrasies.

After these preparations were complete, we went to one of the 65th Aggressor Squadron pilot's homes for a squadron party with families. What a nice group of people! And the food was very good as well.

The alarm was set for 6:30 a.m.; 65 years after Chuck woke up to break the sound barrier for the first time. His life would change that day in 1947. But this day, we were up at 6 a.m.

I gave Chuck a t-shirt to wear under his flight suit—one of the Oak Ridge Boys. They were going supersonic with the General today. Okay. They weren't. But their photos on the T-shirt were.

The guys picked us up at 7:15 a.m. for a 7:30 briefing. The briefing was outstanding. General Yeager gave them the best route to Edwards AFB, California and some pointers on how and where to make the sonic boom so that Edwards AFB folks would best hear it.

The Nellis AFB pilot had had some concerns about pinpointing it. I pointed out that, after 65 years of breaking the sound barrier, sometimes for air shows for the Air Force, General Yeager knows exactly.

The guy asking conceded.

We finished the briefing and went to put on the gear. General Yeager: "Miles of string." Then we headed out to the planes. The day before, I had been asked if General Yeager wanted stairs or a ladder. I said, "Ask him. He often surprises me." (I personally would take the stairs).

When they asked him, he said ladder—it was already up. And he was the mountain goat, as Prince Malik would say—he raced right up the ladder. Now, getting into the cockpit is no easy feat. For anyone. At any age. But he did it carefully and quite gracefully. The maintenance guys helped with the gear, making sure everything was connected. We waited because we had gotten through everything early and they didn't want to take off early and run out of fuel for the whole mission. Chuck called out—he wanted to give me his blue hat with the star to hold onto. I asked the maintenance guy to toss it down—but he didn't want to risk it, so carried it down to me. After another several minutes, Chuck called to me to come on up. I did. That was challenging—that ladder and getting to a sitting position on the wing. I prayed I didn't fall—that would hurt…if I survived. I peered into the cockpit—as Chuck explained the different gauges and buttons. Most of the basic flight gauges were very familiar—since I was now a licensed pilot. The weapons systems were an addition to my knowledge. He pointed to the attitude indicator and said, "That's stupid. If you don't know your attitude…"

The time drew near. Getting onto the ladder from my sitting position… made it. I climbed down and moved off quite a distance. One sure doesn't want to get sucked up into those engines and spit out. They closed the canopy and started the engines. We all put our earplugs in. After they started moving and turned the corner, we jumped into a van and sped out to the runway to watch them taxi past. They went to a holding area—still seven minutes early for takeoff. Time stood still. Finally, they started rolling again to take position on the runway. Chuck waved at me. My heart skipped a beat.

The PIC did a sort of yee-haw wave…and they started racing down the runway. The engines spewed fire as they lifted off and raced toward the blue sky. What a sight! The second aircraft took the active (runway) and followed. Within seconds, you couldn't see them. Nothing to do but wait until they returned. We wouldn't hear the boom—I had tried to get someone to Skype or call me so I could hear it, but to no avail.

But at exactly the minute, if not the second, when Captain Chuck Yeager broke the sound barrier 65 years before, General Chuck Yeager broke it again Sunday, October 14, 2012. Later, reports from some celebrants at Edwards AFB confirmed it was a loud sonic boom. As I said…

At the appointed hour, we raced back to the end of the runway. Our choice was: be where General Yeager would do his razor turn after his fly-by, before he landed, or be where General Yeager would land. Hard choice.

After flip-flopping as well as any politician, I chose the turn. Others chose the landing. We were chatting when I saw the two-ship coming right at us. Looking beautiful! With my extensive vocabulary (kidding), all I could say was: "Wow!…Wow!…Wow!"

Everyone looked at me, looked where I was looking. They flew right over us and Yeager broke first. Quite a backdrop with the Las Vegas skyline behind him. The other broke. They weren't all that low. Darn. We watched Yeager do the approach and suddenly, he was taking off again! This time, he flew by much lower and that razor turn was even more spectacular...with the Las Vegas skyline again in the background. Joy! General Yeager came in for a landing and we watched him roll out. He turned in front of us and waved. Beautiful. After he passed us, we scrambled in the car and raced to a good spot. After stopping for a check, General Chuck Yeager taxied the F-15E through the arch of water from the fire trucks. A magnificent sight.

After its bath, the F-15E stopped right in front of me and the canopy lifted off. The PIC (pilot in control) turned and shook General Yeager's hand. They each got out—by ladder. The 30 year old and the almost 90 year old—like mountain goats. General Yeager took some photos with the maintenance guys and did a couple of autographs for them—he truly honored them. His father had said, "Never forget where you came from, Son." Yeager came from maintenance and never did forget and never forgot the maintainers kept him safe! Then more people wanted photos, but Chuck took a quick personal pit stop.

The young fighter pilot, the PIC (pilot in command), took Yeager's place in front of the cameras and press. He said it was the best flight of his life—to fly with his hero, General Chuck Yeager.

To one of the questions, he responded, "He held up better than me." Very gracious, truthful fellow. And just the right one to fly with General Yeager.

As the young pilot was talking, his wife and I were standing together, enjoying the moment. Her husband, a maverick, is all about the flying and accomplishing the mission well. Same as my husband. It occurred to one of the press that Chuck was almost three times as old as this fighter pilot.

Chuck returned and regaled the press that had gathered, with stories, answers.

After we were finished, we headed in to grab a bite to eat. Chuck changed into jeans.

After twenty minutes, Chuck gave a talk—about one hour fifteen minutes, including Q&A.

He was his usual witty, fun self, as well as serious when needed. We then took photos with kids and their parents, signed a very few items for kids and the squadron and off we went to the civilian jet.

We piled in—a bit of a delay and we were off to Chino—about forty-one minutes. Beautiful country. I flew copilot. Chuck in the back. We landed and hurried over to the hangar where our one fellow was telling stories about Colonel Russ Schleeh at a Celebration of Life for Russ.

We espied Bob Hoover and Dan, made our way over and said hello. Bob Hoover got up, told a story and introduced Chuck Yeager.

The crowd gasped, thrilled that Chuck Yeager was there.

Chuck regaled the crowd with a few great Russ Schleeh stories—mostly in Chuck's books, *Yeager* and *Press On*.

Russ was a very positive, fun, funny guy. Every time we called, he was so excited and thrilled, so upbeat. Here was a guy who had had a stroke ten years earlier and every day was a great day.

Not only had he been a World War II bomber pilot; but after the war, he became chief of fighter test and chief of bomber test. After that, he also held world speed records racing boats.

## CHUCK YEAGER & FRANK BORMAN SPEAK TO TEST PILOT SCHOOL, EDWARDS AFB

At the Edwards AFB Test Pilot School, Chuck Yeager and Frank Borman, astronaut, first person to fly around the moon; were on the stage. I was stunned at the dumb questions when you had these two brilliant minds graciously giving their time to answer questions, advise, and help the test pilots solve problems.

One was "What was your favorite airplane?"

Seriously?

Colonel Borman was an instructor for then Colonel Yeager at ARPS in the 1960s and was immensely honored to receive the San Fernando Valley Engineers Council General Chuck Yeager Award.

Colonel Borman also came to Edwards AFB for the dedication of the life-size statue of General Chuck Yeager at Edwards AFB on Yeager Boulevard. That day, several modern aviation greats, Frank Borman, Clay Lacy, Bob Hoover, and a great financial supporter of aviation, Barron Hilton, were there to honor Chuck Yeager.

Note: Long before I met Chuck, Frank and I had connected briefly regarding a business deal between two sizable corporations; he knew personally that I had acted with the utmost integrity even when the going got tough.

## NOTHING TO WEAR

***Chuck YEAGER-ism #149: "If they care about what you're wearing, they don't care about you, so forget about them."***

Half kidding, half tired of thinking, I had mockingly said, "I don't have a thing to wear!"

I grew up in a house where we dressed for dinner. Dad was very fastidious, had a unique style, three-piece suit, watch chain and fob, bowler hat in winter, straw boater (hat) in summer. Mom, with her dress-designer friend, had a beautiful style all her own.

At the same time, I probably have never outgrown the tomboy side of me. I loved one of Dad's old wool overshirts. Mom hated it on me—somehow it disappeared.

Eventually, I rebelled against dressing up for dinner every evening.

At the time I met Chuck, he was tired of mess dress and slowly got tired of black tie and then coats and ties. But he sure looked good in those. Heck, he looked good in anything and nothing.

I'm pretty sure the last time I wore a dress was in 2007 or so at a Dining In at Wright Patt AFB in Ohio. I don't know what possessed me. I like wearing pants because I never know when a jungle gym might be calling my name and I want to be upside down or swing high on a swing or…At this dining in, Joanie Reynolds, wife of General Reynolds, now a retired two-star, was wearing pants and exclaimed she was counting on me wearing pants. She always loved that I was so relaxed.

I replied, "I would have gladly had I gotten the memo." We laughed… and understood each other.

I think it was the last time I ever wore a dress—wouldn't want to disappoint the wife of a two-star again, even a retired one.

## MESS DRESS FAUX PAS— PANTS ON BACKWARDS: *2017*

Many years later, at the 70th anniversary of breaking the sound barrier dinner at Edwards AFB, I had asked a friend to pick up, at the BX (base exchange, store on military base), some black silk-like pants for me to wear that evening.

At the dinner, seated with the Commander, of course, the civilian executive, and a few other dignitaries, I voiced my shock that the Commander's aide de camp and the Test Ops receptionist had no idea who General Chuck Yeager was and especially re the celebrations this weekend. The Vice Commander assured me: "We'll be rectifying that."

A few minutes later, I put my hands in my pockets. Oops. I started laughing, exclaiming: "I put my pants on backward!"

Those at the table first looked to see why I was laughing, then, upon finding out, weren't sure how to react. All had stiffened a little. They, hoping no one would catch them wearing their mess dress incorrectly, would have slinked to the ladies' or men's room to fix it. They certainly wouldn't have announced the faux pas.

I continued, "I could go fix it, but the ladies' room is a mile away," and, "Actually, I'm starting a new fashion statement. Backwards pockets. This is great: now I can grab my own derrière and I can just say I'm just putting my hands in my pockets."

My tablemates relaxed and laughed. Many years later, I was in contact with the exec, and I said, "Wait a minute! Aren't you the one I sat next to when my pants were on backward?" He sighed, chuckled hesitantly. "Yeah." I laughed. (Chuck YEAGER-ism #12: "You gotta incorporate fun in your life." Victoria's subset #2: "Sometimes, you just gotta step back and see the humor in life.")

## PART X

## EVENTS

## HONORARY SOUL BROTHER, CAL-ORE FISH DERBY: *March 2001*

Chuck and I participated in the Cal-Ore Fish Derby on the Chetco and Smith Rivers (Oregon and California, respectively). We had to switch from his normal time in February to March that year. Thank goodness! Not as cold. Some of the former Oakland Raiders were also participating in March.

The first night at dinner, the former Raiders and a Raider honoree started the night off by joking with each other. Three white and two black players. It got a little raw for me, so I left early, plus it was going to be an early morning to start the Derby.

Chuck and I fished together — catching and releasing steelhead on barbless hooks. No easy feat, although Chuck made it look easy. The Smith River was beautiful, and it was a sunny, albeit nippy, day. Halfway, there was a lunch spot with chili where we could warm up a little. The boats were not large: room for two fishermen and one rowing guide, sometimes a dog. Many were "Willie" boats made by a friend of Chuck's named, you guessed it: Willie.

Willie was an interesting fellow; lost half his right arm, but that didn't slow him down. I met him a few months before, after Chuck and he had been huntin' elk in Oregon. At the fish derby, we liked to fish near him; he always had gourmet snacks. One female guide, laughing, told me Willie had the foulest mouth. I told her, "Not around me." She didn't believe me. Until she saw it with her own eyes. Or didn't hear it. She even tried to goad him. But it didn't work.

That evening before dinner, the former Raiders pulled me aside and asked if Chuck had a good sense of humor. I said sure. They countered that they were going to tease him and what did I think?

I replied: "Good luck! If he's offended, he'll let you know in no uncertain terms." I always wondered why people asked me and didn't just ask him. Someone once said it's because I don't look like I'd bite someone's head off. Hmmm…I've got to practice that look.

We went into dinner—but first, my favorite of the weekend: barbecued oysters—wow. Garlic, butter, and cocktail sauce. Addictive!

The former Raiders group, which included Raymond Chester (top 1970s tight end), a stellar man; MacArthur Lane (top running back); Errol Mann (top kicker, known for kicking straight on—not the side of the foot), Jack West, Jim Otto, Vance, and a couple others, called Chuck up to the front, gave a small speech and then gave him a bucket of Kentucky Fried Chicken.

Next, they gave him a boom box, a black cap turned around backward, and a pair of dark sunglasses. Finally, they gave him a gray Afro.

Then, they announced that these former and honorary former Oakland Raiders were making General Chuck Yeager an Honorary Soul Brother.

I never knew how much they were in awe of and honored to know General Chuck Yeager. They loved that the General played along and had a great time. It was hilarious.

One year during the fish derby, I was talking with Raymond at the halfway chili spot while getting our chili. He said something that inspired me to ask if he would like to take my place fishing with Chuck. On the rivers, I often got very cold and could easily get sick from the wet, cold weather.

He could not believe my offer. Was I serious? He could FISH with GENERAL CHUCK YEAGER, his hero.

I exclaimed I wish I had known sooner. I very much enjoyed fishing with Chuck, but I also shared well when there was an opportunity for Chuck to have guy energy with someone he enjoyed (especially when it was too cold for me).

They caught and released a bunch of fish and had a great time while I returned to the motel, had a hot shower, and drove up the beautiful coast to one of my favorite used bookstores.

Not to be outdone, the next night, after becoming an "honorary soul brother", Chuck repaid the Raiders.

He pretended to get a call from the Chief of Staff of the U.S. Air Force. "You need night flyers? Camouflage? I got just the guys right here."

Raymond shouted, "I don't know how to land!"

Chuck: "Don't worry; it's a one-way mission. No smiling during the mission—it's night and we don't want any bright lights."

It went on like that. The guys loved it. What a different time when guys of different colors and backgrounds could joke and celebrate their differences and similarities. Errol, Jack, and all—clearly, they all loved each other.

Addendum: After Chuck died, I had dinner with Raymond Chester, who very kindly and admiringly told me about fishing with Chuck. They talked about eyesight, strategy, and more. Beautiful. We both had tears remembering Chuck. I'm grateful to the great tight end Raymond Chester for his friendship with Chuck and for sharing it with me.

## GRAND MARSHAL, SIERRAVILLE, CALIFORNIA:
*July 4, 2001*

Chuck was Grand Marshal of the July Fourth parade in Sierraville. His twelve-year-old granddaughter, Amanda, a clever girl, went with us and rode in the parade with him. I watched. It was great fun, but they hadn't fed us. We were all a little cranky, which really meant quiet and please don't talk to us.

She admired me and wanted to learn more.

After we ate, we went to his friend's, former sheriff Jerry McCafferty's, and his wife's gas station and grocery/knickknack store on the main road in and out of town. I said to Chuck's granddaughter, "Watch, now that he's eaten, he'll be the outgoing, charming guy we know and love." She raised her eyebrows in surprise. And sure enough, there he was. She was stunned. I thought, 'You have known him all of your 12 years and your family much more, and none of you ever noticed what we all do when we haven't eaten and it's sweltering hot?'

## SURPRISE 80TH BIRTHDAY PARTY:
*February 13, 2003*

I had put together a surprise eightieth birthday party for Chuck. I had gone through his address book. I had also asked him if he were going to have a dinner party, who would be the first ten people he would invite.

I invited about twenty-five folks. On our way to the club, we were a bit early, so I told him to pull over; I had to talk to him. He knew I was serious, so he pulled over. Then, I couldn't think of anything to say. I fudged it and gave up. If I blew it and we arrive too early, so be it.

The group was waiting. Someone said, "We're going to be chewed out for sure!"

Well, it was perfect. Someone was the lookout and had rushed back to the group to warn them. As we entered, everyone yelled, "Surprise!"

Chuck gave an upside-down, friendly, special finger wave. Relieved, someone said, "Well, at least we weren't chewed out!" Another responded, "What do you think that (the special wave) was?"

I brought Chuck over to see...Russ Schleeh (World War II bomber pilot, former Chief of Fighter Test, and Chuck's great friend!) We had arranged a special flight from San Diego, California for Russ. That made Chuck's day. What joy!

A local woman, Chuck's great friend's widow, then made her "grand" entrance late, which would have ruined the surprise if we hadn't arrived early. No one noticed her but me. Grand entrance wasted.

I had a G-rated comedian, delighted to be there, perform. Then Chuck spoke. He began, "Victoria, bless her little black heart..." He kept seeing that life with me was going to be eventful and fun. It was a delightful birthday, but I learned that while Chuck liked birthday parties, he also liked the planning and hated surprises. I can understand that when you've fought in combat.

## WOMEN IN AVIATION CONFERENCE: *2003*

Chuck was the main speaker at the 2003 Women in Aviation International annual convention when good friend Dr. Peggy Chabrian, founder, was head of it. Chuck had spoken about being at a WASP reunion and how they had talked about no relief tubes for women when they were ferrying a bomber. The co-pilot went back and sat on the toilet, but it was metal and very cold. She stuck to the seat. The pilot needed her immediately, so she painstakingly got herself off the frozen seat, ripping a great deal of skin in the process. At an after-party in one of the rooms, at the reunion, after a bit of alcohol was consumed, the co-pilot mooned the group, including Chuck, to show the ring around her derrière. Chuck was laughing and telling the story good-naturedly. Somehow, when he told a story, it wasn't offensive or too risqué. He had a knack.

Shortly thereafter, he went to take a quick nap; I went to the WASP seminar. One piped up and said, "That was not me with the ring around the derrière." Each of the five or six stated the same. During the Q&A, I contemplated saying: "Prove it!" but I would have been horrified if they had.

## FIRST (INTERNATIONAL ROBOTICS) CHAMPIONSHIP EVENT, HOUSTON, TEXAS: *2003*

April 10-12, 2003: FIRST (For Inspiration and Recognition of Science and Technology) held its annual national championship event at Reliant Park in Houston, Texas. This "Super Bowl of Smarts" was so large that it required Reliant Stadium and the Astrodome to hold the entire event.

General Chuck Yeager was the Guest of Honor/Speaker. At dinner the evening before, the male emcee, with long gray ponytail and beard, told General Yeager he could speak for five minutes. Chuck replied, "I can't say my name in five minutes!"

By the end of the evening, someone got word to this aging hippy, who then told General Yeager he could talk as long as he liked.

FIRST is a nonprofit organization founded in 1989 by Dean Kamen, renowned inventor of the Segway Human Transporter. Teams come from all over the world. The competitions are high-tech spectator sporting events resulting from lots of focused brainstorming, real-world teamwork, and dedicated mentoring.

The FIRST competitors and their mentors start with a box of various items and an assignment to build a robot to perform specific tasks to compete against other teams.

The FIRST competitors in attendance at this event had worked their way up through a series of regional and national contests. At these Finals, the teams were to compete against each other by using their robots to stack boxes, knock their competition's boxes down, and then end up on top of a ramp before the allotted time ran out. There weren't enough parts to build a robot that was perfect at all these tasks, so many decisions and strategies had to be worked out to construct these robots.

The first thing General Yeager said in his speech to the young competitors was: "I don't see why you don't just put nuke weapons on these robots and blow the competition out of the water."

The MIT announcer (now in tuxedo and sneakers, still with white beard and long ponytail) was speechless. Sitting next to me, then-Governor Rick Perry covered his face from his eyebrows down, looked at me under his hand in mock horror, and managed a tense laugh.

But the kids ALL stood up and CHEERED!! General Yeager got no less than FIVE standing ovations from these students during the fifteen minutes he spoke. Everybody was reminded that the whole purpose is to encourage kids to major in science, as our country is sorely lacking in this arena.

The FIRST program is a life-changing, career-molding experience as well as a lot of fun.

## 100TH ANNIVERSARY OF WRIGHT BROTHERS' FIRST FLIGHT AT KITTY HAWK, NORTH CAROLINA

*President George W. Bush, General Eberhardt, John Travolta*

Chuck Yeager and I were at Kitty Hawk, North Carolina, on December 17, 2003, for the one-hundredth anniversary of the Wright brothers' first powered flight. It was a huge event.

At the previous night's celebration, CNN's Wolf Blitzer's messenger had asked if Chuck wouldn't mind coming to the tent to be interviewed by Wolf remotely. Sure. The messenger drove us over. The tent was hardly a tent. It had a flap on one side and a cover; the rest was wide open. No one else was there. Nothing to eat. Nothing to drink, let alone warm to drink. It was freezing. We waited. And we waited. After twenty minutes, we asked the kid what was going on. He didn't know. We said, "We're leaving." The kid scrambled and found out that Wolf wanted us to wait an hour. Chuck's answer was: We left and Chuck refused to ever be interviewed by Wolf Blitzer again.

On the actual anniversary the next day, we had squeezed into the VIP lounge waiting for the re-enactment of the first flight with a replica of the Wright Flyer, which cost a ridiculous one million dollars to make.

As Chuck would say, the weather was stinkin'. It was raining. Hard. When it would lighten up, we would go on the roof to see some fly-bys—then back inside.

The Secretary of the Air Force was inside and wanted to leave. Many, many Air Force generals, colonels, and other personnel were there and unhappy they would miss the day.

Well, he wasn't my boss, so I went to the Secretary and said, "Hello, I wanted to meet you. I'm a newlywed, married to General Chuck Yeager."

The Secretary, barely pleasant, responded: "Nice to meet you."

Me: "Sir, we're enjoying your company today."

He replied, "Thank you."

I continued: "And we'd very much enjoy it for another thirty-five minutes." He wasn't dumb—he understood my point—the re-enactment was set to occur in the next twenty to thirty minutes.

He looked at me, slit his eyes and replied, "The problem is, I broke a tooth, it hurts, and I'm hungry." Ah. That explains his "barely pleasant" response to my greeting.

I looked at his girth—as Chuck and I say about ourselves—we could live off baby fat for a week. He, maybe two or ten. He slit-eyed me, defying me to say anything.

I said, "Oh, that must be miserable. I happen to have two aspirin and a protein drink I often have for lunch I'd be willing to give you. That shouldn't hurt your tooth. I can eat the salad (they were serving)."

And smiled.

He wasn't used to people speaking up like this. His eyes smiled briefly as he said, "I'll think about it."

I replied, "Please take your time."

That wasn't lost on him, either. This time, the corners of his mouth twitched. I decided not to push it anymore—frankly, I didn't have much more in my arsenal.

Oh right. I did. That's when I pulled out the big gun: "Have you met General Chuck Yeager yet?"

He hadn't and would like to. I found Chuck one group over and introduced them.

In any case…the Secretary stayed. Much to the delight of the generals.

I spoke to one general who later became the Chief of Staff and then was fired. I was impressed with his language, or, rather, his vocabulary, or lack thereof—every other word was sh--. And how evil Saddam Hussein was. I loved his clarity despite my amazement at his expression of it.

They tried to start the motor on the Wright Flyer. It wouldn't start. They tried again. It wouldn't start.

One time, they got it started with enough of a push down the tracks, but the pilot over-rotated and the airplane never saw air. (Over-rotating is when you pull up too quickly, which can cause the airplane to lose any possible lift).

BIG letdown.

We learned later that they never bothered to ensure they had a backup motor. A one-million-dollar plane and no extra parts. Poor planning.

We also were told later that rather than a glider pilot, they had gotten two airline pilots not used to the light stuff. The instructor pilot also was not a glider pilot. Chuck remarked to the pilot who had won the coin toss that he (the instructor pilot) was a real S.O.B.. The airline pilot responded, "He hasn't changed."

Well said. Fairly diplomatic. And funny!

Chuck accurately described the scenario re the motor not starting: "Look at the (airline) pilot's face. Every time they try to start the Wright Flyer motor, he's saying, 'Oh, sh--!' Every time it wouldn't start, you could see the pilot's face: big sigh of relief."

After the big letdown, the Secretary of Defense left with his entourage.

One very impressive general, General Ralph Eberhardt, remained. We had eaten lunch with him—his was the only empty table. I appreciated his intelligent, non-evasive answers to my questions.

At this point, it was pouring. President Bush was expected to be onstage soon. Onstage was covered. The audience chairs were not. Regardless, General Eberhardt went outside in the rain in December (somewhat chilly) to honor his Commander-in-Chief.

Chuck and I had debated whether we were required to do so. I kept saying: "You're almost 81; I don't think it's expected. We could catch pneumonia."

When Chuck saw General Eberhardt out there, he decided that was the right thing to do, so we went outside. They supplied us with blankets, which helped. A little—they weren't waterproof.

President Bush arrived in Marine One. He got up on stage and gave a nice speech in which, of the top one hundred aviators honored at this event, the President mentioned only Chuck Yeager. Wow. What an honor. Sure glad we did go outside. (Thank you, General Eberhardt!)

After the President left, we saw his plane fly by and dip its wing. That is always cool to me.

The organizers requested us on stage for the next part of the presentation.

We made our way there and waited for the rain to abate.

The first person we saw was John Travolta. I first interacted with John Travolta (JT) on *Urban Cowboy* while I was in my last year at university in 1979—long story how I became a day player, which ended up on the cutting-room floor. He was eyeing me, but clearly, he wasn't the pilot for me, nor I the partner for him.

JT had been trying for a long time to meet his hero, General Chuck Yeager.

At that time, JT had a very lucrative deal with Qantas in which he endorsed them. The very first thing JT said to his hero, Chuck Yeager, at their very first meeting was: "Did you know Qantas has the best accident record?"

Perhaps part of his deal was he had to greet everyone with that line. We waited for JT to say something more, as we had nothing in response to that greeting. Neither did he.

I teased him: "We're not in public, John. You can be you."

He looked puzzled. I explained: "The first and only thing you have to say to your hero is…a commercial?"

He looked more puzzled, but Chuck, ever practical and recognizing John being nervous and in awe, jumped in gently: "What's the schedule? What's going on?"

John responded: "I think we're just waiting for it to stop raining."

While waiting for the show to start, we chatted a little.

I asked John if he would take some First Day Covers (FDCs) in his plane for his fly-by over the Kitty Hawk monument and mail them back to me. First Day Covers are envelopes with stamps on the first day the stamp comes out. The idea is you get them postmarked on that day. So on December 17, 2003, the hundredth anniversary of the first powered flight, a stamp with the Wright flyer came out. I had gotten these envelopes with this stamp postmarked for that day in Kitty Hawk, North Carolina, and some for December 12, 2003, at Edwards AFB, the fiftieth anniversary of Chuck Yeager exceeding Mach 2.

John asked where they were. I assured him they were (in my car) on the way to his helicopter ride to his plane. He agreed.

I turned and saw a B-2 through the clouds. Very strange to see such a large plane and hear…absolutely nothing.

I mentioned it was there. Everyone turned. No one else (except Chuck and me) saw it—it had dipped behind a cloud. John said I was imagining things. Eventually, he ate his words—it was almost above us. Very large. And very quiet.

John turned to me, very impressed. "GOOD EYES!"

Like Chuck, I also used to have 20-7 vision as a kid.

Someone called the show—too much rain, so they got John to his limo to get to his plane. He told me to follow him closely to get in his limo to pick up the FDCs. I told Chuck I'd meet him at the VIP lounge after this.

Well. Follow closely. Not.

John got in the limo, but before I could follow, about thirty to forty very pretty boys were trying to climb in ahead of me. Of course, some got left behind. Rather than fight through or pull rank, I espied the escort police SUV in front, opened the door and asked if I could ride with the deputy.

He was stunned. "Don't you want to ride with John Travolta?" Everyone knew I was supposed to.

"Sure!…But I don't want to fight all those very pretty boys to do so."

I gained some serious respect from the policeman, who raised his eyebrows in surprise. He couldn't believe it but was impressed.

We stopped at my car, picked up the boxes, and drove to the helicopter that was going to fly JT to his plane.

I, appreciative of the favor, watched to make sure the boxes got on. I started contemplating—just a personal study on human behavior—if John had even noticed I had not gotten in the limo or worried if I had been crushed or about my safety or even cared.

Just then, JT turned, smiled at me, and waved goodbye. I smiled and waved back. Small gestures; big results. Nice.

I returned to the VIP lounge to collect Chuck. Some guy yelled, "Chuck was worried you had run off with John Travolta."

I replied: "Let's not project!"

That stumped the guy. Chuck laughed.

Meanwhile, JT did a fly-by in his 707 and dipped a wing; not the same as the President of the United States, the Commander-in-Chief, doing it, but still pretty cool.

As we drove out, we passed three helicopters that were supposed to have taken the Secretary and all the generals, colonels, etc. But they hadn't left. We learned later that the helicopter transporting the Secretary had broken down, and the other two didn't want to leave ahead of the Secretary. I asked why they didn't just put the Secretary in one that worked and have two leave. No answer.

Glad I wasn't anywhere near the Secretary and his ailing tooth then. Poor fellow.

It took a while to get the FDCs back—JT's male friend asked me if I wanted JT to sign them all. It had never occurred to me to ask that. And then I understood the delay. I thanked them for this kind suggestion and said, "No, thank you." (I was very fortunate to have another pilot to sign them for me, Chuck Yeager.)

## THUNDER OVER MICHIGAN AIR SHOW, YANKEE MUSEUM: *August 2003*

Around 2002, the P-51 with Glennis' name on it crashed. The plane had been damaged before by a major airline pilot who allegedly defrauded that airline's workman's comp and allegedly misappropriated millions of dollars of memorabilia from the Air Force. She had landed hot (too fast) and went off the runway, damaging it extensively, then sold it to this new owner, Gary. Gary's maintenance guy and a pilot had not followed Chuck's warning. He had told P-51 pilots not to put the radiator coolant door on auto while on the ground; it could easily cause the engine to overheat and seize up. And that's exactly what happened. Instead of dead stick (no power) landing it, the pilot and maintenance fellow chose to bail out. They survived The P-51 did not; it was smashed, totaled. The maintenance guy wanted Chuck to testify on his behalf. Chuck told him no way. However, that major airline pilot told Gary a different story.

We ran into Gary at the Thunder Over Michigan Air Show in August 2003. I was glad to have the chance to set Gary straight on that and on another misinformed issue.

Gary had been told lies by the very jealous major airline pilot, so he went to Chuck and repeated what he had heard about me. Chuck said he knew all about me and set Gary straight. Gary was so embarrassed that he left without going flying with his friend, Chuck, that day.

I set Gary straight on that, too. I thanked him for telling Chuck, his friend, what he had heard. Gary was stunned.

I explained, "You were a true friend. You had concerns and had the guts to voice those concerns to your friend and only your friend. That's what a true friend would do. And you also accepted what your friend, Chuck, said in response. And learned that the concerns you had were based on lies."

# PEYTON MANNING, DARIO FRANCHITTI, INDY 500: *2007*

Chuck and I went to the Indy 500 in 2007. We arrived just in time for the Thursday VIP race around the track. Chuck went first in the backseat of one of the drivers. Getting in and out of those cars is not easy.

After three or four times around at 140+, it felt as if only two seconds had passed: he was back and it was my turn.

I kitted up and got in. Slowly. The crew made sure I was buckled in, helmet on right, etc.

We took off. Those turns created quite some side loads; we pulled a few Gs (pull of gravity). At first, I was worried how much it would hurt if we flipped. This was not how I wanted to go. Fifteen years prior, several car-racing folks had suggested I go into car racing after seeing me drive in Los Angeles on ten-lane highways. Thank you, no. I decided this wasn't my day to die, so I chose to simply enjoy the ride, keep my eyes open and stay present.

Wow. What a sport.

No wonder Chuck called racecar drivers "Professional fender benders". (Chuck YEAGER-ism #119.)

It was over too fast and we were slowing down to one hundred mph, then slower and slower till we stopped where the driver had picked me up. I got out and shook myself. I think someone took a photo, but I can't remember where it would be.

They told me I had gone a few mph faster than Chuck, probably the first time ever, if true. I told the driver, "You probably say that to all the girls."

As I approached Chuck, a tall woman with a very deep voice grabbed him, literally grabbed him, and tried to spin him around for a photo. Didn't ask, just demanded. It startled him and everyone. He wasn't going to take that from no man-woman, no matter that she was twice his size. Before Chuck could drop her and put his foot on her throat, Sheriff McAtee, our host and friend, clued her in re respect and that she wasn't the star that day. Danica then politely asked if she could take a photo with Chuck, and all was well.

The Indy 500 picks the pace car drivers years in advance, but in 2007 wanted to honor Chuck Yeager for the 60th anniversary of Chuck Yeager breaking the sound barrier. Their creative solution was to have Chuck lead the pace car, a first for Indy. The day of the race, the sheriff took us and some friends to the venue. We went straight to the top floor to watch. What a view. We said hello to Peyton Manning. What a gracious fellow as he chatted away with General Yeager.

Before the race, we went down to the field.

Patrick Dempsey's minders approached me to ask if General Yeager would like to come over and meet Patrick, this year's pace car driver. I was pretty sure Chuck had no idea who Patrick was. Even so, I told the minder: "No, courtesy and proper etiquette would suggest that Patrick come over here and introduce himself to General Yeager."

The minder wasn't used to that but knew I wasn't kidding. I watched the minder return to Patrick, who immediately came over, graciously stuck out his hand and introduced himself to General Yeager.

Chuck chatted with Patrick a little, then asked: "Are you a pro driver?"

Patrick politely chuckled (being unknown didn't happen often to Patrick "McDreamy"). "No, sir, I'm an actor."

Chuck gave Patrick some tips about driving the pace car and not running into him as Chuck would be ahead of him.

Just before the race, Chuck sat on the hood of Dario Franchitti's race car. That year, Dario won his first Indy 500 and gave some credit to his hero Chuck Yeager—"Chuck Yeager sitting on my car was good luck!"

The Indy 500 was fascinating to watch in person—television does not give it justice—you just don't get the sense of speed on TV as they zoom by.

Note: I was thrilled when, in 2022, Peyton Manning, on his show, aptly called General Chuck Yeager one of 3 G.O.A.T.S. (greatest of all time) daredevils and "Dude"!

## MAKE A WISH KIDS, EAA'S AIR VENTURE, OSHKOSH

At Oshkosh, EAA's Air Venture, Chuck flew Make-A-Wish kids in a Ford Tri-Motor. Each child got to fly right seat, with Chuck flying left. He told about one kid so little; he could barely reach the steering wheel (yes, it is a steering wheel in the Ford Tri-Motor) and certainly couldn't see outside the airplane. When Chuck told him to push on the wheel to make the plane descend, he dutifully pushed with all his might. Then, when Chuck told him to pull the wheel to make the airplane ascend, this little kid, with great determination, pulled as hard as he could. Chuck could just imagine the other ten kids in the back lifted out of their seats. To see Chuck mime all this was hilarious.

I suggested they add a second flight for the families of the Make-A-Wish kids—they are suffering, too. That was a big hit.

On one Tri-Motor flight, I got to fly right seat with Chuck flying left seat. That was exciting.

Then we suggested Barron Hilton, an avid photographer, go to take photos.

One year before Barron rode in the airplane, he was there with Carroll Shelby in his air-conditioned loaner car. It was extremely hot and muggy that day, so after Chuck taxied off with the kids—shyness be damned—I knocked, cautiously opened the back door and asked if I could sit in the car with them. Barron said, "Sure." I kept quiet, listening to the two men talking about airplanes. We watched as a little plane taxied in.

Barron asked Carroll, "Isn't that a mail plane?" Carroll said, "Yes, I think so."

I couldn't help myself. I piped up: "How can you tell the difference between a female plane and a male plane?"

Absolute silence in the front seat. Were they regretting letting me sit in the air-conditioned car with them?

I added, in my best Chuck Yeager voice, "That's a joke, Son."

Carroll spoke first, "Oh," and chuckled.

Then Barron chimed in with a smile. I think they were seriously used to Hollywood bimbos who might have asked that question in all seriousness.

## CHUCK YEAGER'S AWARD WINNING VERSION OF GRANDMA YEAGER'S BUTTERSCOTCH PAH

Chuck would make great butterscotch pah (pie) from Grandma Yeager's recipe. But not often or not often enough.

To get Chuck to make some, I entered him in the men's-only baked goods contest for the Nevada County Fair. He grumbled.

There are some tricky maneuvers to make butterscotch pah, but even a bad one is pretty good. The first one didn't turn out great. The second one did.

We certainly weren't going to give up the perfect one—we were going to eat it! So, we kept the second and entered the first—you can see our priorities.

We went to the fair after the judging to see how Chuck had faired (yup, I said faired).

After some searching, we finally realized that the one with the entire pie gone save a tiny sliver was Chuck's butterscotch pah! with a giant blue ribbon that overshadowed the sliver. The judges had liked it so much that rather than just a couple of tiny pieces missing for tasting, au contraire, only one small piece was left! Obviously, it tasted too good to stop. I understood this completely—I can resist anything but temptation.

The local radio celebrity, who had won every year for decades with his apple pie...until this particular year, said on air, "I bet he won 'cause he's

Chuck Yeager. I guess if you have to come in second, coming in second to Chuck Yeager isn't bad."

Well, them's fightin' words. Through an intermediary, we sent him a piece of the perfect pie and he sent us one of his now-second-place apple pie. The intermediary ate the apple pie, so we never did taste it. However, we had been wise enough to give the intermediary a second piece of the butterscotch pie for him.

The radio personality said on the air, "I'm going to taste this, have my first bite, in front of all of you so you know my live, genuine reaction." He took a bite and there was silence for twenty seconds, a lifetime in radio. "Well, I guess that is pretty darn good. Maybe he won it regardless of his great name."

I confess I did have an ulterior motive. I had in mind to write a cookbook and now I can say Chuck Yeager's award-winning version of Grandma Yeager's butterscotch pah.

## MARIA SHRIVER, CALIFORNIA FIRST LADY, COMES A-CALLIN': *2009*

First Lady Maria Shriver is very personable, with great energy. One of my first encounters with her long ago was at a Hollywood black tie fundraiser show at the Beverly Hilton Hotel. I gave her my seat. She was pregnant, VERY pregnant. She was surprised and grateful.

Another time, I met her at the Washington, DC Ford's Theater show during Clinton's inauguration festivities.

It was pretty funny when she called us to ask if Chuck would accept the award of being inducted into the California Hall of Fame. (Her people had called a few times before and we hadn't had a chance to think about it, get some answers, and respond.) Being the skeptics that we are and with good reason (experience), I asked, "What does Chuck have to do, give a talk?" (Often awards can be bought or they want you to do a talk because it's a façade for a fundraiser, so basically, they are using you to draw the crowd and the money.)

First Lady Maria, being a celebrity herself, understood: "No. All he has to do is accept a medallion from my husband."

Me: "Okay. Just a minute." I went out to the back deck, where Chuck was enjoying our view and his handiwork (clearing, mowing, etc.) and briefed him.

Chuck: "Oh...kay."

I handed him the phone.

He pushed it away: "You tell her."

Me: "No, you tell her."

Chuck: "YEAGER!"

Maria: "OH! OH! I'm actually talking to you. OH. Well. Oh. I wanted to..." and then she went into warp speed like any respectable New Englander and TV journalist who has only a few seconds before "they" cut to commercial.

But Chuck is from West Virginia, where many speak more straightforwardly and slowly. He almost threw the phone like it was a wiggly, nipping animal trying to get loose.

Wonderful! They enjoyed a nice talk together.

On August 25, 2009, Governor Arnold Schwarzenegger and Maria Shriver announced that General Chuck Yeager would be one of thirteen California Hall of Fame inductees in The California Museum's yearlong exhibit. The induction ceremony was on December 1, 2009, in Sacramento, California.

## GENERAL CHUCK YEAGER INDUCTED INTO THE CALIFORNIA HALL OF FAME: *December 2009*

The day started out with an interview from a Sacramento radio station. Two radio personalities talking a mile a minute. I worried Chuck would just tell them to cut it out. He didn't. He kept up and talked fast himself.

Unusual for a West Virginian country boy—they like to smell the roses.

Chuck told a story about Carol Burnett—she, as a very young girl, was in the first USO or similar show that came to his base. Every one of the millions of GIs fell in love with her and wanted to marry her—she represented the girls they had left behind.

The female radio host said: "You have just melted the hearts of millions of females listening to our radio show."

The evening was beautiful.

As we drove there, I considered wearing makeup but doing other fun things with my husband left no time.

We arrived early as usual (don't want to miss the tanker) and were led into the Chuck Yeager display. Chuck's flight jacket and some of his medals, including the Presidential Medal of Freedom, were on loan from the Smithsonian to which Chuck and Glennis Yeager had donated many of his historic items in 1986.

Thank goodness the Yeagers did; or the historic Chuck Yeager items would, most likely, all have gone missing.

We spied Carol Burnett and I introduced myself. She was very pleased to meet me—a very special, gracious woman.

I quickly introduced my husband. They had met a few times before and gave each other a huge, larger-than-life, joyous hug, as only Carol Burnett can do. I mentioned I had met her on the set of the movie *Four Seasons* in Virginia. She contemplated that and later said: "That was in 1980." I replied, "1979 wasn't…it…no! You are so right: 1980." I was graduating. She is quite sharp.

She told me she has her second book coming out in April and she goes on tour—"An Evening with Carol Burnett—to keep the gray matter active. And boy, is it active.

When she walked the red carpet, she was very vivacious and engaging with all the fans. When I met Carol Burnett the first time in 1980, I was so in awe. I was the executive producer's assistant and driver.

Carol Burnett just turned to me, stretched right into my face and said, "Hello, I'm Carol Burnett." My role model was speaking to me up close and personal. Wow! I remembered myself just in time to prevent fainting and introduced myself but could not find any words to continue the conversation.

I always heard that stars hate to be reminded of their age—so I didn't say I was allowed to stay up late to watch *The Carol Burnett Show*. I LOVED her and her show as a kid. After seeing her in person and on stage, I still love her.

I met Harvey Korman a few years after my first encounter with Carol

Burnett—what an amiable, kind fellow. He thought I was very talented and had sought me out after seeing me perform. I *really* liked him after that!

At the California Hall of Fame rehearsal, which was more confusing than enlightening, I sat with Carol Burnett's assistant. She was saying what a real man Chuck is, even at 86. She wishes she could find a man like him. I told her, "Then you would understand why I didn't marry until I was 45, after I met him. Met him at 41."

I told Carol and her assistant that Chuck wears me out! He needs a younger model. They all laughed and could easily agree.

We also saw Coach John Madden—Chuck and he had done a public announcement commercial together for space technology under President Bush '41. John Madden won't fly; he takes buses. And the idea was pairing opposites. Coach John coached a lot of our friends: Jim Otto, Raymond Chester, MacFarlane Lane, Errol Mann and others. Coach John said he could tell me a story or two about those guys. I guess not in front of so many people.

So I told him about the three black players—Raymond, MacArthur, and Jack—making Chuck an honorary soul brother! Gray Afro, boom box, big sunglasses. Coach John got a kick out of that.

John also played on my childhood hometown team—the Philadelphia Eagles, so I felt a kinship—two degrees of separation twice!

His wife is delightful—we enjoyed some time together, too.

Secretary George Shultz was there. I first thought Charlie Brown—and thought he was dead. And then remembered some more U.S. history. I said to his wife, "You should be in his position. I always think the wives understand more and can solve problems better."

She smiled and replied, "But let's not tell them." We had a good laugh. I didn't know then that she was the Chief Protocol Officer for the State of California. Very elegant lady.

At one point, it was our turn to walk the red carpet—there were many autograph seekers to whom I said: "Not today. Please go to our website, www.chuckyeager.com; it tells you how to get an autograph…. Thank you very much!"

We stopped at the first media station—Comcast. She asked the usual:

"How does it feel to be honored tonight?" Ho hum.

I fed her some questions to ask, such as what Chuck gave to John Madden and what Chuck says about Carol Burnett. The interviewer got far more interesting answers. And she thanked me profusely. Smart, perky, attractive girl. I wish I could convey to all reporters, especially those starting out: 1. Do your homework (especially easy now with the internet but must do a deeper dive) and 2. Most people, but especially of Chuck's generation, don't express their feelings or even analyze them, so it's a boring question. But the answers are the same.

I am honored…or…others say I am humbled…boring canned response.

While working in Russia, I did the same as a young (age 21) interviewer when I didn't know the subject. A producer took me aside and had me watch an interview by an experienced journalist who had done his homework and then some. What a far more interesting interview!

The next stops were a few TV and radio stations. Same question: "How do you feel about being honored tonight?"

By the sixth one, I felt bad. I had run out of new pertinent questions myself and we were tiring of the exercise. When Chuck replied, "It was duty," the last interviewer, not understanding that concept, got tongue-tied.

And that's why we prefer to do press conferences—the same repetitive questions answered all at once instead of many times in a row.

Kudos to these reporters, though, for being eager for help and thanking me. A famous interviewer was awful when interviewing General Yeager, so I fed good questions to the producer, who then fed them to the famous interviewer. This elicited great, very interesting answers from General Yeager. About the fourth time, the arrogant interviewer angrily yelled at the producer to cut it out and the interview questions got boring again. General Yeager, who brilliantly was able to gear his talks and interviews to varied audiences, then resorted to essentially interviewing himself.

A note re fake media: When Chuck Yeager was involved with classified programs at Edwards AFB, in the 1940s-60s; the press would try any which way to get information. One way was to print false, nasty information to lure Col Yeager into correcting them. He never took the bait. Smart man.

In the museum, they took a photo of the thirteen honorees in front of their larger-than-life photos. The incredible, prolific author, Danielle Steel, and Chuck Yeager graciously and discreetly helped the bodybuilder, Joe Weider, stand between them for the photo. Joe was in his nineties and looking pretty good, but not too keen on standing too long. He was one of the first to popularize getting in shape and healthy eating and was Arnold Schwarzenegger's sponsor and patron. Gov. Schwarzenegger owes his biggest breaks to Joe Weider.

We all stood for all the honorees as they walked on stage. Chuck got the biggest cheer, Carol Burnett the second biggest. John Madden the third, George Lucas a close fourth. But who's counting?

Coach John Madden, introducing Chuck, said, "Only in California can a guy who doesn't fly introduce the greatest pilot of all time!" (John would get severe claustrophobia when he flew, so quit flying.) Then Coach John read the rest of the introduction and ad-libbed: "Just before he got in the X-1 to break the sound barrier, go into the unknown, faster than anyone, they asked him what he wanted...and he said a stick of Beemans! Now just think about this: he's about to attempt the most dangerous thing in a plane and he asks for a stick of gum!?!?!?"

Outstanding!

Chuck reciprocated and gave Coach John a photo of the largest civilian airplane in the world at the time, which Chuck had been flying a year before, doing stall work over the Pyrénées, and signed it with the note: "I finally found a plane that could lift you off the ground"—Chuck Yeager.

Chuck told some great stories in accepting his award. He should have been the one to introduce his friend Carol Burnett, but it didn't work out that way. Carol and Chuck had sung "Old Lang Syne" beautifully together to Jimmy Stewart at the Kennedy Center many years before.

After the ceremony, George Lucas talked with Chuck about George's movie re the Tuskegee Airmen. Chuck said: "Are you going to tell the truth? They shot down about one hundred and seven planes, not the thousand some historian was saying."

To me, if you overstate, you diminish their real contribution. The group shooting down one hundred and seven planes is great—107 fewer planes to harm the Allies. However, if you state 1000, it signifies you don't think 107 is impressive enough. I do.

At Maxwell AFB, one of the Tuskegee Airmen was there with Chuck for the Gathering of the Eagles seminar in 2001. The Airman was ostracizing himself, obviously some personal issue. I had found some posters in the history office that were being given away, one beautiful one about the Tuskegee Airmen. And only one of those. I wanted to keep it, but after much debate within myself, decided to give it to the Tuskegee Airman. When I knocked on his door just down from ours (all rooms faced outside onto a walkway) and gave it to him, he was stunned and exceedingly grateful; he couldn't speak. It brought him to tears, which brought me to tears. I'm sure glad I won that debate with myself.

George Lucas also was very gracious—I had met him before; when he had just had a baby, in 1991, he reminded me. This evening, he was wearing a suit—I would not have guessed he would dress up. But he looked downright almost too straight to be creative. Honestly, he looked good.

Rafer Johnson, 1960 Olympic gold medalist in the decathlon and actor, was pretty funny, too. An inductee with Chuck, his next job was to introduce George Lucas. He ad-libbed: "At rehearsal, a beautiful blond lady was sitting next to me where George was supposed to be. And I thought, 'Well, he is renowned for special effects; maybe that is George Lucas.' George, could you bring her back?"

## EAA AIR VENTURE: *Oshkosh 2011*

"I just had to come tell you that you are wonderful." Of course, I liked her right away.

She was in her sixties and had seen Chuck give a talk the day before and watched me handle the Q&A.

"You humanize the experience. You two are quite a team."

Wow. Thank you!

This happened several times during the long weekend. Nice. No…very nice.

I meet a lot of interesting people this way, frankly. One of the women gave me some homeopathic patches for different ailments: new studies, new business, acupressure theory. I checked them out online and they appeared harmless, so I dutifully tried the one for insomnia. It kept me up all night, of course.

I left her to do the last Q&A. The questions were pretty interesting.

One very young man, aged eight, was so nervous that he whispered. I waved him close to the stage, bent down, and put the microphone to him. He said: "Like what plane…Like which is…like your most like favorite like plane?"

I stage-whispered conspiratorially, "Did your dad tell you to ask that because he was too scared to do it but knew you were brave?"

The son gave me a huge smile and nodded. We bonded.

I repeated the question exactly in my best imitation cute kid voice. Chuck raised one eyebrow but followed the gist.

Chuck usually answered: "Depends on the mission (for what purpose)?" but this time, he was more explicit: "To fight a war—the F-15E. The P-51 I dearly love. The accomplishments re the X-1, of course."

Another fellow had an accent and also wasn't very loud. So I jumped off the stage and ran over to him. He talked about being in Berlin as a kid on the first U.S. daylight raid of Berlin. As he continued, I was about to ask if there was a question when he asked if Chuck had been on that raid.

Chuck confirmed that he had—one of two P-51s from his squadron that made it through the soup (bad weather) to protect the bombers.

We hadn't been to Oshkosh in four years. Many, many people were very glad to see us. We attended a few events to thank all the volunteers who contributed to the 50,000 young kids per year becoming Young Eagles (over 150,000 kids per year when General Yeager was Chairman) getting their first flight and learning about aviation. And we attended a few fundraisers for these programs.

It's quite gratifying (and exhausting) to do things for others in need and/or for programs for kids and pilots.

At Oshkosh that year, George Lucas brought the trailer for his film *Red Tails* about the Tuskegee Airmen to Air Venture. At the big dinner raising funds for Young Eagles, the announcer introduced the three Tuskegee Airmen who were guests of honor at the dinner. They stood. There was polite applause.

Then the announcer showed the trailer. There was a lot of flying but not much story or character. After it finished, the audience gave a rousing, cheering, standing ovation.

I couldn't believe the make-believe got a bigger response than the actual Tuskegee airmen. The world had officially gone mad.

We had a great week: We toured some airplanes. Chuck visited with the engineer of the largest commercial plane to date at show center. The engineer appreciated Chuck's stories, expertise, and advice.

We saw the winning Staggerwing Beech—exquisite. Classic. We knew the pilot and the owner.

We toured the warbirds. And Chuck explained to our guests the different attributes of each.

We watched the night air show, modeled after the one we saw in Australia. Looked like the fireworks were being discharged from the airplanes themselves. Quite splendid, colorful and exciting.

We saw so many aviation friends. What fun! Although, for most of them, it was a bit like passing ships in the night—often just catching them while they were zigging and we were zagging. We were lucky enough to have lunch with Martha and John King.

One of our favorite events was the Young Eagles volunteer dinner, honoring those who fly the Young Eagles—giving kids their first introduction to flying a plane. EAA had asked Chuck to be chairman to accomplish the mission of giving one million kids their first flight by December 17, 2003, the hundredth anniversary of the Wright brothers' first powered flight. True to form, under General Chuck Yeager's leadership, Young Eagles got over 1.3 million kids flying.

After this, we went to the party for Bob Hoover. Mike Herman graciously culminated a few days of special honors for Bob Hoover by throwing a barbecue for Bob. Chuck ate one of the delicious steaks.

We also got to do some helicopter flying, reviewing the grounds.

Chuck did seven talks with 2000-7000 people each, even though there was seating for only 1000.

For one of the talks, Chuck sat on top of a P-51 at show center. The crowd was very respectful and enthusiastic.

Someone asked: "What was it like to fly Mach 2?"

Chuck: "Twice as nice as flying Mach 1."

The crowd laughed, enjoying the experience. Great answer to a challenging question.

Yes, it was a fun week.

## 449TH BOMBER GROUP REUNION, HORRIFIC P-51 CRASH, RENO AIR RACES: *2011*

I had wanted to go to the Reno Air Races because I had never been and Bob Hoover and Barron Hilton were known for setting up motorhomes with lots of good food.

Chuck was not a fan of the races. One year, General Yeager had been invited to speak, so we put together a list of what was required to make it feasible—nothing extraordinary: a designated golf cart, all-access passes for him and me, a set time for us to fly in and out of Stead each day so we could stay at home and not drive (traffic to the airfield was a parking lot congestion). The talk the night before—the monies raised went to charity. We wanted it to go to our charity in lieu of a speaking fee. We got the run-around and, when the organizer started balking, we were apprised by others that that money really goes to the organizer's bonus. The organizer, with bonus, made at least a quarter million dollars to organize one event a year. We declined.

The reason Chuck was not fond of the races themselves will become obvious in this story.

When Chuck was invited to speak to a World War II bomber group, with

Chuck's lackluster okay, I investigated going to the air races that day or the day before, but it just seemed too hard to do so—thank goodness.

Chuck retired from active duty with the Air Force in 1975 at the age of 52. He continued as a consultant test pilot and continued to do so at 88. He did his best to stay in good health and still had a current medical for military flying.

By this time, I had only ever asked one thing of Chuck—please always fly with an experienced pilot. Just in case, although I'd trust Chuck in a semi-conscious state more than anyone else. He trained his entire life to be able to handle emergencies in a semi-conscious state, which is what saved him after going 2.44 Mach when he was doing three snap rolls per second in the X-1A, caused by inertia coupling. So by this age, 88, especially when flying high-performance aircraft, General Yeager always had a co-pilot or IP (military language for "instructor pilot").

In small single engine aircraft, that second pilot was usually me. Blessed.

His last job on active duty was as Director of Safety. He did not like seeing P-51s, many decades-old aircraft, being stressed beyond their capabilities and/or auguring in, especially for no good reason.

He did not like seeing the P-51 modified, especially without authorization or oversight. The P-51, with its Packard-built engine, helped establish air superiority and turn the tide of World War II in the Allies' favor. It did its job well. You can't improve on that on that airplane.

Further, today's P-51 pilots are not test pilots nor trained as such, yet they modify their airplanes dangerously and perhaps illegally.

Racing these airplanes does not advance aviation. "Nothing you can do in a P-51 that hasn't been done before, including a smoking hole." (Chuck YEAGER-ism #36.)

During the Reno Air Races, a P-51 that had been modified crashed in the audience, wiping out a whole section. It was horrific. During the crash, General Yeager and I were visiting with members of the 449th Bomber Group from World War II for their reunion banquet. The day before, those members had been in the exact spot where the P-51 crashed. Imagine you survive World War II in a bomber, only to be cut down at the Reno Air Races by an illegally modified "friendly"

P-51. Fortunately, there was a full day (24 hours) between the two events.

That evening, the Oak Ridge Boys, a very patriotic group, showed up (a surprise) to honor these veterans and sang a great song, *G.I. Joe and Lillie*, a true World War II love story, also one of service and sacrifice, about his parents, both World War II veterans.

After dinner, Chuck gave a talk honoring these veterans for whom he had all the respect in the world, flying in those sitting ducks to bomb the enemy, doing their duty, protecting and serving their country.

In one bombing run during World War II, Chuck saw sixty bombers shot down by flak—that's 600 airmen. This group, the 449th, lost twenty-five percent of their men. Another twenty-five percent had been shot down but ultimately survived.

And these veterans were grateful to P-51 pilots like Chuck Yeager, who protected the bombers. Chuck's 357th Fighter Group also suffered great losses while shooting down the most enemy aircraft for time in the sky, serving and protecting their country: doing their duty.

There but for the Grace of God...

# HONORED GUESTS, PACIFIC AVIATION MUSEUM:
*Hawaii 2011*

What an evening!
The Pacific Aviation Museum sold out for Chuck's talk. The crowd was eclectic—kids to seniors.

It was also an FAA Safety talk, so at least one hundred people enrolled in the FAAST system—(great continuing education for pilots and anyone interested in aviation)—attended. Civil Air Patrol members, National Guard members, Coast Guard, the general public, veterans and the general public. The youngest I met was eight, in third grade.

We had planned to go to our friend's hangar for a little nosh before the event, but traffic precluded that. And Chuck does not like to be late—"Hawaiian time" doesn't compute. As I said, he doesn't want to ever miss his tanker—a euphemism for when he would need to refuel in the air—if you're late, the tanker isn't there and you're toast—or fuel-less.

Also, when General Boyd said meet at 6 a.m., he meant wheels up in the air after takeoff, so you'd best be getting there at 5 a.m. or earlier.

We got to the museum around 5:30 p.m. and ate some supermarket sushi we had brought.

We thanked Scott, FAA, for such a good job getting the word out to the FAA Safety pilots. Ken, the Museum's Executive Director and a war veteran pilot, and his wife, Tanya, welcomed us again.

Admiral Hays, one of my favorite people, kind, very intelligent, elegant, generous, honored Chuck Yeager, was quite the war hero himself. He had received many medals similar to General Yeager—including the Distinguished Flying Cross, the Silver Star with oak leaf cluster, Bronze Star with a "V" for Valor. Every now and again, one could glimpse the Admiral in him—he hadn't completely retired.

Chuck introduced his DVD documentary, very succinct select highlights of Chuck's life till 1997. After it played, Chuck got up and said, "Hard to watch yourself age 75 years in 26 minutes." He then explained in more detail some of the events. After, he waved me over to help with the Q&A.

The questions were good or unusual this time. First one: What was the worst plane you flew?

Chuck, in a room of Navy veterans, said without skipping a beat: "There was this Navy plane…"

And we were off and running for quite a ride.

As someone in the audience, and several emails since, said: "Lots of informative stories, heartwarming stories, funny stories."

The whole program was probably about two hours. We had planned to leave right afterward (we had an early morning schedule the next day) while people were having poupous and drinks but…we couldn't.

While we didn't do any autographs (takes far too much time; you can't get all 600 people, and one sees many on eBay the next day so the purpose is lost), we did take photos and talk to many of the audience members. We stayed over an hour.

It was a special evening—everyone most appreciative that General Chuck Yeager would donate his time and energies for fundraising for the historic Ford Island Field Control Tower at the Pacific Aviation Museum Pearl Harbor. And everyone was most appreciative to get photos with him as well.

We headed out the back door—with a fine escort of our good friend and honorary Fighter Ace, General Ben Cassiday, USAF (ret.), Admiral Hays, and Ken DeHoff.

A very enjoyable evening for all!

## CHUCK YEAGER'S 89TH BIRTHDAY

It was Chuck's 89th birthday.

After the Las Vegas pre-birthday dinner, we walked to the Bellagio and watched three different shows of water fountains "dancing" to the music. Stunning; alternatively powerful, lithe, and sensual.

The next day, in Laughlin, Nevada, Chuck and I sat on our corner room balcony, enjoying the peaceful view; the river and the sun setting over the desert and hills. It was a bit confusing—the airport across the river was an hour ahead in Arizona from where we were in Nevada.

We watched the ferry going back and forth between the banks so fast it skidded into the docks. I guess it provided a little excitement for a monotonous job—clearly the skipper had done this a few times.

Chuck made his quick assessment: "His clock must be going wild," (having to change the clock back and forth mid-river).

At the birthday dinner in Laughlin, Nevada, the table was decorated with little birthday baskets/cups with candies, silly spray stuff, balloons, blowers, and water pistols, although Chuck's was a water machine gun!

At the start of that evening's show, DK introduced General Chuck Yeager. One could feel the comprehension ripple through the audience as the cheering increased to a crescendo and a standing ovation.

Chuck opened with, "You won't believe this. I can't believe it myself. But I turned 89 today." A huge roar of laughter from the audience and backstage.

Chuck then talked about shooting down his first enemy aircraft during World War II—a great story. The audience loved it.

Joe Bonsall talked about hanging out with Chuck Yeager telling stories (which we had done earlier in the day in their bus).

Mid-show, Joe Bonsall announced: "Whenever the General is attending a show, he 'requests' us to sing his favorite song. And when the General' requests…you don't say no!…" The first time we requested it, Duane was quite touched since he was lead, but also since it was about the Boys' relationship, too. Very personal.

And with that introduction, Duane sang "It Takes a Little Rain" with Ron on piano. Chuck, very appreciative, personally thanked Duane.

For another song, *Love Song*, I noticed the band in the back doing some coordinated steps—very fun. Hilarious. Appropriately so. The ORBs also sang one of my favorites: *"And The Shade Comes Free with the Tree."* Great beat. I even forgot where I was.

At the next morning's very early breakfast; one fellow, Steve, asked me to call his wife to get her there. Steve elaborated as I was calling: "She said she might take a walk by the river. Did you ask her where she was?"

Me: "No…I was afraid she might tell me." This made us all burst out laughing. We obviously were all a little punch drunk from the early morning start.

Our pilot was a real trooper. He had no idea what he was in for when he agreed to fly us down to Vegas. Grab your hat; here we go! We flew home through the High Sierra. A glorious Valentine's Day—perfect day for flying.

When we got home, Chuck said, "Now that was a great birthday!" And that was the real icing on the cake.

## $100 FISH AND CHIPS FRIDAY

It was "Fish and Chips Friday" at nearby Auburn Airport, California, *February 24, 2012;* so we flew down to partake. I did the takeoff and flying to Auburn. It was bumpy. Wow. As we got close, I was making the calls.

Or trying to. I handed the controls over to Chuck and, on final, broke in on the personal conversation: "Guys! A- — Traffic, x-plane, final, full stop." They got the message and stopped chattering.

We landed — not easy — lots of variety of wind.

It was crowded! I mean the parking, but we slipped into the last spot. I ran ahead to get us on the list for lunch. I checked the tables to see if we knew anyone we might be able to join.

G was there with the guys — a group of about six to eight. I teased them and asked where our seats were. They all tried to squeeze but, fortunately, the table next door became available.

The fish and chips were great, as usual.

Chuck said: "Good takeoff. Just the right amount of rudder."

Yay me!

We counted the cars at the airport — inside the fence, where they should not have been. Ten or so. Kinda crazy. We watched a guy take the covers off an aircraft with very long, low wings. Looked like it hadn't been flown in a looooooong time. Two guys were going somewhere — the couple bags tipped us off. Took 'em a while to get all sorted and taxi out.

Noisy. Crowded. And a dog was barking. Loud. Made your brain rattle.

We headed to our plane. The first person who creates a new cockpit configuration, especially for getting in and out, will make a fortune.

Again, I made the takeoff and we quickly turned north out of the way of all the air traffic. It was even rougher. We heard our buddy on the radio so called him: "Arriving in ten."

He understood. It was code for "Could you help us put our friend's airplane back when we get back?"

We got to downwind first and I handed it off to Chuck on base. Did I say it was rough?

Chuck, of course, made it feel like the wind was smooth.

We were coming in for a perfect landing when the air dropped out — huge downdraft. Chuck cobbed it. Then stabilized. The wind changed directions 180 degrees and back again.

We started to land and a gust picked us up.

Later, Chuck said he was just deciding whether he'd go around when he brought it down and stabilized.

Wow. Rather exciting. A GREAT lesson in flying, too. I followed along on the controls while staying out of the way.

I had been having a little trouble trying to feel when one needed to add power, cob it, or let it float, so had been paying very close attention to the landings, since we had had some interesting winds.

What a wonderful thrill!

## OAK RIDGE BOYS INDUCTED INTO THE COUNTRY MUSIC HALL OF FAME: *2015*

After a great deal of effort, the Country Music Hall of Fame gave us two tickets. Three days before the Oak Ridge Boys induction in 2015, we found a pilot honored to fly the General and me to Nashville.

Everyone kept our appearance secret from the Boys sequestered for the show.

General Yeager and I walked the red carpet. It took a while for each of the media to grasp who this was. This was a music industry event, not an aviation event. Several jumped to shake his hand, as did the fans in line; so excited to see a true American hero.

Like an Elizabethan theater, we had box seats on the balcony over the side of the stage—a great view of the audience and the performers.

Rex, band member, waved. He, while quite pleased, didn't look stunned at all—just an everyday occurrence that General Yeager would be nearby. The rest of the band looked up and waved.

All new to me; I was not brought up in the country music appreciation world. In fact, it wasn't until age 41 that I asked a Southerner if they liked country western music. He said, "Yes. Both." Whaaaa—? Oh.

Finally, we saw the Oak Ridge Boys walking in with their wives.

After hugging his son, Chris, William Lee (WL Golden) followed his gaze. As he realized who I was and to whom I was pointing (General Yeager), a big grin spread across his face and you know it was big because we could see it under his beard.

Then Duane (Allen) looked up. I waved. He looked at me as if he was clearing cobwebs…I know her…As I could see the "penny drop" and he was realizing who I was, Duane looked over and saw the General. His jaw dropped.

I called Joey (Joe Bonsall). One could see the gears slowly grinding. I know her…not a famous singer…uh oh, is she trouble…I'm with my *family*…wait…I was vigorously pointing to General Yeager…He got it. I know this because he opened his mouth in shock and pointed at General Yeager.

By this time, Richard Sterban and his wife Donna had grasped the situation and were smiling and waving at us.

General Yeager had nodded to each and given his version of a wave.

Joe eventually put his pointer down and shook his head in amazement. The show was starting. During the show, I could see Joe tear up, so moved that General Yeager had made the effort and, at 92 ½, not a small effort, to be there for his Boys.

General Yeager was pleased that the Boys were pleased. Me, too.

Grady Martin's (a well-known guitar player) son, hiding a handsome face with his long hair, gave a magnificent speech. To prepare for this speech; he let his Bible open randomly. Oddly, the passage was about music. He had to look up a word. And that led to another word. Well, he had to look that word up, too. He truly honored his father and his father's memory.

I looked over to Duane. He had caught my eye and was nodding, tapping his heart with his hand, smiling. I smiled back. A lot of love between General Yeager and the Boys. And some spilled over onto me. Words can't describe…

Other well-known country stars there were Roy Clark, looking grand in his royal blue suede blazer and black hat; Kenny Rogers, the presenter for the Oak Ridge Boys; Trisha Yearwood and Garth Brooks, Jim Ed Brown's sisters (honorees); and more.

Joe led the Boys' acceptance speeches by introducing and acknowledging General Chuck Yeager, America's hero. The audience stood up in great respect, cheered and clapped and cheered and clapped. And cheered. And clapped. Joe and the Boys were honored. So honored. Joe had to stop for a moment as he felt his voice about to break and tears of joy and deep emotion about to fall.

Joe related: "The General is 92 and he TWEETS! Just recently General Yeager tweeted me and said 68 years ago today, at age 24, I was breaking the sound barrier. What were you doing at age 24?"

The audience laughed. General Yeager chuckled at the memory.

At the after-party, a beautiful woman said hello. Chuck nodded. Duane stepped in to explain this was not just an ordinary fan: this is Nora Lee, Duane's wife. Chuck quipped, "Yes, didn't you notice my nostrils flaring." Duane and Nora laughed.

Before they left, Trisha Yearwood and Garth Brooks took the time to brave the aggressive fans surrounding them, to honor and meet General Yeager. They each said a quick hello to General Yeager and Roy Clark, sitting with us: Hello. Hello. Hello. Hello. Goodbye. Goodbye. Goodbye. Goodbye. They all knew that this was not the time for a longer meeting—it was too loud and crowded.

On our way out, Joe introduced his wife, Mary. Chuck responded: "Not too shabby. I wouldn't cull her."

## CHUCK YEAGER'S 93RD BIRTHDAY PARTY:
*February 13, 2016*

What a blast! We had a great 93rd birthday party for Chuck in Laughlin, Nevada, with the Oak Ridge Boys. We invited seventy folks.

Barbara Eden's schedule allowed her and her husband, Jon, to be there. What a lovely woman; gorgeous inside and out. Fun, funny, insightful. I can see why Chuck and she were friends. They met on the set of *I Dream of Jeannie* when it was filmed out at Edwards AFB while Chuck was the Commandant of ARPS (Aerospace Research Pilot School, precursor to the Test Pilot School) in the 1960s.

Colonel Yeager had told Barbara Eden that they would have a man on the moon by the end of the decade. She thought he was being a bit fantastical, especially given her show. He was right, though.

I was in charge of the seating and sat Barbara to Chuck's right, the place of honor. I also asked her if she would introduce Chuck at the Oak Ridge Boys concert. She was thrilled, honored and did a wonderful job introducing Chuck and singing "Happy Birthday" to him.

## CHUCK YEAGER THROWS PITCH BEGINNING OF THE 3RD INNING: *2017 Dodgers Playoffs*

Steve Yeager, an outstanding, well-known catcher in the late 1970s, early 1980s, and our cousin, invited Chuck and me to the first game of the playoffs in 2017. Chuck threw a pitch to Steve before the third inning when they honored veterans.

As we were headed to the VIP box, Tommy Lasorda, well-known Dodger baseball player, then manager, a colorful, energetic character, came up beside us in his motorized wheelchair. He saw Chuck was the center of attention and wanted to get in on it. He was one of those guys who punched you (not tap) when he talked to you. Very annoying. "I met you many times. We had a great time together." Whap whap whap!

Chuck quickly and deftly moved out of reach of the punching and responded truthfully, "We've never met." That had Tommy stunned and frothing at the mouth literally, yelling all sorts of four-letter words. We made our getaway as quickly as possible.

We met many former Dodgers in the VIP box—what fun. One fellow strutted in, puffed up with his chest out, trying to impress Chuck and anyone else around. Steve introduced the team's lawyer. Chuck immediately said, "Oh, you're the janitor!"

The lawyer deflated instantly. It was a very amusing sight to see.

Steve, trying to avert a problem, jumped in, "Well, you do do a lot of cleanup," which caused the lawyer to tentatively inflate again, almost to a normal person's size.

We went to another Dodgers game where they were honoring Vin Scully, a well-known sports commentator. He was to throw the ceremonial first pitch, but being very wise, he got a great retired pitcher to pinch throw it for him, which created a great show. I had worked with Vin in my twenties when I was working part-time for ABC Sports. It was wonderful to see Vin, a positive, kind fellow, again.

## THANKSGIVING — FEEDING THE HOMELESS:
*Houston, Texas, 2017*

We were in Houston, Texas, for Thanksgiving and invited by the owners of a high-end restaurant for dinner. The food was overflowing on each of our plates. I find that too difficult to maneuver and usually instantly lose my appetite.

Unfortunately, the food wasn't very good; too salty. But we did eat plenty and were both full without putting a dent in the pile of food.

Ignoring our courteous protests, they gave us food for an army to take home.

We were passing under a bridge on surface streets and saw a group of black homeless folks. Having grown up in Philadelphia in a neighborhood that morphed from mixed white Jewish and white Christian, ultimately to all black Christian families with three white mixed religion families, us being one of them, I felt right at home. We stopped. They came up to our window—very respectfully. I rolled down the window just a little to be safe since I didn't know them and asked, "Would you like some Thanksgiving dinner; turkey, stuffing, mashed potatoes, green beans, gravy?"

Resounding "YES!"

I said, "You all have to share with those folks over there, okay?"

"Yes, ma'am."

I apologized, "I'm sorry we don't have utensils."

I had to laugh when the five of them raised their hands and each had a fork in their left hand and a knife in their right, confirming enthusiastically, "We do!" The Boy Scouts had nothin' on these intrepid homeless folks; they were definitely prepared. And hopeful, I guess. And definitely grateful as they each thanked us, making this one of our most favorite Thanksgivings ever.

The next day, the restaurant realized they had not given us dessert, so we dutifully went back and picked up dessert. On our drive back to our hotel, we realized neither of us needed any more sugar. We drove by our new best friends, giving them Thanksgiving dessert. I joked with them; apologizing for the delay on dessert. "Thas all right, Ma'am! Das all right! Thank you, Sir, Ma'am." Big smiles.

## PHILLIES HOME GAME: *2018*

On our way home from Paris in June 2018, we went to a Phillies game. I knew the owners from childhood. We were invited to sit in the owners' box and to invite others. We included other childhood schoolmates' mothers, the "Moms", keen baseball fans and friends of the owner's deceased father. It was quite a delight for them. One mother had gone to every game with her daughter, who had died a few years before this—such great memories for her. We met them in the private dining room—the food was excellent—and then we all went to the box. We still had to have hot dogs halfway through the game. It's mandatory at a baseball game and the only place they taste good.

We did the same the following June (2019). We had invited another "Mom" who was starting to have dementia, but it still was a nice outing for her. We also invited one of Chuck's male friends—Chuck and he had a great time.

As we were leaving, one Mom, clearly having enjoyed our day each year, asked enthusiastically, "Are we going to do this next year, too?" I responded, "I sure hope so." We both knew we were at the mercy of the generosity of our friends, the owners, who were kind and generous indeed.

Sadly, we did not do it in 2020. The pandemic severely limited travel and participation. And the Moms haven't done it since.

## WEST VIRGINIA—MEETING YEAGER SCHOLARS, JOYFUL NIGHT AND FINDING CHUCK YEAGER'S BIRTHPLACE: *2011*

What a hectic week!

We were in West Virginia for the Governor's One-Shot Doe Hunt. We arrived a couple days early to visit with family and the Yeager Scholars. As he, and then we, did almost every year, Chuck met with the Scholars, regaled them with stories, answered some questions, signed their *Yeager* books, and gave some guidance re leadership.

Afterward, we went to Joyful Night—West Virginia's celebration of Christmas—lighting of the tree, choruses singing, dancing.

We visited with the chef of the Governor's Mansion, an old friend, and tasted his delicacies for the evening. The Scholars explored the public rooms of the mansion beautifully decorated for Christmas.

We then walked to the Cultural Center, where we arrived in time for the last performance. And CUPCAKES. I asked the scholars if they had gotten cupcakes. They said, "Oh yes,"—they were first in line.

Great leaders. Kids after my own heart. However, I did mention they could have gotten one each for General Yeager and me. They immediately ran and got some.

They're learnin'.

The next day, we headed out to Grandpa Yeager's house. Chuck had not seen it in 75 years. It is literally up a creek. And the creek was very muddy. And getting worse. We couldn't get there. We gave up—we would have to wait until summer. We did get back there the next year. Chuck enjoyed exploring and sharing his memories with me.

We next went back towards Myra. I was afraid our next stop would be much harder to find—the place where Chuck was born. The driveways all look alike.

I guessed right the first time. Chuck loved it—beautiful views. The house had burned down many decades before, but the foundation was there. Chuck sure appreciated seeing it and that I had taken the trouble to find it a year and a half earlier.

When searching the year before, I had driven up every driveway…and realized this probably wasn't a good idea. Country folk don't take too kindly to strangers driving up their driveways. When I introduced myself though, they were pretty nice.

# PART XI

# GERMANY, FRANCE & SPAIN

## GERMAN GENERAL GUNTHER RALL, 3RD HIGHEST SCORING WORLD WAR II FIGHTER ACE: *2008*

In the fall of 2008, we were invited to give a few talks in France and Germany. I told Chuck I was going to stay afterwards and drive around for two weeks. He was welcome to join me; in fact, I'd love it, but he certainly did not have to if he didn't want to. Well, we had already traveled together a lot by then and on extended trips, so he knew it would be fun and interesting, if nothing else.

While giving some talks, we had the chance to catch up with German General Gunther Rall, third-highest scoring World War II ace, who shot down 275 enemy aircraft. One day, he got shot down multiple times. He'd just go get another aircraft and get back in the sky. The Germans saw the enemy on every mission, which explains why their scores were so high. During World War II, Captain Yeager only saw enemy aircraft on five or six of his sixty missions.

Gunther was a special person. Chuck and he were great friends from when they were stationed at Ramstein AFB, Germany, at the same time in the 1960s. Gunther was part of NATO then.

Gunther was always very gracious to me and a great admirer of Chuck's. After a plane incident, he looked at me and said, "That was probably a bit too exciting." "Yes, indeed." And all he said to Chuck, who had saved our lives, "Nice recovery," and hugged him. Gunther knew just the right things to say.

He was thoroughly disgusted with the people who had caused the incident and who were frighteningly bad pilots and dishonest people. He was quite frightened flying with them.

Once, when we went on a walk together, he looked up at the telephone and electrical wires and exclaimed, "America is so antiquated." I was about to take umbrage when he explained: In Germany, their lines are underground; in the U.S., the telephone and electric wires are mostly above ground and, as such, can cause horrible aircraft accidents if the pilot doesn't see the wire. I couldn't disagree with him—often when flying, looking for a place to land in an emergency, roads are hazardous due to the poles and wires.

# F/O CHUCK YEAGER'S P-51 CRASH SITE:
*France 2008*

In 2008, the first time we visited the site where Chuck Yeager's P-51 crashed, the property owner was having a hunting party and had not been forewarned of our visit. Fortunately, Philippe and his wife, Jacky, are warm people who were thrilled to meet General Chuck Yeager.

There was a hole there; no, not from when the plane crashed, but from when the Germans and later "historians" came to dig the plane out.

We visited an area where folklore says Chuck came down in his parachute. The forest had been cut down within the prior ten years. About five elderly men started arguing as to where the actual spot was. It was this tree, no, that tree. No, that area. No, over here.

We often had five to ten people talking at me—all in French. That was a challenge.

Chuck was very gracious—he told me later this was not the spot where he came down—it was too close to houses. He steered clear of houses. And the trees were too short.

Next, we went to La Rode, where the Russian Lady, the first English-speaking person Chuck met in France in 1944, interrogated F/O Yeager. There were many photos of the house as it had been in 1944. Today, while most of the building still stands, the area where the Russian Lady had lived had already crumbled.

We met the Russian Lady's granddaughter in 2008. She was the youngest of the Maquis we had met—and she was the first one to die—in her seventies—in 2009, before we could get back. We were very sad but glad we had met her. She had some useful insights.

We visited Gabriel's house and Raoul's house, two places where Chuck had hidden.

We saw the tree under which F/O Yeager had sat watching the Germans walk by, after which Gabriel was apoplectic and vehemently warned the young evadee not to go outside again upon pain of death.

Relatively near Raoul's house was the field where several Allied drops were made, one of which Raoul and Yeager had helped collect and load into trucks loaned from the pencil factory.

## HÔTEL DU PALAIS *(Palace Hotel), Biarritz: 2008*

We had driven to Sort, Spain, where F/O Yeager had been put in jail for a few hours during World War II after being shot down and evading the Germans by climbing over the Pyrénées in three feet of snow while carrying a wounded airman. And now we were in Biarritz, a place I had wanted to visit since my third (junior) year at university spent in Paris. I had wanted to stay at the Hôtel du Palais, where all the kings and queens had stayed in centuries past.

We walked in the front door in our usual attire: clean jeans, button-down shirt, vest, jacket, walking shoes. The doorman looked down his long Aquiline nose, which seemed to get longer with each second, as he asked in arrogant, nasally, lockjaw French, "May I help you?"

I responded in French, "No, thank you," and we kept walking.

By the time the snobby doorman recovered, we were well on our way. I remember when I lived in Paris while at university, the designer stores would let in folks dressed like us in jeans but maybe even in ratty jeans with holes because, often enough, those were the kids of the wealthy rebelling but still with plenty of money to purchase something.

I asked the receptionist how much a room was. We spoke in French.

The receptionist asked: "With a view or without a view?"

I replied, "Well, each, your least expensive."

The receptionist said, "With a mountain view (no ocean), it's 450 euros." (The equivalent of about $600/night at that time.)

I waffled a little: it's just one night. But we'll be in the room less than twelve hours, so won't be able to take advantage. But Chuck is worth any amount of money.

I turned to Chuck and told him: "It's $600 for the night."

He looked at the receptionist and exclaimed, "I want to rent the room, not BUY it! (Chuck YEAGER-ism #150.)

The receptionist and I burst out laughing. The receptionist clearly agreed with us.

We left. The place we found for the night was right across the street from the best breakfast place ever, with an incredible ocean view. The breakfast was one I hadn't had since I was little. My Dad made it: fried eggs on bacon—literally crack the egg on the almost fully cooked bacon and let it fry that way.

Next, we went to the tourism office, which recommended a great, inexpensive place to stay for a few nights south of town with another beautiful ocean view. Several years later, she found us a great château on a lake slightly inland. The rooms were beautiful and large with a great view of the lake and trees. Rumor had it a plane with nuke weapons had gone down in the deep lake. That made staying there a little more lively.

I also asked the woman at the tourism office to contact Cazeau Air Base and ask them if General Chuck Yeager and his wife could visit. She thought I was kidding, but after I politely insisted, she acquiesced. She hung up and informed us Cazeau Air Base personnel would call her back later—we were to check in with her before 5 p.m.

We drove the coast down to Spain, had lunch on the way—beautiful drive—then returned to the tourism office. The woman's tune had changed significantly; she was in awe and very respectful. Could we come to Cazeau for lunch tomorrow, please?

## CAZEAU AFB: *France 2008*

The following morning, on our way to Cazeau, we climbed the Grande Dune of Pilat, the tallest sand dune in Europe, near Arcachon. For centuries, the French had tried to make a seaport in that area, but the sands kept shifting and it was too dangerous.

Cazaux Air Base could not believe General Chuck Yeager was in their midst. Cazeau AB was established in 1914 during World War I, the largest air base in France, where many U.S. volunteers and units trained and where Chuck Yeager had been assigned briefly in the 1950s. They rolled out the red carpet, fed us a delicious lunch, took us on a tour, took many photos and gave us a case of wine. General Yeager signed some photos, after which we went back to our hotel, for which they paid.

The next day we tried to have petites fritures poissons, a delicacy that Chuck had had when he was there in the 1950s. After many tries and no one knowing what we were talking about, we finally learned that it wasn't the season. Tiny fried fish—you ate the whole thing, tiny bones and all. Delicious. It's fried with herbs. Say no more. I had had something similar in Indonesia.

## FRANCE: *2010*

Unfortunately, when we returned two years later, Raoul's house had been remodeled beyond recognition and beauty. The eaves where Chuck had hidden were still there with cans of food from the 1940's.

We also visited Gabriel's grave. That was a somber moment. Chuck was quite moved. Gabriel had saved his life oh so long ago. The grave was beautiful and elegant.

We visited the site where we have a photo of Gabriel and Chuck from 1955-56, when Chuck returned to visit while stationed in Germany.

Gabriel must have felt great joy when he saw Chuck in 1955-56—that one of the many men he had saved (because there were a few he couldn't) had not only survived but had gone on to do great things.

I know Raoul when he saw Chuck for the first time in 64 years and then this year, had tears of joy. Charlie—with a French accent: *Sharlee*—had survived.

We visited the field where the German airplane that had shot down F/O Yeager had allegedly crashed. We learned the German pilot's parachute had allegedly not opened, so he did not survive. We wondered if, in fact, it had not opened or if the Maquis had killed and buried him upon landing. That unlucky German pilot was shot down over the stronghold of the French Maquis.

We visited the farm where Charlie played soccer with the little boy Jean. And met Jean-Pierre, now a grown man with grandchildren. And we visited the house in a large town, Casteljaloux, where Charlie had spent his second night in France hiding in plain sight. Turns out the owner had been a collaborator (collaborated with the Germans) but not this time. The current owner is a larger-than-life woman with a big personality, thrilled to see us and know her house has some importance in history. We looked at the wine cellar with two egresses where Charlie had hidden.

We visited the defunct pencil factory—from the outside. So picturesque.

We visited the farm where the Maquis assembled the evadees to take south to the Pyrénées. The present-day farmer was resistant to strangers. But after just a few minutes of meeting us, he and his wife invited us inside for a drink.

We visited the Saturday market and saw where Gabriel had his booth and where the French Underground passed most of its messages. Other messages were passed at Gabriel's house—another had the radio and he would come by to relay the messages such as "It's raining." This meant the Allies were going to do a supply drop that evening.

## MONSIEUR ET MADAME BELLOC'S TRYST:
*France, 2010*

November 2010: France: While we were in Southern France visiting places where Chuck had been shot down and worked with the Maquis during World War II, we met or revisited several of the Maquis and French Underground. What a courageous bunch! Three of them were still alive. Raoul, Guy, and Nico. (Sadly, none are alive today. Even Chuck outlived them all; but I met some of their kids and grandkids in July 2023.)

We also learned an elderly couple, Monsieur and Madame Belloc, had quite a story to tell.

On March 5, 1944, Chuck had flown on a mission to Bordeaux to take out the Bordeaux Merignac airfield, munitions factory, German submarine pens, and warships in the harbor.

He was pretty stoked. The day before, he had shot down his first two enemy aircraft, a German Me-109 and a Heinkel 111, although he only got credit for one.

The next day, when Chuck was shot down, his plane, what was left of it, screamed towards the ground, flying pilotless and creating a smokin' hole next to a small barn (still there) where the elderly couple, then a very young couple, were…well…having a tryst.

Monsieur was avoiding being conscripted by the Germans so he had to be very careful bicycling around the countryside. In fact, the Germans came that day to his parents' house looking for him, so it's a good thing he was… out. His parents got word to him, "Son, love you, don't come home." Monsieur called Madame his lucky charm.

I asked Madame if she would discuss the tryst on camera. She was reluctant because, in 1944, one just didn't have sex before marriage, or at least one didn't admit it. During the war, though, one never knew if one would survive.

I tried to convince her it was okay today—there would be no stigma. In fact, au contraire, it was a wonderful love story as they got married just three months later, after D-Day, and were still happily married that day 66 years later.

To convince her, I called in the "cavalry." Or, in this case, the fighter pilot.

I translated Madame's story into English for Chuck.

After listening to this, without skipping a beat, with that mischievous twinkle in his eye, Chuck asked: "Now let me get this straight; did you have the best view? Were you on the bottom?"

I tried to refrain from laughing so I could translate.

Madame burst into giggles, tickled that the General would tease her like that, becoming that young girl titillated that he would flirt with her, waving a finger up at him in mock remonstration.

The cavalry had succeeded. She'd tell the story on camera.

Monsieur and Madame were two peas in a pod. Both were little, about the same height, maybe four feet ten, incredibly agile and alert.

I would ask questions from behind the camera. I wondered if my French was understandable—I had spent time in the south, where the accent and some vocabulary are different.

Monsieur would respond: "What?"

By the time I had reformulated the French, Madame was repeating the question…verbatim.

And Monsieur understood. Like so many couples who have lived together for some time, one can understand only through the voice of their loved one.

I was thrilled! I had gotten it right. Or right enough.

Monsieur would then answer. Or Madame would if I specifically directed a question to her.

They were delightful.

When we finished filming, we had sandwiches for lunch. It had started to rain, so we stayed put to ride it out.

The couple offered us coffee and water. A sign of genuine hospitality. Very kind. They were not rich, but they had provided for their family and survived.

The rain abated, the stories slowed, the gear packed up, the coffee drunk, and after bidding farewell, we left the young, elderly couple—just imagining them when they were lovers before a lifetime together as true married partners.

We returned in 2013 to visit our little friends. We had heard that someone had muddied the waters and they might not be so welcoming. But I ignored the rumors and insisted we go. Contrary to the rumors, they were thrilled to see us. We were like long-lost friends. We sat down, had coffee, and chatted as they continued peeling their quince apples.

Addendum: In 2018, we returned to the area looking forward to seeing our friends and learned they had died about three months earlier—within a week of each other. And so the love story continues.

## CHRISTIANE ET ETIENNE SAW F/O YEAGER DESCENDING IN PARACHUTE: *March 5, 1944*

In Cours-les-Bains, France: Another woman, Christiane, at the young age of 4, along with her brother Étienne, age 6, heard the dogfighting above the clouds and saw F/O Chuck Yeager descending in his parachute after he had been shot down on March 5, 1944; a P-51B disabled by three German Me-109s. The children, who had never seen a person in a parachute, thought he was a bomb and ran inside.

While we were watching Chuck and Étienne, now mayor of Cours les Bains, interviewed on film with the window from the canopy of F/O Yeager's P-51B, which their father had found 66 years before, the day F/O Yeager was shot down, Christiane leaned towards me, watching, clearly enraptured by Chuck, and whispered in French:

"He was worth saving."

I smiled and nodded in agreement with perhaps different or additional personal reasons.

I thought she was about to say because of all the contributions he has made to history and the world, saving men's lives, breaking the sound barrier, but instead, she gave her reason simply and concisely: "So handsome!"

I agreed with her on that point, too. Yet I couldn't help wondering: "Good thing Chuck wasn't ugly. Otherwise, would he have been a throwback?" (Sold him to the Germans?)

## MADAME GABRIEL LAPEYRUSSE – PAULETTE: *2010*

Paulette was the widow of Gabriel Lapeyrusse, the Mayor of Nerac and head of the Maquis, who had kept Chuck safe after he was shot down during World War II. Gabriel had been quite a character; larger than life.

She had at first refused to see us. She was worried we'd be bringing in the cameras and film crew and she wasn't looking her best. Her son assured her it was just Chuck and me. She still hesitated. She still wasn't looking her best – and Chuck Yeager was one of her young woman crushes.

Our last evening in the area, we got the call from her son: Paulette will see us. *Without* cameras or anyone else – just us!

So we told our film crew to go ahead and eat without us and took off. Chuck wasn't so sure about this – didn't know what we would find at the hospital. He's seen too much, been to too many hospitals, as well as to too many funerals. I assured him we wouldn't be there too long, but it would mean so much to her and me.

We were meeting her son at her house for him to lead us to the hospital. He is a very lively, gracious fellow. His wife is also kind and fun, a naturopath and healer.

I seem to always remember where that house is, even this time in the dark night. I don't know why, but it made a big impression on me when we first went in 2008. A large square stone house with ivy – classic. It had a trap door to the attic – very hard to see.

Although many did, Chuck himself never hid there – it was too entrapping – no way out a back door or opening if the Germans searched.

Paulette's son and daughter-in-law (one of my favorite people!) were there and led us to the hospital. We went up the stairs and walked miles – like most hospitals – good for exercise, I guess – and came to Paulette's room.

She was nervous. Chuck lit up when he saw her. She was radiant; frail, small, but lovely. Even more so when she saw Charlie. And in the dim evening hospital light, she emanated an ethereal, brilliant light. She beamed. I don't think a smile was ever broader or more sincere.

I was introduced. Chuck said hello. We chatted a bit. And then Chuck exclaimed: "You are beautiful!"

She knew he was saying something nice; she could see it in his twinkling eyes and elated smile, but she didn't speak English, so I translated.

And added: "And you know it must be true because he is saying it in front of his wife!"

We all laughed.

Me: "And he's right! No wonder Charlie wanted to see you." She beamed with joy and, blushing, shyly remonstrated me, "You shouldn't say such things in front of your husband."

Paulette was so delighted to see "Charlie" (Sharlee)– and to see him as handsome and kind as she had remembered. And telling her he still remembered and still saw her as beautiful and lovely.

We talked a bit about 1956 when she met Chuck—he had returned to Nerac while in France to say hello to Gabriel and Mme Stravorsky, both instrumental in saving his life.

Paulette was Gabriel's third wife. Unfortunately, Gabriel died in a car accident in Eastern France in his early sixties, in the early 1960s. Paulette never remarried.

We asked her about some of the Maquis. There was a question about Dr. Henri's stomping grounds. She confirmed what we thought was true. He did go as far as Cours les Bains.

Some had said: "Oh no, he didn't go that far." But my thought was: an intelligent French Underground member, to avoid capture and a sting, would not tell anyone where he went, so how could any one of the naysayers be so confident of their information?

I trusted Paulette's information, though, because Dr. Henri was good friends with her husband, visited often after the war, and talked about it, including that nothing they ever did again would be as important as those 2 ½ years.

Paulette's son had tears in his eyes—what extraordinary, tender memories. When I couldn't quite arrive at translating well, he helped me. Otherwise, this normally chatty fellow stayed quiet in the background while we felt blessed to witness these two old friends say hello.

After a little more time, we didn't want to wear Paulette out; we bid our goodbyes. Chuck gave her a bise (a kiss on the cheek) and left. It was my turn. We hugged—best we could with her IV. And gave each other a bise. We talked some more, hugged again. And left.

Words can't describe the feelings, the meeting, the energy, really. We all walked on air out of the hospital, Charlie and I knowing we would most likely never see her again in this lifetime.

Paulette Lapeyrusse died shortly thereafter. I can't articulate well how grateful I am that we got to visit with her in the hospital. I still see her as we did: surrounded by and emanating pure brilliant light, ethereal.

## PYRÉNÉES, SORT, SPAIN: *October 14, 2010*

The area of Sort, Spain is rather poor and unemployment in Spain was around 20 percent in 2010, so the people of the region were immensely honored that General Chuck Yeager and his wife came to Sort to celebrate the 63rd anniversary of breaking the sound barrier, October 14, 2010.

After breakfast, Chuck did three interviews with the press. We generally do them all together; they all ask the same questions. As previously stated, we usually ask the interviewers to have read *Yeager, An Autobiography* first or at least review the official website: www.chuckyeager.com—it answers most questions. And then, if the interviewer still has a question, it is usually interesting. This time, there wasn't time, nor is *Yeager* translated into French.

When the interpreter herself had to translate the same question and the same answer many times, she understood and was exhausted. We teased she could just do the interviews now and we could retire.

Chuck was a real trooper.

The first stop was the Town Hall. We met the mayor, the president of the region, Catalonia, some Guardia Civil, the organization to which F/O Yeager had surrendered when he had trekked over the Pyrénées far enough into

Spain to be safe. In 1944, he hadn't expected a hero's welcome, but he sure didn't expect to be put in jail.

In 1944, after being shot down, helping the Maquis, evading the Germans by climbing the steepest part of the Pyrénées in three feet of snow carrying a wounded airman—hiking for four days and nights over 50 kilometers—he came off the mountains, jumped on a bus to Sort, turned himself into the Guardia Civil, the Spanish police, and was promptly put in jail.

We also met some other officials, a Spanish Air Force General and Colonel Lopez, who had grown up in this town. Col Lopez had not been seen in these parts in his uniform, so it was quite a thrill for the town to see one of their own looking so handsome and distinguished.

Next, we went to the jail, now a museum. They unveiled a plaque in Chuck's honor. We then went into the next room, very small, the actual jail cell. There is a sanitized, defunct stand-up toilet there—a hole with two places to put your feet and good luck.

I was the first one in and stood on this (no longer in use, of course, and quite clean) to stand out of the way of the group and the photographers. Chuck and the Spanish general entered next.

I exclaimed: "Do you mind? I'm busy in here."

The two-star Spanish general, striking and elegant in uniform, ever a gentleman, apologized and started to walk out. Blocked by General Yeager laughing, he looked, saw where I was merely standing (fully clothed, of course), and joined in the laughter.

Next, followed by a large crowd like the Pied Piper, we stopped at the most likely place where, in 1944, Chuck slept in a bed for the first time in a month, Hotel Pessets. The façade is the same—Chuck said he didn't remember the hotel itself, but he sure remembered the façade ornaments; mermaids (naked breasts), which had the Catalonians laughing.

The hotel has moved, but this building kept its cafe's name—Cafè Pessets.

We met the owner's mother. 89 years old and now in a wheelchair, she had been there when F/O Yeager came through in March 1944. Thrilled, almost giddy, to meet General Yeager this day, especially when he good-naturedly teased her, she admitted she didn't remember Yeager specifically;

so many came through going both ways as refugees. This area was a smuggling area—refugees, evadees, contraband. When the Germans lost the war, Germans were the refugees. One of the Sort men said he traded a pack of cigarettes for a watch.

Next, we stopped at the police station. Chuck made a joke; our photographer laughed.

Then, everyone laughed.

I told the photographer: "Good thing you give the sound effects signaling that Chuck is kidding…just in case."

The two-star general turned to me, smiled, nodded, and repeated: "Just in case."

Then we went to the auditorium. Several folks gave speeches honoring General Yeager. The Spanish Air Force gave General Yeager Honorary Wings, a striking, ornate design.

General Yeager's response: "Where's my airplane?" The local Spanish, not used to a quick, slightly irreverent wit from someone in the military, laughed heartily.

Chuck gave a short speech. Col Lopez translated with paraphrasing. Fortunately, most of the audience was familiar with English and Chuck spoke slowly and distinctly when he was in front of people for whom English was not their native language. So they got his jokes.

We presented the mayor of Sort and the head of the museum with a lithograph of General Yeager, three of the 361 different makes and models of airplanes he has flown, and fish, elk, and mule deer. Superb lithograph signed to the museum.

Divinas, a trio of dazzling Spanish women dressed like the Andrew Sisters, sang and danced beautifully, energetically, coquettishly. One couldn't decide with which man to flirt—on either side of me: General Yeager or the Spanish two-star general, two extremely handsome, elegant, witty, stellar, real men. (Lucky me!) She looked at me questioningly to see which one was mine. I hesitated; of course—both! Very amusing.

The women posed for a photo with General Yeager and gave a signed copy of their CD, *Chocolat*, 90% swing and 10% country. It's great!

We walked to Cafè Pessets for lunch.

I told the two-star general, seated to my left: "Wait until our Deputy Air Attaché tastes the mushrooms before eating them (to check for poison)."

The general was getting used to us and our humor by now, so he laughed. But then he was reminded of a Thai family of seven that ended up in the hospital after eating mushrooms. I admitted I was only half kidding.

We had salad in a glass and a small main course of tender lamb shank. Dessert was ice cream with yogurt and a fruit puree.

I asked one of the Spanish Air Force members their opinion about Iraq and Afghanistan. Our American military that were present were stunned at how direct I was. Why not? I can say: "Nice weather" to anyone, but since I'm sitting there, might as well learn something.

The Spaniard was quite eloquent. And diplomatic. Excellent. And informative if you listened carefully, which I did.

After lunch, a helicopter ride over the Pyrénées to trace the route again, to complete the unbelievably fantastic day.

## RAOUL RENAUT, FRENCH UNDERGROUND/MAQUIS, WORLD WAR II HERO

In 2008, 2010, 2012 and 2013, we were lucky to meet Raoul François Renaut, head of the Ambrus Maquis, who protected Chuck in 1944 after he was shot down. Raoul was 92 when we met him in 2008. He was 28, an old man, in 1944 when he picked Yeager, "Charlie", up in Nerac. The two bicycled all night to get to Raoul's parents' home.

They slept during the day and, at night, picked up the supplies dropped by the British Halifax in a field a mile down the road. Having learned from his father drilling gas wells, F/O Yeager taught the Maquis how to use plastique explosives with which the Maquis, under Raoul's direction, would blow up bridges and other targets.

I asked Raoul what work to earn money did he do during the war. He said he worked for the Germans…guarding bridges at night!! An occupying army sure has to be careful when hiring the locals.

I also asked Raoul to tell me something not in Charlie's books. He said Charlie would go off riding his bike by himself, which made Raoul very nervous. The Maquis were told on pain of death if anything happened to the American airman.

The first time I met Raoul was at the spot where the Halifax did its drop. He was with his second "wife," an artist whom he had known as a young girl. When Raoul saw Charlie, he teared up. We went to see his parents' house, a beautiful Georgian style home, in which Charlie and he had hidden during the days, while they worked at night. Unfortunately, he did not own it anymore. His first wife had divorced him after she found him in bed with his future second "wife"...at age 87!

Next, we went to the town hall for a little fête.

We saw Raoul again in 2010 when we filmed more of his story. Each time, Raoul would tear up—a reminder of challenging times and a life saved. Raoul and his wife asked me to call them Papi and Mami—French nicknames for grandparents.

In 2013, at lunch in Casteljaloux, Raoul ordered steak frites (steak and French fries). The rest of the group ordered French fries and assured me there would be enough for me. There wasn't. I love the French fries in France.

I noticed Raoul was eating just his steak and pushing his fries to the side. I was sure he wouldn't mind if I asked for some or reached in and grabbed one while he was talking. But I refrained. I could wait for a break in the conversation to ask.

I asked him about something I had been told: "J'ai entendu vous avez tué 57 (cinquante-sept) gens la derniere semaine de la guerre." (I heard you killed 57 people the last week of the war.)

He looked up, contemplated me and what my reaction might be. "Cinquante-sept? C'est beaucoup." (57? That's a lot.) He returned to eating his steak.

Me: "Oui." (Yes.)

Raoul looked up again and saw I wasn't to be put off so easily.

Me: "Eh, alors...?" (And so?)

He replied: "Je ne sais pas. Je n'ai pas compté...J'étais très occupé." (I don't know. I didn't count...I was very busy.) We laughed. He had gone off to fight in eastern France after folks in southern France were liberated.

After the war, Raoul became mayor of Ambrus, where he grew up.

After finishing his steak, Raoul went on to polish off his French fries. Given his combatant history, I'm sure glad I didn't reach for a French fry—as Chuck would say, "I would have drawn back a bloody stump!" (Chuck YEAGER-ism #151.)

Besides, I would have looked like I was stealing food from an old man! Not a good look for me.

Raoul passed in 2015. I will never forget him proudly saying, "On D-Day, Charlie and I were in the same army (the United States Army) under General Eisenhower (the Supreme Allied Commander of Europe during World War II)."

Raoul had/has a special place in our hearts.

## VISITING NORMANDY: *2018*

Chuck lived his own motto/Chuck YEAGER-ism #14: "You don't give up. If you can't do something, you back up and do the next best thing."

A day after visiting Monet's gardens and pond, Chuck and I visited Normandy for the first time. When people asked him if this was his first time in Normandy, he would respond cheekily, "Does bombing it count?" then smile mischievously.

It was pouring, I mean sheets of rain, the day we went to the American cemetery. Chuck stayed in the car while I kitted up and ran to the ticketing (seemed like miles away) booth, then to another building looking for administration. I saw a man locking up and approached him. "Sir, could you help me? I'm looking for the Superintendent." He said, "You found him."

Yay! I asked, "Do you have a covered golf cart to take General Chuck Yeager around the cemetery?"

He was stunned and thrilled but replied, "I only have a two-seater available."

Me: "Great! I can walk. I have plenty of raingear, as you can see."

He arrived with a six-seater, which he had commandeered. We proceeded to tour the cemetery, considered U.S. territory.

No words. As we saw the beaches, the endless headstones…Chuck, listening to the Superintendent as he pointed out sites, was silent and observant the entire time. He stayed in the cart while I got out to go into the tiny chapel or see the statues and some headstones up close. I did not invade his private thoughts.

I remember Carroll Shelby, who had trained as an enlisted man, like Chuck, to become a fighter pilot but was never assigned to combat, wistfully saying, "I wish I had gone into combat."

And Chuck's response (again): "Twenty-one of the thirty guys I trained with were shot down, most killed."

Chuck lost his closest friends, including Mac McKee, with whom he had met Glennis, in 1944. It was a sobering moment for Carroll Shelby and all of us. Imagine, if you even can, all your friends in just a few months, at age 20 or 21. Gone. Imagine their families.

## STAYING IN VILLA NEAR DAMAZAN, FRANCE: *2018*

For six weeks in the spring of 2018, we rented a beautiful villa in France overlooking a canal, an important thoroughfare lined with trees. We were near a lock in one direction and, in the other direction, not far from the very strategic bridge Chuck had helped blow up during World War II. Beyond the canal, for as far as the eye could see, were luscious green fields of various vegetables, strawberries, and the like.

Each day, we'd have breakfast on the veranda while surveying the view. Then we'd go for a drive, visit friends, stop in a different town each day to have lunch, then visit the town.

Chuck was good-naturedly laughing when he told some friends we stopped in every church in the area where he was shot down. The churches were fairly empty, no ornateness, which I preferred, but very high ceilings and some had stained-glass windows. You couldn't help but feel at one with God sitting quietly in those churches. And, if a service was going on, the acoustics made the music even more magnificent.

## PARIS, DAY ONE: EIFFEL TOWER & TROCADERO

In June 2018, Chuck and I stopped in Paris on our way home.

One day, we took a taxi to the Eiffel Tower from our hotel just north of the Champs-Élysées. The driver took us for a ride, not realizing I knew Paris pretty well, having lived there when I was 20-21. Then the driver dropped us a bit of a hike from the Tower because he saw three guys trying to find a taxi. It was raining, so I wanted to get closer. The driver refused.

Chuck and I both had raingear, so we got out. Chuck was rolling in a wheelchair. At 95, it was just safer on the uneven and crowded streets of Paris.

The cab driver tried to charge us three times the amount. I said no and handed him the correct amount. He refused. The three guys wanting to get in the taxi were American. I warned them that this guy cheated. I asked for the guys to protect us so we could leave. After taking photos because they recognized their hero, they enthusiastically did. They were great.

We zipped to the closest restaurant. The driver ultimately followed us.

Fortunately, I speak French. The waiters were the stereotypical snobbish Parisians and told me to pay the driver. I said in French, to their surprise, "How much do you think it should cost to go from the Champs-Élysées to here? Thirty euros?" The waiter looked at me in horror. I said, "I thought no more than ten and tried to give it to him. He refused." The waiters then were on our side and shooed the driver out. Ah, so glad I spoke French.

We ultimately made it to the Eiffel Tower. One of Chuck's World War II squadron mates had said that during the war, he had chased a German fighter under the Eiffel Tower. The story was new, so I wanted to see the space under the Tower, which spurred us there.

We considered going up the Tower, but it was so foggy and ultra-expensive; it would have wasted our time and money. Moreover, there was too much construction and it was drizzling, so we kept moving. We got to the Seine River, where we had a clearer picture. Under the Eiffel Tower, there was a lot of space. No big deal for a skilled pilot to fly a P-51 through there. Even I could have flown the small taildragger I fly, under the Eiffel Tower. The bigger question was *why* would a fighter pilot chase someone under there? Make the German go under, but you go around and pick him off when he comes out. Otherwise, he could turn and pick you off as you come through—nowhere to go. Chuck was clear long before we visited Paris—the squadron mate was telling a tall tale late in life, but it got him some attention and accolades.

We continued across the river and to the Trocadero. We got only partway up and then there was no wheelchair access. I commandeered four or five strapping young men who carried Chuck in the wheelchair up to where access was again. Nice young men. Honored to do it. I think they were from Poland. We met a lot of folks this way. Great pleasure.

We looked at the view, the Eiffel Tower, the Seine, Paris. By then, we were hungry, so we went to the restaurant on the circle with a view. Literally, the one next door without a view was half the price.

Afterward, only halfheartedly, I looked for a taxi. I wanted to avoid a repeat of earlier. We kept rolling towards our hotel, down grand boulevards and eventually, we made it to the hotel on foot. We had walked over six miles that day.

A nice day. Mission accomplished.

## PARIS DAY TWO: NOTRE DAME, ILE SAINT LOUIS, ANGELINA'S; BEST DESSERT EVER

The second day in Paris, we took a taxi to Notre Dame Cathedral and made our way through the crowd to the wheelchair entrance. The Parisians are very, very respectful of an obvious veteran in a wheelchair. Inside, we looked around and then decided not to take the American guys' offer to lift him up the two-three stairs to the dark, crowded chancel. But how would we get down in twenty or so minutes?

Instead, we sat in the aisle looking at the nave and altar and quietly took it all in for about twenty minutes—the sounds, the colors, the history, ambiance. I lit a few candles and we moved on.

Thus began our second very long walk in Paris. First, we went to Le Marais, the Jewish area, and had some taramasalata (salmon eggs spread with crème frais—fresh cream, garlic and spices). I lived on taramasalata when I lived in London in 1981. Then we went to Île le Saint Louis, well-known for its great ice cream but still not as good as Chuck's mouthwatering homemade honey vanilla ice cream

We rolled along the Seine and crossed the bridge past the Île le Saint Louis. Chuck wanted to stay by the river, so I checked out the candy store across the wide, fast-moving, traffic-laden boulevard. It was Portuguese. Not quite my favorite. I looked at Chuck across the street and thought we must look like homeless people. I'm surprised no one offered us money. I should have put out a hat. Paris is expensive. I had plastic bags on the back of the chair and he was wearing his raincoat and a rain sheet over his pants. It was a pleasantly warm day with occasional drizzle, more like misting—a facial—that was refreshing.

We crossed back over the river and then went down a ramp to level with the Seine River: such history, great architecture. Last time I had been along there was when, as a 15-year-old, I was on a six-and-a-half-week barge trip from Toulouse to Paris with 29 other 15-16-year-olds, four counselors and 34 bicycles; our barge parked on the Seine.

We then turned to go up to the regular road, but the cobblestone was prohibitive and dangerous in the end, so we turned and walked along at the level of the Seine back to whence we had come and found a smooth ramp.

We then walked along where they had their outside booths with books, magazines, and souvenirs. I still have some posters of Paris in the Roaring Twenties from my first time there.

We finally reached Angelina's, across from the Louvre, where you can find

Mont Blanc—best…dessert…ever that isn't ice cream. We had soup first, tea and hot chocolate. Then Mont Blanc.

I had taken my mother here when she visited during my junior year in Paris. Most of my education junior year at university was spent exploring Paris on my own and submitting essays for my classes. The professor, considered the foremost authority in semiology, had said I was brilliant in one class because I noticed something he had not in the 30 years he had been studying a particular film. I thought it can only go downhill from there. In another class at the venerable Institute of Political Science, the professor said a lot, but the one thing I remember understanding clearly (in French) was: "My heart is on the left; my pocketbook is on the right." Sounds about right.

Chuck and I started walking/rolling again. When we came to the five-star Hôtel Crillon, where I wanted to have tea, the direct route was blocked. Crowds were waiting for some glimpse of a music superstar, so we had to backtrack, go around, and forgo tea.

We passed all sorts of expensive stores with all kinds of the latest fashion that you didn't know you needed and for those who didn't know what to do with their gobs of money. We resisted temptation (quickly and easily) and continued.

Eventually, we got to our hotel. What a day.

We had walked six-and-a-half miles. Easy when there's delicious food along the way. My real education from my third (junior) year abroad in Paris had served us well.

## JEAN PIERRE JOLIS AND FAMILY: *2018*

Through our friend Ken, who was truly bilingual, we tried to see if Jean Pierre would receive us, as he had had some serious medical issues and was recovering. Finally, on the day before we were leaving, we got word. Yes.

Trying to rearrange packing up and saying our goodbyes was challenging, but I felt we had to make it work. JP had quite a history with Charlie Yeager.

For several days in 1944, Charlie hid out at JP's parents' house deep in the forest, obscured from the road. JP, age 5, thought the American was swell because Charlie got JP's bed, which meant JP got to sleep with his parents whom he adored. During the day, JP took Charlie fishing and played soccer with him.

We met JP again in 2010, 2012, 2013, 2018, and 2019 when we returned to the area.

Charlie and JP were fairly safe—the Germans didn't venture into the forests where there was a high chance they'd be ambushed. The Maquis were thick in this area, not far from the zenith of activity.

Neither spoke the other's language, although they both picked up a few words together. Physical activity doesn't require much re words.

JP once said, "Don't thank me; my parents protected him." I responded, "Jean Pierre, you kept him safe and occupied. Otherwise, he might have gone off to try to shoot a few Germans and might have gotten killed. History and I needed and wanted him."

We understood each other. JP, a confident, honest, humble man, had become mayor of his little town of Pompogne. Clearly, his family had not profiteered off the war or its aftermath. There were a few folks in town who had and they were still somewhat shunned.

The Jolis were land poor. After the war, JP had gone to Paris to be a butcher with his brother. He met his wife, Claudine, there. Within a few years, his father could not work the farm, so JP brought Claudine from the big city of Paris to the countryside of Lot et Garonne and a farm. To her credit, for love of this man, she adapted, not so happily, though. Now, they were tightening their belts a little more since he was incapable of working the farm. We stopped at the grocery store and picked up some staples and some foie gras, which JP's wife loved but rarely had; it was too expensive.

We arrived to find JP, Claudine, their daughter and young grandson sitting outside their home on the patio. A beautiful day. They spoke no English, so they relied on me to translate. To his credit, JP would correct my French in a way that was not condescending and was extremely helpful. We all had established a mutual respect and deep friendship over the years and, although five years had passed, we jumped right back in.

JP teased at one point, after his daughter was insistent Papa do more rehabiliation, "Vous savez, en France, vous avez le droit d'écraser vos enfants même s'ils sont adultes." ("You know, in France, you are allowed to swat your children even if they are adults.")

I teased right back : "Pourquoi pensez-vous qu'elle est assise de l'autre côté de la table à plus d'une longueur de bras?" ("Why do you think she is sitting across the table farther than arm's length!")

The grandson was learning English, so we conversed a little in English.

After much fun, gaiety, and laughter, JP, when it was nearing time for us to go, with tears in his eyes, said, "Mon cœur est tellement touché que le grand général Chuck Yeager prendrait le temps de venir me rendre visite."

I translated for Chuck, "My heart is so touched that the great General Chuck Yeager would take the time to come visit me!" I had no clue how Chuck would respond. Often he'd say, "There's no 'THE' in my name." (Chuck YEAGER-ism #104) and other such YEAGER-isms.

This time, Chuck looked straight at JP, smiled his beautiful, warm smile that embraced his lovely eyes, as we waited…and said, "That's what friends do."

JP, still looking at Chuck, leaned towards me to translate. I could barely. I was so moved. Trying not to cry, I managed to be understood; "C'est ce que les amis font."

JP about lost it with emotion. So did I. So did the entire family. With those four little words, Chuck gave this man a will to live and gave the entire family hope. A priceless gift.

As we left, Claudine ran after us and thanked us again and again. Her burden had been great and would be greater moving forward. But we had alleviated some of the emotional burden for a time.

I then took out the groceries and told her, "We are leaving tomorrow, as you know. Could you please take this food off our hands, so it doesn't go to waste?"

JP, who is very wise, knew exactly what we had done and quietly thanked us with a smile and a sage nod.

Note: In July 2023, I visited Jean Pierre, now age 85, fairly often in the hospital and then his family and him at his home—he had been quite ill, but his mind is intact. We laughed, teased, reminisced, toasted with water, discussed life and death; a stellar man. I felt like I was channeling General Yeager, lifting the Jolis' spirits once again. When JP started correcting my French again, I knew he was on the mend.

# PART XII

## OTHER VOICES

## NATALIA

We met Natalia and her husband in a very small village in France.
"My husband and I were so lucky to meet General Chuck Yeager and his wonderful wife, Victoria, in Larresingle, France, in 2019. We were sitting at a restaurant celebrating my husband's birthday. So you can imagine what happened when Mrs. and Chuck entered the restaurant, my husband being a pilot himself…My husband could not believe his eyes and started crying for joy!!!…

"The owner came over and said someone had bought my husband his birthday cake and wanted to remain anonymous. But we insisted and he told us it was General and Mrs. Yeager.

"After we finished and were leaving the restaurant, we went to their table in the back. Mrs. Yeager invited us to sit at their table to talk with them and they made us feel like "family!" (While my husband usually does most of the talking, he does not speak English, so I, a professional interpreter, did most of the talking. General Yeager laughed, telling me I talk too much, which also delighted my husband.)

"My husband was so happy—he could tell all his colleagues and pilot friends that: 'General Chuck Yeager had bought him his birthday cake!' This was his best birthday ever and we will never forget that day! Thank you, Victoria, we've been thinking of you a lot in the last months and are very sorry for your loss. Love from Italy, Elia & Natalia."

## ÉTIENNE LABARDIN, FORMER MAYOR OF COURS-LES-BAINS

*Near where Charlie Yeager landed in his parachute after being shot down.*

We met Étienne Labardin in 2008 and our friendship continues to this day. Étienne and Chuck admired each other greatly.

Étienne had been mayor of his town, Cours-les-Bains, the first few times we met him. We would stop by, bring him some milk, cheese, or ice cream, sit on his porch and have coffee. As we were leaving, he'd give us fresh eggs.

Whenever we visited, even with the film crew, Chuck would talk to Étienne about his farm and farming equipment. Basic, normal stuff. They bonded.

The last year we were there, Étienne invited us to the small town of Grignols to his friend's restaurant/bar to have coffee with his sisters, Christiane and Josette, and friends. His sisters both had a crush on Chuck and kept smiling broadly at him. I don't blame them.

Christiane, one year (2010), made us foie gras—it was delicious. We had a little left when we ran into some U.S. Air Force guys in Madrid, so we gave them their first taste of foie gras. Luckily for them, it was top of the line. They could not stop eating it.

I espied Étienne watching Chuck at that bar/restaurant, Chuck's and my last year together in France. Étienne had a profound look of sadness, almost tears. I think he knew that might well be the last time he would see his good friend alive. And it was. He sent me these words after General Chuck Yeager passed (translated from the French):

"Here are some thoughts on my meetings with the general: I would like to bear witness to the memories that I keep of him since 2008, having had the privilege on several occasions, to meet at home.

"I had the impression of a very simple and pleasant man. I think he did not like to talk too much about his aerial exploits. He was especially interested in the farm where I live, in the equipment (tractors), corn or animals; he told us about his rural origins. I want to keep the general's image of an exceptional man who participated in the liberation of France without asking any questions.

"His life is so full that we are very small next door. In spite of everything, he kept his feet on the ground and loved nature. Christiane joins me for this testimony.

"Be assured, dear Victoria, of our sincere friendship and our gratitude for what General Yeager accomplished."

In July 2023, I visited with Étienne and his two delightful sisters,

Christiane and Josette, for Sunday lunch. It lasted four hours of wonderful friendship, reminiscing, conversation, laughter, a few tears as we all missed General Yeager (my first time visiting without him), and food.

## ALMOST FINAL NOTE

I'm ever so grateful to Chuck for all the adventures, our life together, our great friends around the world, and the amazing memories that keep me company. I fully understand his feelings when he used to say, "I get up and smoke it out to Mach 2, see from the Pacific to Mt. Charles, from Baja to the High Sierra, and I own it all." When I fly (only 120 mph), it's so peaceful. I feel Chuck with me.

And we own it all.

What a ride!

## AFTERWORD *(And Another Thing)*

Chuck used to say, "When it becomes unbearable, I won't be around anymore." I'd say, "But honey, I'm still here," (although it was always a toss-up as to who would outlive whom).

December 7, 2020, America and the world lost a hero's hero. And I lost my great love.

Yet the truth is, he is still around...not just in the history books, but in my heart and, I hope, in yours.

## CONTINUING GENERAL CHUCK YEAGER'S LEGACY *(And Yet Another Thing)*

I am enlisting all of you to help keep General Chuck Yeager's great legacy alive and pass it on through all the generations forever.

I have written one book—*101 Chuck YEAGER-isms: Wit & Wisdom from America's Hero*.

This is my second.

I am working on the first in a series of documentaries; the first is on Chuck's life from birth through World War II.

There are many people and groups, institutions, public monuments, and more that truly honor Chuck Yeager, including the Women in Aviation 1st General Chuck Yeager Chapter, the Air and Space Force Association General Chuck Yeager Chapter, the American Legion General Chuck Yeager Post 111, and various General Chuck Yeager scholarships. The Governor of West Virginia re-dedicated the Chuck Yeager Bridge recently renovated, first-of-its-kind, and only, bridge—painted two different colors with state-of-the-art paint. There are several Chuck Yeager Roads.

Folks around the world have celebrated and continue to celebrate General Yeager's birthday and have held air shows and events honoring General Chuck Yeager, including. the annual Chuck Yeager Aviation Festival Day. The first one was successfully held all around the world including West Virginia's Jackson County Airport.

My talks on General Chuck Yeager's history are very well-received. After the Q&A, no one wants to leave—they just want me to continue telling stories. I don't blame them. General Yeager's history is fascinating and amazing.

Among other endeavors.

I trust folks will continue to honor General Chuck Yeager as his legacy lives on.

For updates: www.chuckyeager.com
Contact: editor@chuckyeager.com

# PART XIII

# ACKNOWLEDGMENTS

Thank you very much to everyone who helped me in getting this book written, edited, presentable, and to market.

A very special thanks to Brenda Love from Prague, who gave/gives invaluable advice & suggestions; Claudia Furlow, who generously imparted her expertise; Rear Admiral Rick Grant (ret.), very knowledgeable about a whole host of subjects, who kindly guided me every step of the way; Susan House, who had valuable insights; Kermit Weeks, a creative soul; Peggy Chabrian, great friend of Chuck Yeager; Caleb Deschanel & Phil Kaufmann, superb story-tellers; Sandi Ball, my 2nd "Mom" & great encourager; Denise Forbes, imparts common sense patiently; Brigadier General John "Dragon" Teichert USAF (ret.), who always gives me a different, interesting perspective; General Ricardo Rallo, extremely talented cover, logo & concept artist; Tara Mayberry, layout & cover artist extraordinaire; Brigadier General "Mookie" Walker WVANG (ret.), who is forthright, bold, and trustworthy.

Thank you very much, too, to everyone who helped me find photos (what fun to see all those photos of Chuck Yeager!): Roger Penske, Doug Boles, Indy 500, Aimee Maruyama, Meagan Scharrer, National Aviation Hall of Fame, Allison King, Pearl Harbor Aviation Museum, Mike Fonseca, Amanda Meeker, California Hall of Fame, Hickory Aviation Museum, Dick Knapinski, among others.

PHOTO CREDITS:
IMS Photo
National Aviation Hall of Fame
Victoria Yeager
General Chuck Yeager
Nellis AFB
Joe da Silva
Stu Shepherd
Bob Tarn
California Hall of Fame
Bill Baker

## PART XIV

## PHOTOS

*Alaska*

*Golden trout, High Sierra*

*Alaska*

*Chuck & Victoria Yeager: High Sierra, 2000*

*Chuck with Patrick Dempsey ("McDreamy") Indy 500: 2007*

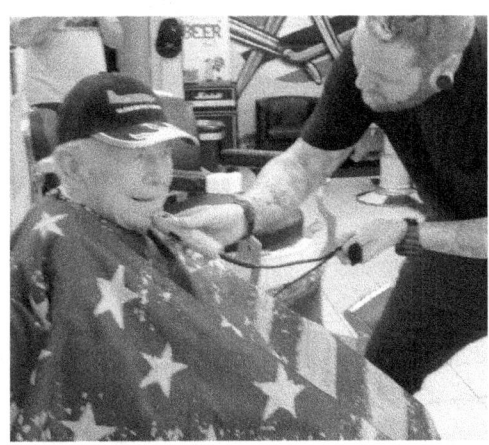

*Chuck Yeager & Neil Armstrong*

*General Chuck Yeager*

*Chuck & Victoria Yeager under tarp, High Sierra hail storm: 2000*

*Cape Town, South Africa: 2010*

*Chuck Yeager flying with Young Eagle in Tri-Motor: Oshkosh WI*

*South Africa: 2010*

*South Africa: 2010*

*Chuck with schoolteacher, Namibia: 2013*

*South Africa: 2010*

*Balloon races with Bruno: Flying M Ranch (Hilton), Nevada*

*Chuck Yeager, pace car drive in Corvette, Indy 500: 1986*

*Indy 500: 2007*

*Aerospace Walk of Honor: Lancaster, CA*

*Chuck with Barbara Hershey
The Right Stuff 20th Anniversary*

*Chuck Yeager and Vincene, organizer
Veterans Day parade: Sacramento*

*Victoria & General Yeager—WV Governor's Mansion with Yeager Scholars: December 2009*

*Chuck Yeager on P-51, Air Venture, Oshkosh, WI: 2011*

*National Aviation Hall of Fame*

*Grand Marshal, National Memorial Day Parade: Washington, DC*

*Chuck & Victoria Yeager, glacier & crevasse: Alaska, August 2000*

*Gen McGillicuddy presenting Chuck Yeager Road sign.*

*General Chuck Yeager gives talk in front of mock X-1; SRO*

*Chuck Yeager in flak in helicopter, Afghanistan*

*Yeager talking to airmen in Afghanistan: 2012*

*General Chuck Yeager with Prince Malik: Pakistan 2012*

*General Chuck Yeager, Mumtaz. Prince Malik: Pakistan 1973*

*General Chuck Yeager on palace veranda: Pakistan*

*Victoria cantering inside Palace grounds: Pakistan*

*Bull races in Pakistan*

*Prince Malik's Palace: Pakistan*

*Prince Malik bringing horse to Victoria*

*Prince Malik Atta Muhammad Khan of Kot Fateh Khan tent pegging*

*Tea in the back of the truck at bull races in Pakistan. Very civilized.*

*Bulls hurtling straight for us.*

*Chuck & John Madden. CA Hall of Fame*

*Gov. Schwarzenegger & Gen Chuck Yeager*

*General Chuck Yeager being inducted into the California Hall of Fame: 2009*

*Victoria & Chuck Yeager on red carpet at California Hall of Fame*

*National Air & Space Museum: 2000*

*General Chuck Yeager & Victoria Yeager in P-51: 2005*

*Chuck & Jean Pierre Jolis: Pompogne, France*

*Etienne & Christiane. Window from Yeager's P-51: Cours-les-Bains, France*

*Victoria in Biarritz, France
Photo by Chuck Yeager*

# PART XV

## INDEX

# A

Ace, 74, 80, 92, 157, 240, 327, 339
Afghanistan, 137, 138, 142, 275, 278, 280-285, 287, 289, 353, *371*
    Kabul, 280-281, 284-285
    Maz-i-Sharif, 283
    Shindand, 283
Africa, viii, 2, 16, 58, 146, 171, 174, *371*
Afterword, 366
Airplanes
    B-2, 307
    F-15E, 46, 118, 207, 247, 266, 290, 293, 321
    F-22, 209, 250-251, *371*
    NF-104, 48, 112, 238
    P-51, 74, 76, 92-93, 182, 192-194, 220, 230, 240, 242, 247, 250-251, 258, 275, 309, 321, 323-325, 340, 347, 357, *371*
    X-1, 3, 53, 59, 90, 94, 110, 112, 209. 210, 264, 319, 321, *371*
    X-1A, 324
Alaska, 23-24, 30, 32-33, 35-38, 113-114, 131-133, 137, 156, 179, *371*
Allen, Duane, 328, 331-332
Almost Final Note, 366
Armstrong, Neil, 89-91, *371*
Astronaut, 89, 109, 208, 254, 294
Australia, vii, 2, 78, 322, 98, 100, 113, 251-252

# B

Balloon (racing), 109, 195-196, *371*
Barnes, Pancho, 97, 165
Beale AFB, 74-75, 223, 252, 258, 260-263, 265-269, 271
Beatty, Warren, 155-156
Belenko, Viktor, 21, 126-127
Belloc, M. et Mme., 344-345

Bening, Annette, 155
Biarritz, 243, 341
Biography–Victoria Yeager, vii-viii
Birthday (party), 11, 71, 73-76, 98, 103, 119-121, 225, 265-266, 301, 327-328, 332-333, 364, 367, *371*
Bochkay, Don, 157-158
Bochkay, Larry, 157-158
Bonsall, Joe, 328-331
Borman, Frank USAF Col (ret.), 294
Boyd, Albert "Al", 96, 326
Bristol Bay, 33
Burnett, Carol, 315-319
Bull Races, 142, 144-148, *371*
Bush, Barbara, 87-89
Bush, George H.W., 36, 82-89, 161, 317
Bush, George W., 130, 304, 306

# C

California Hall of Fame, 155, 314-315, 317
Cassiday, Ben, Brig Gen USAF (ret.), 121, 124-125, 327
Cats, Chuck Yeager's opinion of, 58
Cazeau AFB, 342-343
Celebrity Quail Hunt, 160
Château Margaux, 133-134
Chile, 41-43, 197
Christiane, 347, 365-366, , *371*
Chuck Yeager Road, 9, 260, 263, 367, *371*
Chuck YEAGER-ism, 7, 17, 33, 51, 53, 59-60, 62-63, 80, 91-92, 159, 167, 177, 180, 183, 186-188, 199, 201, 208-210, 247, 251, 272, 275, 277, 282, 295-296, 310, 324, 342, 354-355, 362, 367
Clark, Roy, 72-74, 331-332, *371*
Clifford Family, 127-129

Congressional Medal of Honor Society Dinner, 254
Crossfield, Scott, 110
Crystal Cathedral, 106
Cusack, Mike, 156

# D

D-Day, 256, 345, 355
Dempsey, Patrick "McDreamy", 311, *371*
Dining In, 117, 118, 233-234, 295
Disagreement, 49
Dogfighting, 347
Dogs, Chuck Yeager's opinion of, 57-58, 101, 149, 167-168, 273, 335
Dunham, Archie, Chairman, ConocoPhillips, 33-34, 36-37, 65

# E

Eden, Barbara, 332
Edwards AFB, 92, 117, 165, 232-233, , 238, 247, 250, 253, 264, 291-292, 294, 296, 307, 318, 332, *371*
    Open House Air Show, 232, 238, *371*
    Yeager Boulevard, 294
Egress systems, 260-261, 277, 290
Eisenhower, Dwight D., 288-289, 355
English, Doug, 160

# F

Faulkner, Von, 161
Fighter ace(s), 80, 92, 157, 327, 329
First Foundation, 302

Fishing, 16, 22-23, 28, 30-33, 35, 37, 39, 41-42, 69, 103, 111, 113-114, 121-122, 131, 136, 156, 165, 197-198, 202, 215, 228, 252, 254, 256-257, 299-300, 360, *371*

Flight officer (F/O), 10, 36, 92-93, 128-129, 155, 340-341, 343, 347, 350, 351, 353

Flight test(ing), 179, 253

Ford, Harrison, 105-106

Formation Flying, 104, 192, 194-195, 199, 250

Fossett, Steve, 111-113

449th Bomber Group, 323-325

France, 2, 22, 62, 106, 214, 241, 243-245, 287, 338-340, 342-344, 347, 349, 354, 356, 261, 364-365

Franchitti, Dario, 310-311

French Resistance, 60, 241

French Underground, 60, 344, 349, 353

# G

German American Glider Club, 248-249

Gold digger, 68,

Golden trout, 16, 19, 22, 26, 213-214, *371*

Grand Marshal, 272-274, 287, 289, 300, *371*,

Grandpa Marion General Yeager, 128, 131-132, 336,

Grandma "Adeline" Yeager, 131-132, 313-314

# H

Hamlin, (West Virginia), 81, 111, 131-132

Hawaii, 122, 124-125, 179, 325

Hays, Admiral Ron, 124-125, 326-327

High Sierra, 2, 13, 15-16, 20, 24, 27, 46, 71, 78-79, 101, 110, 191, 213, 215, 328, 366, *371*

Hill, David "Tex", 154-155
Hilton, Barron, 91, 101, 103, 109, 113, 119, 131, 167, 191-192, 195, 197, 210, 229, 254, 284, 295, 312, 323
Hilton, Paris, 103
Honorary Soul Brother, 75, 298-299
Horseback riding, vi, 41-42, 109, 148, 191, *371*
Hôtel du Palais, 341
Huntin', 7, 58, 69, 71, 80, 97, 104, 121-122, 127, 131, 159-163, 165, 167-171, 197, 215, 248, 298, *371*
    Elk, 8-9, 69, 100, 115, 155, 163-164, 298, 352
    Pig, 71, 162, 167

# I

Indian Fighter Pilot, 132
Indy 500, 121, 310-312, *371*

# J

Jarrett, Kenny, 79-80, 180,
Jolis, Jean Pierre, 344, 360-363, *371*

# K

Kevorkian, Korky & Irene, 71, 190,
Kittyhawk, NC, 304, 307
Knight, Pete, 93-94, 247-248

# L

Ladd, Karol, 161
Labardin, Etienne, 347, 364-365, *371*
Legacy, 366-367

LaPeyreusse, Paulette, 347-350
Legion d'honneur, 241, 244, 367
Lucas, George, 319, 320, 322

# M

Mach, 110, 112, 241, 247, 253, 271, 290, 307, 323, 324, 366
Madden, John, 317-319, *371*
Manchin, Joe, Governor, 82, 116-118
Manning, Peyton, 310-312
Maquis, 10, 60, 241-242, 244, 262, 340, 344, 347, 349, 350. 353, 361,
Marriage, 4, 44-45, 47-48, 58, 61, 65, 73, 87, 99, 345
Maul Rock, 111
McKee, Mac, 127
Mentzelopoulos, Corinne, 133-134
Merbold, Ulf, 109
Mess Dress, 295-296
Mildred & Dick, 95-96
Military decorations and awards, 257, 316, 326
Mondavi, Janice, 157
Mondavi, Marc, 156-157, *371*
Mondavi, Peter, Sr., 157
Monday, Humpy, 111
Montana, Joe, 155
Montegna, Joe, 287
Myers, Johnny, 119-121, *371*

# N

Nabors, Jim, 121-124
NASA (National Aeronautics and Space Administration), 208, 238
Namibia, 148, 175, , *371*
National Air & Space Museum, 90

National Memorial Day Parade, 287, *371*
Nerac, (France), 347, 349, 353
New Zealand, 170
Nicoletti, John, 260-263

## O

Oak Ridge Boys, 291, 325, 330-333
O'Brien, Obie, 92-93
Olds, Robin, Brig Gen USAF, 80-81

## P

Pacific Aviation Museum, 121, 325, 327
Pakistan, 132-133, 137-143, 148, 150-151, 153-154, 164, 251, 270, 280, 282, 285, 287, *371*
Palace Hotel, 341, *371*
Panther Branch, 131
Photos, *371*
Prince Malik Atta Muhammad Khan, 137-142, 144-153, *371*

## R

Renaut, Raoul, 340-341, 343-344, 353-354
The Right Stuff, iii, 3, 52, 91

## S

Sacramento Veterans Day Parade, 272, 274
Schleeh, Russ, Col USAF (ret.), 96-97, 153-154, 294, 301,
Schuller, Robert, Reverend, 106-108
Schwarzenegger, Governor Arnold, 94, 315, 319, *371*
Sexwale, Tokyo, 36, 135-136

Shelby, Carroll, 114, 153, 312, 356
Shultz, George, 317
Sinatra, Frank, 103
Sinatra, Barbara, 103
Sinise, Gary, 255-157, 278
65th Aggressors Squadron (Nellis AFB, Nevada), 290
Skinny Dipping, 6
Smith, John, MD, 121-122
Smith, Pip & Dick, 98, 252
Smith, Mrs. Terri, Mr. Terry, 136
Sort, Spain, 341, 350
Sound barrier, breaking of, 3, 96-97, 110, 117, 230, 232-233, 237, 246, 250, 351, 258, 264, 291-292, 296, 311, 319, 332, 347, 350
South Africa, vii, 135, 171-173, 176, 265, *371*
Spain, 262, 287, 339, 341-342, 350
Squirrel, 46, 104, 165-166
Statues of Yeager, Chuck, 294, 355
Steel, Danielle, 319
Stone Cabin Ranch, 127, 129

# T

Tahr, 170-171,
357th Fighter Group, 128-129, 157, 239, 325
Tonopah, (Nevada), 127-128, 130
Tsiu River, 38, 113, *371*
Tuskegee Airmen, 274, 319-320, 322

# U

USAF (United States Air Force), 96, 111, 115, 117, 119, 121, 125, 138, 153-154, 277, 282, 286, 327, *371*
U.S. Air Force Academy, 276

## V

Vietnam war, 79, 167

## W

Wedding, 32, 45, 47-48, 67-69
West Virginia, 81-82, 111, 116, 131, 160, 177, 192, 199, 315, 336, 367
Women in Aviation International, 302

## Y

Yeager, An Autobiography, 113, 139, 350
Yeager, Glennis, 6, 17, 21, 45, 52, 76-79, 90, 107, 139, 190, 203, 253, 309, 316, 356
Yeager, Steve, 333

www.ingramcontent.com/pod-product-compliance
Lightning Source LLC
Chambersburg PA
CBHW081207170426
43198CB00018B/2874